Controlling the State

Controlling the State

*Constitutionalism from
Ancient Athens to Today*

Scott Gordon

Harvard University Press

Cambridge, Massachusetts, and London, England | 1999

Library of Congress Cataloging-in-Publication Data

Gordon, Scott, 1924–
    Controlling the state : constitutionalism from ancient Athens
to today / Scott Gordon.
        p.   cm.
    Includes bibliographical references and index.
    ISBN 0-674-16987-5
    1. Separation of powers. 2. Authority. 3. Liberty.
4. Constitutional history. I. Title.
    JF229 .G67 1999
    321.8'01—dc21
                                                    99-30812

In all government there is a perpetual intestine struggle, open or secret, between Authority and Liberty, and neither of them can ever absolutely prevail in the contest. A great sacrifice of liberty must necessarily be made in every government; yet even the authority which confines liberty can never, and perhaps ought never, in any constitution to become quite entire and uncontrollable . . . It must be owned that liberty is the perfection of civil society, but still authority must be acknowledged essential to its very existence.

    —DAVID HUME

Acknowledgments

I wish to express my thanks, for assistance in various ways, to Byrum Carter, the late James Christoph, J. A. Gunn, H. H. J. Kiesling, Kenneth McRae, Robert Patterson, James Riley, Dan Usher, George W. Wilson, Frank Zeller, two anonymous readers for Harvard University Press who offered valuable criticisms and suggestions, and to Julie Carlson for her meticulous and constructive copyediting.

Contents

Controlling the State

Introduction

Numerous theories have been advanced to explain the nature of government by suggesting how it might have arisen out of a "state of nature" in which there was no social organization beyond that of the family. Such hypothetical scenarios have played an important role in Western political thought ever since Thomas Hobbes and John Locke employed them to demonstrate that the authority of the state rests upon a "social contract"—that is, an agreement among the people to form a political entity and endow it with the exclusive authority to exercise coercive power. Hobbes and Locke constructed their theories not as purely abstract speculations, but in order to provide guidance for their fellow Englishmen during the great political upheavals of their time. They drew very different implications from their theories, but their fundamental conception of the state was the same: political authority derives from the people who are governed by it, and the state is a utilitarian social artifact, created by the people to enable them to enjoy the benefits of a peaceful and orderly civil society. This conception of the state originated long before the seventeenth century, but its expressions by Locke and Hobbes constituted a large step in the development of modern political theory.[1]

As a historical phenomenon, the origin of the state as distinct from locally confined tribal organizations has been traced by archaeologists to the valleys of the Nile, Tigris-Euphrates, and Indus rivers, where opportunities existed for greatly increasing the yield of agriculture by large-scale irrigation projects that could only be constructed and managed by a comprehensive coercive

1. The utilitarian conception of the state can be found at least as early as Greek and Roman antiquity. Historians have discovered expressions of the idea that the state is founded upon a contract as far back as Thucydides (Ostwald, 1986, 111; on the history of contract theory, see Gough, 1957; Lessnoff, 1986 and 1990). The most common form of the theory conceives of a contract between the people and the state, but the Hobbesian-Lockean notion of a contract among the people themselves also has earlier antecedents, and has recently been revived as a modus for establishing the limits of legitimate state authority (see Rawls, 1971; Nozick, 1974; Buchanan, 1975).

authority (Daniel, 1968; Service, 1975). From the standpoint of political theory, the most important work of this genre is Karl Wittfogel's *Oriental Despotism* (1957), which traces the origin of the "managerial state" (as well as urbanization, social stratification, and the invention of writing and numerical record keeping) to the innovation of "hydraulic agriculture." Wittfogel regards all early states as highly concentrated centers of despotic power, in contrast to smaller political organizations in which something like a democratic system of governance may have obtained. Wittfogel describes "The Terror of Hydraulic Government" (1957, 140f.) in graphic terms, pointing out that it springs not from economic necessity but from "the corrupting influence of power whenever circumstances permit." In the West, a better mode of political organization has come into existence, not because occidentals are different from orientals, but due to developments such as feudalism and capitalism, which split the monolith of power and led to the creation of a pluralistic polity with numerous competing and mutually controlling institutions (78, 100, 140f.).

The thesis that power corrupts its possessor may be as good a "law" as any that we have in political science, but the emergence of states in which political power was significantly distributed among competing institutions antedates feudalism and capitalism in Europe. The need to control the exercise of state power, and the notion that it can be done by institutional design, is evident in the political systems of Periclean Athens and republican Rome. The idea of a "constitutional" political order has a provenance as old as Western political thought. Its modern revival attended the emergence of nation-states in western Europe in the fifteenth century, a development that was not driven by economic imperatives as much as by the fact that large polities are superior to smaller ones in the conduct of warfare.

Even after the nation-state came into existence, its domain of operation was for a long period largely directed at the furtherance of dynastic aims by diplomacy, marriage, and warfare. Until the end of the eighteenth century (at least), most of the common people were engaged in agriculture and domestic crafts, and only encountered the power of the state if they had the misfortune to be where armies marched. They lived out their lives impervious to the shifts and changes of state policy. They identified themselves as members of local communities, and the institution that most influenced their daily lives was the church. Today, "citizenship" is defined in terms of the nation, and nationalism is the dominant political sentiment of our time. Local and regional organs of government continue to exist, and religious institutions continue to be regarded as centers of moral authority, but the hegemonic dominion of the nation-state is uncontested.

Until the middle of the twentieth century, the domain of government remained small. Prior to World War II, less than 10 percent of U.S. national income was taken in taxation by all levels of government. Today, it is 35 percent, a proportion that is low in comparison to most other industrialized countries. Moreover, such figures understate the degree to which modern states exercise their coercive authority. In addition to taxing and spending, the modern state imposes a vast array of regulations whose impact is not reflected in its fiscal accounts. Such regulations range from the provisions of criminal law to the requirement (in Norway) that parents seeking to register the birth of a child choose a name from an official list. Nevertheless, there is little evidence that the people of the United States, Norway, Great Britain, and other modern states feel themselves oppressed by tyrannous government. There may be a widespread view that, in general terms, the domain of the state should be reduced, but on specific matters, popular demand is persistently for more government action rather than less.

This demand is surprising, but it is not incomprehensible. The state (in some parts of the world at least) is not what it was even little more than a century ago. Except for England and the Netherlands, the nations of eighteenth-century Europe were ruled by absolute monarchs who, with a small cadre of assistants, determined state policy with little reference to the people's welfare and no concern for their freedom. The belief that the state has been transformed by the development of political systems in which "the people" exercise political power is however, an illusion. Modern government is not at all like the town governments of New England in colonial America. Nevertheless, in a substantial number of countries today there is widespread participation by the citizenry in the formation of public policy, and the exercise of political power is controlled by means of an established constitutional order. It is no mystery that the citizenry of constitutional democracies are willing to accept such a large role of the state in their lives.

Many theories of the state have been advanced by political philosophers, ranging from William Godwin, who viewed the state as the primary source of all social evils and called for its total destruction, to G. W. F. Hegel, who reified the state as the fundamental social "organism" with moral purposes that transcend those of its individual citizens.[2] Between the extremes of anarchism and idealism, there is the utilitarian view, which construes the state

---

2. In his article for the *International Encyclopedia of the Social Sciences* on the state as a social institution, Morton Fried observes that the concept of the state has been employed in a wide variety of ways by scholars. "At one extreme of argument the state is identified with one or more highly specific features, such as organized police powers, defined spatial boundaries, or a formal judiciary. At the other end of the definitional spectrum the state is regarded simply as the institutional aspect of political interaction; no concrete structures are specified, and the state, being coterminous with society, vanishes in universality" (1968, 143).

as a pragmatic device through which the people can act to service their mundane needs for "collective goods." This phrase covers a large domain of commodities and services that cannot be provided by private market transactions, from foreign policy to roads and bridges (Gordon, 1994). In recent years, economists and political scientists have developed and employed the "theory of public choice" as a vehicle for the analysis of public policy. The conception of the state as a useful instrument for making decisions on matters that are inherently collective is an underlying assumption of this book, but I am not concerned with the mechanics of public choice. I address a different problem, which springs from the fact that, as an instrument of social organization, the state operates by means of coercion. The most significant feature of political organization is not that the nation-state has supplanted all other forms, nor that the domain of the state has grown so large, but that ways have been found to control its coercive power.

The most common definition of the state encountered in modern literature construes it as the institution in society that possesses monopolistic authority to employ legitimate force. This definition stems from Max Weber, who emphasized the words "monopoly" and "legitimate" in his definition. Every system of political authority must rely upon a considerable degree of voluntary obedience to supplement its ability to employ coercive force, and this voluntary compliance is derived from the habiliment of legitimacy that clothes the state. Weber's definition of the state is essential when considering a nation's *legal* system, but may be misleading in analyzing its *political* system more broadly. In all political orders, the source of law is the state, but law is not the same thing as policy. In the dynamics of politics, policy precedes law. Only after public policy has been determined are lawyers called in to draft a statute and construct a set of administrative regulations for its implementation. In nations such as the United States, the formation of public policy is a pluralistic process involving many institutions that are not part of the formal apparatus of government, such as the media, private interest groups, religious organizations, and a large array of nongovernmental public-policy research and advocacy institutions. These private institutions are centers of political power. Describing the state as having a monopoly of coercive authority may be misleading because doing so diverts attention from the complexity of politics in modern constitutional democracies. The essential property of political organization in such polities is not captured by describing them as democracies, *tout court*. They are "democratic" in the sense that there is wide participation by the general citizenry in the formation of public policy; but they are also "constitutional" in that they contain institutionalized mechanisms of power control for the protection of the interests and liberties of the citizenry, including those who may be in the minority.

The term "constitutionalism" is fairly recent in origin, but the idea can be traced back to classical antiquity.[3] Briefly, I take "constitutionalism" to denote that the coercive power of the state is constrained. C. H. McIlwain, who a half-century ago was one of the most widely acknowledged authorities on the history of constitutionalism, stressed its long lineage and complex manifestation, but maintained that a simple generalization was nonetheless possible: "In all its successive phases, constitutionalism has one essential quality: it is a legal limitation on government . . . The most persistent and the most lasting of the essentials of true constitutionalism still remains what it has been almost from the beginning, the limitation of government by law" (1940, 24). In focusing on the constraint of state power, McIlwain faced in the right direction, but in stressing *legal* constraints, he came close to destroying the coherence of his view. If there is a body in the state that makes all law, then the only legal constraints under which it operates consist of laws that it itself makes; that is, there are no constraints at all. One would have to modify this assertion for nations like the United States in which there is a written constitution that cannot be changed by the passage of an ordinary statute, but McIlwain was not thinking of the United States; in fact, he was highly critical of the American political system and preferred the British one, which has no written constitution and no *legal* limitations on the lawmaking powers of Parliament. If we were to insist on defining "constitutionalism" in terms of written constitutions embodying constraints such as the Bill of Rights in the American Constitution, we would have to exclude British and other parliamentary systems, which in terms of the operation of state authority are not clearly less "constitutional" than that of the United States. Paradoxical though it may seem, constitutionalism has little to do with the existence of a written constitution.

Closely akin to McIlwain's in its emphasis on the law, but a much broader contention, is the oft-repeated formula that a good political order is "a government of laws and not of men." This is a very old notion, with a provenance that extends back to classical antiquity. In republican Rome, the consuls and other magistrates, on taking office, were obliged to swear an oath to obey

3. According to the *Oxford English Dictionary,* the word "constitutionalism" was first used in 1832. Berman (1983, 9) asserts that the word was coined in America during the Revolution. Chrimes (1949, 475f.) notes that the adjective "constitutional" was a novelty even in the mid-eighteenth century, but the noun "constitution," with a political meaning, came into use during the English debates that led to the outbreak of Civil War in 1642. The *OED* reports uses of that word sense as early as the twelfth century, but it was the English debates of the Civil War period, and after the "Glorious Revolution" of 1688, that firmly established "constitution" and its cognates as elements of the modern political vocabulary.

the laws and were expected to declare, at the end of their tenures, that they had done so (Brunt, 1988, 16n.). The sixteenth-century Venetian historian Gasparo Contarini attributed the success of the Venetian political system to the fact that, unlike other states, its government was based "on laws, not men" (Bouwsma, 1968, 149f.).[4] In the mid-eighteenth century, David Hume offered the opinion that of all kinds of government, the monarchical had made the greatest improvement. He also claimed that "it may now be affirmed of civilized monarchies what was formerly said in praise of republics alone, *that they are a government of laws and not of men*" (1953, 106; Hume's italics). The phrase was popular in revolutionary-era America as an expression of the political aspirations of the colonists, and it was promoted especially by its incorporation into the Massachusetts state constitution of 1780 (Cunliffe, 1959, 34). It still surfaces occasionally in American political debate; Milton Friedman, for example, has used it as a general expression of a political ideal and, specifically, in support of his contention that economic policy should be operated through the promulgation of "rules" rather than by the establishment of "authorities" with discretionary powers of action (1962, 51f.).

As a slogan, the phrase "a government of laws and not of men" is appealing, but like most political slogans, it makes better sound than sense. The plain fact is that all government is, unavoidably, the exercise of coercive power by some people over others. Laws do not spring into existence spontaneously, nor are they interpreted and applied by nonhuman agents. The kinds of laws here described are not like the "laws of nature" to which scientists refer. The law of gravitational attraction acts with complete objectivity and cannot be stayed. A stone that comes loose from the cornice of a building is more impartial in its behavior than a drunken driver. It falls immediately, without regard to who might be beneath it, and without reference to the morality of falling heedlessly upon a crowded street, or the deservingness, or otherwise, of whomever it might hit. Legal laws, unlike scientific ones, are made for a human purpose, by people who have to consider the merits of the purpose; and they are applied by human policemen, judges, juries, and others who, at all these stages of law administration, exercise moral, utilitarian, and pragmatic judgment. The only thing that can be salvaged from the slogan "a government of laws and not of men" is the notion that good laws should not place power in the hands of authorities to act arbitrarily or capriciously. This

---

4. The proposition "was endlessly stated and almost universally believed by city-state Greeks and Romans alike, even by Plato and Aristotle, [that] the essential condition for a genuine political society, for a true *polis* and therefore for the good life, is 'Rule by laws, not by men.' Innumerable statements of the slogan can be quoted down to Cicero in the last days of the Roman Republic" (Finley, 1983, 135f.).

brings us back again to the central issue of constitutionalism: the problem of *controlling* the power to coerce.

The notion of "the rule of law" is not the same thing as that of "a government of laws and not of men," though the two are often conflated. The first of these ideas refers to the proposition that laws enacted by lawmaking authorities should apply to *everyone:* legislators, executive officers from the highest rank to the lowest, policemen, judges, military personnel, and so on. The wisdom of this proposition, and the necessity of public vigilance to see that the rule of law is not flouted, is illustrated almost daily in the United States and other constitutional polities. If a part of the apparatus of the state becomes immune to the law, there is little doubt that at least some of the officials so protected will abuse their authority. But the principle of the "rule of law," even if it were rigorously adhered to, would not suffice to create and sustain a constitutional political order. If a nation's legislature were dominated by fundamentalist Baptists, for example, the fact that laws apply to all offenders without exception could not be relied upon to constrain them from prohibiting the celebration of the Catholic mass. In the modern state, we have innumerable cases of legislation that have little or no impact on the legislators who enact it, or on the officials who enforce it. The preservation of the rights of minorities cannot be absolutely guaranteed, but more can be done than simply asserting the principle of the rule of law.

The framers of the American Constitution had no doubt that all legitimate governmental power derives from the people, but they were equally certain that even a government that meets this test of legitimacy should be constrained. Prominent French political thinkers such as Mirabeau, Turgot, and Condorcet, observing American efforts to rebuild the political order after the success of the Revolution, disapproved of what they saw because, in their view, control of the power of the state is necessary only in monarchies. In a republic, where "the people" have taken over the reins of government, such constraints are not only unnecessary, but positively injurious (Wood, 1969, 236). Political developments in France after the downfall of the Bourbon monarchy demonstrated, however, that declaring the state to be a "republic," describing it as dedicated to "liberty, equality, and fraternity," and celebrating the "sovereignty of the people" are insufficient to guarantee that political power will not be abused.

The two great revolutions at the end of the eighteenth century accented two quite different lines of political thought. The French Revolution was in the utopian tradition; its philosophical leaders embraced the view that a wholesale reconstruction of society is necessary and that this great task can only be accomplished by a determined and relentless government with unbridled power. Marxism, and the takeover of the Russian Revolution of 1917 by Lenin, were the most prominent post-Napoleonic developments in this line of thought. Political developments in America, though frequently garbed in a romanticist visionary rhetoric that celebrated the intention to build a new Jerusalem in a new land, were much more conservative and pragmatic in actuality. The political inheritance of England was not rejected; on the contrary, the architects of political reconstruction in America sought to preserve it and improve upon it. The internal disturbances that punctuated American life after the success of the War of Independence convinced the men who met in Philadelphia in 1787 to find a way to form "a more perfect union"—they believed that a strong central government was necessary. But equally necessary was a system of constraints that would effectively control the power of the government they proposed to establish.

The central problematic of political science, from antiquity to the present day, has been the examination of how the authority of the state is exercised. Aristotle set his students to work collecting and analyzing as many political systems as could be studied in order to investigate this empirically. Jean Bodin, one of the most important of early modern political scientists, responded to the social upheavals of sixteenth-century France by investigating "sovereignty," that is, ultimate power, in terms of what was required to maintain the order and stability of society. Power remains today the main focus of both academic and vernacular political studies, whether they wear a philosophical, normative, or positivistic habit.[5]

Because the concept of "power" occupied such a central position in an important branch of Western thought over so long a period, one might expect that it would have been subjected to intense examination, but this is not the case. There is virtually no literature dealing generically with political power that dates before the twentieth century, and very little earlier than World War II. Since then, however, a considerable volume of literature has been generated, some of which has attempted to subject the notion of power to semantic and epistemic, as well as social, analysis. Although this literature has made some important contributions to political science, it has not won a central

5. "At one extreme an analysis of power may simply postulate that power relations are one feature of politics among a number of others—but nonetheless a sufficiently important feature to need emphasis and description. At the other extreme the analyst may hold that power distinguishes 'politics' from other human activity; to analysts of this view, 'political science, as an empirical discipline, is the study of the shaping and sharing of power' " (Dahl, 1968; Dahl's quotation is from Lasswell and Kaplan, 1950, xiv). Bertrand Russell went further in introducing his *Power: A New Social Analysis:* "In the course of this book I shall be concerned to prove that the fundamental concept in social science is Power, in the same sense in which Energy is the fundamental concept of physics . . . Power, like energy, must be regarded as continually passing from any one of its forms into any other, and it should be the business of social science to seek the laws of such transformations" (1938, 10–12).

place in that discipline, mostly because the concept of power remains imprecise and ambiguous. The *Encyclopedia of Philosophy* contains only a brief article on "Power" (Benn, 1967), the chief import of which is that the concept is subject to severe difficulties of definition. William Riker contends that these difficulties are insoluble, being "rooted in the very conceptions of power and causality themselves" (1964, 348).[6]

Social problems will not go away, however, or even diminish, because social scientists and philosophers have been unable to provide conceptual tools as precise as good scientists and scholars would wish.[7] The word "power" denotes, even though vaguely, a highly significant property of the relations between the members of a society; and the phrase "control of power" refers to a issue of exceptional practical importance, as any person who has lived under an absolutist government is likely to certify.

In his essay on "The Origin of Justice and Property," David Hume began by noting that "of all the animals with which this globe is peopled there is none towards whom nature seems, at first sight, to have exercised more cruelty than towards man, in the numberless wants and necessities with which she has loaded him and the slender means which she affords to the relieving of these necessities." As individuals, humans are very weak contestants in the struggles of nature but, Hume pointed out, these deficiencies have been overcome by social organization. "By the conjunction of forces" that society makes possible, he writes, "our power is augmented" (1953, 29). Social scientists address the subject of power in this sense—the aggregate power of a whole community—in considering a community's ability to deal effectively with its natural environment, or its capacity to defend itself against other communities, or to attack them.[8] But the notion of power that is germane to the subject of this book is different; it concerns the distribution of political power within a community. The concept of "political" power sometimes refers to the policies and operations of a particular social institution, the state. But other social institutions such as churches, business firms, research insti-

6. Of the literature on power that has seen print during the past forty years, the most comprehensively useful that I have encountered is Dennis H. Wrong's *Power: Its Forms, Bases, and Uses* (1979). On the difficulties involved in using the concept of power in political analysis, Bell et al. (1969) is an excellent collection of papers.

7. Ideally, one would like to have an operationally quantitative measure of power, so that the comparative powers of different social actors could be assessed. Robert Dahl (1957) expressed the view that at least ordinal rankings of power are possible, but his proposed method of constructing these has met with little response.

8. Talcott Parsons, the leading American sociologist of the mid-twentieth century was, according to Wrong, primarily interested in power in this "aggregate" sense (1979, 239–247). This is certainly the main focus of Parsons's paper "On the Concept of Political Power" (1963).

tutes, and public interest associations are also repositories of power. As important elements of the system through which the apparatus of the state is actuated, these institutions must come under consideration in any comprehensive investigation of political power. In considering the lawmaking authority of the state, it is well to keep in mind that the power to coerce is a relationship between individual persons. Saying that "the state" wields power is metonymous speech; it is not the state that acts, but the persons who are endowed with the authority of the state. Recognition of this fact is essential if one is to appreciate that the citizen is often coerced by decisions made by even minor officials.

In his discussion "The Fundamental Concepts of Sociology," Max Weber gave a comprehensive definition of "power" and distinguished it from "imperative control" and "discipline," as follows:

> "Power" is the probability that one actor within a social relationship will be in a position to carry out his own will despite resistance, regardless of the basis upon which this probability rests.
>
> "Imperative control" is the probability that a command with a given specific content will be obeyed by a given group of persons.
>
> "Discipline" is the probability that by virtue of habituation a command will receive prompt and automatic obedience in stereotyped forms, on the part of a given group of persons. (1947, 152)

In Weber's definition, "power" refers to a *general* capacity, one not restricted as to the specific matter or occasion upon which it is exercised, or the sustaining foundation of the power in question, or the nature of the obedient response it can command.

Bertrand Russell defined power as "the production of intended effects" (1938, 35), thus making more explicit the notion of "will" in Weber's definition. Dennis Wrong adopts a modified version of Russell's definition— *"Power is the capacity of some persons to produce intended and foreseen effects on others"*—and gives a schematization of the forms of power in terms of "Force," "Manipulation," "Persuasion," and "Authority" (1979, 2, Wrong's italics; ch. 2). The first and last of these are especially important in investigating political power and the activities of the state, but in any comprehensive analysis of power, it is as inadvisable to neglect "manipulation" and "persuasion" as it is to disregard the role of nonstate institutions. In an early paper in the development of the modern discussion of power, Robert Dahl noted that the "intuitive idea" suggested by the term is that "A has power over B to the extent that he can get B to do something that B would not otherwise do" (1957, 203).

Max Weber was a strong believer in the epistemic principle that has since come to be called "methodological Individualism." This doctrine contends that all explanations of social phenomena must be derived from propositions that refer to individual persons. It is salutary in warning against reification—in particular, the error of treating social institutions and groups as if they possess properties and capacities like those of individual persons (such as will, intention, choice, and moral judgment). The wording of Weber's definition of power, focusing as it does on "one actor within a social situation," displays his epistemic concern, but it is seriously deficient in that it fails to recognize what is, in fact, the most vital feature of political power—that while it is exercised by individual persons, it is most effective when mediated through organized groups.

The single individual, as Hume emphasized, has very little power. But even where general social organization exists, individual members remain powerless unless they can associate with others to engage in joint action to further their particular interests. The individual can exert some influence upon others by exhortation, argument, example, and so forth, but *political* influence—that is, influence upon the determination of state policy—requires organization. A large populace may be ruled by a small number of persons, if they are organized as a cohesive group, but such organization is absolutely indispensable to the exercise of political power. "Power," claims Hannah Arendt, "corresponds to the human ability not just to act but to act in concert. Power is never the property of an individual; it belongs to a group and remains in existence only so long as the group keeps together" (quoted by Wrong, 1979, 39). This point is of such vital importance in the investigation of political phenomena that it might well be given the status of a general sociological "law," which maintains that "the organized few can invariably dominate the unorganized many."

This "law" is at odds with the concept of democracy. That term was coined by the pre-Socratic philosophers to refer to a society in which the citizenry at large control the policies and operations of the state, as distinguished from "monarchy" and "aristocracy," the other two basic forms of government. Plato and Aristotle regarded democracy as inherently unstable, degenerating unavoidably into anarchy. This view was almost universally embraced in the political literature until the seventeenth century, when the notion of democratic government was stated by Gerrard Winstanley and other Leveller radicals of the English Civil War period in remarkably modern terms (Hill, 1975). Their fame (or notoriety) was brief, and a historian of political thought might well be more inclined to name Jean-Jacques Rousseau as the important early figure to develop the modern presentation of the concept of democracy. Rousseau joined the notion of democracy to the conception of society as resting upon a social contract (1913). In his construction, the social contract confirms the fact that the people at large possess an inalienable right of sovereignty and, therefore, that government exercises coercive power legitimately only to the extent that it acts in accordance with the "general will." A variant of this idea—which came to be called "popular sovereignty"—played a prominent part in the political literature of the revolutionary period in France. Despite subsequent events there that seem to substantiate the view of democracy that Plato and Aristotle had stated, the notion of the inalienable sovereignty of the people became deeply embedded in the political thought of the West. As one modern historian of the subject puts it: "Revolutionary in its origins, the theory of popular sovereignty was destined in the course of the nineteenth and twentieth centuries to become the only widely accepted basis of political legitimacy" (Watkins, 1968).

Rousseau's notion of the "general will" neglects the fact that the individuals who constitute "the people" are not identical, or even complementary, in their interests and values. The Spanish political theorist José Ortega y Gasset made the same error in reifying "the masses," and in contending that government is, and moreover always has been, controlled by "public opinion."[9] Leaving such notions aside, it is evident that the most that can be done to make state policy "popular" is to adopt the principle of majority rule as a pragmatic device of collective decision-making. This highlights the problem of minorities who do not share the values, interests, or interpretations of the majority. Moreover, *every* member of a political order is almost certain to experience minority status on some occasions; because there are many issues that demand state action, and people are exceedingly varied, the majority-minority split is very unlikely to be the same on all issues. The problem of minorities generates the most difficult issues of practical politics, and must be coped with in a civilized social order. Hardly anyone would contend that a "democratic" political system is satisfactory if the pragmatic principle of majority rule is so rigorously employed that minorities are summarily disregarded. John Stuart Mill began his famous essay "On Liberty" by noting the "tyrannous" capacity of "public opinion," and went on to warn that "In England . . . the majority have not yet learnt to feel the power of the government their power, or its opinions their opinions. When they do so, individual liberty will probably be as much exposed to invasion from the government, as it already is from public opinion" (1977, 222f.).

The problem that Mill pointed to was the central concern of the first im-

---

9. "It is necessary to distinguish between a process of aggression and a state of rule. Rule is the normal exercise of authority, and is always based on public opinion, to-day as a thousand years ago, amongst the English as amongst the bushmen. Never has anyone ruled on this earth by basing his rule on any other thing than public opinion" (Ortega y Gasset, 1950, 92).

portant book on power published in the post–World War II period: Bertrand de Jouvenel's *Power: The Natural History of Its Growth* (1948). In speaking of the "natural history" of power, de Jouvenel advanced the thesis that history shows a steady growth in the magnitude of state power. In the modern era, he contended, this growth has been substantially accelerated by the development of the theory of democracy: "The history of the democratic doctrine furnishes a striking example of an intellectual system blown about by the social wind. Conceived as the foundation of Liberty, it paves the way for tyranny. Born for the purpose of standing as a bulwark against Power, it ends by providing Power with the finest soil it has ever had in which to spread itself over the social field" (1948, 204). Only a revival of the rule of "natural law," writes de Jouvenel, can counter this growth of power (256). This proposition is one that Friedrich Hayek later resorted to in his own sustained attack on the growth of the modern state (1973, 1976, 1979; see also Gordon, 1981). Neither de Jouvenel nor Hayek explains how the doctrine of natural law is to accomplish this task. It seems that natural law (as they conceive it) speaks so plainly on the question of state power that all rational citizens, if they are taught its precepts properly, will oppose any further growth of the state, and indeed demand its reduction. This is doubtful. The specific content of natural law is contained in no document, and those who invoke it are free to proclaim whatever they have a mind to. If the history of the doctrine since it was first developed by Thomas Aquinas in the thirteenth century is any indication, the concept of natural law merely serves to increase the power of any institution whose members are bold enough to claim exclusive authority to interpret it. There is more than one way by which the organized few can dominate the unorganized many.

If not by reestablishing the authority of a so-called natural law, how may power be constrained? Responses to this question constitute one of the central topics in the history of Western political thought. It was not an important issue for Karl Marx and Friedrich Engels, who favored absolute power in the hands of the "proletariat" but viewed this as merely a transitional state to a society in which there would be no state at all. Aside from utopian visions such as this and other forms of anarchism, the issue of the control of power remains a central problematic of political theory.

One line of thought on this issue was clearly expressed by James I of England, commonly regarded by historians as a prototypical defender of absolute power. In his *Trew Law of Free Monarchies,* James acknowledged that a monarch has a duty toward his subjects. He is not authorized to behave capriciously, willfully, or selfishly in regard to his subjects' welfare. But should he fail to meet this duty, no earthly being has any right to oppose him, or even to refuse obedience to his commands, for he has been made monarch by God and to God alone is he answerable. In James's construal, the authority of the monarch to exercise the power of the state is only constrained by his fear of divine punishment. One might well be skeptical concerning the operative force of such a constraint. History shows that the fear of God has had little influence upon the exercise of power, even by princes of the church, let alone secular rulers. Indeed, monarchical absolutism would seem to be privileged, because it can be justified by direct reference to holy writ; any monarch who claims absolute power can quote 1 Samuel, as James I did, in clear support of his demand.[10]

How about a statement of the *purpose* of government, to exercise a moral constraint upon governors? At the dawn of the Roman Republic, the "Twelve Tables" (as close as the Romans came to writing a constitution) asserted that *salus populi suprema lex esto* (the welfare of the people must be the supreme law). This principle has been reiterated often by political philosophers since Roman times, most notably by Jeremy Bentham and James Mill in explicating the political implications of the philosophy of utilitarianism. But the principle is mere exhortation; it is toothless, without power to constrain state authorities who are free to declare what does, and what does not, serve the welfare of the people. In Republican Rome, state power was indeed subject to significant constraints, but these derived from the institutional structure of Roman government, not from the principle of *salus populi*.

Perhaps we are pursuing the wrong object here. Plato, the first systematic political theorist, construed the fundamental problem of government to be the selection of the right governors. If that were done, constraining the exercise of political power would be unnecessary, and indeed absurd. Why should one bind the hands of governors who are wise and good? The notion that the best form of government is a benevolent dictatorship has appeared often in the history of Western political thought since Plato and, indeed, it would be difficult to find any despotic ruler who did not sincerely believe that his great labors were devoted to improving the welfare of his subjects. But the history of dictatorial government indicates that, whatever the ruler's initial intent, dictatorships invariably degenerate into repressive tyrannies. The desire for power is not, at bottom, the desire to possess the power to do good, but the desire to possess power *tout court*. Whether exercised by a monarch or by a small group, persons who regard themselves as especially wise and virtuous are probably the worst custodians of power.

Historical experience, however, is not an unrelieved record of failure to

10. Chapter 8 of 1 Samuel tells how the children of Israel, having become dissatisfied with the direct governance of God as mediated by the prophet Samuel, asked that a king be established to rule them "like the other nations." God acceded to the request, but only after warning them that their king will, in effect, treat them as little more than slaves.

deal with the problem of power. A number of societies have succeeded in constructing political systems in which the power of the state is constrained. The key to their success lies in recognizing the fact that *power can only be controlled by power.* This proposition leads directly to the theory of constitutional design founded upon the principle most commonly known as "checks and balances." The general use of that term originated in the debates over the establishment of the American Constitution, but the central idea is older, and wider in its application. In the political domain, it was clearly stated by the Baron de Montesquieu in his interpretation of the English Constitution in his *Spirit of the Laws* (1748). In the preceding century John Locke, in his *Second Treatise of Government* (1689), advocated a separation of legislative from executive powers as a structural device to prevent government from becoming arbitrary and tyrannical. Gasparo Contarini used the concept of checks and balances in his analysis of the governmental system of Renaissance Venice (1543), and back as far as the second century B.C., the Greek-Roman historian Polybius interpreted the constitution of the Roman Republic in terms of checks and balances (von Fritz, 1975).

As it has been usually employed in the modern literature of political science, the theory of checks and balances refers to the control of power within the domain of the formal structure of government. Politics, however, is broader than government, and political power is not just a matter pertaining to the institutions of the state. The operation of the political "law" that the organized few can dominate the unorganized many is not confined to the formal institutions of the state. Private institutions such as the National Rifle Association, the American Association of Retired Persons, and the Southern Baptist Conference are organized groups whose political power in America is considerable. In all constitutional democracies there are hundreds of such groups. Individual citizens, if they wish, can be members of many of them, and may participate in their activities in different ways and degrees, from merely paying annual dues, to occupying positions on governing boards or executives. The result of these forms of power dispersion is an intricate political system whose power relationships are not only complex, but also constantly shifting. If such a system were sketched as a proposal for a new state, it would probably be rejected as unworkable, but complex pluralistic political systems of this sort are in fact working in some parts of the modern world, with no less effectiveness, and more security of individual freedom, than polities built upon simpler and neater designs.

No two governments are identical in their institutional structures or modes of operation. The study of "Comparative Government," a standard topic in the modern academic curriculum, reveals an enormous variety, even excluding polities now defunct. Some scholars object to any attempt to classify these governments under a limited number of generic headings, but radical empiricism in social science, as in other disciplines, fails to serve the need to understand what one is observing. I would contend that there are only two basic models of social organization. In one, the authority to command is structured in hierarchical order, with each entity in the system obligated to obey those superior to it; at the top is an entity that is supreme. The other model depicts a network of independent entities that interact with each other, with no supreme authority. The operational concept that drives the analysis of the first model is the notion of "sovereignty." Its counterpart in the second is "countervailance," or the dynamics of checks and balances. In the next chapter, I shall review the history of the theory of sovereignty; in the rest of the book I shall examine specific cases of polities that adopted the countervailance model and attempt to trace the provenance of the *theory* of checks and balances. In preparation for this discussion, some brief further remarks on these basic models may be useful to the reader.

The second model is clearly "pluralist" in that it conceives of a polity operating with numerous centers of political power. That term has, however, been used in various ways in the modern literature. It often refers to communities whose populations are heterogeneous in respect of their racial, ethnic, linguistic, religious, or cultural compositions. This is an important subject, engaging the attention of practicing politicians as well as social scientists.[11] But I do not deal here with such pluralistic properties. Nor am I concerned directly with socioeconomic class differences, though these are also important in themselves. Ethnic, linguistic, class, and other dimensions that differentiate groups from each other are not irrelevant to the countervailance model, but they are subsumed in it as factors that may affect the distribution of political power.

In examining the historical and contemporary examples of constitutional orders, we must not lose sight of the fact that they contain a great deal of social organization that is hierarchically structured. Indeed, this is the standard mode of organization employed by business firms, churches, labor unions, government departments, and even the most loosely structured social arrangement—universities. In such a scheme of organization, every level is subordinate to a higher level, until one comes to a level that is subordinate to none—that is, none within the command structure of each particular institution. The doctrine of sovereignty holds that these chains of authority extend beyond the domains of the individual institutions and continue

---

11. Social pluralism, or "muticulturalism," became a major focus of attention in the 1960s, energized by belated concern for the plight of black Americans. *Beyond the Melting Pot,* by Nathan Glazer and Daniel Patrick Moynihan (1963) was especially influential in making this topic a priority of social research and policy.

into the political system, where they are incorporated in a singular institution that has the ultimate authority to compel obedience. That extension is inapplicable to constitutional polities, and insistence upon it only leads to a search for a "seat of sovereignty" that does not exist.

The prevalence of hierarchical organization is easy to explain. It is necessary for administrative efficiency, indeed it may be necessary for any orderly administrative functioning at all. For a ship at sea, or an army in battle, it is obvious why there must be a clear chain of command. Ambiguity of authority is as dangerous to a ship at sea as an uncharted reef in its course. Is it not likewise with the ship of state?

To resolve this issue, we must distinguish between two kinds of activities: immediate operational activities, and the determination of general objectives and a comprehensive strategy to achieve them. The administration of policy is not the same as the determination of policy. A ship at sea is operating under very different circumstances from the board of directors of the shipping company that must decide what kinds of ships to buy, what routes and schedules to set, what prices to charge, and so forth. The shipping company, in turn, is not coping with the same problems that must be addressed by the state in determining the nation's maritime law. At the level of the ship there are few, and only very minor, policy decisions to be made; effective administration is the paramount concern, and to secure it, a hierarchy of authority is necessary. At the level of the shipping company, a mixture of administration and policy exists. With respect to policy, the hierarchical order becomes much less self-sufficient because attention must be paid to the views of shareholders, customers, and "public opinion," as well as maritime and company law. Within the domain of the state, hierarchical order is necessary to effective administration by the executive departments, but the formation of public policy results from a complex set of interacting influences, with no identifiable "ultimate" authority.

The conception of a network of independent but interacting entities is not unique to political science. It is, in fact, the fundamental model employed in a number of modern disciplines, most notably in physics, biology, and economics. Newtonian celestial mechanics depicts the solar system as a stable order in which the sun and the planets interact with forces determined by their masses and the distances between them. The sun is "fixed" only in degree. It is not the "center" of the system in the sense that the earth was in Ptolemaic cosmology. Copernicus was a great innovator in transferring the locus of centrality from the earth to the sun, but not so innovative as Newton, in whose system there is, conceptually, no center at all. In biology, the concept of countervailance has also been productively employed in ecological analysis. The various organisms and species are modeled as interacting with each other and with the nonorganic environment in a shifting equilibrium that is the product of competitive, predatory, and symbiotic relationships. Standard microeconomic theory construes the economic system as composed of independent individuals and institutions that generate a "general equilibrium" by interacting in the markets where factors of production and final goods and services are exchanged. The countervailance model in political science is essentially the same. It can be defended simply as an effective instrument for the positive analysis of constitutional polities, but it has normative implications as well, which will engage our attention persistently in the following pages.

1

The Doctrine of Sovereignty

In scholarly literature, law, and common discourse, the term "sovereignty" has two quite different meanings. One refers to the status of a nation-state vis-à-vis other nation-states, indicating that each has autonomous jurisdiction within its own geographical area. The other refers to the notion that within each individual state there is a entity that constitutes the supreme political and legal authority. To say that the United Nations or the World Trade Organization is composed of sovereign states is not analogous to saying that in Great Britain sovereignty resides in its Parliament. Both of these notions of sovereignty are problematic, but the focus of this chapter is on the systems of authority within the state and, more specifically, upon the analytical and empirical problems that are encountered when sovereignty is construed to be the central concept that must be employed in understanding the governmental system of a nation such as Great Britain or the United States.

The Classical Doctrine of Sovereignty

The provenance of the concept of sovereignty in its domestic reference goes back at least to Justinian's codification of Roman law, and the issues it raises were prominent in the political literature of the late medieval period, but I will begin the discussion here with what, for the modern era, can be called the "classical" doctrine of sovereignty, as formulated by Jean Bodin and Thomas Hobbes.

Jean Bodin

Bodin's *Six Livres de la République* was published in 1576[1] and was an immediate success, in England no less than on the continent.[2] In France it appeared to address a matter of great contemporary importance, the political instability produced by the violent religious animosities of the period. J. H. Burns observes that the *République* was "a work of political propaganda as well as a theoretical inquiry. Bodin's polemical purpose was to vindicate royal authority and central power against a number of enemies" (1959, 176). But however strong his desire to influence contemporary political affairs, Bodin had also hoped to write a comprehensive treatise that would have a longer and broader influence in the sphere of universal political thought. He succeeded to a truly extraordinary degree.[3]

French legal scholarship in the sixteenth century was strongly focused on Roman law, with the object of discovering the principles of law that could be regarded as universally valid. This orientation must have been prominent in the instruction Bodin received as a student of civil law at the University of Toulouse in the 1550s. He formed the view that although general legal principles could not be derived from Roman law alone, a scheme of universal law could be constructed synthetically from a comparative and historical study of the laws of the most important states. His early publications were inspired by this objective. The *République* has a more restricted aim: the comparative study of legal systems in terms of a central heuristic concept—the concept of sovereignty.[4]

---

1. This version was written and published in French. Bodin prepared a Latin edition, somewhat enlarged, which was published in 1586. The only complete English translation that exists was prepared by Richard Knolles from both the French and Latin texts, and published under the title of *The Six Bookes of the Commonweale* in 1606. Kenneth D. McRae reprinted the Knolles translation (edited somewhat), with an introductory essay, in 1962. The parts of it dealing specifically with the issue of sovereignty have recently been translated afresh by Julian Franklin, and published in 1992, with an introductory essay. All direct references to Bodin in the following text are to Franklin's translation and will be indicated as "(Bodin, 1992)."

2. Within four years of its initial publication, the *République* was reprinted eight times. Sixteen reprints appeared during the next two decades (Kossmann, 1981, 5). "It was known and read all over Europe, and was promptly made a textbook in English universities" (Clark, 1915, lxi; see also Burgess, 1996, 65).

3. Bodin's *République* "is, in a very real sense, an attempt at a general system of politics, and contemporaries were not far wrong in likening it to the *Politics* of Aristotle" (McRae, 1962, A9).

4. "In Bodin's design," notes Franklin, "the basis for comparing states, and explaining their schemes of public law, was to determine and describe the locus of sovereignty in each" (Bodin, 1992, xvi).

Bodin broadened the traditional domain of legal scholarship in two respects: his strategy required that legal systems other than the Roman be consulted, and that the inquiry be diverted from examination of the laws themselves to the political system that generates laws. Bodin assumed without question that every stable political system is necessarily hierarchical in organization as, indeed, are the domains of the natural and the divine. Analysis of any political system must therefore begin with the most basic question: What person or body of persons is at the apex of the hierarchical order? The entity that occupies this position has the authority to make binding laws and, in exercising its lawmaking powers, it is not subject to constraint by any other human agent. This is the status of the political institution in a state that can properly be described as its sovereign authority.

Although Bodin leans toward monarchy as the best type of state, he does not contend that this is the only stable form of political organization. He adopts the ancient classification of basic types of states as monarchies, aristocracies, and democracies: government by one, few, or many, respectively. In all cases, however, there exists a sovereign authority. Bodin does not, at bottom, derive this from empirical evidence. Every state, in his view, *must* have a seat of sovereignty. This proposition serves as an axiomatic principle that is necessary in directing the empirical investigation of particular states. In pursuing such an investigation, it is essential to determine at the outset whether the state in question is a monarchy, aristocracy, or democracy. This determination can be made if, and only if, one ascertains where the seat of sovereignty lies. There may be cases, Bodin notes, where the locus of sovereignty is uncertain because the predominance of power may shift from time to time, but in most cases it is plain who has the authority to make laws, the fundamental power of a sovereign.[5] He categorized republican Rome as a

5. "This same power of making and repealing law includes all the other rights and prerogatives of sovereignty, so that strictly speaking we can say that there is only this one prerogative of sovereignty, inasmuch as all the other rights are comprehended in it—such as declaring war or making peace; hearing appeals in last instance from the judgments of any magistrate; instituting and removing the highest officers; imposing taxes and aids on subjects or exempting them; granting pardons and dispensations against the rigor of law; determining the name, value, and measure of the coinage; requiring subjects and liege vassals to swear that they will be loyal without exception to the person to whom their oath is owed. These are the true prerogatives of sovereignty, which are included in the power to give law to all in general and to each in particular, and not to receive law from anyone but God" (Bodin, 1992, 58f.). McRae notes that, prior to the *Six Books,* French jurists had been inclined to construe sovereign power in terms of the traditional prerogatives of the crown. "Bodin was the first to emphasize . . . that the most fundamental of these various rights was the power to make laws" (1962, A14).

democracy, and contemporary Venice as an aristocracy.[6] But aristocracies and democracies were not construed by Bodin to be systems in which sovereign power is shared among a number of independent political entities. It is still unified, in the body of the nobility as a whole in contemporary Venice, and in the people as a whole (or "the greater part" thereof) in republican Rome.

Bodin's assertion that all stable polities have a definite seat of sovereign power was not what made the *République* one of the most influential works in early modern political thought. Its importance was due to his explication of what the term "sovereignty" *means*. In Bodin's view, to describe an entity in a political system as "sovereign" denotes that its authority is absolute, indivisible, and permanent. A political entity that lacks any of these properties is not a supreme authority, and one must look elsewhere for the true locus of sovereignty. In order to understand the fundamental nature of a political organization, whether monarchical, aristocratic, or democratic, one must recognize that its sovereign authority necessarily possesses these three attributes.

In describing a sovereign as "absolute," Bodin meant the term to be taken literally: there are no limitations on what a sovereign may do. "Sovereignty given to a prince subject to obligations and conditions," writes Bodin, "is properly not sovereign or absolute power." He continues: "The main point of sovereign majesty and absolute power consists of giving the law to subjects in general without their consent . . . For a sovereign prince has to have the laws in his power in order to change and correct them according to the circumstances" (1992, 8, 23f.). There are no procedural or substantive constraints upon the power of the prince, and his decrees must be implemented by state officials and obeyed by the citizenry. There is no "right of resistance," as the persecuted French Protestants claimed, no matter how bad the government of the sovereign might be.[7]

The absolute power of sovereignty, explains Bodin, must be concentrated in a single entity. It cannot be shared; it is by its very nature "indivisible."[8]

---

6. It seems to me that whenever Bodin encountered a case where the seat of sovereignty was difficult to locate, classifying it as an aristocracy or a democracy provided an easy escape. In his discussion of federal forms of political organization, such as the German Empire, Bodin comes close to abandoning the concept of sovereignty. As we shall see, federalism has posed especially great difficulties for modern adherents to the sovereignty doctrine.

7. Franklin contends that in Bodin's earlier book, *Method for the Easy Comprehension of History* (1566), he specifically repudiated the notion that sovereignty must be absolute. Franklin suggests that Bodin amended his view of sovereignty in reaction to the "revolutionary movement set off by the Saint Bartholomew's Day Massacre of 1572" (1973, 23, 41). Quentin Skinner makes the same assessment of Bodin's change of view between the *Method* and the *République* (1978, 2:284f.).

8. "Just as God, the great sovereign, cannot make a God equal to Himself because He is infinite and by logical necessity . . . two infinities cannot exist, so that we can say that the

A sovereign may delegate power to subordinate officials, but those officials do not thereby acquire any sovereignty of their own. All actions of the state are the direct or indirect expression of the will of the singular sovereign authority. Bodin's central doctrine was crisply embodied in the statement that *imperium in imperio* (power within power) is a logical impossibility. This Latin tag was frequently cited as a negating axiom in Western political literature down to, and including, the debate on the American Constitution in the 1780s. Reification is necessary to apply the principle of indivisibility to polities such as ancient Athens or republican Rome, but this does not appear to have worried Bodin. He conceived of sovereignty as held by one person or a tightly organized group of persons.[9]

Numerous passages can be quoted from the *République* that express Bodin's concept of sovereignty in unambiguous terms (see, e.g., 1992, 15, 23, 25, 27, 46, 57f., 117). But there are also passages in which he contends that the command of a sovereign authority is not valid if it violates the laws of God or nature, disregards the commitments of previous sovereign authorities, or unilaterally breaks a contractual agreement (1992, 31f., 35f., 39, 43–45). Commentators on Bodin have noted the inconsistency of his views, and efforts to provide a coherent interpretation of his political theory persist to the present day.[10] I will not review these studies here; for our purposes it is sufficient to note that what entered the literature as "the Bodinian theory of sovereignty" was the unqualified version: sovereignty is absolute, indivisible, and permanent. This was the notion of sovereignty that engaged the attention of subsequent writers, defenders and critics alike.[11]

---

prince, whom we have taken as the image of God, cannot make a subject equal to himself without annihilation of his power" (Bodin, 1992, 50). This passage shows clearly that, for all the illustrative historical material in Bodin's discussion, his concept of sovereignty was analytical—that is, the properties of sovereignty are construed by him to be logically inherent in the concept itself.

9. "Bodin held . . . that the powers of sovereignty were indivisible and consequently that they must all be possessed by some identifiable human being or organization of human beings . . . Bodin thought that there had to be a sovereign, not just sovereignty, in every state" (Goldsmith, 1980, 39).

10. David Parker is perhaps more critical than most: "Jean Bodin's *Six Books* . . . has a well established reputation as one of the most confusing works of political theory ever written. Ambiguities and contradictions abound; so much so that even the pivotal thesis that sovereignty is indivisible and absolute, plainly enunciated early in the work, becomes problematic because of the equally clear retention of a framework of natural law and divine law within which a just monarch is morally obligated to operate" (1981, 253; see also Allen, 1949). For a systematic examination of Bodin's apparent inconsistencies in terms of contemporary juristic theory, see Shepard (1930). For an attempt to acquit Bodin of the charge of inconsistency, see Lewis (1968).

11. On the basis of a detailed examination of the European political literature from the

In addition to classifying states as monarchies, aristocracies, and democracies, Aristotle had noted a fourth form, a mixture of these basic types. Bodin flatly rejected this notion on the ground that such a state would violate the principle that sovereignty is indivisible.[12] Noting that various authors had described ancient Sparta and Rome as mixtures, as well as contemporary Venice, the German Empire, and the Swiss states, Bodin contends that they were mistaken. Closer examination of the locus of sovereignty in these polities, he says, reveals that they were (are) pure forms, either aristocracies or democracies (1992, 93–106).[13]

Thomas Hobbes

The writer best known to English-speaking students of intellectual history as the author of the classical doctrine of sovereignty was not Jean Bodin but Thomas Hobbes. His *Leviathan,* in which that doctrine is advanced and amplified, was published in 1651, two years after Charles I, the sovereign of England, had been executed at the order of Parliament. Hobbes was born a commoner, but he succeeded in getting to Oxford University and from the time of his graduation was connected with members of the high aristocracy. He was mathematics tutor to the Prince of Wales, followed him into exile in 1640, and continued on close personal terms with him after he became King Charles II in the Restoration of 1660. Hobbes first expounded the essentials

---

beginning of the thirteenth to the end of the sixteenth century, Kenneth Pennington contends (contrary to other scholars such as Skinner, McRae, and Franklin) that virtually all that Bodin had to say on the subject of sovereignty had been developed by previous writers. "His definition of absolute power was taken from earlier jurists, and the limitations that he placed upon it were adopted from their thought." In Pennington's judgment, Bodin's contribution was "conceptual rather than substantive" in that he used the concept of sovereignty to draw together the issues relating to princely power, which his predecessors had discussed extensively, but less systematically (1993, 283). If this is correct, Bodin must be mainly credited for establishing the methodological view, which persists to the present, that sovereignty is an indispensable heuristic concept in the study of political systems.

12. "To combine monarchy with democracy and with aristocracy is impossible and contradictory, and cannot even be imagined. For if sovereignty is indivisible, as we have shown, how could it be shared by a prince, the nobles, and the people at the same time?" (Bodin, 1992, 92). For a summary of Bodin's views on mixed government, see Franklin (1968) and (1991).

13. Before we take leave of Bodin, we might note that he did not regard the political instability attending any dilution of sovereignty as the only, or indeed the greatest, threat to European civilization. Like many others of his time, he believed that Satan's covert votaries were numerous among professed Christians. His *Démomanie,* calling for unremitting effort to discover witches, and to extirpate them, was more immediately influential than the *République.* The former is seldom mentioned by historians of political thought, but it helps one to understand Bodin's Manichaean view of the world.

of his political theory in 1640 in his *Elements of Law*. Although he restated it yet again in numerous writings thereafter, it is the *Leviathan* that most clearly and completely contained his famous statement of the contract theory of the state, and the doctrine of absolute sovereignty.[14]

"As a defense of absolute sovereignty," declares Irving Zeitlin, "the *Leviathan* remains the outstanding philosophical essay of the century, unsurpassed for its intellectual rigour and logical consistency" (1997, 110). In its basic argument, the *Leviathan* parallels that of Bodin's *République* (see Hampton, 1986, 239f.). Hobbes was a scholar and cannot have been ignorant of of the *République,* but he makes no reference to it in the *Leviathan*. It is tempting to regard Hobbes as merely a clever political hack who engaged in the manufacture of royalist propaganda, with secondhand materials, for service in the contemporary struggle between the Stuart monarchy and Parliament. But there are a number of reasons why the *Leviathan* should not be so summarily dismissed.

First, Hobbes used his contract theory of the state to bolster the doctrine of absolute sovereignty. In view of the important role that contract theory has played (and continues to play) in the history of political thought, this gave a significant measure of weight to Hobbes's exposition of the doctrine that Bodin's lacked. Most contract theorists, before and after Hobbes, employed it in defense of the right of the citizenry to disobey, and even to rebel against, established political authority. A few earlier writers had resorted to the theory of contract in support of absolutism, but no one had provided anything comparable to Hobbes's systematic argumentation. This being the case, it was virtually inevitable that when Locke's contract theory was embraced as the foundational doctrine of English constitutionalism after the Revolution of 1688, Hobbes would be singled out as the archetypical exponent of the contrary view. In modern textbooks on the history of political thought, Hobbes and Locke are invariably coupled, like Siamese twins who share vital organs but face in opposite directions.

Second, of the flaws in Bodin's contention that every stable polity must have a *singular* seat of sovereignty, the most conspicuous in his era was the empirical fact that authority to exercise coercive power was, in France and most other countries, divided between the state and the church. In England,

14. The term "Leviathan" appears in the Old Testament as a sea monster of incomparable ferocity (Job 41) that only God can slay (Isaiah 27:1). According to Catherine Armstrong, the Hebrew "Leviathan" derives from an earlier mythical creature called "Lotan," a seven-headed dragon that "symbolizes the latent, the unformed and undifferentiated" (1993, 10). From this, as a political notion, "Leviathan" would seem to be an appropriate term for the state of nature, but Hobbes used it to refer to the sovereign, and this has become standard.

this division had been dissolved in the reign of Henry VIII, with the separation of the English church from the authority of Rome and its formal incorporation within the domain of the state. Hobbes approved of this arrangement, and the subordination of the church to the secular authority was one of the most notable features of his doctrine of sovereignty. In the *Leviathan*, he delineates twelve "rights" that the secular sovereign holds by virtue of the social contract (1968, 229–236). These include the right to determine what "doctrines" and "opinions"—presumably including religious doctrines and opinions—are to be promulgated by anyone. The first of the rights he there lays down denies the Puritan doctrine that there is a "covenant" between the individual and God. One can only come to God through the mediation of "God's Lieutenant who hath the Sovereignty," writes Hobbes, declaring "this pretence of Covenant with God is so evident a lie, even in the pretender's own consciences, that it is not onely an act of an unjust, but also of a vile, and unmanly disposition." Hobbes appears here to have been concerned with the claims of the nonconformist Protestant sects to exemption from secular authority in matters of conscience, but he must also have been aware that the opposite doctrine—that the state was subservient to the church—was widely held by Catholic theologians, and by some Protestant ones as well. Hobbes's personal faith is somewhat uncertain, but he left no doubt as to his views on the relation between church and state. He was a fully committed "Erastian," holding that religious institutions are, and must be, subject to the authority of the secular monarch. There is much discussion of religion in the latter part of the *Leviathan*, but its main object is to show that God intends man to obey his secular sovereign, and him alone, and unconditionally.

Hobbes's position on church and state was simply an application of his insistence on the indivisibility of sovereignty. All social institutions, without exception, must be subordinate to the secular sovereign for, in Hobbes's view, any recognition of independent authority leads inevitably to the degeneration of the political order and a return to the state of nature—where there is constant warfare and, in the much-quoted passage, the life of man is "solitary, poor, nasty, brutish, and short." In the *Behemoth*, an analysis of events leading up to the Civil War, which Hobbes wrote in the later 1660s but did not publish,[15] he attacked the notion of divided power at length, and attributed the breakdown of the English political system as due to Parliament's insistence on sharing power with the king (see Hampton, 1986, 111).

Third, as a political theorist, Jean Bodin had one foot, and part of the other, in the Aristotelian mode of analysis. He did not derive the properties

---

15. It was published posthumously, in 1679.

of sovereignty from empirical evidence; they were construed as metaphysically "essential" properties, and sovereignty, therefore, *by virtue of its very nature,* must be absolute and indivisible. Hobbes's argument is very different: sovereign authority is viewed as a pragmatic necessity. Without it, the terrible evils of the state of nature cannot be overcome. All self-interested persons are endowed with the capacity to reason know this, and in entering upon the social contract, they are fully aware that the sovereign they establish will be a despotic authority. They have no need for God to warn them of this, as the Israelites of biblical times had been warned; their own reason tells them that it must be so. In consulting their self-interest, they conclude that subjecting themselves to such an authority is worth doing, in order to obtain the prerequisite social conditions of "commodious living." Thus we see that the foundation of Hobbes's political theory is his conception of humankind, and his mode of analysis is to deduce the consequences that must flow from man's egocentric nature, and his rationality.

One may question whether Hobbes's conclusions flow compellingly from his psychological assumptions. The French Protestant political theorist Philippe du Plessis Mornay, writing earlier than Hobbes, expressed the view that it is absurd to suggest that rational people would freely choose to place themselves under an absolute sovereign. And John Locke, writing later, argued that, upon contracting to form a civil society, rational people would reserve the right to rebel against the established order if it proved to be tyrannous. But even if he was wrong in his inference, Hobbes's *procedure* is highly significant. It anticipated Jeremy Bentham's contention that social analysis must be based upon the psychological principle of rational self-interest, a view that has had a momentous and enduring influence on the analytical social sciences.[16]

Hobbes's procedure, moreover, was not merely opportunistic; it derived from carefully considered principles of scientific epistemology. He was a great admirer of Galileo and even went to visit him in Italy, in 1636, to obtain advice about how to apply the methods of the natural sciences to the study of politics. In the *Leviathan* and other writings, he employed Galileo's method of resolution and recomposition (Peters, 1967, 35); he adapted to the social domain Galileo's principle that motion, not rest, is the natural state of affairs; defined the human passions as "voluntary motions"; and in nu-

---

16. "For all its ambiguities, oversights, and obvious defects, Hobbes's psychology was remarkable, for he attempted to establish it as an objective study untrammeled by theological assumptions. To suggest that man is a machine was a great step forward in thought. Even though the hypothesis is probably untenable, it marked the beginning of the effort to use scientific methods and objective concepts in the sphere of human behavior. In the seventeenth century this was a novel undertaking, as well as a dangerous one" (Peters, 1967, 39).

merous other ways attempted to utilize the "geometrical method" of the new natural sciences. He was the first of a long line of writers to consider himself to be the Galileo (or, later, the Newton) of social science.[17] In this fashion Hobbes constructed a doctrine of sovereignty that, despite its growing irrelevance as constitutional polities developed, helped to persuade many political scientists and jurists that the concept of sovereignty in some form or another is indispensable in political analysis.

Finally, we should note that one of the outstanding merits of Hobbes's reasoning is that he maintains a steady focus upon the crucial issue of *power*. In the state of nature, the power to coerce is dependent only upon personal capacities. The social contract, however, establishes a system or *organized* coercive power. Bodin construed sovereignty as the power to make law, but Hobbes treated it as the power to coerce, by law and in accordance with law, or without law and in disregard of it (McIlwain, 1950, 115). In recognizing the significance of organization—that the organized few can invariably dominate the unorganized many—Hobbes laid his finger upon the central issue in political science. Machiavelli is sometimes called the father of political science, but his focus upon power consists only of ascertaining the means by which a prince can keep his crown when surrounded by others who aspire to wear it. With Hobbes, a much broader, and potentially more fruitful, approach to the study of political power is opened. Unfortunately, Hobbes's insistence that sovereignty must be indivisible precluded him, and many others after, from following a line of thought that leads to the pluralist conception of politics.

The literature I shall now proceed to examine is concerned not with the nature of sovereignty, but (accepting as given that there must be a sovereign authority in every stable state) what entity should be regarded as morally entitled to occupy the seat of sovereignty, or, what is in fact the sovereign authority in a particular state. There are a number of answers to the normative question that can be found in the literature, but the most important of these is the view that "the people" constitute the proper repository of sovereign authority. For the positive question, the literature that demands our attention contends that in the particular case of Great Britain, sovereignty resides in Parliament.

17. As Macpherson puts it, "He was sure that politics could be made a science. He believed that he had done it, and that he was the first to have done it" (1962, 10). This view of Hobbes has not gone unchallenged. Leo Strauss in particular, to whom the very notion of a scientific study of politics was anathema, rejected it categorically (1962).

The People as Sovereign

The provenance of the doctrine of popular sovereignty in Western thought is long, going back to ancient Greece and Rome. The Athenian democracy of the fifth and fourth centuries B.C. is, even today, commonly instanced as its classical existential expression. The notion that the sovereignty of the state resides ultimately with the citizenry was often expressed in republican Rome, and it continued to be expressed after the fall of the republic, when political power became concentrated in the hands of one man, the emperor.[18] The idea reappeared in the late medieval literature, often in a form derived from the maxim in the Justinian code that "what touches all must be approved by all."[19] J. W. Gough discerns "a definite theory of popular sovereignty" in the writings of Manegold von Lautenbach (later eleventh century), the first writer to express clearly the notion that government is founded on a contract between the people and their governor (1957, 31). The oft-expressed formula *vox populi, vox dei* (the voice of the people is the voice of God) goes back much further; according to Monahan, at least to Alcuin in the eighth century, though he warns that the "people" in such expressions probably meant the nobility rather than the populace at large (1987, 56). Thomas Aquinas maintained that while the authority of the pope comes directly from God, that of the secular authority derives from the people (Merriam, 1972, 12).[20]

Marsilius of Padua's *Defensor Pacis* (1323) deserves special note in tracing the provenance of the idea of popular sovereignty. An Erastian two centuries before Erastus, Marsilius was a vociferous critic of the papacy. In developing his attack on the contemporary ecclesiastical order, of which he was himself a member, he advanced some propositions of considerable significance in the general history of political theory. Following Aquinas, he applied the holistic metaphysical concept of "bodies corporate" in medieval philosophy (which was frequently used to describe the church) to the people. According to this view, a society is not a mere aggregation of individuals but an entity in itself (Monahan, 1987, 209f.). Though it is the "weightier part" of the populace that must represent the whole in political matters, the authority to make law must lie with the people (Lloyd, 1991, 256). There can never be a plurality of governors, for that would only lead to "civic discord and strife," but the

18. James Bryce points out that the Justinian Code referred to the people as the supreme legislative authority, and construed each successive emperor as having personally received it by delegation (1901, 525).

19. "From the eleventh century on, the principle of popular sovereignty became increasingly familiar as a result of the revival of Roman law and the scholastic study of classical philosophy" (Franklin, 1969, 12).

20. "St. Thomas Aquinas recognizes sovereignty as originally and primarily vested in the people, hardly less explicitly than the Declaration of Independence" (Bryce, 1901, 529).

singular executive authority of the state has only a delegated power; the people never alienate their sovereignty (Skinner, 1978, 1:57, 61f.).[21]

In the early seventeenth century, Johannes Althusius, writing in defense of the Dutch rebellion against Spain, adapted Bodinian theory to the task of establishing the principle of the sovereignty of the people (Cooper, 1960, 68; Kossmann, 1960, 93; Franklin, 1991, 312). The fact that seventeenth-century writers such as Pufendorf (Dufour, 1991, 575) and Filmer (see Chapter 7) singled out the doctrine of popular sovereignty for special criticism attests to its prevalence.[22] The phrase "the sovereignty of the people," and its equivalents, appears often in the English literature preceding and during the Civil War (see Morgan, 1989, esp. pt. 1).

One must constantly bear in mind that in earlier times the phrase "the people" did not mean what it (usually) does today in political discourse. In Periclean Athens, slaves and women were excluded from political participation, as were many adult free males. In republican Rome, in addition to excluding slaves and women, membership in the popular assemblies was restricted to Roman citizens, a designation that qualified only the Latin-speaking tribes, and not even all of those. The "people" of Rome in the ubiquitous acronym *SPQR* (*Senatus Populusque Romanus*—the Senate and People of Rome) included less than a majority of the peoples of Latium, let alone the Italian peninsula as a whole or the vast colonial empire under the sway of the Roman Republic. Late medieval and Renaissance writers who espoused the sovereignty of the people would have been hard put to name any continuing polity in Europe in which more than a small fraction of the population actually participated in political processes. In England, well up to the end of the eighteenth century, literary use of the phrase "the people" commonly referred to a small portion of the population. Even in America, in the literature of the Revolution and Constitution periods, the ubiquitous locution "the people" was commonly construed to exclude slaves, and though there was no hereditary aristocracy and few that corresponded to the English gentry, the founding fathers regarded the business of governance as best confined to "the better sort" of the populace. Nevertheless, semantics aside, the early proponents of popular sovereignty, like more recent ones, claimed that, in some unspecified fashion, the ultimate power in a state resides (or ought to reside) with those whose lives are impacted by it.

---

21. On the importance in Marsilius's philosophical thought of the notion that political power derives from the people, see Gewirth (1951).

22. Filmer quotes a striking passage from Cardinal Bellarmine stating that "by the Divine law," secular and civil power is vested "immediately in the whole multitude" (1949, 56).

Except for Marsilius of Padua, none of the early proponents of popular sovereignty undertook to explicate its meaning. In the mid-eighteenth century, just a short while before the American and French revolutions made the notion of popular sovereignty the cynosure of democratic political thought, this issue was addressed by Jean-Jacques Rousseau, who followed a similar path to that which Marsilius had taken by arguing that an organized political community ceases to be a mere collection of individuals and becomes an entity in itself. But Rousseau extends the idea much further. He reifies the abstract concept of a community into a real existent that has properties of purpose and value judgment like individual human beings. In the ideal social collectivity, as he conceives it, the opinions, interests, and preferences of individuals are amalgamated into the "general will," which is the only legitimate sovereign authority—legitimate because it contains, and transcends, the wills of the individual members. In such a regime, laws that are in accordance with the general will are not coercive, and they are never unjust, for no one can coerce or be unjust to oneself (Rousseau, 1913, 33). The freedom of the individual is preserved intact, even if force is required to administer the laws of the state. Rousseau retains the Bodinian properties; the sovereign power is absolute, indivisible, and permanent, but the locus of power is displaced from a concrete political entity such as a monarch or a council to a collective abstraction, "the people."

The modern democratic notion that the "ultimate" locus of sovereign authority is the people derives mainly from the American and French revolutions. Michael Kammen observes that in America, "in the years 1774–87 . . . popular sovereignty became a standard refrain sung by a swelling chorus" (1988, 18; see also Bailyn, 1967, 198f.). George Mason wrote for the Virginia Declaration of Rights (1776), "That all power is vested in, and consequently derived from, the People; that magistrates are their trustees and servants, and at all times amenable to them" (Kammen, 1988, 19). For some, the American Constitution constructed the first government in history based on the principle of popular sovereignty. Speaking at the convention called in Pennsylvania to ratify the proposed Constitution, James Wilson declared: "The supreme, absolute, and uncontrollable authority *remains* with the people . . . The practical recognition of this truth was reserved for the honor of this country. I recollect no constitution founded on this principle . . . The great and penetrating mind of Locke seems to be the only one that pointed towards even the theory of this great truth" (Richards, 1989, 96). In opening his examination of the doctrine of popular sovereignty in revolutionary-era American thought, a modern historian observes, "From the perspective of European monarchists as well as Enlightenment thinkers, the proclamation of the principle of popular sovereignty in the American founding documents was a momentous innovation" (Adams, 1980, 129).[23]

In assessing the role of the doctrine of popular sovereignty in late-eighteenth-century American thought, one must distinguish between the initiation of the Revolution and the drafting of the Constitution, events separated by two decades of war and social instability as well as the generation of much political literature. During the first period, when the main preoccupation of American political thought was to justify rebellion against established authority, the writer most frequently quoted was John Locke, whose social contract theory embodied the notion that sovereignty resides ultimately with the governed, an authority that they have a right to invoke in extreme conditions. Locke's reasoning is clearly evident in the argumentation of the Declaration of Independence, but it is worth noting that "the sovereignty of the people" or equivalent expressions are not present there. Thomas Jefferson, who drafted it, and his colleagues who revised and approved it, were conversant with European literature and must have been familiar with Rousseau's writings, but his formulation of the doctrine of popular sovereignty makes no appearance in the important documents of the American revolutionary period.

The literature of the 1780s provides even less ground for reading popular sovereignty into American political thought as more than a superficial locution. The Constitution itself begins grandly with the phrase "We the people of the United States," but when it proceeds to the more prosaic task of constructing the working machinery of government, it blueprints a system in which neither the people nor any other entity has sovereign status. Institutional devices are created to detach the state from direct control by the people, such as in the establishment of an electoral college to serve as an intermediary in choosing a president, and in the procedure (then) prescribed for filling seats in the Senate. No political entity is given power that could possibly be construed as absolute, indivisible, or permanent, let alone all three. Instead, the various entities are awarded equal and independent status, in order that they may act to constrain each other. So far as the people at large are concerned, they are not even given authority to amend the Constitution, which would seem to be the one power, more than any other, that lies within the province of any entity considered to be "ultimately" sovereign. One of the main objects of the Constitution, reinforced by the first ten amendments, was to protect the people from the state, not to place Bodinian sovereignty

23. The doctrine of popular sovereignty was especially prominent in the public debates over the procedures for ratifying the proposed national Constitution by the states. On this, see Rakove (1997, ch. 5).

in the hands of the people at large, or their representatives. The individualistic temperament of the Americans, engaged in conquering a wilderness without the leadership of established authorities, was not hospitable even to the abstract concept of popular sovereignty, and certainly not to the formulation of it that Rousseau provided.[24]

The story of the French Revolution is very different. It rapidly degenerated into a bloody tyranny, for which the sovereignty of the people was flagrantly invoked as moral justification. The Estates General were called to meet in the spring of 1789, for the first time since 1614. After such a lapse, there was hardly anything that could be resorted to as conventions of procedure. Members of the elected body, the Third Estate, adopted the view that they, and they alone, represented the nation. After withdrawing from the other estates and meeting separately, they declared themselves to be a national assembly and proclaimed the principle of popular sovereignty. This was reiterated two months later in the foundation document of the new regime, the *Declaration of the Rights of Man and the Citizen,* in terms that were "to confer on popular sovereignty the sacredness which had always accompanied the acts of the monarchy by appealing to universal principles and the authority of God" (Fontana, 1992, 115). From that point on it was all downhill; the Revolution degenerated into the Terror. The revolutionary slogan "Liberty, Equality, Fraternity" became a propaganda mask for official murder on a grand scale, and it was retained to do like service by Napoleon, who having become dictatorial master of France, turned the country's revolutionary energies to the military conquest of Europe.[25]

24. In dealing with the "Changing Concepts of Popular Sovereignty, 1764–1788" in America, Kammen admits that it is uncertain "whether popular sovereignty is most sensibly referred to as a theory, a concept, or simply a shifting set of attitudes" (1988, 14). Of the three, the last appears to be the most that can be claimed. Nevertheless, it cannot be denied that, in modern American thought, the notion continues that governmental authority is derived from "the people," and finds expression even when its empirical foundations are highly dubious. For example, in the elections of 1994, when the Republican Party won control of both houses of Congress, party leaders confidently contended that they had been given a "mandate" by "the people" to carry through a program of radical reform, despite the fact that only 39 percent of the electorate voted and, in the aggregate, Republican candidates received only 52 percent of the votes cast.

25. In his "Lectures on Heroes" Thomas Carlyle remarked, approvingly, that "The French Revolution found its Evangelist in Rousseau" (1888, 325). The American historian of sociology, Robert Nisbet, offers a more detailed appraisal: "Rousseau's relation to the Revolution is an interesting one. To think of him as one of the 'causes' of the Revolution is, of course, absurd. He was too little read, too little respected in France during the years that preceded the Revolution. Even in 1789, when the Revolution broke out, there is little evidence that his ideas mattered very much. But by 1791, . . . he had become the Grey Eminence of the Revolution: the most admired, most quoted, and most influential of all

There was, of course, a reaction, led by the church and expressed in French political theory most strikingly by Louis de Bonald's *Théorie du pouvoir politique et religieux* (1796) and Joseph de Maistre's *Considérations sur la France* (1797). De Maistre far outdid Hobbes in reading the political upheaval he was living through as certifying the necessity of monarchical absolutism. Secular power, when sanctified by the true religion, he contended, partakes of divine authority. It is absolute and indivisible, and the duty of the citizen is total submission to the state and unquestionable obedience to its officers. The doctrine of the sovereignty of the people is atheistical and must be rejected by all adherents of the true religion. He warned that correction of the Revolution's errors would not be easy. The Terror evidenced the fact that a great evil had entered the world, one that could only be combatted by the further shedding of blood, even that of innocents, for all members of the body politic were tarnished with collective guilt. And, for de Maistre, the reconstruction of the social order demanded yet more: firm rejection of the intellectual principles of the Renaissance and the Enlightenment; the suppression of science, rationalism, and utilitarianism; the ending of religious toleration; and the submission of the state to the supervision of the Catholic Church.[26]

Yet despite the excesses committed in the name of popular sovereignty, the idea was quite impervious to criticism by dithyrambic intellectuals like de Maistre, and also by more sober observers. The doctrine retained, and still retains, a prominent and honored place in Western political thought.[27] It is common opinion in democratic states that the best form of government is self-government, and that this is achievable if sovereign authority rests, at least ultimately, with the people. The contrary notion—that all government

the *philosophes*. His exciting combination of individualistic equalitarianism . . . and of a General Will that gave legitimacy to absolute political power . . . was made to order for revolutionary aspirations" (Nisbet, 1966, 35).

26. An excellent essay on de Maistre is Isaiah Berlin's "Joseph de Maistre and the Origins of Fascism" (1991, 91–174). For a brief, but more comprehensive, examination of the reactionary school, see Merriam (1972, ch. 3).

27. "Since the American and French Revolutions . . . it [popular sovereignty] has sooner or later come to be the prevalent doctrine, at least in all the more advanced political societies" (Hinsley, 1986, 154). Hinsley regards Rousseau's expression of the doctrine as one that will remain definitive: "it can be modified in detail, but it cannot in essence be outdone." That popular sovereignty continues to have appeal in normative political theory and empirical political analysis is clearly shown in Mostov (1992). The use of the notion in American constitutional jurisprudence also remains undiminished. In a recent judgment of the Supreme Court, which denied to state governments the authority to limit the terms of office of federal senators and congressmen, Justice John Paul Stevens, author of the majority decision, declared that "a critical postulate" of the American system of government is "that sovereignty is vested in the people" (*New York Times*, May 23, 1995, A10).

is, unavoidably, the exercise of power by the few over the many—is a proposition that wins explicit acceptance only among anarchist ideologues and (some) professional political scientists. But the popular sovereignty doctrine must confront a problem that Rousseau evaded: A regime of direct democracy, such as that of the early New England town governments, is impractical in a political community that is geographically extended, with a large population. In Rousseau's time, France had a population of 27 million. To imagine "the people" (even if restricted to adult males) meeting together for effective deliberation of public policy is a hallucination. It is equally illusory to regard the principle of popular sovereignty as maintained in a polity where legislators are chosen by popular vote to "represent" the people. Representative government is not "self-government" and does not dispense with the need to investigate the dynamics of political power. In discourse on representative government, observes McIlwain, "the phrase 'popular sovereignty' contains a contradiction in terms; for, whether we like it or not, in choosing a legislature we are choosing a master, and because we choose it, it is no less a master than a monarch with a hereditary title" (1950, 111).[28]

Edmund Morgan's detailed survey of the history of the notion of popular sovereignty (1989) gives it a major place in the development of modern political thought by displacing the view that monarchs held sovereign power as God's lieutenants on earth. The English parliamentary opponents of the early Stuart kings invented the sovereignty of the people, says Morgan, as a fiction that, in effect, endowed *themselves* with sovereign authority as the people's representatives (1989, 49f., 169). Morgan errs in tracing the origin of popular sovereignty to seventeenth-century England, but he is on solid ground in claiming that its invocation there was very important in the subsequent development of Western political thought. In order to appreciate its significance, however, one must distinguish between two ways in which the doctrine was employed (and continues to be employed) in political discourse: (1) as a normative principle that legitimizes the exercise of coercive power by the state, and (2) in accord with Bodin's contention that, as a matter of empirical fact, there is a seat of sovereignty in every state, and the positive study of politics must attend to its locus.

As Morgan shows, most of the English and American devotees of popular sovereignty argued the first of these propositions. Only the Levellers of the English Civil War period (1989, 66–77), and the occasional utopianist since, have entertained the idea that "the people" can literally perform the

---

28. In the concluding essay in his collection of papers on the "unfinished journey" of democracy, John Dunn expresses the view that the only real democracy is direct democracy. Although he sees some merit in representative government, he suspects it of being a "conjuring trick" designed to keep the masses docile (1992, 248f).

hands-on tasks of governance. Even in a small community, "self-government" must be, as a matter of pragmatic necessity, the exercise of political power by the majority, or some other subset of the populace. In a large community, it is ineluctably the exercise of political power by the few over the many.

Rousseau evaded this problem by construing "the people" to be a singular living entity, with mind, will, and purpose. In the history of political thought, this is not the only concept that has been reified in order to declare it to be the seat of sovereign authority. Over the years since Bodin, various other loci have been suggested: the state, the nation, the cultural community, the constitution, the law, and, by philosophical idealists, "reason."[29] Examining these would only lengthen this review without advancing our political understanding. Bodin contended that the a sovereign authority must be a "*visible* ruler," a singular monarch or a group small enough to constitute a cohesive center of political power. I shall consider next a theory of sovereignty that meets this requirement. Because that theory was almost exclusively the product of writers who reformulated the doctrine of sovereignty in terms appropriate to the English political system, I shall consider it as postulating the "sovereignty of *Parliament*."

Parliament as Sovereign

The notion that Parliament is the sovereign authority in England has been traced back to Sir Thomas Smith in the later sixteenth century,[30] and to Richard Hooker, one of the most prominent theologians of the era. Hooker asserted that the sovereign authority to make law properly belongs to Paliament as the agent of the whole people (Lloyd, 1991, 282), thus anticipating the contention of the parliamentarians of the early Stuart era that the prerogative powers of the Crown were subordinate to the those of the House of Commons. The Revolution of 1688 was construed by Whigs as having firmly

29. On the first and last of these, see Merriam (1972, chs. 5–7 and 10); on the notion that the seat of sovereignty is "the nation," see Cohen's discussion of one of its main proponents, the prominent early twentieth-century French jurist Adéhar Esmein (1937, ch. 2).

30. "Sir Thomas Smith set forth [in his *De Republica Anglorum* (1583)] the legal supremacy of Parliament in words to whose clearness and amplitude nothing can be added today" (Bryce, 1901, 553). Bryce gives a quotation from Smith that would seem to bear this out. Sabine, however, noting that Maitland and Pollock have given similar interpretations, disagrees, because Smith clearly recognizes that the monarch has powers which do not depend upon Parliament. "The most striking feature of Smith's book," Sabine adds, "was that it regarded the constitution as consisting mainly of the courts and represented parliament itself as the highest court in the kingdom" (1937, 449). If Sabine is correct, then Smith must be credited for asserting (and perhaps originating) yet another theory of sovereignty: that its seat is occupied by the judiciary.

established the sovereignty of Parliament and, by the end of the second decade of the eighteenth century, even Tories had accepted it (Dickinson, 1976).

William Blackstone referred to Parliament as sovereign in his *Commentaries on the Laws of England* (1765–1769), but his concept of "Parliament" was ambiguous and his notion of "sovereignty" unclear. Not until the mid-nineteenth century was a coherent theory of parliamentary sovereignty expressed in print, by Walter Bagehot in *The English Constitution* (1867). Bagehot's analysis was shortly superseded by A. V. Dicey's *Introduction to the Study of the Law of the Constitution* (1885).[31] Bagehot and Dicey both embraced the theory that Parliament is the locus of sovereignty in England, but there is an important difference between them. Bagehot regarded sovereignty as a *political* doctrine, while Dicey contended that it is essentially a *legal* one. This disjunction between political scientists and lawyers on the nature of constitutionalism persists today in academic scholarship. The theories of Bagehot and Dicey will be examined separately in order not to obscure that distinction.

Walter Bagehot

Walter Bagehot (1826–1877) was a veritable prototype of the Victorian man of comprehensive intellectual competence. He was a practicing banker, a lawyer (though he never practiced), the editor for sixteen years of the outstanding weekly magazine *The Economist,* for which he regularly wrote its two main articles (Buchan, 1954, 768), and, in his short and unhealthy life, he also wrote a large number of books and essays that embraced such diverse fields as literary criticism, biography, Darwinism, the relation between the social and natural sciences, contemporary economic and political events, monetary and banking theory, and the English constitution. No fewer than three editions of his collected works have been published since his death; the the most recent (1965–1986) runs to fifteen substantial volumes. Handsome, charming, articulate in speech and the possessor of an engaging literary style, he seems to have been universally admired in his lifetime (except by the voters, who defeated all three of his attempts to enter Parliament), and that admiration

31. A recent textbook on the British political system observes: "If Bagehot's *The English Constitution* has been regarded as the authoritative constitutional account for the golden age of parliamentary government between 1832 and 1867, then Albert Venn Dicey's *Introduction to the Study of the Law of the Constitution* . . . has come to be regarded as the authoritative text for the period of parliamentary democracy since then and his account still occupies the high ground of British constitutional theory today" (Dearlove and Saunders, 1992, 32).

continues to the present day. G. M. Young called him "The Greatest Victorian" (1937), and Asa Briggs, leading authority on the Victorian era, ranks him with Anthony Trollope as a premier observer of English society in the mid-nineteenth century (1972, ch. 4). Studies of his life and work, some unabashedly hagiographic, continue to be published. I call attention to Bagehot's repute because the modern reader of *The English Constitution* may be inclined to wonder why it has not long since been consigned to the dustheap of works that viewed the democratic trend of English politics with undeserved alarm.

Bagehot greatly admired the English system of government as not only the best that had so far been produced in the world, but one that was nearly perfect (1928, 143–149). In his view, however, the system as it actually operates had not been properly understood by previous writers. It was to repair this deficiency that he undertook to write *The English Constitution*. But the reader of it will quickly appreciate that it is more than a positive analysis of the mechanics of English government. It has two normative objectives as well, which are indeed so dominant that one might describe it as a tract aimed at objectives that were of immediate political concern at the time of its composition. One of these was to persuade English admirers of American government (the only alternative system then meriting consideration by a civilized society) that the English system was indisputably superior; the other was to defend the principle that the best form of government is that which places the levers of political power in the hands of the small part of the population who possess the qualities of intellect and character necessary to the operation of efficient government in a modern state. This latter principle, Bagehot felt, was in danger of being subverted by the franchise reforms that were then being advocated and, despite his persuasive analysis, were subsequently implemented by the Reform Act of 1867.

Bagehot embraces the Bodinian principle that there must be, in *every* state, an ultimate sovereign authority, which he attributes to Hobbes: "Hobbes told us long ago, and everybody now understands that there must be a supreme authority, a conclusive power in every state on every point somewhere. The idea of government involves it—when that idea is properly understood" (1928, 195).[32] If we take the phrase "on every point" to mean what it would seem to mean, a sovereign power must be unlimited in the scope of its authority. His description of the Cabinet as having fused the legislative and executive branches of the state into a singular authority, and his criticism of

---

32. In another passage he seems to soften this view somewhat, writing not that there *must* be, but that there *should* be, such a power: "There ought to be in every Constitution an available authority somewhere. The sovereign authority must be *come-at-able*, and the English have made it so" (Bagehot, 1928, 87).

the notion of separation of powers (as produced by the American Constitution), indicate that Bagehot also thought that sovereignty in England is undivided. Thus he construes the political system of England as one in which the Bodinian properties of absoluteness and indivisibility characterize the sovereign authority.

The mid-Victorian readers of *The English Constitution* were most struck by Bagehot's contention that the development of the Cabinet was the most important institutional change that had taken place in the English system of government since the Revolution of 1688. Bagehot regarded this recognition as his most significant insight. He begins his analysis with a discussion of this new institution, which had, he emphasizes, eliminated the previous separation of the legislative and executive branches of the government, and combined them into a singular locus of political power.[33] The most glaring defect in the voluminous literature on English government, in Bagehot's view, is its failure to appreciate the momentous import of the development of the Cabinet. That institutional innovation, together with a steady decline in the influence of the monarch and the House of Lords, had elevated the House of Commons to supreme authority in the state. The prime minister and the members of the Cabinet, he notes, are drawn from occupants of seats in Parliament, and they retain their offices only as long as a majority of the members of the House of Commons are willing to let them do so. It is not altogether clear, from Bagehot's discussion, what entity he would name as the sovereign power: the House of Commons at large, the political party holding a majority of the seats in the Commons, or more narrowly still, the Cabinet. He definitely did not mean to include the Lords, so when one says that Bagehot espoused the doctrine of "parliamentary sovereignty," some qualification is necessary because the word "Parliament" is often construed to include the House of Lords, and sometimes the monarch as well.[34] Resolution of this issue is, moreover, complicated by the fact that some members of the Cabinet were then selected from the Lords. At the time that Bagehot was writing *The English Constitution*, the Earl of Derby, a member of the House of Lords, was prime minister.[35]

33. "The efficient secret of the English Constitution may be described as the close union, the nearly complete fusion, of the executive and legislative powers . . . The connecting link is *the cabinet* . . . The cabinet, in a word, is a board of control chosen by the legislature out of persons whom it trusts and knows, to rule the nation . . . The first and cardinal consideration is the definition of a cabinet . . . a cabinet is a combining committee—a *hyphen* which joins, a *buckle* which fastens, the legislative part of the state to the executive part of the state" (1928, 9–12, Bagehot's italics).

34. In *The English Constitution*, Bagehot frequently refers to "Parliament" when he clearly means the House of Commons (see, e.g., ch. 5).

35. Bagehot was perfectly aware that the traditional definition of governmental functions

Next to Bagehot's emphasis on the Cabinet, the most striking feature of his book is its distinction between the "efficient" and the "dignified" parts of the English constitution. The queen and the House of Lords have very minor roles to play in "efficient" duties, he contends; their main function is to provide objects of awe and reverence that engage the attention of the common people and unite them in submissive deference to superior beings. It is only by historical accident that England has acquired a monarch and aristocracy that can exercise such an "imaginative attraction upon an uncultured and rude population" (1928, 186). But it is a great boon, for with the "dignified" part of the constitution, the people of England can be ruled without much use of coercive force. Amused, and bemused, by the behavior of the royal family and the aristocracy, the masses of England cheerfully submit to be governed by the "efficient" part of the constitution—the Cabinet and the House of Commons.[36]

Bagehot's essential political theory is that in a modern and large political community, the mass of the people deserve to be efficiently governed, but they lack the personal qualities that such governance requires. These qualities are very scarce, confined to the "educated ten thousand" (1928, 6), to whom, alone, the government of the nation should be entrusted. In the introduction written for the second edition of *The English Constitution* in 1872, Bagehot argues that the 1832 extension of the franchise to ten-pound householders had not significantly altered the English system of government, as it might have done, because the new electors allowed themselves to be guided in their political views by "the better educated classes" and voted for candidates who were members of those classes. The vital question for Bagehot, after the franchise had been significantly extended by the Reform Act of 1867, was whether the new electors would show the same "deference . . . to their betters" (1928, 263f.), which was the only way that England could continue to enjoy the best government in the history of the world.

Bagehot was pessimistic, but he was not of the opinion that the Rubicon had been irremediably crossed in 1867. There was a way of handling the new situation. "Our statesmen . . . have to guide the new voters in the exercise of the franchise; to guide them quietly, and without saying what they are doing, but still to guide them." All is lost if, at this time when "great ignorance has an unusual power in public affairs" (1928, 270), the statesmen of

---

was tripartite, composed of the judiciary as well as the executive and legislative "branches" of government. But it is curious that he does not devote a chapter to the judiciary; indeed, he hardly mentions it at all in *The English Constitution*.

36. Bagehot does not systematically present his theory of the English constitution as "a double set of institutions" (1928, 148) in any one place. Reference to it is frequent, though *passim*. For some distinctive passages, see 6f., 53f., 80f.

the two political parties should try to compete with one another for the favor of the lower classes, or if those classes should form a political party of their own. An "evil of the first magnitude" will ensue; for "*Vox populi* will be *Vox diaboli*" (268f.).

Bagehot's hope (it cannot be called "confidence") that rule by the select few might still be maintained derived from what he had described, in the first edition of *The English Constitution,* as the "dignified" part of the constitution. "A free government is essentially a government by persuasion" (1928, 185), and in its queen and aristocracy, together with the lower classes' unthinking reverence of them, England possesses an instrument of popular persuasion of unique efficacy. If the attention of the lower orders is kept fixed upon the "theatrical show" of "pomp," "spectacle," and "wealth" (236)— the visible evidence of government to their limited understanding of it—the hidden "efficient" part of the constitution, the real government, may continue to be left alone to exercise quietly the sovereign powers of state. Other nations are less well equipped to deal with the rising tide of democracy; more coercive methods may be the only means by which they may preserve rule by the few over the many. In essence, Bagehot embraced Plato's proposal that the mass of the people should be held in check by the inculcation of a "noble lie." It is not quite the same lie that Plato proposed—it is psychological and sociological rather than metaphysical—but it is "noble" because its object is efficient government.

Needless to say, Bagehot had a low view of the American Constitution. Federalism in itself, he believed, violates the principle of indivisible sovereignty, a transgression compounded by the adoption of the separation of executive and legislative authorities within the central government (1928, 196f.). The "principal thought of the American constitution-makers," writes Bagehot, was that "they shrank from placing sovereign power anywhere. They feared that it would generate tyranny" (199). Relying, unwisely he thought, upon the principle of checks and balances instead of unified sovereignty, they produced a governmental system incapable of dealing with the serious problems that confront the community, as evidenced by the degeneration of the dispute over slavery into civil war. The English system attracts better talent to politics than does the American, Bagehot declares, and in quiet as well as unquiet times, the policy-making and administrative efficiencies of the English political system are distinctly superior (24–29). It is unfortunate, he observes, that the only other major nation with a system of "government by discussion" had chosen to construct a constitutional system that is inherently unviable.[37]

---

37. See (1928), 299–312, for Bagehot's most extended comparison of the English and American systems.

It is perhaps unnecessary to conclude our examination of Bagehot with a critique of his central political theory, because the modern reader will be well aware that the extension of the franchise to the English lower classes did not have the disastrous consequences that he feared. In fact, today the universal adult franchise is commonly taken to be an essential property (and, unfortunately, by some as the *only* essential property) of a constitutional democracy. *The English Constitution* is now seldom referred to in the scholarly literature on political theory. In this domain, Bagehot retains the interest of only a small band of uncritical admirers, and the occasional commentator who regards the American system of government as persistently running into deadlock and needing reforms that will reproduce the centralizing features of British Cabinet government.[38] But some brief observations on *The English Constitution* are in order before we leave it.

First, the doctrine of parliamentary sovereignty is not dependent upon Bagehot's theory of the double constitution, with "efficient" and "dignified" parts. In fact, the most commonly held view of the English constitution today is that it is fundamentally based upon the sovereignty of Parliament. But few, if any, of those who hold this view would argue that it requires the support of the ancient institutions of monarch and aristocracy in the way that Bagehot claimed. Moreover, the nations of the British Commonwealth, and a number of others, have systems of government like England's, which operate as effectively without such institutions.

Second, the greatest merit of *The English Constitution* is that it maintains a strong focus on the issue of political *power*. Unlike Dicey, Bagehot does not allow himself to be diverted from this theme, and there is no author I have encountered who is more attentive to the fact that the organized few can dominate the unorganized many. Indeed, his analysis of the role of the "dignified" element in the English constitution serves to highlight the fact that there are more ways in which this may be done than by physical coercion and the threat thereof.

Third, *The English Constitution* occupies a place in the history of political organization as containing the first clear statement of the mechanics of Cabinet government, but despite Bagehot's perceptiveness in seeing the great significance of the Cabinet, he was not correct, even for his own day, in construing the English political system as one of unified sovereignty. Even if we restrict attention to the formal machinery of government, his depiction is inaccurate, and if we regard the "governmental system" of England more

---

38. Among these, the most prominent was Woodrow Wilson, in the days when he was an academic political scientist (see Hofstadter, 1954, 241f.).

broadly to include also the nonofficial institutions that can exert significant influences on the formation of public policy and its execution—the mass media, political parties, trade associations, organized minorities, religious institutions, and so forth—that system quickly appears to lack a singular seat of sovereign power, and to consist instead of a network of competing institutions. The English and American systems are much more alike than Bagehot appreciated.

Fourth, the exclusive focus of Bagehot's study of the English constitution is governmental *efficiency*. The protection of individual freedom and the civil rights of minorities, which surely must be one of the main objectives of a constitution, whether written or unwritten, receives no attention. We know from Bagehot's other writings that he was much concerned with this matter; he was a "liberal" in the tradition of Milton, Locke, Burke, and Mill. If in writing *The English Constitution* he took this for granted, it only serves to show how easily a political community that has won its way to liberty can forget the hard struggle by which it was achieved. In leaving the impression that the English are so secure in their liberty that there is no longer need for vigilance, he did a disservice.

Finally, Bagehot's failure to consider the role of the judiciary is a serious defect. In a polity such as England, operating under the rule of law, the ordinary citizen comes into direct contact with the coercive power of the state most hazardously in the courts. No adequate examination of constitutionalism can do without an appraisal of the role of the courts. In the next section, I consider a theory of British constitutionalism that focuses heavily on the judiciary.

A. V. Dicey

"Sovereignty," writes McIlwain, "is the central formula of our political thought, and the key to much of our constitutional history. We must at least be clear on what we mean by it." And what we mean is clarified if we recognize that "'sovereign power' as distinct from any other power is the highest *legal* power in the state. And this being so, the term 'sovereignty' has no proper application beyond the domain of law. It is a purely juristic term and it should convey a purely juristic idea" (1939, 68, 29f.). The outstanding figure in the development of this version of the sovereignty doctrine was Arthur Venn Dicey, but modern historians are in general agreement that its originator was John Austin.

Austin was an academic jurist who taught at University College, London. His lectures there formed the basis of his *Province of Jurisprudence Determined* (1832) and the enlarged *Lectures on Jurisprudence* (1861–1863). Merriam describes him as "the keenest of English jurists since the time of Hobbes" (1972, 133). Philosophically, he was a disciple of Jeremy Bentham and embraced without reserve the notion that the state can, and should, be vigorously employed in the promotion of "the greatest good of the greatest number." In developing this view into a doctrine of legal sovereignty, however, Austin espoused a theory of the state that many, including Henry Sidgwick, the leading utilitarian philosopher of the late nineteenth—early twentieth century, found severely defective and, indeed, odious.

Austin adopted, from Hobbes, the view that there must be a definite center of absolute sovereignty in every state. He rejected the notion that sovereignty can be ascribed to transcendental entities such as those proposed by Rousseau and the idealists. The sovereign authority must be "a determinate body . . . capable of corporate conduct . . . The distinction between ruler and ruled must stand out clearly and distinctly; there must be no doubt as to where the sovereign power really is" (Merriam, 1972, 142). The key to its locus is the "habitual obedience" of the mass of the people. A "law" is a command, but the entity that issues it does not possess the true mark of sovereignty unless the people are accustomed to obey.[39]

It would seem to follow from Austin's definition that the sovereign entity in Britain is Parliament, or the House of Commons, a locus that would make his theory of sovereignty indistinguishable from Bagehot's. But despite his insistence on a determinate body, Austin shrinks from naming one. In reference to the United States, he appears to contend that the sovereign entity is that which has power to alter the Constitution, but the procedures of amendment laid down in that document cannot be realistically described as identifying a determinate body of persons. Austin seems to have been trying to construct a jurisprudence that depicted law as a self-contained intellectual system, independent of anything that is not itself within the domain of law. His effort to do so would have had little more than antiquarian interest, if not for Dicey. Dicey recognized, without attempting to gloss over the matter, that the legal system of a nation cannot be construed as completely independent of nonlegal factors, but he carried the attempt to formulate the doctrine of sovereignty in purely legal terms as far as would seem possible.[40]

39. Sidgwick summarizes Austin's definition with his customary clarity: "Every Positive Law of any State is a general command to do or abstain from certain acts, which is issued directly or indirectly by the Sovereign of the State to a person or persons subject to its authority: the Sovereign being that determinate person, or body of persons combined in a certain manner, that the bulk of the members of the State habitually obey, provided that he, or it . . . do not habitually obey any one else" (1969, 651).

40. Austin's jurisprudence has been subject to a many severe critiques, which we cannot take time to review here. I would refer the reader especially to Sidgwick (1969, app. A); Bryce (1901, ch. 10); Merriam (1972, ch. 8); and, for a rather more idiosyncratic appraisal, Dewey (1894).

A. V. Dicey was a jurist of great distinction. As Vinerian Professor of English Law at Oxford from 1882 to 1909, he occupied the most prestigious academic post to which any lawyer could aspire. His *Introduction to the Study of the Law of the Constitution* was developed from the course of lectures he devised to instruct students in the basic principles of English constitutional law. Dicey retained this didactic focus in writing the published text, thereby making it more accessible to nonprofessional readers than many other books of law. For more than a century, it has been an immensely influential book. First published in 1885, it went through eight revised editions during the author's lifetime, and two more have been published since. Wade's 1959 edition of Dicey's book has been reprinted eleven times, and a century after its first appearance, it was still selling at the rate of 600 copies a year (Blackburn, 1985, 681). It continues to be regarded as a definitive work on English constitutional law, and is studied by students of jurisprudence in America as well as in countries with constitutions of the English type (McEldowney, 1985, 39–41).

Dicey was also the author of another important book: *Lectures on the Relation between Law and Public Opinion in England during the Nineteenth Century*. First published in 1905, it is still referred to by intellectual historians as a major work on Victorian England. In view of his eminence as the most important jurist to attempt to construct a legal theory of the English constitution, Dicey's *Law and Opinion* demands at least passing note here because its main thesis is that the making of law by Parliament, even before the Reform Act of 1867, was, and continues to be, driven by the extra-legal factor of "public opinion." One might speculate that his lectures on this issue were composed in response to critics—perhaps especially his friend Henry Sidgwick—who had chided him for giving inadequate attention to it in his *Law of the Constitution*.

Students of the English constitution, writes Dicey, have reason to envy their counterparts in countries like the United States that have written constitutions, for their teachers know precisely what must be discussed. The English student, even after consulting the most distinguished legal, historical, and philosophical authorities such as Blackstone, Hallam, and Bagehot, will find that "the whole province of so-called 'constitutional law' is a sort of maze in which the wanderer is perplexed by unreality, by antiquarianism, and by conventionalism" (1960, 4–7). The way out of this maze is to distinguish between political and legal sovereignty. These two domains are not, in practice, separable, but they are conceptually distinct, and it is the latter that one must attend to in examining the *law* of the constitution. In countries like the United States, which are federal unions and have written constitutions, there is no definable locus of legal sovereignty (Dicey, 1960, pt. 1, ch. 3). In the English system of government, however, the sovereign authority is clear: it is

Parliament, which possesses the sole authority to make law and is not restricted, in the subject or substance of its legislative acts, by anything that lies within the domain of law.

In the final pages of his large book, Dicey summarizes his essential theory: "The law of the constitution . . . is in all its branches the result of two guiding principles . . . The first of these . . . is the sovereignty of Parliament . . . The second . . . is what I have called 'the rule of law,' or the supremacy, throughout all our institutions of the ordinary law of the land . . . which means at bottom the right of the courts to punish any illegal act by whomsoever committed" (1960, 470f.). Dicey devotes part 2 of the *Law of the Constitution* (almost half of the book) to the "Rule of Law," under which heading he discusses "The Right to Personal Freedom," "The Right to Freedom of Discussion," "The Right to Public Meeting," and other topics that have been central concerns of the doctrine of constitutionalism since its beginnings in the later Middle Ages (and even before, in Periclean Athens and republican Rome). The liberties of the people are secured in England, Dicey argues, not by a written constitution, but by the rule of law conventions of its unwritten one, which, like the legal supremacy of Parliament, "have been gradually worked out by the more or less conscious efforts of generations of English statesmen and lawyers" (470). As Dicey construes it, Parliament may legally pass any law that it pleases, but by well-established convention, all laws must be general as to the scope of their domains, not exempting anyone within the jurisdiction of Parliament (especially the lawmakers themselves) from the responsibility to obey them. According to Dicey, that is the way in which the power of the state is effectively constrained in England. Legislators will not pass odious laws if they themselves will be subject to them. In effect, it places them, like other citizens, under the jurisdiction of a court system that impartially applies the law.[41]

The courts come into Dicey's theory of the law of the constitution in a fundamental way. What *is* a "law"? Dicey is not satisfied to define it as a

41. Dicey's *Law of the Constitution* was very influential in promoting the doctrine of the "rule of law" in English jurisprudence and political science. I should note, however, that there is some inconsistency between it and the principle of legal sovereignty. The rule of law focuses on the *properties* of legal enactments, whereas the notion of legal sovereignty refers to the *source* of law, and there is nothing in it, as such, that restricts the lawmaking authority from exempting anyone from its provisions (see Wormuth, 1949, 211f.). On the evolution of the rule of law doctrine since Dicey, see Jowell (1994). Sir Ivor Jennings was rather disingenuous in titling his appraisal of Dicey on the fiftieth anniversary of the publication of the *Law of the Constitution* "In Praise of Dicey," because it is mainly a harsh critique. But he was perfectly sincere in saying that "the Constitution was for him an instrument for protecting the fundamental rights of the citizen, and not an instrument for enabling the community to provide services for the benefit of its citizens" (1935, 132).

statute passed by both houses of Parliament and given royal assent. But he was too much of a positivist to consider seriously the notion that a putative law must pass the test of conformity to "natural law." He defines a law as any rule or command that the courts of England will recognize as a valid law: "A law may, for our present purpose, be defined as 'any rule which will be enforced by the courts' " (1960, 40). In a nation that has no written constitution limiting the lawmaking power of the legislature, is this not a distinction without a difference? To common folk it would seem so, but to the perceptive lawyer, it opens the possibility of arguing that for some reason (such as failure to follow prescribed procedures), a particular statute or administrative regulation is not a "law," and the courts can properly decline to enforce it. In effect, it imports into the English legal system something like the American system of judicial review.

The rule of law principle is not the only "convention of the constitution" that Dicey discusses. Indeed, for a jurist who purports to instruct his students in law, he devotes a remarkable amount of attention in his *Law of the Constitution* to the nonlegal elements of the working constitution of England.[42] In Jennings's appraisal, "Dicey's analysis of constitutional conventions (he invented the term) was a magnificent contribution to English public law." But, he adds, this drew the book outside the limits that Dicey had imposed on it. "It is a discussion not of law, in his narrow sense, but of political science and jurisprudence. The conclusions which he reached were based essentially upon political theory" (1935, 130).

The conventions of the constitution posed a great puzzle for Dicey. His empirical realism demanded their recognition, but his legal approach to the constitution forbade their inclusion because conventions are not recognized as binding by the courts. "By far the most perplexing of the speculative questions suggested by a study of constitutional law," he admits, are "the sanctions by which the conventions of the constitution are enforced" (1960, 439). Dicey failed to answer this question satisfactorily. He notes that constitutional conventions are widely respected and obeyed, even more so than some laws are (440), but he does not explain why this is so. Nevertheless, in concluding this chapter he writes, with undiminished confidence in his approach to the English constitution:

> Let us cast back a glance for a moment at the results which we have obtained by surveying the English constitution from its legal side.
>
> The constitution when thus looked at ceases to appear "a sort of

---

42. Part 3 of the book concerns "The Connection between the Law of the Constitution and the Conventions of the Constitution." This, together with part 2 on the "Rule of Law," constitute almost two-thirds of the text.

maze"; it is seen to consist of two different parts; the one part is made up of understandings, customs, or conventions which, not being enforced by the courts, are in no true sense of the word laws; the other part is made up of rules which are enforced by the courts, and which . . . are laws in the strictest sense of the term, and make up the true law of the constitution.

This law of the constitution is, we have further found, in spite of all appearances to the contrary, the true foundation on which the English polity rests, and it gives in truth even to the conventional element of constitutional law such force as it really possesses. (1960, 469f.)

It appears therefore that, in Dicey's view, the law and the conventions do not share equal status as elements of the English constitution; the former dominates the latter. This is the heart of the notion of sovereignty as a legal doctrine. But I should note, again, that Dicey is concerned only with the *law* of the constitution. He explicitly states that "the fundamental dogma of modern constitutionalism [is that] the legal sovereignty of Parliament is subordinate to the political sovereignty of the nation" (1960, 453), which resides in the people or, at least, in the electorate (430–436). He does not appear to have perceived any conceptual conflict between these two sovereignties.

From the first appearance of Dicey's *Law of the Constitution* in 1885, it was the object of a great deal of discussion in the legal and political literatures. Much of this attention consisted only of fulsome praise, but some was critical of particular points, especially its comparison of the English rule of law to the French *droit administratif* (see, e.g., Lawson, 1959). A trenchant comprehensive critique of Dicey's approach to the constitution—Sir William Ivor Jennings's *The Law and the Constitution* (1933)—did not appear until almost fifty years after the publication of Dicey's first edition. It would be tedious, and of very little profit, to review these criticisms of Dicey in detail, especially since, at bottom, his doctrine of sovereignty is the same as Bagehot's in focusing upon the supremacy of Parliament as the nation's lawmaker. A few brief comments must suffice to conclude the discussion.[43]

43. In this discussion of sovereignty as a legal doctrine, I have concentrated upon Austin's and Dicey's presentation of a view that many other jurists also advanced. I cannot review this literature here, but should note one writer at least, Hans Kelsen, the leading luminary of what is sometimes called the "Viennese School of positive law." Kelsen migrated in 1940 to the United States and taught for a number of years at the University of California in Berkeley. He insisted upon defining sovereignty solely in terms of law and went much further than Dicey had been prepared to go in construing a nation's law as a self-contained system, independent of its political and social constituents. Every such legal system, in his view, rests upon a "Grundnorm," a basic normative principle, which in England is the sovereignty of Parliament and in America is the sovereignty of the Consti-

Having come to the end of our survey of the doctrine of sovereignty since Bodin, it is striking how little it was modified over four centuries. Modern adherents to the doctrine appear to be as convinced as was Bodin that the central problematic of political analysis and the comparative study of political organization is the discovery of the locus of sovereign authority. In modern democratic polities that locus may not be as evident as it was in the sixteenth century, but it *must* exist. Bagehot acknowledged that the political system of the United States has no such locus, but he regarded it as therefore fundamentally flawed and, in the long run, likely to prove unviable. It might be argued that Dicey's most important contribution to the theory of sovereignty was that he followed Bagehot only halfway; he acknowledged that there was no unified seat of sovereignty in federal political systems, but he did not regard them as unviable on that account—thereby, in effect, he abandoned Bodin's central principle. The number of federal states had grown appreciably during the forty-eight years between the first edition of Bagehot's *English Constitution* and the last revised edition of the *Law of the Constitution* that Dicey prepared. The British North America Act (1867), establishing Canada as a federal state, was passed in the very year that Bagehot's book first appeared, so it appears that his negative appraisal of federalism was not generally shared by his contemporaries. Once the Bodinian insistence on indivisibility is abandoned, however, there seems to be nothing in political theory that serves to specify the limit to which the dispersion of political power might be carried; without indivisibility, the whole doctrine of sovereignty is fatally undermined.

In Dicey's view, the significance of the American Constitution did not lie in its inclusion of a Bill of Rights, but in its establishment of a federal form of government, with legislative powers divided between national and state authorities. If a constitution is such a vital part of a political system as Dicey clearly thought, then one should expect that the political and social orders of federal states would develop very differently from unitary ones. But this is obviously not so. The outstanding feature of the United States and Great Britain as political communities is their similarity in effectively controlling state power, not their institutional differences. Moreover Canada, a federal state but one having a parliamentary system modeled after Britain's, is more like the United States than Mexico, whose political system is modeled on the United States. Britain and the United States differ in the structure of their governmental systems, but, as Dicey himself writes, "in every other respect

---

tution. His ideas are most accessible in English in his *General Theory of Law and the State* (1945). For useful reviews and appraisals of Kelsen see Cohen (1937), ch. 5; Beinart (1952); and Ebenstein (1968).

the institutions of the English people on each side of the Atlantic rest upon the same notions of law, of justice, and of the relation between the rights of individuals and the rights of the government, or the state" (1960, 140).[44]

Moreover, when Dicey writes of "Parliament" as the *legal* sovereign, and Bagehot refers to it as sovereign without that qualification, they seem to regard its House of Commons as a unified institution. Neither comments on the role of the "Loyal Opposition," though this is surely one of the essential features of constitutional government. It is difficult to see how a modern legislature, as a deliberative body, could function properly without general acceptance of the notion that opposition to the proposals of the majority, or the executive, is not treasonous but an indispensable part of good government. Nor can the ruling party stifle opposition simply by claiming that it had been given a "mandate" to rule in the preceding elections. But does this not mean that the majority party lacks morally valid sovereign authority and, indeed, that even a majority of the electorate does not have truly sovereign political authority? Majorities are most assuredly not unanimities. Unless one is prepared to accept Rousseau's doctrine of the "general will" under the sway of which dissidents are merely being "forced to be free," a constitutional order must allow room for political minorities to influence public policy formation.

In defining a law as a command that the courts will enforce, Dicey recognizes that the authority to interpret the law gives to the judiciary powers that are, in effect, legislative. "A large proportion of English law is in reality made by the judges," he explains, and this weighting of the judicial branch is compounded by the system of case law in which judges regard the judgments rendered in previous cases as precedents that should be followed. "The appeal to precedent is in the law courts merely a useful fiction by which judicial decision conceals its transformation into judicial legislation," writes Dicey. This "judicial legislation," however, does not violate the principle of parliamentary supremacy in his view, for it is only "subordinate legislation," carried on with the assent and subject to the supervision of Parliament (1960, 19, 60f.). This process in effect reduces the common law of England, which jurists since Coke have regarded as the main repository of the constitution,

44. On similar grounds, one might reject the contention that the distinction between a written and an unwritten constitution is fundamental. "However that may be, and if it pleases the British to emphasize the fact that they have a constitution which is not written, this question is of secondary importance . . . What really matters is the end, the *telos*. And the purpose, the *telos*, of English, American, and European constitutionalism was, from the outset, identical . . . a fundamental set of principles, and a correlative institutional arrangement, which would restrict arbitrary power and ensure a 'limited government' " (Sartori, 1962, 855).

to the status of "subordinate legislation." There is no getting away from the fact that laws must be interpreted, and whoever has the authority to interpret them has power that only casuistic reasoning can deny to be legislative in nature. One commentator, indeed, goes so far as to suggest that the judiciary is the real sovereign: "As long as it is for the courts to ascertain and apply the law, so long will parliamentary [sic] sovereignty rest with the courts" (Gray, 1953, 61).

More important still is that "courts" consist of juries as well as judges. In most cases where individual citizens become seriously engaged with the law, they will have to face a jury composed of laymen as well as a judge learned in the law. Legal theory holds that judges and juries have distinct responsibilities: judges decide matters of law, and juries decide matters of fact. This legal fiction fails to recognize that juries are under no sanction to confine their attention to the determination of guilt or innocence as a "fact." In practice they regularly disregard the limits that legal theory places upon their authority, despite the lectures that presiding judges may give them concerning their restricted role in the judicial process. The point uppermost in the minds of jurors when they retire to consider their verdict (without the judge being present) is not whether the accused is guilty or innocent, but whether he or she deserves to be punished, and the probable consequences of that punishment. There is an endless number of cases in which juries have rendered verdicts that are in plain defiance of palpable facts, and this is not because they have embraced the epistemic doctrine that all facts are opinions. They refuse to convict if to do so would seriously violate their own sense of what is just or expedient. Historians have pointed out, for example, that in the early nineteenth century, when there were scores of capital crimes on the statute books of England (including pickpocketing and counterfeiting), juries acquitted the accused on many occasions when his guilt was all but certain. What does it mean then to say that Parliament is the legal sovereign because it makes laws that the courts will enforce?

Moreover, between Parliament and the courts stand the law officers of the state. They do not have the protection from summary dismissal that judges have, but it would be absurd to contend that they behave as automata, exercising no discretion at all as to whom to arrest, whom to bring before the courts, and what charges to prefer. In fact, there are many laws still on the statute books that are simply not enforced for one reason or another, including the view of law officers that they are unwise or unjust. When social mores change, allowing laws to fall into desuetude is one of the ways in which they are repealed, without any act of the legislature. In such cases, are not the law officers *making* law?

When Dicey wrote the *Law of the Constitution,* the body of "administrative law" in England was small; today it has become the most important instrument by which the lawmaking authority exerts power over individual citizens and business firms. Legislatures pass general laws, leaving it to the appropriate executive departments to construct the specific regulations by which the law is actually implemented. Citizens who find themselves afoul of the taxing authority, or the administrator of health and safety regulations, may ask to be shown by what authority they are being charged, but they will then be referred not to a statute, but to a small passage in a large volume of regulations written by civil servants. Such a citizen may, of course, appeal to the courts, but they will inform him that the regulations have the same legal status as statutes do. Who, then, actually exercises the powers of legal sovereignty in the polity? Anyone who has a taste for coercive authority might well decide there are better opportunities to satisfy it in becoming an official of the taxation authority than in standing for election to the legislature. In modern democracies, protection of the people's liberties from arbitrary exercise of official authority requires as much, or more, attention to the pedestrian activities of minor officials than to the majestic proceedings of a Parliament or Congress.

The large apparatus of administrative law that has developed in recent years concurrently with the great extension of the scope of the state highlights the proposition that the main problematic of political analysis is political power—its institutional distribution and the mechanics of its exercise. Focusing upon the discovery of the seat of sovereignty, even if only in the domain of law, dissipates one's energies in the attempt to capture a wraith.

It is perhaps understandable why lawyers find the concept of sovereignty indispensable: their profession is dedicated to bringing disputes to definitive settlements. Our sense of justice requires that appeals to higher courts be permitted in order to prevent miscarriages of justice. But the process must, at some point, be brought to an end, and an ultimate judicial authority is established in order to accomplish this. The political process is very different. It deals constantly with problems that can never be finally resolved. They can only be coped with, for the nonce, in some reasonably satisfactory fashion. Even if construed simply as an instrument for efficiently permitting collective action, let alone the protection of minority interests, politics is very different from law (see Gordon, 1980, ch. 1).

As always in such matters, one must beware of carrying a good argument too far. In the enthusiastic search for flaws in Dicey's doctrine of legal sovereignty, it would be absurd to conclude that in a modern constitutional polity, the law, and the legislatures that make the law, are of negligible importance. McIlwain defended the doctrine of sovereignty by construing its pluralist opponents to be advancing such a contention (1939, ch. 2). But it is not necessary for any pluralist to embrace such a view. Law is the main vehicle by which the political organization of a society is effectuated, and it is a vital component of its economic and social organization as well. Only the most doctrinaire devotees of laissez-faire believe that the market mechanism of economic organization can work without the support of a legal framework, and only utopian romantics believe that spontaneously developed customs and conventions are sufficient to generate sociocultural organization in a large and heterogeneous community.

The central point here is that law works as it does because it is an instrument through which the organized few can effectively dominate the unorganized many. Government is, of necessity, government by the few. The inference that Hobbes took from this, however, is not logically impeccable. It does not follow that the only alternative to unending anarchic disorder is the rule of a singular sovereign with absolute powers. Organization, which conveys power, may be employed as a technique in fields other than the making and administration of law. A great weakness in Dicey's books, both the *Law of the Constitution* and *Law and Public Opinion,* is that he leaves such things as the "conventions of the constitution" and "public opinion" in an amorphous state, failing to recognize that they become powerful agencies in a constitutional polity only when mobilized and directed through purposive institutions. In a modern democratic society, the protection of the citizenry from the abuse of state power is not only effectuated by the broad franchise and fair elections. An equally vital element is the ability of citizens to associate freely with others of like opinion and interest, forming institutions to supply the power of organization.

Critics of Sovereignty

Bodin's specification of the properties of sovereignty are secondary to his insistence that there must be a seat of sovereign power in every stable state. If no such seat exists, it would be otiose to discuss its properties. We have found, however, that ascribing a definite locus to sovereignty in modern democratic states is highly problematic, and even in the restricted domain of law, there is little agreement as to where sovereignty is lodged. It is not surprising, therefore, that some political scientists have suggested that the concept be abandoned altogether. I proceed now to review, briefly, three prominent writers who have taken this stance: Henry Sidgwick, Harold Laski, and Jacques Maritain.

Sidgwick was primarily an ethical philosopher. His *Methods of Ethics* (1874) reformulated utilitarianism as a less egocentric doctrine than Bentham had advanced, and was a dominant influence on English ethics for the next half-century. He wrote important books on numerous subjects, played a leading role in the development of the Charity Organization Society (from which the modern profession of social work stems), and pioneered the application of scientific methods to the empirical testing of alleged psychic phenomena. His *Elements of Politics* (1891/1969) was intended, as he says in the preface, to "expound, within a convenient compass, and in as systematic form as the subject-matter might admit, the chief general considerations that enter into the rational discussion of political questions in modern states." Sidgwick's "convenient compass" extended to 650 pages, concluding with a final chapter on "Sovereignty and Order." This chapter appears to be largely an afterthought, added perhaps after Sidgwick realized, or a reader of the manuscript observed, that he had written what purported to be a comprehensive book on politics without discussing a concept that many professional experts regarded as indispensable. Whatever the reason for its inclusion, the chapter was, I believe, the first general attack on the doctrine of sovereignty to appear in the literature.

Sidgwick did not call for the abandonment of the sovereignty doctrine in so many words, but he criticized it so vigorously that it is difficult to believe that he regarded it as serving any useful function in political analysis. He flatly rejects the notion that the locus of sovereignty in a state can be identified by ascertaining what body has the power to alter the law. Supremacy is a question of political power, broadly construed, not merely the power to make new law. But this is a very complex and difficult question, he notes, because there are many entities besides the legal authorities that are able to exert political power. John Austin's simple answer will not serve. "My view, on the contrary," writes Sidgwick, "is that in a modern constitutional State, political power is not merely exercised at the discretion of a political superior . . . [but] is usually distributed in a rather complex way among different bodies of individuals" (1969, 638). In a country with a "flexible constitution" such as Britain, the issue becomes even more complex, for the distribution of political power can alter without any explicit action having taken place. He enlarges upon this in the rest of the chapter, making no attempt to suggest how the matter might be resolved. It is evident that Sidgwick derived no political insight from the doctrine of sovereignty and believed that attempts to locate the seat of sovereign political authority in Britain were wasted effort.

The writer that most demands our attention as an early critic of the doctrine of sovereignty is Harold Laski. Foremost luminary in political studies at the London School of Economics and a leading adviser to the British Labour Party, his influence on students and others with whom he came in personal contact was unsurpassed by any other English political thinker of the interwar period, and his essays and books were widely read on both sides of the Atlantic. His comprehensive *A Grammar of Politics,* first published in 1925, went through five editions and a number of reprintings, and was used for a long time as a textbook on political science. While yet in his early twenties, Laski projected a series of volumes that would systematically examine various aspects of the theory of the state in the modern world. The first of these (the only one of the series to be completed as planned) was *Studies in the Problem of Sovereignty* (1917/1968), evidencing the central importance of that issue in Laski's view.[45] At the time of writing this book, Laski described himself as a "pluralist." He later rejected this label when, in the mid 1930s, he became a committed Marxist, but this conversion did not lead him to modify any of the strong criticisms he had made of sovereignty as a positive or normative concept.[46]

The basic point of departure for Laski's critique of sovereignty is John Austin's contention that the key to the problem is the "habitual obedience" of the people. The seat of sovereignty in England, claimed Austin, is Parliament, because it issues commands that are habitually obeyed. Laski points out that the state is not the only social institution able to command obedience. This might be the case if the state were to become, as Hegel envisaged, an "all absorptive" unity (Laski, 1968, 1), but this is far from the case in political communities like modern Britain and America. The citizens of such polities retain their individual powers of judgment and do not render automatic obedience to the laws passed by legislatures. Moreover, and more important, a pluralist society is one in which the independence of the individual from the state is organized through other social institutions that command his loyalty to a degree rivaling that of the state. Laski was especially struck by the role of religious institutions in this respect. He devoted more than a third of his *Studies* to a review of the controversy over the relation between church and state that had punctuated nineteenth-century political thought, and a substantial part of the remainder to similar issues.

In Laski's view, the status of religious institutions, and the loyalty they obviously receive from their members, clearly show that there is no such thing as a singular locus of undivided sovereignty in a state where people are free to form religious (and other) institutions and give their allegiance to them.

---

45. In the preface, Laski writes that "the starting point [for a theory of the state] is the belief that in such a theory, the problem of sovereignty is fundamental, and that only in the light of its conception can any satisfactory attitude be adopted." Laski's later work continued to be strongly focused on sovereignty. In the *Grammar of Politics,* the first chapter after the introduction deals with this topic. The chapter is a good summary of the views that he had developed at much greater length in the *Studies.*

46. On his change of political stance, see Laski's preface and addendum to the fourth (1937) edition of the *Grammar of Politics.*

Bodin's property of indivisibility is empirically false, and without it, the whole doctrine of sovereignty falls apart as a useful analytical construct. It also fails as a normative one because it cannot deal with the fact that people are so constituted as moral beings that they regard churches and other nonstate institutions as deserving their loyal support. The following passages may serve to summarize Laski's views on sovereignty:

> The sovereignty of the State does not in reality differ from the power exercised by a Church or a trade union . . . [They] are exercising a power that differs only in degree, not in kind, from that of the State . . . The force of a command from the State is not, therefore, bound to triumph, and no theory is of value which would make it so. (1968, 270)

> The division of power may connote a pluralistic world. It may throw to the winds that omnicompetent State for which Hegel in Germany and Austin in England have long and firmly stood the sponsors. (68)

> The modern theory of sovereignty is . . . a theory of political organization. It insists that there must be in every social order some single center of ultimate reference, some power that is able to resolve disputes by saying a last word that will be obeyed. From the political angle, such a view . . . is of dubious correctness in fact; and it is at least probable that it has dangerous moral consequences . . . It would be of lasting benefit to political science if the whole concept of sovereignty were surrendered. (44f.)

Laski was not a systematic political theorist. Although he made numerous suggestions concerning the content of a pluralist theory of the state, he did not develop his ideas sufficiently to enable pluralism to stand as an alternative to the doctrine of sovereignty. When he became a Marxist and embraced Marxian economic theory (which he little understood), his basic ideas concerning the state, nonstate institutions, and the autonomous individual became entangled in contradictions, multiplied by his undiscriminating admiration for the route to social reconstruction taken by the Soviet Union under Josef Stalin.[47]

The critiques of sovereignty by Sidgwick and Laski bear most heavily on the Bodinian property of indivisibility. For Jacques Maritain, the fatal error

---

47. For critical appraisal of Laski on the issues noted here, see Cohen (1937, ch. 8); and Sarma (1984, ch. 4). There is a clear similarity between Laski's critique of sovereignty and that made by J. N. Figgis in his *Churches in the Modern State* (1913) and by the prominent French jurist Léon Duguit in his *Les Transformations du Droit Publique* (1913). Laski translated Duguit's book (published under the title of *Law and the Modern State*, 1919). On Figgis and Duguit in respect to sovereignty, see Ward (1928).

in the doctrine as it had developed after Bodin was its insistence that sovereign authority must be absolute. Maritain was one of the most distinguished French intellectuals of the mid-twentieth century. A youthful convert to Catholicism, he became the leading, and most widely read, neo-Thomist philosopher of the era. He opposed the collectivist and authoritarian tendencies of Catholic philosophy and developed a highly individualistic social theory, founded upon Christian principles, that defended democracy as essential to the moral regeneration of politics. His most important book on political theory was *Man and the State* (1951), in which he attacked the doctrine of sovereignty as philosophically erroneous, morally pernicious, and a threat to the development of democratic systems of government.

In the first chapter of *Man and the State*, Maritain lays the foundation for his rejection of the sovereignty doctrine by advancing an "instrumentalist" view of the state. He rejects altogether the notion of Hegel and other idealists that the state is "a kind of collective superman" that transcends the individual persons who are its citizens. The state, he insists, is not a "moral person" in any sense; it is simply a device that the people use to service their need for peaceful communal association. The idealists, however, are not the only ones who have undermined this fundamental principle. In modern democracies, the state has been elevated to transcendent status by those who deny that there are limits to its legitimate power. "Power tends to increase power," he observes, and in the modern democratic state, like in the government of the church, there are strong incentives for those in authority to enlarge their domains without limit. Since the French Revolution, the state has become identified with the nation, and with the people considered as a whole, a notion that ascribes to it the property of transcendence, which in older times was attributed to monarchs. "That concept of the State," he declares, "has forced democracies into intolerable self-contradictions" justifying totalitarianism as effectively, or more so, than have the philosophies of Fascism, Nazism, and Russian communism. Maritain does not argue for a minimal state, for the institution has important work to do in promoting social justice. "The problem," he says, "is to distinguish the normal progress of the State, from the false notions, connected with the concept of sovereignty, which prey upon it" (1951, 12–23).

Maritain opens the following chapter, "On Sovereignty," by observing that "no concept has raised so many conflicting issues and involved nineteenth Century jurists and political theorists in so desperate a maze as the concept of Sovereignty." If the concept is subjected to philosophical analysis, it becomes clear that the notion of absolute authority is inadmissible. Only God, who stands above the human polity, has such a property. All human governments are part of the polity they govern, and even if they are not practically limited in what they may do, they are morally bound by divine and natural law. Bodin recognized this, Maritain points out, but modern supporters of the sovereignty doctrine have failed to do so. The doctrine of popular sovereignty has been especially pernicious, in Maritain's view, because it converts the valid proposition that the people have the right to determine how they shall be governed into the notion that the state, which is really only their instrument, is a moral entity *in se*, outside the polity and ruling it "from above." It was Rousseau, with his doctrine of the general will, who infected democracy with this philosophic error. The state is, indeed, the highest authority in the polity, but describing it as "sovereign" carries the ineradicable connotation, due to the provenance of the term, that it is like unto God. "The two concepts of Sovereignty and Absolutism," writes Maritain in concluding this chapter, "have been forged on the same anvil. They must be scrapped together."

In the modern literature, one encounters numerous other expressions of the view that the concept of sovereignty is unserviceable to political science,[48] but so far as I know, no one has developed a critique of it that goes beyond what one finds in Sidgwick, Laski, and Maritain. Other writers have come to its defense; some by embracing the full doctrine of sovereignty, little altered from the formulation that Bodin had provided—others by contending that it can be rescued as a serviceable conceptual instrument in political science by relieving it of much of its Bodinian freight.[49] The central weakness in the attack on sovereignty reviewed earlier is that its protagonists failed to develop an alternative to sovereignty as a heuristic concept. The basic lines of such an alternative were only suggested by Sidgwick's and Laski's pluralistic conception of society.

W. J. Stankiewicz observes that criticism of the doctrine of sovereignty derives basically from the fact that the notion of a supreme authority cannot be fitted into the theory of democracy, or of constitutionalism (1969, 35). But he does not share the critics' conclusion that the concept of sovereignty must therefore be abandoned. On the contrary, Stankiewicz defends it, on heuristic grounds, as an integrating concept that makes possible the empirical study of politics in a society in which there are many kinds of power. More-

48. Some references: Bryce (1901, 503f.); Ward (1928, 178); Beinart (1952, 102); Marshall (1954, 209); Crick (1968, 81); and Benn (1969, 85).

49. See, e.g., McIlwain (1939); Schmitt (1985); Hinsley (1986); and the articles by Wilks, Simon, Middleton, and especially the editor's introductory essay, in Stankiewicz (1969). The most penetrating and thorough examination of the concept of sovereignty I have encountered is Rees (1950) which is reprinted in Stankiewicz (1969). Rees concludes that the great faults in the concept of sovereignty can be repaired, but only at the cost of making it an excruciatingly complex notion.

over, he contends, the concept of sovereignty not only makes plain what is meant by "power," but also renders meaningful and serves to integrate other terms that are essential in political discourse, such as "community, obligation, legitimacy, authority, state, government, and constitution" (298). This is a bold claim and, if sustained, would compel one to regard sovereignty, in essentially its Bodinian form, as the most fundamental instrumental concept in empirical political science.

Observation of research practice in political science, however, fails to sustain this contention. With respect to democratic countries, the dominant agenda of professional political analysis consists of the examination of the various institutions that influence the formation of public policy, their interaction, and the changes that take place in the weight of their influence. A pluralist structure of political power is assumed as obvious, without specific recognition. Even scholars who assert that identifying the locus of sovereignty is essential to the study of a polity make little or no use of it when they come to empirical analysis.[50]

In the remainder of this book, I shall examine the history of constitutional government since its origin in ancient Athens. It will appear that the diverse cases reviewed share a common factor: the distribution of power among multiple political institutions. I shall argue that the operational dynamics of their governmental systems is rendered intelligible by construing them in terms of the countervailance model of political organization.

50. Some modern authors defend Bodinian sovereignty as a purely analytic proposition. See, e.g., Wilks (1969, 200f.) for an attempt to sustain it by an exercise in *modus ponens* logic.

2

Athenian Democracy

The English word "democracy" translates the Greek *demokratia,* which derives from *demos,* "the people," and *kratos,* rule or authority. Literally, it would seem to mean government of the people by themselves. Because this is an impossible method of governance, even in a relatively small city like ancient Athens, the term is likely to mislead, as one can see from its use in the political discourse of our own time. But we do not have a better term to refer generically to political systems in which there is free and widespread participation in government by the citizenry. It is in this broad sense that I use "democracy" here, as elsewhere in this book.[1]

The beginning of a regime of democratic government in Athens cannot be dated precisely because it was not initiated by a singular event, but through a series of constitutional reforms that took place over a lengthy period. Some historians regard the reforms introduced by Solon in 594 B.C. (henceforth in this chapter "B.C." will be taken as understood, where appropriate) as its beginning, others the reforms of Kleisthenes in 508, while still others point out that important elements of the political system were not in existence before the reforms of Ephialtes in 461. The end of the Athenian democracy is more distinct because it did not gradually degenerate, as republican Rome did, from indigenous difficulties, but was overwhelmed by the superior military force of Macedon, in 338. The Athenian democracy lasted (with a few brief interruptions) for roughly two centuries—long enough to qualify as more than a transitory experiment in democratic government.

Even before Solon, Athens had become the largest and most powerful city in Greece, dominating the whole of Attica, a region of about a thousand square miles. Subsequently, it embarked on a policy of territorial conquest and assembled a large empire, with dependencies around the whole coast of the Aegean Sea, and westward, in Sicily and southern Italy. When one speaks of the *political* system of Athens, it was, indeed a city-state whose boundaries did not go beyond Attica, at most, but one must bear in mind that its government had to

1. On the evolution of the term in classical Greece, see Hansen (1991, 67f.).

administer an extensive colonial region and defend its hegemony there in almost constant warfare. The empire provided Athens with a large flow of wealth, but the city would not have been able to maintain its hold on it for as long as it did without an efficient system of home government.

The imperial achievements of Athens are impressive as signifying a powerful state, but more impressive still, and totally unprecedented, was the intellectual and cultural efflorescence that took place there during the democratic era. Names that are familiar more than two millennia later include not only the great philosophers Plato and Aristotle, but numerous others: the historians Herodotus and Thucidides; the dramatists Aeschylus, Aristophanes, Sophocles, and Euripides; the sculptors Praxiteles and Policlitus. And, of course, there are many whose creations we admire but whose names are lost: the sculptors whose works were copied by the Romans; the architects whose buildings still survive; and, judging from the enormous amount of Attican red-figure pottery in European and American museums, scores of talented artists. Athens was a city in which independently minded intellectuals were able to flourish—a society sufficiently stable, secure, and confident to tolerate philosophers, historians, and playwrights who scorned its political system and derided its political leaders.

The influence of Greek thought and political practice was a significant factor in the almost contemporaneous development of the Roman Republic, but it would be inaccurate to say that, either directly or via Rome, Greece exerted a continuous influence upon the history of the West. Indeed, that influence was suppressed, almost to the point of extinction, during the many centuries that elapsed between the beginning of the Christian era and the late Middle Ages. With the rediscovery, editing, and translation of ancient texts, Greek philosophical, scientific, and political ideas became distinctive properties of Western civilization. We might note the following as "Hellenistic" features of modern constitutional democracy (without undertaking to determine what was inherited and what was indigenous):

1. A secular and utilitarian view of government as an instrument for making collective choices on matters of general interest.[2]

---

2. The increasing secularization of Greek thought in the fifth and fourth centuries is stressed by Ostwald (1986, chs. 2 and 3). The ancient dominance of religion, and the religious authorities, was replaced by, or at least subordinated to, the secular authority of the state. The greek term *nomos*, which had meant divinely mandated laws of conduct, came to refer, in respect of constraints on personal behavior, to the ordinances of the state. More broadly significant for the Western intellect, *nomos* also began to acquire the connotation of "laws of nature," signifying a shift from theology to "natural philosophy" as the modus for explaining worldly phenomena.

2. The concept of an entrenched constitutional order, which, though a fixed feature of political organization, can nevertheless be changed to adapt to new circumstances.

3. The participation of a wide spectrum of the citizenry in the process of lawmaking.

4. A polity in which "public opinion" plays a continuous role, not restricted to explicit acts of formal legislation.

5. The rule of law in two senses: that the law of the state applies to all citizens without exemption, and that the power of the state must be exercised through established formal procedures.

6. A system of justice in which individual citizens can plead cases before independent courts that have the authority to make binding decisions.

7. An institutional structure that constrains the ability of state officials to exercise their power arbitrarily.

When we add to these political elements the more general characteristics of the modern *mentalité* that derive from the Greek philosophers and historians of the fifth and fourth centuries—secularism, rationalism, and empiricism—it is evident that the foundations of Western civilization are inadequately described as "Judaeo-Christian" without adding "Hellenistic."

One cannot complain that the intellectual, cultural, and political achievements of classical Greece have gone unrecognized. On the contrary, no philosophical texts have been, and continue to be, examined more intensively and more widely than those of Plato and Aristotle; and works of the great Athenian dramatists have not only been objects of scholarly study but are also still frequently performed on the Western stage. Nor can one contend that Athens has received insufficient credit as the *fons et origo* of political democracy. But the common understanding of Athens in that role is highly unsatisfactory. The Athenians are frequently depicted as meeting together periodically in an open forum to consider and determine all matters of state. Such a view of political organization might be credited if one is speaking of small self-contained communities, like the towns of early New England. But to regard such a system as working effectively in fourth-century Athens, with some 40,000 men eligible to attend an assembly to determine civil and military policy and administer a large empire as well as local affairs, defies rational belief.[3] In fact, the Athenian system of government was much more complex. But detailed knowledge of its institutional structure and functions is quite

---

3. The figure of 40,000 adult male citizens is a "ball-park" estimate. Hansen says that in the time of Pericles (d. 429) the number was about 60,000, but declined to about 30,000, largely as a result of losses in warfare, a century later (1991, 55).

recent; only in the past half-century have historians been able to construct a systematic picture of it, and some important details still remain unclear.[4]

The main reason is that, with one exception, the surviving Greek texts provide only bits and pieces of information. Historians have had to resort even to oblique comments put into the mouths of characters by Athenian playwrights, and to the iconography of coins and medallions to furnish important facts.[5] The exception, a comprehensive review of the Athenian political system and its historical development, is "Aristotle's" *Athenaion Politeia* (Athenian Constitution, 1984). In addition to his other intellectual achievements, Aristotle initiated the empirical study of comparative government. Sometime after 335, he set his students to work compiling descriptions of all known political systems. Reports on more than 150 polities were compiled, one of them on Athens (Davidson, 1992). Of these documents, only the *Athenaion Politeia* has survived. Judging from references to it by writers such as Plutarch, it was well known at least as late as the second century A.D., but it was subsequently lost, and only came to light again in 1891 when an incomplete copy, written on the obverse of a first-century A.D. statement of financial accounts, was discovered during the excavation of an ancient rubbish dump in Egypt (Rhodes, 1984, 11; Murray, 1994, 3). On some matters it is rich in detail, but on others that are vital it offers no information, and some modern scholars regard it as seriously misleading in certain respects (see, e.g., Hansen, 1991, 49f.).[6] Nevertheless, the *Athenaion Politeia,* and the intense scholarly work on other sources of the past few decades, has generated broad agreement among historians as to the institutional structure of the Athenian political system, though not, as one might perhaps expect, its theoretical interpretation.

Constitutional Development

Even as early as the late seventh century, some of the institutions and practices that were to form essential parts of the Athenian political system were in place. The *Athenaion* reports that "under Draco . . . laws were written out for the first time," and that by his ordinances of 621–620 a council of 400 called the Areopagus was established, members of which were chosen by lot from

4. Hansen (1991) is the most complete account of the Athenian system of government now available.

5. On the materials that are available for a study of the Athenian political system, see Hansen (1991, ch. 2), and Davies (1993, 214f.).

6. The English translator of the *Athenaion Politeia,* P. J. Rhodes, concludes from internal evidence that it was not written by Aristotle himself (1984, 33f.). This view is shared by most scholars, but it is usually cited under Aristotle's name.

the small class of large landowners who were authorized to bear arms. But the common people had no political rights and, writes the author, "the harshest and bitterest aspect of the constitution for the masses was their enslavement . . . there was nothing in which they had a share." The reforms of Solon (a half-century later) constituted "the change that brought about the origin of the democracy" ("Aristotle," 1984, 43, 45, 86).

Solon replaced Draco's law code by one of his own. Debt bondage, which in effect had made slaves of the poorest citizens, was abolished by forbidding loans on the security of one's person. Four classes of citizens were established, based on the produce of one's land. Though the lowest of these could not hold office, they could attend meetings of an assembly at which affairs of state were considered.[7] Perhaps the most important of Solon's reforms was to deprive the Areopagus of much of its judicial power by creating a system of law courts, with juries composed of men from all classes. These juries, among other things, could adjudicate charges of unjust treatment by officials ("Aristotle," 1984, 48f.; Ostwald, 1986, 14f., 67; Hornblower, 1992, 4f.).[8]

Ostwald claims that "Solon's measures were accepted by both sides" (1986, 175), but the *Athenaion* contends that both rich and poor were dissatisfied: the former because they had expected him to sustain, and even increase, their power; the latter because they "thought that he would carry out a complete redistribution of property" ("Aristotle," 1984, 51). At any rate, civil quietude did not ensue. Peisistratus attempted to seize power on three occasions and, in 546, finally succeeded in establishing a personal dictatorship that was not ended until his successor was deposed thirty-six years later.[9] During this period, however, the Solonic reforms were not rescinded, and when Kleisthenes achieved political leadership in 507 with the support of the general populace and the army, he instituted additional constitutional changes that definitely set Athens on the route to democratic government (Rhodes, 1984, 55; Farrar, 1988, 21; Stockton, 1990, 21f.).

Kleisthenes established a new system of tribal organization. Every Athenian

7. For a discussion of the significance of the Solonic class structure, see Hansen (1991, 43–46). By the fourth century, restrictions on office holding by the lowest class had become a dead letter (88, 107f.).

8. Stockton regards Solon's greatest contribution as the setting down in writing of the rules of governance. Whether or not he made truly significant reforms, "from his day forward the rules were defined and visible and hence capable of being used as an objective check . . . In that respect, Solon had a just claim to be regarded as the father of Athenian liberties, and struck a heavy blow at a traditional ruling class which had not hitherto been cabined, cribbed, and confined by published rules" (1990, 20).

9. Peisistratus is more favorably remembered by intellectual historians as having sponsored the collection, in writing, of the Homeric epics, the first of the great literary works of the West to be embodied in "hard copy."

citizen was made a member of one of ten tribes based on his residence, like modern political constituencies. The Areopagus continued to exist, but a new Council of Five Hundred was created, which served as an organizing committee to prepare the agenda for meetings of the Assembly, which all citizens were entitled to attend. There were nine senior officials, the Archons, who supervised the day-to-day administration of the state. Decision-making remained in the hands of the wealthy, and the archonships and other major magistracies continued to be held exclusively by the nobility, but the creation of the Council of Five Hundred and the corresponding reduction in the role of the Areopagus were important movements in the direction of popular government. The Assembly became more effective as a policy-determining institution, and the fact that Kleisthenes had introduced his constitutional changes via Assembly approval established a precedent that made it thenceforth the recognized lawmaking body, under whose statutes the Archons and lesser officials had to function (Ostwald, 1986, 24; Stockton, 1990, 25f.; Hornblower, 1992, 8).

The constitutional reforms of Ephialtes (462) are more difficult to specify than those of Solon and Kleisthenes because they consisted of incremental changes in practice rather than discrete alterations in the institutional structure of Athenian government. Their effect was to reduce still further the power of the Archons and the political role of the Areopagus, through which the exclusive class of aristocratic families had maintained their political dominance; to increase further the effectiveness of the Assembly and the Council; to enlarge the role of the jury courts in matters of state; and to widen the participation of the citizenry in these central organs of government (Farrar, 1988, 22). At the end of the fifth century the Athenian code of laws was revised and systematized, thus making the binding power of law on the activities of state officials more certain and easier to apply. Historians agree that during the period from Ephialtes to the city's conquest by Philip of Macedon, Athenian democracy had its fullest development. It is often called the "Age of Pericles," after the political leader (from 443 to 429) who initiated further important changes in political practice, used state funds to support impressive public ceremonials and entertainments as well as the construction of magnificent buildings, and in other ways aimed to make Athens the cultural center of the civilized world.

This great era of the first democratic state in history was interrupted on two occasions. Class conflict had not ceased to exist, and in 411 the aristocrats engineered a successful coup that established an oligarchy—the rule of "The Four Hundred," a term that is still used in some societies to refer to a pretentious social and economic elite. The new regime was short-lived, however, and the democracy was restored within a few months. When the Peloponnesian War finally ended in 404 with Athens's capitulation, the victorious Spartan commander established a new government, which subsequently became known as the rule of the "Thirty Tyrants." At first, according to the *Athenaion,* the Thirty "were moderate towards the citizens, and pretended that their aim was the traditional constitution . . . But when they had firmer hold on the city they left none of the citizens alone, but put to death those who were outstanding in their wealth, birth or reputation, cunningly removing those whom they had cause to fear and whose property they wanted to plunder" ("Aristotle," 1984, 80). Despite their cunning, however, the Thirty were overthrown within a year and the democracy restored.[10] These episodes show, more than anything else could, how firmly established and widely supported the democratic constitution had become. Even after the debacle of 338, with their city garrisoned by Macedonian troops, the Athenians did not abandon hope that their political system might be restored. When news was received in 323 of the death of Alexander, they rose in revolt under the leadership of the great orator Demosthenes, but to no avail; "the Glory that was Greece" was over.[11]

The Athenian Political System

In writing, as I have, of Athens as a "democracy" with the *demos* occupying positions of political power, one must not lose sight of the fact that, even at its fullest development, participation in politics was reserved to male citizens over the age of eighteen (thirty was the minimum age for holding state office). Women and slaves were excluded. Moreover, "citizenship" was strictly defined to include only persons born of parents who were both Athenian citizens. The total population of fourth-century Attica was perhaps as high as 300,000, a third of whom were slaves. Less than 15 percent had the right to attend the Assembly. Even without taking into account inhabitants of the subject territories, the Athenian political system was government of the many

10. Hansen contends that the political system was significantly altered in the course of being restored in 403 and that the high period of Athenian democracy described by most historians only applies the to last sixty-five years of Athens's independent political existence (1991, 21f.).

11. For more than a half-century after the unsuccessful revolt, writes Finley, "there was still a remarkably strong drive to restore the old political way of life, and enough leaders willing to make a go of it. The old institutions and methods kept coming back to life. But superior power told: Macedonian garrisons in Athens and armies swirling about and in the area made the decisions in the end . . . After 261 B.C. Athens permanently entered the ranks of the subject city-states with paltry politics, the victim of superior force" (1983, 117).

by the few (Hansen, 1991, 90–94; see also Finley, 1983, 59; Farrar, 1988, 6; Davies, 1993, 23).[12]

Before proceeding to examine the institutional structure and functional dynamics of the Athenian political system, I should also note that much of the income of Athens was derived from sources other than the productive effort of Athenian citizens. Rich silver mines in southeast Attica, owned by the state and worked by slaves, provided the wherewithal for Athens to build the navy that enabled it to conquer an empire (Finley, 1983, 16). The empire, in turn, produced revenue from tribute, the sale of slaves, ransoms, and so forth (Stockton, 1990, 185f.). Only the richest Athenians were subject to regular taxation (Hansen, 1991, 108, 112). Common employment, even of a skilled sort, was not held in high esteem by Athenians, and a large proportion of the citizenry were state employees or were supported in other ways from the public purse, while slaves did most of the work.[13] Participation in politics takes time, and the Athenians were able to engage themselves in government at least in part because the pressure to earn a living was not as great as most people, even those in wealthy "developed" societies, find it to be today (Stockton, 1990, 17f.; Hornblower, 1992, 4; Finer, 1997, 363). It remains an open question whether a political system like Athens's "democracy" can function without slavery and foreign exploitation. At any rate, we must be cautious in determining what general political lessons can be learned from the Athenian democracy.

The centerpiece of the Athenian political system was the Assembly *(ekklesia)*.[14] It normally met on four nonconsecutive days in each month (thirty-six days) of the Athenian calendar, perhaps more frequently in times of emergency. The meeting site was the Pnyx, a hill near the Agora, the city's central market place. Six thousand constituted a quorum. A stipend equivalent to about a half-day's wages was paid to those who attended, and apparently there was little difficulty in achieving a quorum—though there are some reports of officials "driving" citizens to the Pnyx from the Agora (Hansen, 1991, 5). Because the number qualified to attend was many times the quorum, and the total capacity of the Pnyx was much too small to accommodate all of them,

12. For a good brief description of Athenian government, see Finer (1997, 34f.).

13. There was also at least the rudiments of a welfare system. The *Athenaion* records that "there is a law which prescribes that men who possess less than three minas and are so maimed in their bodies that they cannot do any work are to be scrutinized by the council and given a public maintenance grant of two obols a day" ("Aristotle," 1984, 95; see also Hansen, 1991, 98f.).

14. The secondary literature on Athens makes little effort to accommodate the nonprofessional reader. Greek terms (sometimes in Greek lettering) are often given for institutions and practices without their English equivalents, and in a few cases, I have had to invent such equivalents myself. There is a useful glossary of Greek terms in Hansen (1991, 348f.).

the composition of the Assembly would have been different at each meeting, undoubtedly affected by its agenda, which was announced several days in advance. Anyone in attendance had the right to speak, but discussion was limited to the items placed on the day's agenda by the Council. The meetings were usually over by midday, or shortly thereafter, and items of business could not normally be postponed for decision from one meeting to the next (Finley, 1962, 10f.; Stockton, 1990, 67–84; Hansen, 1991, 167f.). Decisions were made by majority vote, indicated by a show of hands. A specific decree passed by the Assembly was final, but if a proposal were adopted that involved a general change in law, it had also to be approved by a body known as the Nomothetai. This institution was constituted by lot, separately for each meeting of the Assembly, from among the general panel of law-court jurors. Its size was invariably large, on one occasion numbering 1,000 (Ostwald, 1986, 521; Hansen, 1991, 161f., 362).

The political authority of the Assembly was comprehensive.[15] But a distinction must be drawn between the *ultimate* authority of the Assembly and the actual day-to-day conduct of Athenian government. Much of the latter was in the hands of officials, but it is difficult to believe that general policy determination could be done effectively by a gathering of more than 6,000 persons meeting for only a few hours forty times a year. A moderate degree of rational skepticism suggests that a meeting of this sort, where everyone and anyone was able to speak and to make motions, would have quickly degenerated into a riot. The orderly conduct of business by the Assembly was only possible because, in fact, the ordinary citizen did not exercise his rights of participation, except to vote after the discussion was concluded. The discussion itself was monopolized, apparently with general consent, by a small number of prominent citizens who almost exclusively belonged to the higher socioeconomic classes.[16] These men, who had no formal status in Athenian law, were called "demagogues" (from *demos*—people and *gogos*—leader), a descriptive term that originally did not have the negative connotations it later, but apparently quite quickly, acquired.

15. Stockton specifically notes its authority to determine taxes and public expenditures, to choose the officials not selected by lot, to impeach offending officials, to make treaties with other states, to declare war and make peace, to dispatch military expeditions and specify their composition and command, to determine public construction projects and choose their architects and overseers—in short, "just about everything that affected the state in matters both large and small" (1990, 83). Hansen, however, describes a variety of ways in which its power was limited (1991, 151).

16. "It is broadly true that down to the generation of Pericles all political leaders, whether aristocratic or democratic in sympathies, were from the aristocracy themselves, whereas after his death aristocratic families tended to withdraw from politics and new families came to occupy the foreground" (Rhodes, 1984, 137).

There is little doubt that the role of the demagogues in Athenian politics was of great importance, but it is not at all clear what that role was. Most historians view them simply as men of extraordinary personality and rhetorical skill, capable of dominating a large audience by speeches in which content was subordinated to eloquence. Modern political experience surely suggests that "public opinion" responds more readily to the art of "communication" than to rational substantive argument. Nevertheless, it seems unlikely that Athenian government could have been as effective as it was if its lawmaking body was as pliant as this interpretation implies. M. I. Finley suggests, with Pericles particularly in mind, that the Assembly deferred to such political personalities because they came to its meetings well informed about the matters that were to be considered and displayed capacities for systematic analysis and sound judgment as well as speaking ability (1983, 73–76). But this explanation does not fully account for the orderly conduct of Assembly meetings. Finley's argument would have somewhat more weight if demagogues were leaders of political parties. Each of them undoubtedly had committed supporters among the *demos,* but so far as is known, nothing resembling organized party blocs of citizens existed in Athens.[17]

A clear picture of how the Assembly functioned in the determination of state policy continues to elude us, but its role in combatting concentration of political power in the hands of a demagogue, a public official, or a military commander is evident. The jury courts were the main institution that served this function, but via the mediation of the Assembly, the citizenry at large were able to declare any person "ostracized," which meant that, while not deprived of any of his property, he had to leave the city and not return for ten years. One ostracism a year was permitted. At a meeting in the sixth month, the Assembly regularly voted on a motion to hold an ostracism. If it passed, a day was designated in the eighth month on which any citizen could scratch the name of whomever he wished to ostracize on a piece of broken pottery and deposit it at the Agora. The person named by the highest number, provided that the total was 6,000 or more, was ostracized forthwith, with no appeal. Candidates for ostracism were not publicly nominated, but obviously the two-month period allowed ample time for private discussion to coalesce upon a limited number of men who had incurred the displeasure of a wide segment of the populace.[18] Many thousands of potsherds with names scratched upon them have been unearthed by archaeologists, but it is not known how frequently a vote of ostracism was held, or how often it was

17. This issue is still disputed by historians—see Hansen (1991, 277f.).

18. Ostracism was introduced by Kleisthenes in the late sixth century, probably as a response to the Peisistratid dictatorship. It fell into disuse after the ostracism of the demagogue Hyperbolus in 416 (Finley, 1983, 55; Hansen, 1991, 35).

successful. One historian notes that there are only about ten well-documented cases of actual ostracism, half of which are concentrated in one decade of the early fifth century (Roberts, 1982, 143), but it is evident that the threat of ostracism could have been as effective in controlling the concentration of political power as the act itself. Anyone whose name appeared on the potsherds with some frequency, even if not frequently enough to be ostracized, would have been effectively warned to modify his behavior.

The most powerful organ of state was, almost certainly, the Council (*boule*). It prepared the agenda for meetings of the Assembly and coordinated the administrative activities of the government (Rhodes, 1984, 178; Finer, 1997, 347f.). Financial control, an especially important function in any government, was exercised by the Council. It consisted of 500 members, fifty from each of the ten tribes into which Attica was divided.[19] Its members were chosen annually by lot from the pool of male citizens over thirty. No one was permitted to be a councilor more than twice in his lifetime. One of the important contributions of the Council to Athenian democracy was a by-product of this rule: at any point of time, a substantial number of citizens would have served on the Council and been familiar with the business of state. The councilors, who received pay for their services, met daily, except on festival days and holidays. Though it was more manageable than the Assembly as a policy-making and administrative body, the Council would still seem too large for efficient action. A large part of the detailed work must have been done by its standing committee, called the "Prytanes." In monthly rotation, one of the tribal contingents of fifty constituted the Prytanes for the period. Too little seems to be known to enable one to obtain a clear view of the operative relationship between the Council and its standing committee.

The courts played a role in the Athenian political system that goes well beyond their function in a modern state. There were two classes of cases. *Dikai* were cases in which charges could be brought only by an injured party. This was a wider category than modern torts because it included charges such as theft and murder, which in modern systems of jurisprudence are prosecuted by persons acting on behalf of the state. The other category, *graphai*, were cases "which were held to involve matters of public concern . . . interpreted very widely" (Stockton, 1990, 99). *Graphai* included cases in which charges were made against state officials, which could be initiated by any Athenian citizen, not necessarily the injured party. Such cases were processed only in a jury court *(dikasteria)*. The extraordinary importance of these courts in the

19. The selection process was actually more complex than this, designed to assure that the local parishes *(demoi)* of Attica were represented on the Council in proportion to each one's relative numbers in the tribe (see Rhodes, 1984, 130; Ostwald, 1986, 24f.; Hansen, 1991, 46–49).

Athenian political system derived from their authority to hear and determine cases of political import, and their role in constraining the power of the Athenian bureaucracy. The constitutional significance of the jury courts is indicated by the attention devoted to them in the *Athenaion,* which describes, in mind-numbing detail, the elaborate judicial system of later fourth-century Athens ("Aristotle," 1984, 109–114). Modern historians agree that after the Areopagus was deprived of most of its judicial functions, the jury courts significantly affected the determination of public policy and its administration.[20]

The Athenians were an exceedingly litigious people, making full use of the jury courts to give vent to their personal grievances and political concerns. There were no professional lawyers at Athens, and no official prosecutors with special authority to act on behalf of the state. Any adult male citizen over age thirty could bring a case before a jury court and plead it himself, or induce another citizen with greater knowledge and/or oratorical skill to prosecute it. The same conditions pertained on the defense side. If an official was charged before a court, he was on his own; there was no body of official defenders to come to his aid. The decision of the court in each case was final; there was no provision for appeal.[21]

The determining entity in an Athenian *dikasteria* was the jury. The presiding officer (an Archon, or his deputy) was not a "judge" in our sense of the term. No distinction was made between matters of fact and matters of law, and the presiding officer did not instruct the jury as to its responsibilities. There were rules limiting the length of speeches, and each case was apparently disposed of in a single day, or less. When the two sides had concluded their

20. Davies observes that, despite the oath that jurors had to take to attend only to the case in hand, they "were swayed by considerations of public policy" and "it came to be as much in the lawcourts as in the Assembly that quarrels between politicians, and even debates over national policy and direction, were carried out" (1993, 227f.). Hansen goes further, contending that "the courts had unlimited power to control the Assembly, the Council, the magistrates, and political leaders" (1991, 179, 203f.). Ostwald quotes Aristotle as describing the courts as "sovereign in all matters," and goes on: "That Aristotle saw the mainstay of popular sovereignty in Athens in the judicial power of the *demos* as vested in the jury courts . . . is evident not only from this passage from the *Politics* but from its presence like a thread through the entire historical part of his *Constitution of Athens*" (1986, 5). Ostwald agrees with Aristotle on this point. The thesis of his book, that late classical Athens should be described as a regime of the "sovereignty of law" rather than the "sovereignty of the people," depends upon his view that the jury courts had become the central institution of the Athenian political system.

21. Ostwald notes that cases were often transferred from one court to another and that, under Solon, this was, in effect, an appeals procedure. But, in Periclean Athens, such "referrals" were solely a matter of meeting the rules of jurisdiction under which each court operated and, in fact, the practice solidified the status of the popular jury courts as bodies of final determination in "crimes against the state" (1986, 28f.).

presentations, the jury voted immediately by secret ballot, without adjournment for discussion. The case was decided by a simple majority of the jury votes.

Obviously, the outcome of any judicial proceeding would have depended crucially on the composition of the jury, and its freedom from bribery and other influences on behalf of contestants. The obvious flaws in such a system were remedied, to a degree, by having large juries—*very* large by modern standards—and selecting them by methods that assured their independence. The size of the jury depended upon the seriousness of the indictment. The smallest jury impaneled to hear public cases, such as charges against officials for minor malfeasance, was 500. One case is recorded with a jury of 2,500, and another in which the entire jury pool of 6,000 was impaneled (Ostwald, 1986, 68f.). Any male citizen over age thirty could apply for jury duty, for which a stipend was paid. From these applications, the pool of jurors was selected annually by lot. Jurors were assigned to the various courts each day by lot (Rhodes, 1984, 137; Ostwald, 1986, 68; Stockton, 1990, 96f.). It must have been impossible for anyone to manipulate the composition of the jury assigned to hear a case, or to bribe its members.[22]

In describing a state in terms of its institutions, one must bear in mind that a collective entity, *eo ipso,* has no ability to make judgments and perform actions. The constitutional significance of such entities is that they supply means by which individual persons may become *organized* into a cohesive combination that greatly multiplies the power of its members. The Athenian institutions we have so far examined could not have become continuing centers of organized power. For the Assembly that goes almost without saying—unless we consider it as an institution that exercised power over those who were not qualified to be members: women, slaves, noncitizens, and the peoples of the conquered territories of the empire. The Council was too large, and the method by which it was constituted would have prevented it from becoming such a power center. The Prytanes—the standing committees of the Council—had the minimum requisite of small size and, representing only one tribe, some initial cohesion. A specific committee could have exploited the power-augmenting capacity of organization, but each committee held office for only one month, and that alone would have sufficed to prevent it from achieving any significant political aggrandizement.

The concentration of power is an especially important matter when one considers the role of officials who act in the name of their governmental

---

22. For a more extended account of the Athenian judicial system, see Finer (1997, 354f.). He remarks that "of all the ways a citizen could participate in affairs, the most accessible was as a juror in the popular courts."

departments or, more generally, "the state"—including most obviously military officials, who possess the skills and the ready means to exercise coercive power in its most primal form. No description of a political system is complete without considering the composition, organization, and powers of its military and civil bureaucracies. This is a facet of Athenian politics on which important information is lacking, but enough has been brought to light by historians to enable one to address the main issue here: the mechanisms by which the power of the bureaucracy was controlled.[23]

From the description of the bureaucracy in the *Athenaion*, there were a large number of state officials in Athens ("Aristotle," 1984, 96f.). It lists the nine Archons, the most senior magistrates; the ten top military commanders and some forty commanders of infantry regiments, cavalry, and naval squadrons; ten city magistrates with various duties; twenty magistrates regulating the corn trade and other markets; eleven magistrates in charge of prisoners; forty officials empowered to hear and decide private lawsuits for small sums; an unspecified number of "arbitrators" who attempted to settle suits of higher value without resort to the jury courts; five officials in charge of road building and repair; ten auditors of public accounts and another ten "advocates" who had the responsibility of preferring charges if irregularities were discovered; two "secretaries" in charge of state documents; and twenty in charge of religious festivals, expiatory sacrifices, and the taking of auspices. Rhodes notes that the *Athenaion* misses a few (1984, 95), and it is obvious that it does not include the clerical and administrative staffs that these officials must have had. Davies gives a list that differs somewhat from the *Athenaion* and estimates that "over a thousand . . . were holding an accountable public post of some kind" (1993, 232). If one defines an "official" as one who receives pay from the state treasury for services rendered, which would including jurors, clerks, and minor administrators, Davies's contention that one-third of the Athenian citizenry were civil servants of one sort or another would not appear to be an overestimate.

It seems likely, on grounds of efficiency, that the clerical and administrative staffs of the magistrates held their posts for a lengthy period, but most of the important officials had tenure of only one year, could not be reappointed, and were selected by lot.[24] The nine Archons, selected by lot, held office for

23. This subject is examined specifically by Jennifer Tolbert Roberts in her *Accountability in Athenian Government* (1982).

24. Most accounts of the Athenian bureaucracy that I have consulted claim that most officials were chosen by lot, but Ostwald contends that "only those magistrates were chosen by lot who had routine duties to perform; the important offices that required special political and diplomatic skills were filled by direct election, usually of members of rich and well-born families who had for generations given service to the state" (1986, 82).

only a year, but became members for life of the Areopagus, which, on account of this method of recruitment, must have numbered at least 150 and perhaps as many as 300 at any point in time (Forrest and Stockton, 1987). The most important exceptions to the rule that a person could not be reappointed to the same office were the *strategoi,* the ten senior military commanders who were elected, not chosen by lot. In fact, many commanders were repeatedly reappointed and there was no convention, as in modern democratic states, that such officials must not engage in political activities. Athens would have been exposed to the same circumstances that brought about the downfall of the Roman Republic if there had not been effective methods of controlling the power of the *strategoi.* The Assembly could rescind their commands at any time, but the most effective controls upon them were procedures that applied to all officials.

Whether elected or chosen by lot, before assuming his office the designee had to appear before a jury court to undergo a process called *dokimasia,* which might be freely translated as a "confirmation hearing." The purpose of this process was to ascertain whether the candidate met the established criteria for holding Athenian office (Roberts, 1982, 14; Adeleye, 1983). At such a hearing, any citizen could raise objections to the candidate. The jury then voted on his candidature and a majority was necessary to confirm him. During an official's term of office, any citizen could initiate a "denunciation" *(eisangelia)* against him for personal impiety or for embezzlement, treason, conspiracy, or other high crimes, which, if sustained, could carry the death penalty. A denunciation was first placed before the Council, but more serious cases were usually referred by it to a jury court for final disposition. Extremely serious denunciations, such as for treason, were heard by the Assembly. Even the revered Pericles was denounced on one occasion and tried before a jury court (Ostwald, 1986, 193f.; Hansen, 1991, 353).[25]

If an official survived these tests, he was not yet home free. Upon the conclusion of his year, he had to submit to a *euthenai*—a review of his conduct in office. A board of ten public accountants examined his records, and if they

---

25. For the *strategoi,* denunciation was a highly probable condition of office. "Demosthenes maintained that every general was tried for his life two or three times in his career and that the danger of being sentenced to death by an Athenian court was greater for a *strategos* than the risk of dying in battle" (Roberts, 1982, 19f.). "The sources seem to show that a fifth of all generals were confronted sooner or later by an *eisangelia.* . . . And their first *eisangelia* was usually their last, for it usually ended with condemnation and the death sentence" (Hansen, 1991, 217). The most celebrated case was the treatment of the Athenian commanders after the naval battle against Sparta at Arginoussai in 406. Despite the victory of the Athenian fleet, the six surviving commanders were charged with having made insufficient efforts to rescue Athenian sailors whose ships had been sunk. All were convicted and sentenced to death (Hansen, 1991, 8, 216).

found no financial irregularities, the review would be handed over to a board of ten examiners, selected by lot, to hear any charges of a nonfinancial nature. Any citizen could bring such charges against him, including the complaint that he had been personally mistreated by the official, which would be heard first by a ten-member committee of the Council, and then by a jury court. If the ex-official failed to pass these tests, a condemnation proceeding would be undertaken against him in the jury courts. Only when the whole process was complete and his conduct was declared legally impeccable was he free to sell any of his property and/or leave the city if he so wished (Roberts, 1982, 17f.; Hansen 1991, 355).

The most striking, and politically the most significant, feature of Athenian government was not its method of determining state policy, but its use of the jury-court system as a means of controlling the exercise of power by state officials. In any society, personal liberty is more exposed to the power of bureaucrats, who deal directly with the citizenry, than to the power of legislators, who make general rules. In a hierarchical political system, each level of the bureaucracy is responsible to its immediate superiors, which creates a chain of accountability that culminates at the top with a "sovereign," who is not accountable to anyone. Clearly, the Athenian bureaucratic system was not a hierarchical chain of responsibility. All officials, high and low, were accountable to the citizens who sat on the jury courts. Every society must have a judicial system for the purpose of settling private disputes, and to apply general laws to specific cases. The Athenian judicial system was designed to perform a third function: the control of state power in the hands of officials. This function of the courts is widely accepted today as an essential feature of democratic government. As a standard practice, however, it dates back no further in Western history than the seventeenth century when, in England, the judges of the common-law courts began to achieve a degree of independence from the monarch (see Chapter 7). Athens anticipated this vital role of the modern judiciary by more than two thousand years.

The Theory of the Athenian Constitution

The Athenian system of government described here was the culmination of a series of constitutional changes that took place over a long period, in piecemeal response to contemporary problems. Solon, Kleisthenes, and Ephialtes must have had some rudiments of political theory in mind in devising their reforms, but no documents exist that provide more than fragmentary clues to the general principles that lay behind them. There appears to have been widespread agreement among Athenians that the purpose of government is to serve the interests of the citizenry, but no systematic analysis of Athenian government, or of *demokratia* as a generic political model, has as yet been unearthed by scholars. Plato and Aristotle were the founders of secular political theory as an intellectual discipline, and they lived in Athens, but their writings on politics contain no analysis of the Athenian political system. Even the Aristotelian *Athenaion,* which describes the structure of Athenian government in great detail, contains nothing that could be called a political "theory" of the Athenian constitution. Historians have devoted a great deal of effort to elucidating the implicit theory of the Athenian constitution from the available texts, but the quarry remains elusive. Greek terms such as *politeia, demokratia, nomos,* and *isotes* carry mixed cargos of meanings: the state, community, self-rule, majority rule, the rule of law, freedom, equality, equality of opportunity, justice, and more—making all inferences in terms of modern political theory questionable.[26]

Thucidides quoted verbatim Pericles's celebrated oration in praise of Athens in his *History of the Poloponnesian War,* but nevertheless he consistently depicted Athens as disorderly and badly governed. In this view, he was not alone. It is ironic that Periclean Athens, revered by its citizenry and still widely admired today, was condemned by its own historians, ridiculed by its poets and dramatists,[27] and rejected by its philosophers.

Plato regarded democracy as fatally flawed in that it allowed the ignorant masses to determine public policy—which, in his view, was a specialized function that could only be properly performed by the few men of philosophic talent who had been selected in youth and trained for the task. "Justice," which Plato regards as the fundamental principle of social life, is construed by him to limit every individual in a community to that work for which he is suited, and in such terms, democracy is unjust (Zeitlin, 1997, 4f,). The ideal state depicted in Plato's *Republic* contains no assembly, no courts, indeed none of the institutional elements of contemporary Athenian government. There is no rule of law, and the "guardians" and their agents are neither constrained nor accountable. The key to good government, in Plato's view, is to select the best men as governors and, once this is done, it would be "ridiculous" to control them. Nevertheless it is incorrect to regard Plato, as Karl Popper and others have done, as favoring totalitarian government. He did not admire Sparta nor recommend its institutions. In his ideal state the

---

26. See Saxonhouse (1996) for a recent attempt to sort out some of these ideas in the writings of Herodotus, Thucidides, Plato, and Aristotle. Saxonhouse's object is to combat the view held by most historians that these authors were hostile to democracy.

27. Hansen notes that the Greek tragedies consider the *ideals* of democracy and treat them favorably, but the comedies focus on Athenian *practice* with a harsh, satirical eye (1991, 16f.). On this score, ancient Athens would not have differed much from modern democracies.

individual citizen would be free to do much as he pleased, because there would be no need for the guardians to do much, and their own philosphic wisdom would suffice to limit the domain of state authority. From this angle of view, Plato's political theory resembles that of modern radical "libertarians" more than it does that of Hegel and others who view "state" and "society" as one.

Aristotle was not as hostile to Athenian democracy as Plato was, but in the *Politics* he gave it only a few brief, and begrudging, remarks of praise and, on the whole, construed it as having deteriorated since Solon's time. On democracy as a generic form he had numerous criticisms, one of which deserves special note. A democracy cannot, for pragmatic reasons, adopt the rule of unanimity in making public policy decisions, but majority rule, the best workable alternative, subjects individual citizens, and minority groups, to coercion by laws that may be inimical to their interests. As Saxonhouse puts it, Aristotle felt that "we cannot really distinguish between an assembly [of the people] and a tyrant; neither has a claim to authority based on anything besides power" (1996, 140).

The romanticization of Athenian government is a fairly recent development in Western political thought. Prior to the mid-eighteenth century, "democracy" was a term with negative connotations, and Ancient Athens was frequently cited as exemplifying its defects. Today, democracy is celebrated in the West as the *ne plus ultra* of political systems, and the most common test is whether the governors of a nation have been selected by majority vote in free elections. This general approbation masks the fact that majority rule has the defect that Aristotle noted so long ago.[28] Periclean Athens deserves to be regarded as a forerunner of modern political systems, but not, or not mainly, because its laws were passed by majority vote in a popular assembly. More important was that the Athenian citizen participated in the business of governance in many other ways as well, especially through the jury courts, and that the institutional structure of Athenian government was the first major polity in history to have a nonhierarchical system of plural and mutually controlling authorities.

Only in recent years have significant efforts been made to analyze the Athenian political system in theoretical terms.[29] One of these warrants some special

28. For example, John Dunn says that "It was literally [sic] true that the citizens of Athens ruled themselves" (1992, 241).

29. Writing in 1962, M. I. Finley noted two then-recent attempts to extract a theory of Athenian democracy from "the fragmentary evidence available in the surviving literature" and concluded that they did not succeed. "I do not believe that an articulated democratic theory ever existed in Athens. There were notions, maxims, generalities . . . but they do not add up to a systematic theory . . . the systematic philosophers of this period had a set

attention: Martin Ostwald's book, *From Popular Sovereignty to the Sovereignty of Law* (1986). It is a valuable work on the Athenian political system that, as the references given in the preceding pages attest, I have freely quarried for information. Its aim, however, is not merely to describe the institutional structure and practice of Athenian government, but to advance a theory of its development in terms of the concept of sovereignty.

Ostwald's thesis is that the reconstitution of the Athenian democracy in 403 involved an important change in its political system. What had developed after the reforms of Kleisthenes was a polity in which "the people" were the sovereign power; but after 403, the seat of sovereignty resided in "the law."[30] Ostwald does not mention Bodin, but in effect he employs Bodin's proposition that there is a seat of sovereignty in every state to argue that, from the constitutional standpoint, Athens was a significantly different polity after the end of the Peloponnesian War and the brief regime of the Thirty Tyrants than it had been previously. The reader of the preceding chapter on Sovereignty will already be aware of my hostility to the notion that "the law" can be regarded as constituting a locus of sovereignty. This idea is a reification; it attributes material existence to an abstract idea and, in effect, diverts attention from the issue that is most fundamental in the study of a political system— the mechanism by which the coercive power of the state is exercised.

The notion that sovereignty resides in the people is more credible with respect to Athens than to a modern nation-state with a system of representative government.[31] In Athens there was such a wide degree of participation

of concepts and values incompatible with democracy. The committed democrats met the attack by ignoring it" (1962, 9). More recently, another such attempt has been made, by Cynthia Farrar, identifying Protagoras, Thucidides, and Democritus, who lived before Plato, as having put forward the elements of a theory of democracy in their writings. "Protagoras," she declares, "was, so far as we know, the first democratic political theorist in the history of the world" (1988, 77). The textual evidence Farrar provides is very oblique, however, and thin, and her conception of "democratic theory" is focused too much on political psychology and too little on the institutional structure and operative mechanics of government to make a convincing case.

30. "The purpose of this book is to trace the growth of popular power in ancient Athens to the point at which it became popular sovereignty, to investigate the challenges popular sovereignty had to face, and to show how a principle of the sovereignty of law emerged from these challenges" (Ostwald, 1986, xix). Without using the language of "sovereignty," Sealey (1987) similarly emphasizes the importance of the "rule of law" rather than "democracy" in the Athenian system of government.

31. "The sovereignty of the people" was a phrase used by the Athenians themselves, if Rhodes's translation of the *Athenaion* is acceptable: "The people have made themselves masters of everything, and control all things by means of decrees and jury-courts, in which the sovereign power resides with the people" ("Aristotle," 1984, 86). But Hansen points out that there is no clear equivalent to "sovereignty" in classical Greek and advocates avoiding the term (1991, xi).

by the citizenry in the processes of governance that one might perhaps regard it as an empirical counterexample against the general critique of the notion of "popular sovereignty" made earlier. I do not think that such a contention is sustainable, however. The fact that *anyone* could speak in the Assembly, serve on a jury, bring a charge against an official, and so forth, does not warrant the proposition that Athens was ruled by *everyone*. The participation of the citizenry in Athenian government was mediated by the institutional structure of the state. A theory of Athenian democracy, like that of any other polity, must be a theory of how its coercive authority is effectuated through its established political institutions. Ostwald construes the Nomothetai as the innovation that shifted the locus of sovereignty from the people to the law (1986, 521f.), but it is more instructive, in my view, to regard the Nomothetai as simply one of the numerous institutions of the Athenian polity. Ostwald's thesis concerning the change in Athenian government after 403 could be better described simply as an increase in the power of the courts vis-à-vis the other institutions. In any pluralistic polity, there are shifts and changes in the relative powers of its constituents.

The structure of the Athenian political system cannot be modeled in hierarchical terms. The various organs of government were not arranged in a line or pyramid of superiority and subordination, and where there is no hierarchical ordering of authority, there is no sovereign. The only extant alternative to the hierarchical model of political organization is the countervailance model. Epistemologists warn us that facts are "theory-laden," that a strongly held theory predisposes one to read the data in accordance with it. Nevertheless, I think that a good case can be made for interpreting the political system of ancient Athens as exemplifying the countervailance principle. Its various institutions were independent of each other, yet linked in their functions. Because of this, no overweening center of power could develop; each institution was able to act as a check upon its companion institutions. The Assembly could generate law, but not without the work of the Council, and the law that it generated was interpreted and applied in concrete cases by the jury courts, where in turn the pleadings of accusers and defendants could, and did, raise important issues of public policy that demanded the attention of the Council and the Assembly.[32]

---

32. Hansen (1981) makes the interesting suggestion that the organs of Athenian government can be modeled in terms of the notion of separation of powers, some being able to *initiate* public policy proposals, others having the authority to *decide*, whereas still others undertook to *implement* the policy decisions. The concept of separation of powers has the potential for development into a countervailance model of government, but Hansen does not explore this. He models Athenian government as a linear structure of functions that,

The countervailance model cannot explain all features of Athenian government, however. For example, the provision that no citizen could be a member of the Council more than twice in his lifetime would seem to be a grossly excessive restriction if the sole object were to prevent concentration of power. Historians agree that one of the main objectives of the Athenian constitution was to achieve broad participation by the citizenry in the processes of government. One might note, however, that this objective is feasible only in a rather small city-state, and perhaps only one that, like Athens, restricted political participation to a fraction of the actual population and drew much of its wealth from a colonial empire. Modern democracies permit wide participation in political processes also, but not direct participation, nor by the means that were operative in Athens. In short, we may construe Athens as a participatory democracy, but this does not supply us with a theory of politics that can be generalized.

By contrast, the countervailance theory of power control is not so restricted. It can be applied to polities that are aristocracies like republican Rome and Renaissance Venice, and to modern constitutional democracies such as modern England and the United States. Ancient Athens may have been the first polity in the history of the world to establish a stable and effective democracy, but it deserves to be celebrated also for inventing a constitutional structure that provided for the control of power by means of a network of checks and balances.

The Doctrine of Mixed Government

In terms of the history of constitutional *theory*, the most influential contribution of the Greeks was the doctrine of "mixed government." This derives from the idea that there are three basic or "pure" forms of the state—monarchy, aristocracy, and democracy, or, as they frequently expressed it, government by the one, the few, or the many. In some expressions, these three forms are construed as having different essential properties: respectively, unity, wisdom, and liberty. This classification has been traced back to the pre-Socratic era; Herodotus records it as forming the focus of a debate between Persian nobles on the forms of government in 522 B.C. (Hansen, 1991, 14). By the time of Plato and Aristotle, a tripartite classification of constitutional forms was commonplace, as was the notion that there can be a fourth form, consisting of a mixture of two, or all three, of the pure forms.[33] There are some

___

though implicitly rejecting the notion of a hierarchy of power, does not address the question of power control. This, in my view, was the most striking feature of the Athenian political system.

33. See Walbank (1972, 135–137) for a review of the history of the notion of mixed

variants in different authors, and fourth-century writers sometimes identified three parallel degenerate forms as well. Aristotle named monarchy, aristocracy, and *politeia* as the good forms; tyranny, oligarchy, and democracy as the bad ones. It is not clear what he meant by *politeia* in this connection; in his anxiety to classify democracy as a degenerate form (undoubtedly with contemporary Athens in mind), he muddied more than somewhat the initial conception of one, few, and many. The simple notion that there are three basic forms of government, and that a mixture of these is possible, entered European political thought with the rediscovery of classical Greek literature during the Renaissance. Our interest must center here on the concept of "mixture" *(mikte)* rather than on the pure forms in themselves. To what extent did this notion in the Greek literature contain the idea of a system of checks and balances? A strong claim that it did has recently been made by Panagopoulos (1985, ch. 1). He construes Plato, Aristotle, and other writers of classical Greece as having a clear conception of *mikte* as an institutional structure that, by mirroring the socioeconomic classes in the community, constituted a balancing of interests.[34] Moreover, he contends, this political theory reflects the notions of balance and equilibrium that had a prominent place in Greek metaphysics, aesthetics, and ethics. The argument has its attractions, but it is not sustainable by reference to the original texts. The notion that a checks and balances doctrine can be found in, and was advocated by, Plato in the *Laws* and by Aristotle in the *Politics* seems to me to be a reading into the Greek mind of the fourth-century B.C. ideas that belong to modern political theory.

Plato discusses the monarchy-aristocracy-democracy classification of states in the *Republic*, but his main intention is to show that all (except the special aristocracy of Guardians) are unstable forms: aristocracy naturally degenerates into oligarchy, and that, in turn, into democracy, which finally culminates in dictatorship (bk. 111: 543a–576b). The *Laws*, written much later than the *Republic*, when Plato was almost eighty, is a quite different book, more focused on the pragmatically possible than the ideal. Here Plato represents Persia as the fullest development of the monarchical form and Athens of the democratic, and goes on to claim that "almost all other regimes . . . are woven from these. Both of them should and must necessarily be present if there is

---

government, from the earliest reference to it by Thucidides to Polybius's celebrated statement of it in the second century B.C.

34. On this basis, Panagopoulos regards Athens as having been a mixed polity only briefly, between 460 and 403, when the Council functioned as the balancing element between the Areopagus, representing the aristocracy, and the popular Assembly. After 403, he says, "the omnipresent *demos* rode in the saddle . . . [and] the quest for a balanced government lost its meaning" (1985, 14).

to be freedom and friendship, together with prudence. . . ." (693d–e). But there is no indication here, or elsewhere in the *Laws*, that Plato had come to regard mixed government with favor because it involved a system of checks and balances.[35] There is, however, one passage in the *Laws* (683d–684b) that deserves attention in this connection. Plato is here considering the story of the simultaneous founding of Argos, Messene, and Lacedaimon and explains:

> What happened was this: the three kings and the three cities that were to be governed monarchically, all swore mutual oaths, in accordance with the common laws they set up for ruling and being ruled. The former [the kings] swore not to make their rule harsher as time went on and the line continued, while the latter [the cities—i.e., the people] swore that if the rulers kept their oaths, they in return would never dissolve the monarchies or allow others to try to do so. They also promised that the kings would help the other kings or the populaces if they were treated unjustly, and that the populaces would help the other populaces or kings if they were treated unjustly . . . [The very great advantage of this arrangement was] the fact that there were always two cities ready to take the field against any one of the cities that disobeyed the established laws.

This passage clearly contains the idea that the preservation of the international status quo can be secured by means of a balance of power. It could have been expanded into a general theory of checks and balances, but Plato failed to do so. The *Laws* is certainly more pluralist and more favorable to democracy than the *Republic*, but it falls well short of presenting a countervailance system of political power.

Aristotle's *Politics* is the second part of a treatise of which the first was his *Ethics*. It is a disorderly book—ill-organized, repetitious, inconsistent, and in parts incoherent. It displays the signs of a preliminary draft that the author never got around to revising for publication. Finley suggests that it was left in such a state because Aristotle recognized that he had failed to achieve his aim of constructing a systematic political theory (1983, 124). Nevertheless, after its rediscovery in the thirteenth century, it became the most important work on that subject in Western literature. Indeed, the *Politics* retained its eminence long after the appearance of the much more systematic writings on political theory of the sixteenth and seventeenth centuries.

Since Bodin, the political literature on Aristotle has focused especially on his statement that, in addition to the pure forms of the state, a "mixture" is possible. Indeed, one often finds this notion referred to by modern historians as the "Aristotelian" theory of mixed government. But it is not at all clear

35. For a brief account of the political theory of Plato's *Laws*, see Zeitlin (1997, 23–29).

what Aristotle meant by *mikte*. Different mixtures are suggested in different places in the *Politics*, and one of his pure forms, *politeia*, is itself described as a mixture of oligarchy and democracy (1293b22–1294b14). Neither Aristotle nor Plato give any indication that they regard the government of fourth-century Athens as an effective mixture. In a passage rendered similarly by various translators, Aristotle notes, "There are indeed some who say that the best constitution is one composed of a mixture of all types, and therefore praise the Lacedaemonian. Some of these say that it is made up of oligarchy, monarchy and democracy" (1265b26). Aristotle disputes this interpretation of Sparta, but more significantly, he rejects the very doctrine that later political theorists called "Aristotelian"—that the best government is a compound of the one, the few, and the many. Nowhere in the *Politics* does Aristotle claim, for any mixture, the merit of being a constitutional arrangement that enables political power to be controlled.[36]

Before leaving Aristotle, I should note a passage in the *Politics* that some commentators have construed as suggesting a "separation of powers" doctrine (Finley, 1983, 58). "There are three elements in each constitution," explains Aristotle, "first, the deliberative, which discusses everything of common importance; second the officials . . . and third, the judicial element" (1297b35). This differentiation of state *functions* eventually displaced the concept of a *status* mixture of one, few, and many in constitutional theory, and it is tempting to regard Aristotle as anticipating Montesquieu in this regard by some twenty-two centuries. But such an interpretation is unwarranted. Aristotle does no more here than recognize what must have been obvious even to anyone less devoted to taxonomy than himself: that all orderly government consists of lawmaking, lawadministration, and lawadjudication. He does not propose that these functions should be embodied in distinct institutions, much less that such an arrangement might serve as a vehicle for the control of power through their interaction and interdependence.

In sum then, the classical Greek doctrine of *mikte* cannot be construed as a forerunner of the concept of checks and balances. As the subsequent literature shows, political commentators regularly used the language of "mixed government," but with a variety of meanings. Struggling for escape within this concept, so to speak, was the idea of a political society deliberately designed in its institutional structure to effectuate the control of state power. Two centuries after Aristotle, the Greek-Roman historian Polybius clearly

36. It seems to me that Stockton goes well beyond the text of the *Politics* in claiming that "Aristotle's own preference was for a 'mixed' constitution, in which a citizen's public rights bore some relation to the level of his wealth, but with stringent checks and restraints on any possible abuse of power" (1990, 177).

formulated the concept of countervailing powers, but it was not until the eighteenth century that its escape from the doctrine of mixed government was complete.

The Constitutional Totalitarianism of Sparta

Prior to the rise of Macedon, the arch-rival of Athens for the hegemony of the eastern Mediterranean was Sparta. These two Greek cities are commonly referred to today as exemplifying categorically different polities: Athens as a liberty-husbanding democracy, and Sparta as a polity in which personal freedom was hardly valued at all. In their political and social philosophies, Athens and Sparta were indeed poles apart, but their governmental systems had significant similarities. It is curious that Polybius did not refer to Athens as exemplifying a pluralist form of political organization, but not surprising that he instanced Sparta as having preceded Rome in establishing such a one.

The Spartans viewed their constitution as the singular creation of a great "lawgiver," Lycurgus, about whom in fact so little is known that he may indeed be a mythical figure. According to tradition, the Spartan system of government was established in the ninth century B.C., but most historians would date it later, perhaps not long before Solon in Athens. The system basically consisted of three elements: two kings, chosen for life, one each from the two wealthiest families; a council (*gerontes*—old men) of twenty-eight members representing the aristocracy; and an assembly *(apella)* composed of all adult male citizens authorized to bear arms. There was also a board of five magistrates (the *ephors*), appointed annually, with candidature open even to the poorest citizens.

Cicero contended that the *gerontes* constituted the supreme policy-making body in Sparta and viewed the Roman Senate as an imitation of it (1988, 159). Polybius's description of Sparta disregarded the *ephors* and presented a tripartite view of the constitutional structure that closely followed the notion, by his time ancient, of a "mixed government" composed of monarchical, aristocratic, and democratic "elements." Walter Moyle, a late seventeenth-century English advocate of the countervailance principle, regarded Sparta as an important early exemplification of it: "The true Constitution of [its] Government . . . contained in its Formation a proper Distribution of Power into several Branches, in the whole composing as it were one great Machine, and each grand Branch was a check upon the other, so that not one of them could exceed its just Bounds, but was kept within the Sphere in which it was circumscribed by the original Frame" (quoted in Panagopoulos, 1985, 60f.).

Modern historians are much less certain concerning the operation in practice of Sparta's political institutions (see, e.g., Andrewes, 1966; Powell, 1988,

101f., 238), but there is general agreement that the life of the ordinary citizen, from childhood until old age, was highly regimented; it resembled, according to one commentator, "that of a military camp" (Powell, 1988, 215). This does not mean, however, that Spartans were subject to arbitrary and uncontrolled coercive authority. On the contrary, the rule of law was regarded as a sacrosanct political principle. But Spartan law was extraordinarily comprehensive, leaving no part of ordinary life untouched. As von Fritz observes, Sparta was a totalitarian polity (1975, 350).[37]

The general inference that might be derived from the case of ancient Sparta is that a pluralist distribution of political power and the rule of law, though necessary to personal liberty, are insufficient in themselves to guarantee it. In a pluralist constitutional polity, those who share the power to make and apply law may cooperate in the suppression of individual freedom if transcendant religious, or national, or social objectives are widely regarded as demanding it. In secular democracies such as the United States, where individualism is celebrated and civil rights are stated in a written Constitution, personal liberty is invariably an early casualty of war, and even in times of peace and plenty it has often been significantly eroded when the safety of the state, or the general interest, has been viewed as threatened by iconoclastic views or eccentric behavior. As James Madison perceived, a pluralist distribution of political power may be insufficient to prevent those who make and administer law from abusing their authority, and when popular passions are aroused, even a constitutionally entrenched Bill of Rights may prove to be only a "parchment barrier" against attacks on personal freedom.

37. On the political and social system of ancient Sparta, and the changing image of Sparta in modern European thought, see Rawson (1969). For a brief description of Sparta's political system, and the rigorous militaristic education of its male citizens, see Burn (1979, 112–118); and Finer (1997, 336f.).

3

The Roman Republic

Even as recently as the early twentieth century, it would not have been necessary for any commentator on ancient Rome to remark upon its enormous influence on the history of the Western world. In every European country, and to only a somewhat lesser extent in the British Commonwealth and the United States, the study of Latin language and literature was an essential part of the standard educational curriculum. Though it had been absent from the world scene for fifteen centuries, ancient Rome was deemed by those in charge of the enculturation of the young to have an importance that sometimes even surpassed that of the student's own country. High-school graduates were acquainted with the poetry of Virgil, Ovid, and Catullus and the orations of Cicero; the historical significance of Scipio Africanus, Marius and Sulla was fully understood; and Caesar and Augustus were as well known as native worthies. That many things are comparable to Gaul, in being divided into three parts, was a common cliché; "How long, O Cataline" a recognizable reference to great oratory; "Of arms and the man I sing" a familiar epical pronouncement. The late-nineteenth-century English socialists adopted the name "Fabian Society" confident that its reference to the military tactics of a famous Roman consul-general of the third century B.C. would be widely understood. Now that Latin studies and Roman history have almost disappeared from school curricula, it is well to remind oneself how prominent they were for a long time, and until quite recently.

In the lands that bordered the Mediterranean, the continuing influence of ancient Rome undoubtedly reflects the fact that they were its colonial dependencies for some seven centuries. But the main influence of Rome on "Western Civilization" derives from the Renaissance, almost a millennium after the end of the empire, and was due to the more distinctly intellectual influences that attended the enthusiastic study of the rediscovered classical texts and the investigation of their historical provenance. Rome's hegemony of the Mediterranean world naturally engendered great interest in the political system that had enabled a small city-state to conquer an extensive empire and hold it for many hundreds of years. Our interest centers upon the republican era, from the expulsion of the Etruscan kings in the late sixth or early fifth century B.C. to the effective end of republican government when Cornelius Sulla marched his legions into the city in 88 B.C. (hereafter in this chapter, B.C. will be omitted in the dates given). It was during this period that Rome acquired its empire and established an effective system to maintain and exploit it. My main object here, however, is not to explain how Rome could rule such a vast territory, but to examine the institutional machinery of the government of Rome itself, which politically remained no more than a somewhat enlarged city-state. Understanding Roman government after Augustus is nonproblematic. It was hierarchically structured, with a central seat of sovereignty that fully met the criteria that Bodin later established. Political power was concentrated and exercised through coercive force or the palpable threat of it. The Republic, however, was a different system, operating with a complex set of political and social institutions and established traditions.

As with ancient Athens, scholars have had to construct a picture of Rome's republican government from many diverse sources. There is no contemporary document comparable to the Aristotelian *Athenaion Politeia* that describes the republican constitution. Copies of the "Twelve Tables," a constitutional document establishing the Republic after the end of the Etruscan monarchy, exist only in fragments. Documentary materials for the early Republic, up to the end of the Second Punic War in 201, are very scant; for its later period we have the commentaries of a number of contemporary historians such as Livy, Polybius, and Sallust, and the voluminous writings of Cicero. From these and other sources, a fairly reliable picture of the institutional structure of the Republic at its height has been constructed, but, as one would expect, the actual working of the political system is less clear. Scholars continue to disagree on important points, especially on a general theoretical interpretation of the system.[1]

The Development of the Republic, and Its Fall

From archaeological evidence it appears that the settlement on the Tiber that was to become the city of Rome began in the mid-eighth century. By the late seventh century, the Etruscans, who probably came from the eastern Mediterranean, had established themselves in the area of Latium, and Rome was governed by Etruscan kings until the seventh of these, Tarquin the Proud, was assassinated (or expelled) at the end of the sixth century. Under the Etruscan monarchy, Rome developed into the leading economic, cultural,

---

1. For an account of the original sources available for study of the political system of the Roman Republic, see Taylor (1966, 9f.).

and political center of Latium and, indeed, became one of the richest and most powerful cities of Italy (Heichelheim et al., 1984, 23f., 33; Scullard, 1992, 62). The king was the dominant political, religious, and military authority, and it seems evident that Tarquin and his predecessors exercised their powers without any significant constraint (Brunt, 1971, 44). Nonetheless, political institutions had developed even in the monarchical era that could serve to distribute political power more broadly—notably, a senate, or council of leading citizens, and popular assemblies that all citizens could attend.

Rome was not innovative in establishing a republican form of government. At the time of Tarquin's deposition, there were hundreds of city-republics in the Mediterranean basin, but over the next three centuries all of them succumbed to the hegemony of Rome. Dominance over the area of Latium was achieved in the early fifth century; central and southern Italy were absorbed in the first quarter of the third century; northern Italy in the Gallic Wars of 225–222. After this date, Roman hegemony in mainland Italy was complete. One of its by-products was an end to the warfare, hitherto incessant, among neighboring Italian communities. The subject peoples benefited greatly from this *Pax Romana* in itself, and also from the great roads built by the legions to sustain it, which stimulated economic development by providing an infrastructure of unprecedented quality for overland commerce. Local languages gave way to Latin, local gods were displaced by Roman ones, Roman coinage became the general medium of exchange, a common system of jurisprudence came into being as Roman law spread throughout the peninsula, and the political aspiration of its peoples was to be recognized as full Roman citizens. "Slowly but surely," writes Scullard, "the various races of Italy became a nation" (1992, 150f.).

Some historians have referred to the political system that was established to govern the Italian peninsula as a "confederation" or even a "federation,"[2] but these terms are misleading. The relation between Rome and the other Italian communities was not comparable to that which exists between the levels of government in federations such as the United States and Canada. Rome and its Italian "allies" were not partners in any cooperatively determined political policy, nor can they be regarded as sharing the jurisdiction of the state. The Italian communities were left free to govern themselves in local affairs as they wished, but each region was subject to a governor, appointed by Rome, with unlimited authority *(imperium)*, which he was expected to exercise vigorously if the interests of Rome were threatened. At the time of

---

2. Scullard usually refers to Rome and the Italian provinces as constituting a "confederacy" (1992, see esp. 146–153) but sometimes uses the term "federation" (113, 146). Smith refers to the system as a "federation" (1955, 9, 66). For a firm rejection of this notion, see Millar (1984, 6f.).

the Gallic Wars, the number of people entitled to participate in the popular assemblies (adult males with full citizenship) was almost 300,000, many of whom lived a considerable distance from Rome. Only the technique of representation could have enabled the allied communities of Italy to participate in the political system, but no such process developed in the Roman Republic. In terms of constitutional structure and operational politics, Rome was essentially a city-state, and it remained so even after the boundaries of its power extended beyond Italy to include the whole of the Mediterranean world.

The main threat to Roman dominance of Italy was Carthage, a great military, naval, and trading city situated on the southern shore of the Mediterranean near the site of the present city of Tunis. While Rome was consolidating its hegemony of mainland Italy, Carthage had turned the lands of the western Mediterranean into subject provinces. A larger city than Rome, and richer, Carthage was a deadly enemy, determined to destroy its emerging rival. Rome only survived because most of its Italian allies remained loyal when, in the Second Punic War, a large Carthaginian army under the command of Hannibal invaded the Italian peninsula. There were three Punic Wars in all, beginning in 264, but it was the second (218–201) that was decisive. After it, Rome found itself not only secure in the peninsula, but the unrivaled possessor of the territories that had previously been subject to Carthage. The empire so acquired was easily extended to the east, and by a century after the defeat of Hannibal, the Roman Republic was master of all the lands bordering the Mediterranean, a large part of the entire civilized world.[3]

Rome was an imperial power (in the modern sense of the term) long before it had an emperor. For more than two centuries, from the end of the First Punic War in 241 to the principate of Augustus, the Republic had to deal with the problem of governing a large number of diverse provincial communities, and of compelling their dependency despite the constant threat of internal rebellion and the expansionist ambitions of border states.[4] The treaty ending the First Punic War transferred control of Sicily from Carthage to Rome. The method of alliances was not applied to Sicily, however. There a

3. "The importance of the Second Punic War can hardly be exaggerated. It was a turning point in the history of the whole ancient world. Its effect on Rome and Italy, on the constitution, on economic and social life, on religion and thought was profound. After it no power arose that could endanger the existence of Rome. The Hellenistic monarchies of the east still flourished, but at Rome's touch they fell like a house of cards" (Scullard, 1992, 238).

4. The Latin word *provincia* originally referred to the defined sphere of a magistrate's authority to act in the name of the state, his *imperium*. As Rome's hegemony extended, it came to mean a geographic territory, i.e., an overseas dependency (see Scullard, 1992, 182).

system of provincial government was instituted and extended to other overseas territories as they fell to the Roman legions. From the Italian communities, Rome demanded little more than contributions of fighting men, but the overseas territories were looked upon as sources of wealth, not through commerce, but tribute (Scullard, 1992, 179f.).[5] Like Carthage before it, Rome became a kleptocracy, exploiting the provinces by expropriating their lands and charging rents for their use, taking slaves at will, and levying heavy taxes. In 168, direct taxation of Romans was discontinued because revenues flowing from the provinces met—even exceeded—the expenses of the state: the great public building program that transformed the city of Rome in the second century, and the aqueducts that provided a supply of water unsurpassed by any city until modern times, were financed from the provincial revenues (Brunt, 1971, 16; Crawford, 1993, 74).

The government of this kleptocracy was exceedingly simple and effective. Each province was placed under the command of a praetor sent from Rome with full *imperium* and supported by locally garrisoned legions under his immediate command.[6] Although the praetors were expected to act on behalf of the state, supervision of the work of provincial governors was lax. There were great opportunities for personal enrichment, which the governors quickly learned to exploit. War itself became a source of enrichment, because booty could be used as the army commander wished: to add to his personal fortune, to distribute to his legions, or to send home to swell the Roman treasury. The second of these became highly significant in Rome's political development. Sharing in war booty was, for the ordinary soldier, a far more important source of income than his meager official pay, and a generous commander could create personal loyalties in his legionaries rivaling those

5. "Rome inherited from the former rulers of Sicily a tithe payable in grain. Nearly half a million bushels of wheat, sufficient at first to last the city for half a year, were annually supplied free of charge by the Sicilians. It was imported and sold in Rome, the proceeds going to the Treasury" (Cowell, 1948, 25). If Republican Rome had not previously appreciated that war and conquest could be exceedingly profitable, the large indemnity that Carthage agreed to pay for ten years, plus the steady supply of free grain from Sicily, must have sufficed to convince its leaders that protection from foreign invasion was not the only benefit derivable from them.

6. "Inside the province the powers of the praetor were practically absolute. There was no colleague of equal rank [as at Rome] to oppose his decisions or acts, no plebeian tribune to interpose his veto in defense of private individuals, no senate as in Rome to exercise by its higher authority a moral restraint over his abuse of arbitrary power, and no popular assembly to pass laws that he had to obey. As subjects of a foreign power, the people of a province had neither the right of appeal nor legal guarantees of the rights of life, liberty, and property" (Heichelheim et al., 1984, 95).

they owed to the "Senate and People of Rome." Foundations were thus laid for the ultimate subversion of the Republic.[7]

The immense wealth that flowed from the provinces had a great impact on the socioeconomic structure of the Roman, and Italian, populace, creating a division between rich and poor that far exceeded in political importance the traditional division between aristocrats and commoners. The groups that benefited significantly from provincial tribute were the senior members of the provincial administrative establishments, the tax farmers who were appointed on very lucrative terms to collect the tribute,[8] and those who were awarded state contracts to construct public buildings and other facilities. In effect, these beneficiaries included only two small segments of the Roman citizenry: the members of the senatorial aristocracy, and the wealthiest class of plebeians, known as the *equites* (Kunkel, 1973, 45).

Even after making lavish expenditures for personal gratification and display, a great deal of wealth remained in their hands, which they sought to invest. Rome was not an industrial or trading community with large opportunities for commercial investment, and those that existed were forbidden to senators (Hawthorn, 1962, 57). Moreover, it was firmly established in Roman culture that, aside from military exploits, the only thing that definitely contributed to one's personal standing in the society, one's *dignitas,* was the ownership of land (Cowell, 1948, 41; Brunt, 1971, 21, 34; Heichelheim et al., 1984, 136). As a consequence, a great deal of surplus personal wealth was invested in the acquisition of land. At the same time, the importation of tribute grain from Sicily and, later, from north Africa, undermined the market for this commodity that Italian farmers had been accustomed to supply, making less viable the family farm that had been the mainstay of the early republican economy. Wealthy Romans bought out, or forced out, the small farmers and leased from the state the large tracts of public land that had been expropriated during the conquest of the peninsula. Huge *latifundia* were thus created, which were used as grazing lands for the raising of livestock. Such enterprises did not require a great deal of knowledge, skill, or care, and could be profitably operated by slaves, with a few overseers whose power over them was, by Roman law, absolute. Thus slaves replaced the independent farmers of the Italian countryside.[9] Many of those dispossessed migrated to Rome, where

7. Shatzman (1972) points out that the authority of the generals to dispose of war booty was not illegal and that repeated efforts to bring it under legal control all failed.

8. Brunt says that it may be inferred from available evidence that, in the mid-first century, tax farmers kept for themselves perhaps as much as half of what they collected (1988, 154).

9. One of the important consequences of Rome's overseas expansion is that slavery, of small significance prior to the Punic Wars, became much more important thereafter, and not only in agriculture (Tenney, 1930, 379; Kunkel, 1973, 8). Cowell writes, "We do not

they crowded into the squalid slum of multistoried tenements called the *Sub-ura*, eking out a living as best they could with the aid of the subsidized grain and other welfare benefits that were established to deal with the great numbers of the urban poor (Brunt, 1966).[10]

"The political history of the two hundred years which followed the fall of the monarchy," writes a modern Roman historian, "is mainly that of the struggle of the social orders, as the plebeians sought protection from, and then equality with, the patricians" (Scullard, 1992, 81). The most effective weapon available to the plebeians was the *successio*—in effect a general strike by which the plebs withdrew from all communal activities. Because of the vital military role of the plebs as footsoldiers in the Roman legions, this proved to be a potent instrument.[11] It was, apparently, first employed in 499 and, through numerous subsequent ones, the plebs gradually won large political concessions from the patricians (see Heichelheim et al., 1984, 61–63). But, as we shall see in the next section where the structure of the mature Republican constitution is outlined, the success of the plebs in attaining personal security from the magistrates' arbitrary exercise of power far exceeded their achievement of effective participation in the making of state policy. Rome continued to be a city-state in which all important political issues were determined by a very small segment of the citizenry. Consequently, the functioning government of the Roman Republic was dominated by the interest of the landed aristocracy and the wealthy commercial class in maintaining the socioeconomic regime that had developed with the acquisition of the empire. No significant reforms were instituted to remedy the conditions of the poor (beyond the provision of "bread and circuses"); such reforms could only have been achieved by a policy of land redistribution at the expense of the *lati-fundia*.

In the later second century there emerged, from within the bosom of the

---

know how many slaves the Romans owned in Cicero's day, but they must have covered Italy in hundreds of thousands" (1948, 51). In addition, by this time there were many former slaves (and their descendants), freed by masters who found them unprofitable to keep, who swelled the ranks of the poor. Crawford refers to "the problem of the creation of a slave economy [in the second century] as opposed to an economy in which slavery existed, at a time when free labor was available" (1993, 104).

10. See Heichelheim et al. (1984, ch. 12) for a good survey of "The Internal Effects of War and Imperialism" in the late Republican period.

11. The military importance of the plebs derived from the adoption, in the sixth century, of Greek military tactics, which relied on large numbers of heavily armed infantry. Prior to this the basic fighting unit consisted of cavalry, which was drawn from the patrician class and the *equites,* the topmost property-owning commoners who were wealthy enough to provide themselves with horses and other equipment for their military service (Kunkel, 1973, 7f.).

patriciate itself, two great champions of the plebs: the Gracchus brothers, Tiberius and Gaius.[12] They attempted to redistribute agricultural land and to institute other reforms, by methods that in effect enlarged the political power of the plebeians at the expense of the aristocracy (Cowell, 1948, 55f.; Heichelheim et al., 1984, 162f.; Beard and Crawford, 1985, 6; Crawford, 1993, 113f., 119). The political conflict that ensued degenerated into violence in which Tiberius and Gaius were murdered, along with many of their followers. For the remainder of the Republic, the political power of the aristocracy remained unchallenged (Heichelheim et al., 1984, 164f.).

Historians seem to agree that the Gracchi were most notable for initiating an era of degeneration in Roman government that led to the downfall of the Republic.[13] The political system that had helped Rome become master of Italy, defeat Carthage, and appropriate a vast overseas empire no longer seemed capable of providing the means for the orderly conduct of government. Disregard for established constitutional practices became the rule rather than the exception; violence, not previously unknown in Roman politics (Lintott, 1968, ch. 5), now became an endemic feature of it. The entrenched upper classes, intent upon the maintenance of their wealth and power, were unable to recognize that the Gracchi had identified some serious problems that, in the long run, could not be dealt with by repression.

One of these problems was the political status of the Italian peoples. Only a small number of them had the full rights of Roman citizenship; a larger number enjoyed a kind of partial citizenship known as "Latin rights," but most were not citizens in any political sense at all.[14] This grated sorely upon

---

12. Cornelia, the mother of Tiberius and Gaius Gracchus, was a daughter of the revered Scipio Africanus, conqueror of Hannibal, so they belonged by birth to the topmost stratum of Roman society. In addition, both brothers were connected by their own marriages to two of the wealthiest and most influential patrician families of Rome, which supported them in their political endeavors (Brunt, 1971, 76f.). Cowell notes that they were "among the first children of the Roman aristocracy to get their education under pronounced Greek influence"—which, he suggests, may account for their unconventional approach to the political problems of the Republic (1948, 52).

13. See Brunt (1971, ch. 5).; Brunt remarks elsewhere that the Gracchi "set the revolutionary process in motion [which] was consummated and ended by Augustus" (1988, 87; see also Scullard, 1951, 248; and Finley, 1983, 117f.). Smith (1955) is the most extreme in this regard, depicting the dominance of the patriciate as an ideal government that would have been capable of dealing with all problems if the harmony of the Roman polity had not been broken by the Gracchi. Most historians do not accept this appraisal but, nevertheless, as Scullard puts it, they regard the Gracchi as "without doubt" precipitating "the revolution that overthrew the Republic" (1982, 40).

14. Scullard refers to there being "full citizens and half-citizens." The latter had the same legal status as the former in private matters, but they could not vote in the assemblies or stand for office (1992, 146f.; McCullough, 1991, 855).

the Italians and led in 91 B.C. to the "Social Wars." The insistence of the Romans on preserving special citizenship status for themselves convinced a number of the Italian allies to undertake armed rebellion, not in order to regain their independence, but to persuade the citizens that they should admit others to their ranks. Ultimately their aims were met, but not before Rome first put down the rebellions by force. In the Social Wars, many of the Italian communities were devastated, with heavy casualties on both sides. The century of peace in the Italian peninsula that had followed the defeat of Hannibal was succeeded by six decades of conflict between rival Roman factions. The Social Wars themselves lasted little more than a year, but they initiated a period of political disorder that ended only with the replacement of the Republic by the principate of Augustus.

Without a system of political representation, it is difficult to see how the Italians could have been admitted to full participation in the institutions of government. As of 91 B.C., there were already some 400,000 adult male citizens in a polity that was operating as if it were still a small city-state. Extension of citizenship to the whole of Italy would necessarily have led ultimately either to a fundamental reconstruction of the political system or its breakdown. As it turned out, reconstruction occurred, not in the form of a representative democracy, but by reversion to the form of government that had pertained five centuries before: a monarchy in all but name, with Augustus and his successors holding absolute power.

In the play of events, it was neither the economic problems created by the dispossession of the small farmers, nor the political problems arising out of the extension of citizenship, that was the immediate cause of the fall of the Republic. The operative factor was the failure to maintain political control of the army commanders. Military exigencies rendered it sometimes necessary to prolong a command. In 326 the term of office of the commander beseiging Neapolis was extended, and thereafter this became a common practice (Finer, 1997, 406). Unlike Athens, Rome did not develop other means to control its commanders, and their authority to distribute war booty and provincial tribute to their soldiers enabled them to create armies that were loyal to themselves rather than to Rome. Given this situation, it was only a matter of time before one of the military leaders was to succumb to the temptation to march his army to Rome and, with its backing, establish himself as a dictatorial ruler. Julius Caesar's celebrated military coup in 50 B.C. was not the first of such events; the Roman polity had already been profoundly altered by similar employment of the Roman legions by Gaius Marius and Lucius Cornelius Sulla.

Marius was one of the most outstanding military geniuses of a community that had produced many. Not a scion of a patrician family, he rose to prominence as a consequence of war in north Africa against a Numidian petty-monarch who, in 112, rebelled against Roman domination. The "Jugurthan War" was incompetently conducted and dragged on without resolution until, in 107, Marius was elected consul by the Assembly, in defiance of the Senate, and given command of the Roman legions in Numidia. Jugurtha was speedily defeated and Marius returned to Rome a popular hero. In preparation for his campaign against Jugurtha, Marius had broken with long-standing tradition and enrolled the lowest class of Roman citizens (the unpropertied) in the legions, arming them at state expense. Marius's army had a great sense of personal loyalty to their commander, who, in addition to distributing booty generously and giving them the honor of great victories, had elevated many of them, for the first time in Roman history, to equal rank with the propertied classes. Though Marius himself did not intend to take over the government of Rome by an army coup, he contributed greatly to the development of a military mentality that made this possible. Equally important was Marius's repeated reelection as consul. While the prohibition against reelection had been flouted previously, and undermined in other ways, this vital element in the republican constitution now became a dead letter (Smith, 1955, 62f.; Brunt, 1971, 97f.; Beard and Crawford, 1985, 6f.; Crawford, 1993, 125f.).

The specific events that ended the Republic were a by-product of the Social Wars. An eastern monarch, Mithridates of Pontus, seized the opportunity provided by Rome's preoccupation with the rebellious Italians to invade the Roman provinces of Asia Minor, Macedon, and Greece (Brunt, 1971, 103). Command of the Roman legions to wage war against Mithridates was given to Cornelius Sulla, a companion and rival of Marius since the days of the Jugurthan War. Marius, who coveted this post, succeeded in having the assembly rescind Sulla's appointment and name himself as commander of the Roman forces in the east. Enraged, Sulla marched his army to Rome (88 B.C.) and invaded the city, with much loss of civilian life and destruction of property (Heichelheim et al., 1984, 183f.). After settling accounts with his enemies and assuming the position of dictator, Sulla departed from Rome to deal with Mithridates. In his absence, the consul Cornelius Cinna revoked his decrees and brought Marius back from Africa, where he had fled to escape capture by Sulla. A reign of terror ensued in which many people, both patrician and plebeian, were slaughtered.[15]

After defeating Mithridates and restoring Roman hegemony in the east,

15. "For days he [Marius] ranged the city like a raving lunatic. His followers struck down all the nobles and senators whom he hated. Their mutilated corpses littered the streets and their heads, dripping blood, decorated the rostra. Their houses and property were confiscated and auctioned. His outrages made even Cinna quail and finally stop them" (Heichelheim et al., 1984, 184).

Sulla returned to Rome (83 B.C.) with a large army and initiated an even more ruthless bloodbath of his own, which eliminated all vestiges of opposition. Political power now securely in his hands, Sulla introduced numerous reforms in the Roman constitution. He did not intend to continue a regime of personal rule and, in fact, voluntarily retired in 80 B.C. He regarded his reforms as necessary steps in the restoration of republican government, but in fact that regime was now defunct.[16] The civil wars and riots that punctuated Roman history for a half-century after Sulla were not contests to decide whether Rome should be a republic or a monarchy, but to determine *who* should be its sovereign master.[17] The exact date of the demise of the Roman Republic is debatable, but the disease that killed it, one fatal to any pluralist system of power, was contracted in the latter part of the second century, when the army commanders freed themselves from effective political control.[18]

The Political System of the Republic

Political theory is greatly stimulated by civic disorder and upheaval, and the intellectual historian must deeply regret that no such literature has survived from the period when the Etruscan monarchy was dissolved and Rome became a republic. There must have been a great deal of discussion, at the end of the sixth century and the beginning of the fifth, concerning the purposes of the state and the constitutional forms that would best serve to achieve

16. On Sulla's constitutional reforms and their objectives, see Cowell (1948, 168f.); Smith (1955, 1076f.); Brunt (1971, 108f.); Kunkel (1973, 47); Scullard, (1982, 80f.); and Heichelheim et al., (1984, 187f.).

17. "It was with Sulla that the Republican constitution . . . came to its end . . . Sulla's forces were no longer the Republic's armies but personal ones, men who followed him for booty and reward. All the armies of the contenders in the subsequent civil wars were of this kind" (Finer, 1997, 436).

18. Historians differ greatly in their assessments of the causes of the fall of the Republic. In Cowell's view, the greatness of Rome derived from the superior character of the Romans and their capacity to subordinate personal interests to those of the community. The Republic fell because these qualities had been diluted by foreigners and corrupted by the egocentric emphasis of the patrician classes on personal wealth and social distinction (1948, 14f., ch. 18). Heichelheim et al. contend that political rivalry within the oligarchy had become so intense that it could only end with one person dominant (1984, 181, 208). Beard and Crawford also emphasize the deleterious effects of aristocratic competition (1985, 68f.). Lintott contends that the lack of a police force in Rome meant that violence was condoned as a method of settling personal disputes, leading inevitably to the use of violence in politics, which could only be brought to an end by an army coup (1968, 1–5). Brunt writes that the system of "balance" depended critically upon the existence of "social harmony," which was dissipated in the late Republic with the discontent of the lower orders (1966, 26; 1988, 13, 76f.).

them, but we have no direct knowledge of it, and the best that the historian can do is infer, from the constitution that was actually established, what the dominant political ideas seem to have been.

The most significant single fact in this regard is that the Romans did not replace the Etruscan monarchy by a Latin one. The chief executive authority of the regime established by the new constitution was placed in the hands of two consuls, equal in power, elected by a popular assembly for nonrenewable terms of one year. From this fact alone one might feel justified in drawing a pluralist inference, but the governmental machinery of the Republic was very complex, composed of elements retained from the monarchical period as well as new ones, and it is advisable to withhold theoretical appraisal until we have before us an outline of its structure.[19]

The political institutions of the Roman Republic were based upon a society that was formally stratified. In all, eight classes of citizens were distinguished. The senatorial class, at the top of the social pyramid, was initially an exclusive patrician order based upon birth, but membership in it came to depend on wealth, which given the restrictions imposed on the economic activities of senators, meant wealth in land. Until the reforms of Sulla, only a few hundred Roman citizens were senators. Senatorial status could be lost by falling below the required minimum amount of land owned, and nonpatricians could become senators if they had sufficient landed wealth.

Below the senators were the *equites,* the equestrian class originally defined as those who composed the cavalry units of the army, but later in terms of a wealth criterion judged sufficient to enable one to provide the mounts and equipment required by a cavalryman, whether or not he actually served in that capacity. No restrictions were placed on their permissible sources of wealth, and the *equites* ceased to be only a military elite and developed into the dominant economic class in the Republic.[20] Socially and culturally, the *equites* and the senators belonged to the same class, and though they frequently came into conflict, their interests were essentially the same and differed from those of lower social classes (Brunt, 1988, 147, 162f.). Not all of

19. The structure of the constitution, and the functions of its various elements, changed over the five centuries of the Republic's history. Millar points out that the "established form and functions" of the main institutions came into being between the beginning of the fourth and the end of the third centuries (1989, 140). I shall adopt the latter date as, roughly, the temporal reference point for my description. I should note that historians are not in complete agreement on the institutional details of the political system, and I have occasionally had to choose between conflicting accounts.

20. In addition to forming companies to engage in trade, banking, and other private enterprise, the *equites* acted as collectors of the provincial tribute and rents on public lands, operators of state-owned mineral properties, contractors for the construction of public works, etc. (Scullard, 1992, 319).

those who met the wealth criterion belonged to the class of *equites* because, strictly speaking, this rank was confined to the 1,800 who were enrolled in the equestrian "centuries." Together, in the opinion of Beard and Crawford, the 2,000 or so senators and equites "controlled the political, legal, military and economic processes of Rome" (1985, 44).

The remainder of the Roman citizenry was divided into six classes, ranked in order according to the amount of land owned, a measurement that initially served as an index of one's ability to provide the arms and other things required when called up for military service. The members of the lowest class, too poor to provide even the minimum of these necessities (and, until the time of Marius exempt from such service), were not listed by name as the others were, but simply counted and recorded as an aggregate number (hence their designation *capite censi,* which translates literally as "head-count").

Membership in the various classes was reviewed every five or six years by an administrative staff under the direction of two senior magistrates called "Censors." The work required about eighteen months to accomplish and constituted a periodic population census more extensive than any undertaken by modern nations until the nineteenth century. Obviously, the Romans regarded it as important.[21]

The main institutions of the republican system of government were the Senate, the various magistracies, and the assemblies. From the standpoint of constitutional analysis, the most striking feature of the Senate is that it had no distinct functional responsibility. It was not specifically a legislative, executive, or judicial organ. Formally, its role in the Republic remained what it had been under the monarchy: an advisory body. But unlike its status then, the "advice" it rendered in the republican era carried great weight and, in certain areas—such as foreign policy, fiscal administration and policy, and the governing of the provinces—its views were effectively determinative (Cowell, 1948, 107f.; Heichelheim et al., 1984, 51f.). To understand the political role of the Senate, one must appreciate the importance in Roman culture of what was called the *mos maiorum.* McCullough suggests that this might be regarded as "Rome's unwritten constitution" and crisply defines it as "The established order of things . . . *Mos* meant established customs; *maiores* meant ancestors or forbears in this context. The *mos maiorum* was how things had always been done" (1991, 863). Throughout the history of the Republic and, indeed, even after Augustus, it counted much in Roman political dis-

21. "This census classification . . . was a central element in Roman political and social life. The amount of scribal effort involved in keeping such records of each citizen and updating them was immense . . . Yet even more extraordinary to us is the explicit and open economic base this classification gave to the structure of the citizen body" (Beard and Crawford, 1985, 43).

course to refer to the *mos maiorum*.[22] The status of the Senate rested solely on the Roman people's unquestioning acceptance of a hierarchical social structure and the belief that the topmost class in that structure possessed, by virtue of long-standing tradition, unchallengeable authority in large matters of state.

The composition of the Senate changed during the course of the Republic, due to the opening of the senior magistracies to plebeians in the fourth century.[23] Any plebeian elected to such a post automatically became a senator for life at the end of his term. Over the years, a substantial number of plebeians became senators in this fashion, changing it from a closed hereditary order to a more broadly based aristocracy (Beard and Crawford, 1985, 45f.). One should not conclude, however, that this degree of fluidity in the Roman class structure rendered it less rigid in function. The plebeians who achieved high magisterial office were co-opted into the aristocracy, and their humbler origins had little political significance.

The noncorrespondence between the formal status of the Senate and what appears to have been its actual role in the government of the Republic creates problems in the interpretation of Rome's political system that scholarly research has not yet been able to resolve. Many historians have taken the stance that the Senate was so dominant that one should regard it as constituting, in all essential respects, the government of Rome (e.g., Kunkel, 1973, 19f.). H. H. Scullard goes further, contending that while Rome was ruled by the Senate, the Senate itself was dominated by a much smaller group representing only twenty, or fewer, patrician families (1973, xvii; 1982, 5f.; 1992, 332). According to this view, Rome was governed by a very small, tightly knit, and largely hereditary, oligarchy. Historians have not universally accepted Scullard's depiction of the nature of Rome's republican government, but there seems to be general agreement that the senatorial and equestrian classes dominated Roman politics. Classifying a polity as falling within one of the classical Aristotelian categories, however, tells one little about its governmental dynamics. For this purpose, consideration of the other organs of the state—the magistracies and the assemblies—is essential.

22. Finer avers that it was the *mos maiorum*, which he translates as "the customs of our forefathers," rather than religion, that constituted the Roman standard of moral conduct (1997, 392).

23. The acquisition of property sufficient to qualify one for senatorial rank did not mean that one would automatically become a senator. The Senate itself had authority to decide which, if any, of such persons to admit. It seems that many wealthy *equites* did not apply for senatorial rank because senators were forbidden to engage in the economic activities that were their main source of income.

CONSULS. Two consuls were elected annually by the assembly. Candidature for this office was normally restricted to persons who had already served in the praetorship, the next highest magisterial office. Though the consuls were the highest executive officers of the Republic, their actual duties were largely military, and usually one of them, and sometimes both, were absent from the city, attending to the never-ending problems of maintaining Rome's authority in the provinces and warring against neighboring states. Until Gaius Marius parlayed his popularity into several successive terms, any ex-consul who wished to hold the office again was required to wait for ten years. But because of practical necessities, a consul's authority as a military commander abroad was frequently extended, sometimes for several years, by naming him *proconsul* after his term as consul had ended. Even before Marius shattered constitutional tradition, it was possible for a military commander to hold his post long enough to build up a institutional center of personal power that was denied to magistrates dealing only with domestic affairs (Scullard, 1992, 125). As a domestic official, a consul had great prestige, but remarkably little personal power. His decisions were subject to negation by his fellow consul, and by any one of the ten tribunes, whereas the other magistrates had independent authority that no consul could easily supersede (Brunt, 1988, 16). Abroad, as commander of legions, a consul could effectively "pull rank," but he could not do so at home.

In the early Republic, the consulship was held exclusively by persons of senatorial rank, but after a prolonged political dispute on this matter, the office was opened to others in 367 (Brunt, 1971, 55; Heichelheim et al., 1984, 59; Scullard, 1992, 117f.). Nevertheless, it remained a senatorial monopoly, and even the occasional "new man" who succeeded in being elected to it identified himself with the patrician order.[24] Like other senior magistrates, consuls did not receive salaries, and because campaigning for election was expensive, the only nonpatricians who offered themselves as candidates came from the equestrian class.

PRAETORS. This magistracy was apparently established originally to provide the consuls with assistance, but it developed into one of independent authority, second only to the consulate in the Republic's status system. Until the middle of the third century there was only one praetor, but the growing

---

24. Tenney points out that of the 108 consuls elected between 200 and 146, only about 8 belonged to families that had not previously had members in consular office (1930, 365). Even within the patrician class, the top magistracy was concentrated: over roughly the same period; some 80 percent of the consuls belonged to only 26 family groups (Scullard, 1982, 6).

burden of administering Rome's Italian dependencies led to the establishment of another, a praetor *peregrinus*, as the chief judicial officer to deal with cases outside the city. The other praetor, the praetor *urbanus*, had legal jurisdiction within the city.[25] As Rome's empire grew after the defeat of Carthage, further praetorships were added; the number was increased to four in 277, and to six in 177 (Kunkel, 1973, 17; Heichelheim et al., 1984, 62; McCullough, 1992, 871f.).

To describe the praetorship in modern terms as the "judicial branch" of the Roman state would be accurate enough if it did not suggest the notion of a distinct "separation of powers." In the absence of both consuls from the city, the urban praetor assumed all the responsibilities and authority of the consulship. In addition, after the end of his term of office, a praetor could be given military command as *propraetor* with, as in the case of a *proconsul*, no constitutional restriction on the duration of his appointment (Brunt, 1971, 45; Scullard, 1992, 125). Thus, like the consuls, praetors were viewed as qualified to embody Rome's imperium abroad, with all the potential for financial gain and personal power that such appointments conveyed.

The praetors were elected annually by the assembly. Two years after the conclusion of a person's term of office as praetor, he could stand for election to the consulship, as all those ambitious to ascend the *cursus honorum* (ladder of honor) to its top would seek to do. Only former praetors could be candidates for consular office, but even so, this meant (after 177 B.C.) that each year six men were added to the number of potential consular candidates although there were only two posts to be filled.

QUAESTORS. This magistracy was the first of the three rungs on the *cursus honorum*. Candidates for this office had to have completed several years of military service and be at least thirty years of age. Like the consuls and praetors, quaestors were elected by the assembly for one-year terms. The number of quaestors grew steadily from two when the office was created in the mid-fifth century, to eight in the later third century, to twenty after the reforms of Sulla. Their duties were mainly concerned with financial administration, which, as in all orderly governments, gave them considerable power and authority. They also were responsible for keeping official records and the archive of state documents, as well as for investigating certain crimes. Some were seconded to the staff of military commanders for administrative pur-

25. "During their year's service they [the praetors] would naturally have to make many decisions upon disputed points of legal principle and practice. In these two ways the Praetors laid down the law and so began the slow building up of that great body of Roman law and Roman legal practice to which many countries today owe the core of their legal system" (Cowell, 1948, 136).

poses, but could also undertake military duties if requested to do so (Hawthorn, 1962, 53; Kunkel, 1973, 17f.; Heichelheim et al., 1984, 60; McCullough, 1992, 875; Scullard, 1992, 126).

The ascending order of the *cursus honorum* was, clearly, a rapidly narrowing one, with twenty places on the first rung (after 83 B.C.), six on the second, and only two at the top. As a training system for magistrates, it undoubtedly had considerable merit. Indeed, the competition for higher office generated by the progressive reduction in posts might have led to the development of a significant democratic element in the republican system, but the voting methods used in the assembly (described later) precluded this. Instead, it resulted in intense political infighting among the leading families anxious to move their scions up the ladder. The violence, intimidation, and bribery caused by these rivalries undermined the moral authority of the Senate and contributed to the decline of Rome's ability to govern itself as a Republic.

TRIBUNES. In addition to the magistracies composing the ladder of honor, there were numerous other officials functioning in the city and abroad. Only one group of these, the plebeian tribunes, requires our attention here as a vital part of the Republic's constitutional order.[26] These officials, though lacking magisterial status, nevertheless constituted a vital part of the republican political system, especially if one examines it in terms of how the Roman citizenry were protected against the arbitrary exercise of state power. Despite the strong legalistic component of the Roman political culture, the modern constitutional concept of due process of law was, at best, only a nascent principle. The freedom of the ordinary citizenry, and their property rights, depended upon the authority not of the courts, but of the plebeian tribunes.

26. The most important other officials were the *aediles* and the *censors*. The aediles were responsible for supervising public facilities, regulating markets, and organizing public festivals and entertainments. Some historians include the aedilship as part of the *cursus honorum*, between the offices of quaestor and praetor. The censors, in addition to determining the class membership of the Roman citizenry, were responsible for letting contracts for the erection of public buildings and other large public works, making contracts with private tax farmers, and leasing public land. This office was regarded as highly prestigious and was frequently sought by ex-consuls as the capstone of their careers in public service. Some historians describe it as the topmost rung of the *cursus honorum* (e.g., Finer, 1997, 400). One should note, also, the office of *Dictator*. In times of great crisis, a dictator could be appointed for a term of six months by the Senate. The full imperium of the state was placed in his hands. Such appointments were made on more than forty occasions in the second half of the fourth century, but infrequently thereafter, and never after 202. According to Cowell, Sulla and Caesar were not dictators by formal appointment but "assumed" dictatorial powers (1948, 137). This office can hardly be construed as an element in the working republican constitution because the filling of it meant, in effect, that the constitution was suspended.

The office of *tribuni plebis* came into existence, apparently without specific legal status, at the beginning of the fifth century and, after a general strike in 449, was embodied in law. As of that date, and subsequently, there were ten such tribunes, elected for one-year terms by the Assembly. From the beginning, their main responsibility was to come to the aid of any citizen who may have been treated unjustly by a magistrate. To this end, individual tribunes had the authority to veto a magisterial order of punishment. The tribunes were declared to be personally inviolate by the assembly, which in the form of a *conjuratio* (solemn oath) decreed that "anyone laying violent hands upon him or willfully interfering in the performance of his duties was laid under curse or pain of death." Obviously the plebeians felt very strongly that there was need for protection against the exercise of magisterial imperium (Cowell, 1948, 138; Brunt, 1971, 51; Kunkel, 1973, 21; Heichelheim et al., 1984, 56; Beard and Crawford, 1985, 65; Scullard, 1992, 85f., 89).

The power of the plebeian tribunes was not limited to countering that of the magistrates in this fashion. Over time, they obtained the authority to veto any official act regarded as contrary to the interests of the plebs in general, including bills introduced into the assembly and decrees of the Senate. Scullard remarks that the tribunes "could check the whole state machinery" (1992, 86). The tribunes gradually acquired the right to participate directly in the deliberations of the Senate, first only to attend its meetings, then to speak, and finally, in 216, to act as authorized conveners of its meetings Kunkel, 1973, 22; Finley, 1983, 99; Heichelheim et al., 1984, 56; Finer, 1997, 404f.).

This review of the powers of the plebeian tribunes might suggest that there was, after all, a definite seat of sovereignty in the Roman Republic, which they occupied. But this would be a grossly erroneous judgment. The tribunate might have developed into a collective entity with supreme authority, but on matters of general state policy, the tribunes were in fact pliant instruments of the Senate, except for rare instances such as the Gracchi. In contrast to all other organs of republican government, the Senate had the advantage of permanent membership. Despite the incessant disputes and maneuverings of its factions, this enabled it to maintain sufficient solidarity to preserve the economic and political interests of the aristocracy. The tribunes were elected by the plebs, but by financial necessity as well as tradition, only men who belonged to the senatorial and equestrian classes could stand as candidates. Unavoidably, the personal interests of the tribunes were more allied to those of the aristocracy than to those of the common citizenry. In the second century, writes Scullard, "most of the legislation introduced in the assembly by the tribunes had already been shaped in the Senate, and the tribunes in fact were becoming an instrument of the senatorial oligarchy" (1982, 8; see also

Brunt, 1971, 66f.). In contrast to the senators, the tribunes were not members of an organized institution that met as a body to determine a common policy. All of them had equal status and authority, and one could veto the decrees of another. It was not difficult for a senator or group of senators to persuade or suborn a tribune to exercise his veto power against a colleague when the economic or political interests of the senatorial class appeared to be threatened. It was not always necessary, as in the case of the Gracchi, to resort to violence.

One should not, however, dismiss the plebeian tribunes as unimportant in the Roman political order. They continued, throughout the history of the Republic, to do what they had been established initially to do: to protect the common citizen from arbitrary or excessive magisterial power. Their constitutional function was not to determine public policy, but to maintain personal liberty. They did not run the Roman state; they provided the individual Roman with a means of defense against it.

THE ASSEMBLIES. Up to this point, I have referred to "the Assembly" in the singular, but in fact there were three assemblies that all adult male Roman citizens were entitled to attend, all of which had important governmental functions. The resulting organization was exceedingly complex, and has not as yet been completely defined by historians.[27] Fortunately for our purposes, the differences between them, their historical development, and the fine details of their functions are unimportant, and I shall continue to refer to them collectively, except where specification is required.

The Assembly was the lawmaking institution of the Roman Republic. A bill, drawn up by a magistrate or a tribune, would first be discussed in a number of preliminary meetings, called *contiones,* and then forwarded to an Assembly, formally convened for the purpose of voting upon it. If the bill passed, it forthwith became law, without any requirement of ratification by the Senate. No discussion took place in the Assembly itself; the bill could not be amended; and no other business could be introduced into an Assembly meeting called for the purpose of voting upon a proposed legal enactment. The Assembly also met in other sessions called specifically for the purpose of voting upon candidates for the magisterial offices, the tribunate, and some minor offices. No discussion took place at such election meetings, and they were not preceded by *contiones.* The Assembly also had some other functions: prior to the establishment of a system of standing courts in the later part of

---

27. The most complete study of the assemblies thus far is Taylor (1966). Taylor presents a convenient table summarizing the structure and functions of the various assemblies (1966, 4). A similar table is also contained in Crawford (1993, 196).

the second century, it acted in some judicial capacities.[28] The Centuriate Assembly *(Comitia Centuriata)* possessed the authority to make formal declarations of war.

If, as Bodin asserted (and many since have repeated), the power to make formal law is the essential mark of sovereignty, then the Assembly constituted the seat of sovereign power in the Roman Republic. But, in fact, it would be much less misleading to say that it functioned as little more than a voting mechanism that was itself highly constrained. The political process of debate on legislative proposals and on the relative merits of candidates for office took place outside the Assembly meetings.

The only institutionalized form of such debate was the *contio,* a public meeting that any magistrate or tribune was empowered to call. All citizens— and indeed women, foreigners, and slaves as well—could attend such a meeting (Taylor, 1966, 3), but the only persons permitted to speak were those selected by its presiding officer, a magistrate or a tribune. It seems that the most common speakers at *contiones* were magistrates and senators. Brunt contends that differences of opinion concerning the proposed legislation were freely expressed (1988, 26, 315; see also Taylor, 1966, 18), but obviously as a forum of public discussion, it was severely limited. Shouts and catcalls from the audience, which apparently were not uncommon, may have indicated the state of public opinion, but hardly constituted a substitute for open debate.[29]

The restricted character of the *contiones* might have been unimportant; the plebeian citizenry could, and undoubtedly did, discuss legislative proposals among themselves during the period (a minimum of twenty-four days) between its announcement and the meeting of the Assembly that was to vote on it and, after all is said and done, it was the plebs who were the voters. The view, expressed by some historians, that the Roman Republic had significant "democratic" properties rests upon the role of the plebeian Assembly as the ultimate legislative authority. But the Assembly did not simply ascertain whether a majority of the citizens in attendance approved or disapproved of the bill placed before them. A complex voting procedure was employed that,

28. The first such court, in which only senators were jurors, was established in 149. There was no appeal from their verdicts. Equestrians were apparently admitted as jurors in 123. A sharp conflict developed between these two classes over control of the courts, which was settled in 71 with a clear victory for the equestrians (Brunt, 1971, 65, 119; Scullard, 1982, 8; Brunt, 1988, 144).

29. Millar (1986) regards the *contiones* as important in the Republic's political processes, not as vehicles for discussion, but as providing opportunity for oratorical persuasion. Compare the role of the "demagogues" in the Athenian political system described earlier (Chapter 2). See Finer (1997, 420f.) for an account of the role of the *contiones* in Roman government.

in effect, placed the power of decision in the hands of a small fraction of those entitled to vote.

The Centuriate Assembly was the oldest of the popular assemblies and was derived from a military organization dating back to the monarchical period. When the Republic was established, it elected the first consuls (Taylor, 1966, 5). Until the series of constitutional reforms following the First Punic War, this Assembly consisted of 193 "centuries," of which eighteen were allotted to the citizens belonging to the topmost plebeian class, the *equites;* eighty to the next property class on the census rolls; and the remainder distributed among the other classes. The unpropertied class, the "head-count," were allotted only five centuries, despite the fact it was by far the largest class.

The political significance of this organization derives from the practice of recording votes in centuriate blocks. If the majority of voters within a given century voted in favor of a proposal, that century's whole vote quota was recorded as approving it. Consequently, for example, all of the eighteen equestrian votes could be treated as having been cast in favor (or opposed), even though only a small majority might have voted yes (or no) in every century. The *equites* and the first property class together constituted ninety-eight centuries, so they could make a majority all by themselves. In the Centuriate Assembly, the votes of the equestrians were taken first, then those of the first class, and so on down the census classification. In practice it was seldom necessary to proceed very far into the second class before a majority was obtained. For the citizens classified by the censors as belonging to the lower classes, the right to vote in the Centuriate Assembly was of no significance.

Voting procedures in the other two popular assemblies were somewhat more democratic, but the dominance of the senatorial and upper-class oligarchy could not be effectively challenged (Brunt, 1971, 9, 63). The participation of the mass of the citizenry in the formal political processes of the Roman Republic, if not altogether negligible, was very small.[30] The Gracchi

30. In addition to the voting procedures in the assemblies, I should note that all the processes by which legislation was enacted and magistrates elected took place in the city of Rome. Of the many citizens who lived more than a short distance away, few could afford to take time away from their occupations to attend. Moreover, the motivation to do so must have been small, because exercising one's citizen rights meant that one stood for hours in *contiones* listening to political speeches and, on voting day, stood again for hours waiting for the call of one's voting class, which for the lower classes was unlikely to come in any event. Of the 400,000 adult male citizens at the end of the second century, it is doubtful that as many as one-tenth ever attended a *contio*, or voting assembly, in their lifetimes. Even the urban citizenry showed only small interest in such meetings. When a matter of exceptional interest was on the agenda, such as Tiberius Gracchus's proposal to redistribute land, a large number may have wanted to attend but on such rare occasions a

demonstrated that, with the leadership of a dynamic tribune, a plebeian Assembly could be mobilized in effective support of radical reform legislation, but this does not mean that the lower classes were able to exercise a steady and persistent influence on the determination of state policy. Political power that manifests itself only on exceptional occasions is power that is latent; it is not a significant element in the normal and regular business of government. In the early years of the Republic, the lower orders won significant constitutional concessions by engaging occasionally in general strikes. But the trend in the direction of democratization that these concessions initiated came to a halt after the defeat of the Hannibalic invasion of the peninsula. In the late Republic the urban plebs could, and did, show their disaffection occasionally through rioting (Brunt, 1971, 6), but no stable polity can incorporate riot as part of its regular processes of government. The power of the plebs thus displayed only contributed to civic disorder, which enabled Sulla, and later Caesar, to claim that in breaching the constitution and disregarding the *mos maiorum* they were rescuing a state that had become ungovernable.[31]

Theoretical Interpretation of the Republican System

Political theory as an intellectual discipline was born in fourth-century Athens, but as we have seen, none of the Athenian philosophers undertook a theoretical appraisal of their own political system. For republican Rome, however, we have two writers who did—Polybius and Cicero. Their comments on the republican system demand attention in any history of constitutional theory.

Polybius

Polybius (ca. 203–120 B.C.) was the scion of an aristocratic Greek family prominent in affairs of the Achaean League. He had begun to emulate his father's political career when he was deported in 167 to Rome with a group of a thousand hostages. There he was befriended by Scipio Aemilianus, who belonged to the Cornelian family, one of the foremost of the Roman senatorial class. He remained in Rome for seventeen years as a hostage, and there-

different constraint came into operation: even the largest meeting places available could accommodate, standing close-packed, only a small proportion of the eligible voters (Taylor, 1966, 45f., 113; Brunt, 1971, 8; MacMullen, 1980; Scullard, 1951, 273; Brunt, 1988, 25f., 75).

31. For a fictionalized, yet reliable, depiction of the Roman political system at work, see the fourth of Colleen McCullough's series of novels based on late republican Rome, *Caesar's Women* (1996).

after voluntarily for a few years before returning home. Because he was a foreigner, he was forbidden to engage in Roman politics, but his close personal relations with the Roman nobility enabled him to observe the workings of the republican system of government firsthand. He became a great admirer of Rome, and about the time he was released from hostage status, he began to write a history of the Republic whose main object was to explain, and justify, Rome's dominance of the Mediterranean world. Only a small part of the massive original text is now extant, but it contains comments that are of exceptional importance because they present an interpretation of Roman government as a system of countervailing powers (Taylor, 1966, 10; Larsen, 1968, xif.; Brunt, 1971, 60; Walbank, 1972, ch. 1; Service, 1975, 287; Millar, 1984, 1f.).[32]

In his account of the structure of the republican polity, Polybius employed the classical Greek notion of *mikte,* a political system that is a mixture of the pure forms of monarchy, aristocracy, and democracy. No system of government, writes Polybius, is permanent, for there is a natural cycle of change that dominates history, but a mixed government resists degeneration more effectively than others (von Fritz, 1975, 364). Polybius regarded the Senate as the aristocratic element in the Roman Republic, and the popular assemblies as the democratic one. The monarchical element was more problematic. In Polybius's schema, the consuls constitute this. He perhaps has in mind the dual monarchy of Sparta, but the fact that the Roman consuls were elected for terms of only one year, and by a popular Assembly, would seem to disqualify them from a political role that can properly be described as monarchical.[33] There has been a great deal of discussion of Polybius's categorization in the modern literature, but the important issue is not whether the Republic can be interpreted in terms of the classical scheme, but his description of how the "elements" were related to each other. According to Polybius,

---

32. The relevant passages are contained in app. 1 of Kurt von Fritz, *The Theory of the Mixed Constitution in Antiquity.* This will be referred to hereafter as "von Fritz (1975)." The concluding chapter of von Fritz's book contains a good discussion of Polybius's political theory in comparison to Hobbes's doctrine of sovereignty, plus some penetrating observations on the difference between the classical concept of mixed government and the modern theory of checks and balances. Walbank (1957) is a detailed analysis of the sixth book of Polybius's *History.*

33. The noun "consul" derives from the verb *consulere,* "to consult." It seems therefore, that the adoption in the early Republic of "consul" as the title of its highest magistrates signified a role very different from that of monarchs. Brunt defends Polybius's construal of the consulate as the monarchical element on the grounds that, away from Rome, as provincial governors or military commanders, the imperium of a consul was unrestricted (1988, 15–17). This does not, however, speak to the issue of how Rome itself was governed.

Lycurgus [of Sparta] . . . tried to unite all the advantages and character-istic features of the best governments so that none of the elements could grow unduly powerful . . . since the power of each would be counter-acted by those of the others. In this way, he thought, no element could outbalance the others and the political system would for a long time remain in a state of equilibrium . . . It was as a result of the introduction of this political system by Lycurgus, that the Lacadaemonians retained their liberty for a much longer time than any other people we know of . . . The Romans . . . have arrived at the same result [by piecemeal de-velopment] as Lycurgus, namely the best political order yet realized among men. (von Fritz, 1975, 364f.)

Polybius goes on to describe how the institutions of Roman government function and notes "the power which each of the elements of the state has either to hamper the others or to cooperate with them." He concludes,

All the three types of government . . . were found together in the Roman Republic. In fact they were so equally and harmoniously balanced, both in the structure of the political system and in the way it functioned in everyday practice, that even a native could not have determined definitely whether the state as a whole was an aristocracy, a democracy, or a mon-archy. (von Fritz, 1975, 367)

No clearer statement of the principle of checks and balances could be made so briefly. Despite some passages in which Polybius seems to claim that the supreme power of the Roman state resides in the Senate, and the occasional description of Rome as an aristocracy, he regarded the Roman polity as es-sentially different from any in which the power of the state was embodied in a singular center. Whether or not one should regard Polybius as correct in interpreting Rome (or Sparta) in terms of a model of countervailing powers, he was the first writer to make a clear statement of that model and, as such, occupies a place of exceptional importance in the history of constitutional theory. He employed the language of the classical doctrine of mixed govern-ment, but his reasoning was fundamentally different from that of Plato and Aristotle (Wormuth, 1949, 23; Walbank, 1972, 149f.; von Fritz, 1975, 336).

Polybius made three claims of superiority for a government such as Rome's: it provided political stability, it protected the individual liberties of the citizen, and it facilitated foreign conquest (von Fritz, 1975, 306, 345f.). Sparta, he contended, had equalled Rome on the first two grounds, but was inferior to it in conquest. When Sparta had embarked on a policy of subduing its neigh-bors, it jeopardized the liberty of its citizens, but Rome achieved its great conquests without doing so (von Fritz, 1975, 379). Friedrich contends that Polybius was far more impressed with Rome's stability and military power than with its civic liberty (1968, 320), but a reading of the original text suggests that he did not rank liberty below the other achievements that had persuaded him, a foreigner belonging to a conquered nation, that the Roman system of government was the best ever devised.

Cicero

Marcus Tullius Cicero (106–43 B.C.) was born in Arpinum, about seventy-five miles from Rome, into a family of the equestrian order that was prominent in local politics. He was schooled in Rome and, even as a youth, attracted attention for his intellectual prowess. In 76 he was elected quaestor, thereby becoming automatically a senator. He progressed steadily up the *cursus honorum* thereafter and attained the consulship in 63. He was very active in Roman politics through the disturbed period in Roman history that brought an end to the republican system of government. In the civil wars that culminated in the victory of Octavian (later Augustus), he made powerful enemies and, in 43, was murdered by Roman soldiers (Cowell, 1948, 4; Stockton, 1971, 3, 331f.).

Cicero was an outstanding master of Latin prose and one of Rome's greatest orators. The texts of many of his speeches before the Senate and the law courts have survived, and these, together with a large number of letters, have been important sources quarried by historians for details on the Roman system of government. For our purposes, his most important works are two large books modeled, and named, after Plato's political dialogues. A large part of Cicero's *Laws* has been available to historians for some time, but his *Republic,* though known to have existed, was lost until 1820, when fragments, amounting perhaps to as much as a third of the original text, were discovered in the Vatican library. From these sources, it is possible to ascertain Cicero's views on constitutional theory (Rawson, 1983, 151f.; Heichelheim et al., 1984, 264f.).

There has been some discussion among historians concerning Cicero's originality as a political thinker and especially his indebtedness to Plato, for whom he expressed great admiration, and Polybius, whose history he had studied closely (see Ferrary, 1984), but this need not concern us here. Cicero's *Republic* and *Laws* are important texts in the early history of constitutional theory, whatever the provenance of their ideas.[34] The *Republic* was

---

34. A contrary view is expressed by David Stockton in his *Cicero: A Political Biography* (1971). He restricts discussion of the *Republic* and the *Laws* to a very brief appendix and dismisses them as mere "literary exercises" written in imitation of Plato's two books on politics. Cicero's real interest, says Stockton, was not in such theoretical matters but in the day-to-day play of Roman political events (app. C; see also 304).

written in the late 50s, in the form of a conversation that Cicero presents as having taken place in 129—that is, in the period after the end of the Punic Wars and before the tribunate of Tiberius Gracchus, when the confidence and pride of upper-class citizens in the Roman system of government was at its zenith. The dialogue in the *Laws* is located as contemporaneous with its composition, in the midst of a protracted period of political disturbance and civil war. The *Republic* reflects Cicero's admiration of Rome as it used to be; the *Laws* his hope that it can be restored, and even improved.

In Book 1 of the *Republic*, Cicero repeats Polybius: the Roman system of government is a mixture of the three forms, which is the best of all because it is more stable than any of the pure forms. The consuls supply the monarchical element, the senators the aristocratic, and the assemblies the democratic. As we have seen, Polybius carried his analysis further by contending that the elements of the Roman system of government constituted a set of mutual checks and balances that prevented any one of them from achieving dominance. Cicero could not have been unaware of this appraisal, but he does not refer to Polybius's countervailance theory of the Roman constitution, and the closest he comes to presenting a similar idea is that he often describes the republican political system as "balanced." He recognizes certain countervailance features of the system, such as the power of the tribunes to check the consuls (1988, 169), but he does not present any general theory of checks and balances. No additional light is cast upon this matter by the *Laws*. One cannot say that Cicero accepted Polybius's theory of the Roman constitution, but to contend that he rejected it, as Ferrary does (1984, 91), is not supportable by any explicit remarks in available portions of the *Republic* and the *Laws*. From these materials, it is indeed impossible to specify what he construed the purpose and functional dynamics of a "mixed government" to be. Cicero continued an already established, and long to endure, tradition in political discourse: the use of "mixed government" as a nebulous concept referring generically to political systems in which power is shared among different institutional entities.[35]

The Ciceronian texts strongly suggest that his view of the best government is one in which an aristocracy—or, to use the term he frequently employs, the "optimates"—are politically predominant. He sometimes refers to "the people" as the source of all political authority—*res publica, res populi*—(1988, 64), but his view of the Republic, before the tribunate of Tiberius Gracchus

35. P. A. Brunt contends that Cicero regarded monarchy as, theoretically, the best type of polity, but recognized it to have certain deficiencies in practice. "He therefore preferred the mixed or, rather, balanced, system . . . of which Rome . . . was the exemplar" (1988, 506f.). Brunt does not explain here, or so far as I know elsewhere, the distinction he apparently has in mind between a "mixed" government and a "balanced" one.

"divided one people into two factions" (55), is that the optimates ruled, with the free consent of the people (167, 169; see also 487, 492f.). When Servius assumed power in Rome after the assassination of King Tarquin, writes Cicero, he divided the people into property classes and constructed a voting system that gave the greatest number of votes to the rich, and thus "put into effect the principle which ought always to be adhered to in the commonwealth, that the greatest number should not have the greatest power" (149).

If we focus upon the classical taxonomy of types of states, it appears therefore that Cicero was wrong in applying the term "mixed government" to the republican Rome of the late second century. As he himself describes it, it was an aristocracy pure and simple: government by the upper-class few. Without any doubt, he regarded the greatness of Rome to derive from the fact that its government was monopolized by aristocrats like himself.[36] That he nonetheless called it a "mixed government" may perhaps indicate that by his time, three centuries after Aristotle, the concept of *mikte* had become widely accepted as denoting the ideal form of the state.

Polybius and Cicero are depicted by modern historians as presenting radically different assessments of the power structure of the Roman Republic in the era before the Gracchi. Polybius saw the common citizenry as having a significant degree of political influence, through the role of the popular assemblies in enacting legislation and electing magistrates, while Cicero viewed the senatorial and equestrian classes as all-powerful in practice. This disagreement continues to punctuate the literature on republican Rome. Some historians insist that it was in all essential respects an oligarchy (Smith, 1955, 8f.; Brunt, 1966, 4f.; Heichelheim et al., 1984, 63f., 23; Scullard, 1992, ch. 15, 127, 130; Crawford, 1993, ch. 3). No modern commentator contends, as Jean Bodin had, that the Republic was a democracy (1992, 59f.), but some have strongly argued that it was truly a classical "mixed" polity in which the democratic element was too substantial to be disregarded in the study of Roman history (Millar, 1984; Brunt, 1988, 4, 20; North, 1990).

Although this classification is not unimportant, from the standpoint of constitutional theory it diverts attention from the issue raised by Polybius's interpretation of the Republic as a system in which political power was not only dispersed, but embodied in institutions that controlled each other. To

---

36. Rawson writes of the *Republic,* "The work as a whole is an elaborate theoretical justification of Cicero's long established policy of aristocratic but conciliatory government" (1983, 149). Brunt's judgment is harsher. He contends that Cicero "despised the common people," disdained "anything that savored of democracy," and dissembled on those occasions when, in public speeches, he declared that the people were sovereign and that their right to elect magistrates of their choice could not be derogated without diminishing Roman liberty (1971, 125; 1988, 340).

find that a polity is an oligarchy does not necessarily mean that the governing few compose a unified decision-making entity, a seat of "sovereignty" as Bodin defined it. As we shall see in the examination of the Venetian and Dutch republics, the control of power by checks and balances can be incorporated into a polity that, in Aristotelian terms, is a pure aristocracy, lacking even the "democratic elements" that Rome possessed in its popular assemblies. Perhaps it is because the notion of checks and balances is today so strongly identified with the American Constitution that one is led, erroneously, to construe it as operative only in a regime in which there is broad participation of the citizenry in the processes of government. But before we take leave of Rome, we must ask a more specific empirical question: was the Republic, in fact, a system of countervailing powers—was Polybius correct in describing it as such?

On the whole, historians have been reluctant to adopt this interpretation. Brunt depicts the Republic as a system of plural and mutually controlling centers of power, but he eschews use of the phrase "checks and balances" or any equivalent as a general descriptive term, and refers to Polybius as having focused upon the notion of a mixture of monarchical, aristocratic, and democratic elements (1988, 12–23). In an earlier paper, Brunt specifically criticized the system as having "too many checks and balances . . . which operated in practice only in the interest of the ruling class" (1966, 8). Stockton describes Ciceronian Rome as "a system of checks and balances" only once as a passing remark (1971, 24). Aside from these comments, I have encountered such a description of the republican constitution only in Coleen McCullough's novels dealing with the careers of Marius and Sulla (1991, 1992), and in S. E. Finer's general survey of the history of government (1997).[37] On the other hand, some historians have explicitly rejected the view that the Republic may be correctly described as a checks and balances system and have criticized Polybius for doing so (e.g., Tenney, 1930, 357; Walbank, 1972, 155f.; von Fritz, 1975, ch. 11). Other commentators simply disregard altogether his checks and balances argument and focus upon whether he was correct in describing Rome as a mixture of the Aristotelian pure forms (e.g., Wormuth, 1949, 7; Finley, 1983, 127; Casper, 1989, 214).

If there were available to us some documents even remotely comparable to the American *Federalist* papers, it might be possible to ascertain what the Romans had in mind in constructing their complex governmental apparatus.

---

37. Finer provides an excellent brief description of Roman government (1997, ch. 4), which centers upon the countervailing functions of its various institutions. The Republic, says Finer, "threw up one device after another as time moved on, to *prevent* supreme power from resting in the hands of one man or body of men. What the Romans did was to invent, *avant la lettre*, the device of *checks and balances*" (1997, 388).

Lacking such materials, we can only infer its purpose from the structure itself. This structure, however, speaks plainly enough, it seems to me. The constitution was essentially designed to disperse the imperium of the state among a number of independent agencies, and to prevent anyone from aggrandizing enough power to become dominant. Working with such a system, the city-state of Rome conquered the whole of the Mediterranean basin and extended its northern frontiers into England and Germany, but one could not claim that it was designed for such a purpose. On the contrary, the internal government of the Republic appears to contravene all the basic rules of efficient administration.

The highest office in the republican system, the consulate, was itself divided in two, with one holder of the office empowered to veto the orders of the other. The other magistracies were also plural, with similar powers. Even without professional experts in "administrative science," it must have been obvious to any Roman who gave thought to the matter that this was not the way to determine state policy expeditiously and coherently or effectively administer it. Why, for example, have eight quaestors with equal rank to administer the state finances, instead of a "Chief Quaestor" with subordinate deputies and assistants? There was a degree of hierarchical ordering in the system in that quaestors normally deferred to praetors and praetors to consuls, but they were not legally compelled to do so. All the senior magistrates, including the tribunes, were elected individually by the assemblies, so no one could claim that his authority derived from a source superior to that of another. Why were the terms of office fixed at one year, with (normally) no renewability? Why prohibit a magistrate from immediately succeeding to another office? Such requirements must have worked against the accumulation of personal administrative skill through experience, which is a prime object of modern civil service systems.

Such features of the republican polity can only be explained as constitutional devices to prevent anyone from constructing a hegemonic power base. Obviously, the Roman oligarchy was not satisfied to have a collective monopoly of political power. Even "optimates" cannot be trusted to resist the lure of power. The governing few may have been fearful of the many, but it is also evident that they were exceedingly wary of each other. Subsidized grain, free entertainments, and the authority of the tribunes to countermand magisterial orders of punishment may have been thought sufficient to keep the commonality quiescent, but to protect themselves against the more ambitious members of their own class they constructed a constitution that constrained the magistrates through an elaborate network of mutual control. As the republican system began to disintegrate, the notion of Roman *libertas* became prominent in public debate.[38] The aristocracy, murdered wholesale during the struggle for power that began with the contest between Marius and Sulla, knew that their very lives were threatened by political disorder; but they were also aware that when order is secured by dictatorship the cost in personal freedom is high. Throughout this period, and even for a long time after Augustus had firmly established a regime with a definite center of sovereign authority, the aristocratic class looked back to the Republic as Rome's golden age, hoping, as Augustus himself contended, that the new regime would only be transitory and that the republican system of plural and mutually countervailing political institutions would be restored.

As a political entity, Rome continued after the end of the Republic for another half-millennium. What significantly came to an end in the first century B.C. was the world's first experiment in *constitutionalism*, begun by the Greeks and further developed by the Romans. After Augustus transformed Rome into an unlimited monarchy, constitutionalism virtually disappeared from the political experience of the West for more than a thousand years, until it found congenial soil again in the islands of the Venetian lagoon. Since then, it has enjoyed a more or less continuous, though often tenuous, existence, developing in some parts of the world into "constitutional democracy"—that is, political systems in which the people at large enjoy rights of political participation in the affairs of state, while the power of the state is effectively constrained.

38. See Brunt (1988, ch. 6) for an excellent discussion of "*Libertas* in the Republic."

4

Countervailance Theory in Medieval Law, Catholic Ecclesiology, and Huguenot Political Theory

For a millennium after the fall of Rome, the people of Europe belonged politically to many autonomous local principalities. The various princes were absolute rulers within their own domains, but these were small. The only more widespread authorities were the Bishop of Rome, head of the church throughout Christendom, and the Holy Roman Emperor, who from the tenth century claimed jurisdiction over a broad band of middle Europe. Both of these leaders were too weak to displace the authority of the local princes, however much they wished to do so. The central authority of the papacy was attenuated by repeated conflicts over the succession to the papal throne, which did not end until the Great Schism was resolved in the early fifteenth century. The Holy Roman Emperors were heirs to a political authority that, although not purely honorific, fell far short of "imperial" dominion.[1] The political organization of late medieval Europe, with local princes, the emperor, and the pope all having political power in the same jurisdiction, was essentially pluralist. Jean Bodin's contention that sovereignty must be indivisible lacked empirical foundation before the rise of France and Spain as centrally administered nation-states.

Canon Law and Roman Law

As some historians have recently argued, "constitutionalism" as a theoretical idea can be traced back to the late Middle Ages. In its emergence during that period, a central role was played by the long-established traditions of canon law and Roman law, especially by Gratian's synthesis of canon law in the mid-twelfth century, and by Accursius's new gloss on Justinian's codification of Roman law in the early thirteenth. According to a modern historian of late medieval political theory, Gratian "aimed at nothing less than establishing a

1. Kenneth Pennington notes that the question of the relation between the emperor and the local princes was a matter of protracted debate during the later Middle Ages, which had some significance for the development of political theory (1993, 31f.; see also Ullmann, 1949, 1f.).

116

basis for a Church-dominated society" (Monahan, 1987, 50), but to this end he raised the issue of the appropriate organization of church government. This opened discussion of questions similar to those important in the domain of secular political theory, which subsequent commentators addressed more directly.[2]

Justinian's *Corpus Juris* contained numerous statements appearing to support the doctrine that the emperor had absolute and unlimited power, but Accursius's gloss gave a different interpretation, thus initiating a lengthy literature that advanced a "constitutionalist" theory of the state.[3] Consider, for example, two well-known maxims in the Justinian code bearing on the relation of the prince to the law: *Quod principii placuit legis habet* (What pleases the prince is law) and *Princeps legibus solutus est* (The prince is not bound by the law). Accursius, and others following him, contended that such seemingly plain assertions of absolute princely power, if considered within the body of relevant Roman law taken as a whole, must be construed to mean that the prince is obligated to respect the established laws and customs of the community. The prince was unlimited in the sense that there was no superior magistrate that could force him to respect them, but he was nonetheless "internally" bound by conscience and recognition of the divine origin of all law (Tierney, 1963).[4]

Consider, further, another maxim in the *Corpus Juris: Quod omnes tangit ab omnibus approbetur* (What touches all must be approved by all). This contradicts the notion, also prominent in Roman law, that though the people are the source of all political authority, they had permanently ceded it to the prince, and would seem to provide foundation for essential parts of the ma-

---

2. Gratian's *Decretum,* inspired by Justinian's codification of Roman law, was "an immensely influential work that created an ordered synthesis for the first time out of the chaos of conflicting canons, decretals, and patristic texts that had been accumulating in the Church for a thousand years" (Tierney, 1966, 4f.).

3. Accursius's *Glossa Magna,* writes Pennington, "became the Ordinary Gloss that was read by all students of Roman Law for the next four centuries" (1993, 80). "Accursius did not give an absolutist interpretation to constitutionalist maxims of Roman law. Rather he displayed considerable ingenuity in extracting a constitutionalist doctrine from a structure of texts that was originally intended to buttress Justinian's theocratic absolutism" (Tierney, 1963, 400).

4. Pennington traces the sociological-legal element in this view back to Roman times. "The Roman jurists did not work out a clear and unambiguous doctrine of the prince's legislative authority . . . Any study of law in pre-modern societies reveals that buried deep within the legal sensibilities of the people, learned and unlearned, is the idea that 'good old law' ought to be preserved and protected. Roman law, even in its sophisticated Justinian dress, is no exception to this generalization." In the thirteenth and fourteenth centuries, he writes, "most jurists did not view absolute power as absolute. They did not concede that it granted the prince authority to act arbitrarily" (1993, 78, 117).

chinery of constitutional government such as estates and parliaments (Monahan, 1987, 97f.). The maxim was cited in the royal writ by which Edward I summoned England's first parliament in 1295. It also played an important role in the development of the movement, within the church, to increase the power of general councils vis-à-vis the papacy.

Equally significant, and even more so from the standpoint that a constitution should protect personal liberties, is the view that the authority of the prince must be exercised through established legal procedures. This notion is evident in Magna Carta, and earlier, in the twelfth century, European jurists had begun to argue it, pointing out that even God, who knows all, did not condemn Adam and Eve without a hearing. From this biblical source, together with Roman law practice, an elaborate specification of the requirements of due process was constructed that in the fifteenth century was extended even to the pope's prerogative powers, such as that of excommunication (Pennington, 1993, 142f., 238).[5]

It is evident from recent historical scholarship that during the later Middle Ages there occurred an efflorescence in political thought of considerable importance that, in a general book on the history of political theory, would deserve far more attention than the few pages devoted to it here.[6] For our purposes it must suffice to recognize that the roots of Western constitutionalist thought go back to the juristic literature of the late medieval period. From that standpoint it would appear that the Bodinian doctrine of sovereignty was merely a hiatus in the long evolution of the theory of constitutionalism.

Catholic Ecclesiology and the Conciliar Movement

In the history of political theory, late medieval argumentation over the proper frame of government was more important with respect to the church than to the secular authority. The theological doctrine that all Christians are members of the "one body of Christ" was construed as a holistic notion that supported the hierarchical model of ecclesiastical organization. But some theologians argued that the same doctrine had an individualistic import, which denied

5. "As this study has demonstrated, a doctrine of individual and inalienable rights first surfaced in Western legal thought in the twelfth and thirteenth centuries. Political systems were not democratic, politics were not liberal, but jurists had a common set of norms to which they gave their consent. These norms were the building blocks upon which they constructed rights of property, obligations, marriage, defense, and due process" (Pennington, 1993, 288).

6. One of the notable features of Quentin Skinner's *Foundations of Modern Political Thought* (1978) is the space he devotes to the literature of this period.

that the lesser clergy were subordinate to the pope in the making of church policy (Black, 1980). The latter view energized the "Conciliar Movement," which, had it succeeded, would have restructured the organization of the church along the lines of the countervailance model.

"The Christian church," Monahan reminds us, "was the most important community or society with which the individual medieval person was concerned; its significance for the medieval Christian far outweighed that of the particular political society in which he happened to find himself" (1987, 134). The church was a governing institution, in the full sense of the term, and it is not surprising that many of the issues concerning the authority of the secular state and how it must be exercised, which became prominent as the nation-state developed in Europe, had surfaced earlier with respect to ecclesiastical organization.

The view that the papacy constitutes a locus of absolute and indivisible sovereign power goes back to the early church and is reflected in the ancient Roman law phrase *plenitudo potestatis* (fullness of power) to describe the status of the pope. In the early thirteenth century, Innocent III emphasized this feature of his authority, even to the point of claiming that his actions as pope were those of God, *tout court*. This did not go unchallenged by the canonists (Pennington, 1993, 45f.), but the issue did not come to a head until the Great Schism was finally resolved by the Council of Constance (1414–1418).

This council, summoned at the insistence of the Holy Roman Emperor to deal with the problem of a church to which three persons were claiming papal authority, dispersed the power of the papacy in the process of unifying it. The council successfully dealt with the problem it had been convened to address, deposing all three contenders and electing another, Martin V, as the sole occupant of the papal throne, but it also declared that ecumenical councils, not the pope, held supreme authority in the internal organization of the church.[7] The Council of Constance was dominated by French theologians who embraced the doctrine of conciliar supremacy. Under their influence it promulgated two revolutionary decrees; one asserting that ecumenical councils are superior to the pope in authority, and another ordering that such councils should be convened at least once every decade (Mundy, 1961, 11).

A prominent figure at the Council of Constance was the noted theologian Jean Gerson, under whose influence the University of Paris had become the center of conciliarist thought (Burns, 1991, 420). According to Lloyd, Gerson viewed conciliarism as "a mixed form of rule . . . the means of checking

---

7. The previous Council of Pisa (1409) had expressed similar views, but its efforts to resolve the schism only resulted in adding a third pope to the two then claiming the office.

possible monarchical excesses" (1991, 256). Cardinal Pierre d'Ailly is also worth noting because he asserted that "the best constitution for the Church would be a 'mixed' one in which the papal monarchy would be tempered with aristocratic and democratic elements, in the form, respectively, of the college of cardinals and frequent general councils" (Oakley, 1964–1965, 687). "It is Pierre d'Ailly's particular distinction," writes Jacob, "to have applied to the Church constitutional doctrines which political philosophers used in connection with the State" (1963, 14f.).

Historians have pointed out that the conciliarists traced the provenance of their ecclesiological principles back beyond the canonist literature to the pre-Christian Greek concept of "mixed government" (Tierney, 1975, 230f.). The first council of importance to follow Constance was the Council of Basel, convened by Martin V in 1431. It quickly began to assert its authority, and despite the accommodating stance taken by Pope Eugene IV, Martin's successor, it instituted formal proceedings against him. Eugene thereupon declared it to be heretical and ordered it dissolved. The council, however, continued to meet, condemned Eugene, and elected another pope in his place, but it received little support from the secular princes and dispersed in 1449. Apparently the conciliarists at Basel had overplayed their hand in the game of church power politics. The doctrine of conciliar supremacy was formally condemned in a papal bull issued by Pius II in 1460.

So far as the governance of the church is concerned, the impact of the Conciliar Movement was, and has continued to be, of minor significance. Councils have assembled from time to time but have not become established as part of the essential fabric of ecclesiastical organization. The promulgation of the doctrine of papal infallibility by the Vatican Council in 1870 demonstrated that a council can be used to enlarge the authority of the papal office, rather than to constrain it. The Catholic Church remains today a prototypical example of a strictly hierarchical mode of organization, supported by a doctrine of sovereignty that is essentially Bodinian.

The failure of the Conciliar Movement to reform the church does not mean, however, that it had no effect on European political thought. The movement raised issues that are fundamental in all domains of social organization, and it contributed to the understanding of the general principle of countervailance, which eventually became the foundation of modern constitutionalism.[8]

---

8. "The resemblances between seventeenth century secular constitutional thought and fifteenth century ecclesiastical constitutional thought are too frequent and too close to be mere coincidences. The idea of an indivisible sovereignty inhering in the ruler, the alternative concept of a dual sovereignty co-existing in both ruler and community, the relevance of this concept for arguments about rights of resistance, the idea of collegiate sovereignty,

The Huguenot Political Theorists

The institutional unity of the Christian communion was shattered by the Reformation, with great import for the development of constitutionalism. As I shall note later, the development of religious diversity in the Netherlands and England was the primary reason why those countries enjoyed a greater degree of religious, and secular, freedom than elsewhere in Europe. This diversity cannot be credited to Protestant theological doctrine, which initially offered no improvement over what it had displaced. In their ardor to derive authoritative principles from biblical sources rather than Roman law and canon law, Luther and Calvin employed the first book of Samuel and the thirteenth chapter of Paul's Epistle to the Romans in support of the absolute sovereignty of secular princes. The persecution of Protestant minorities in Catholic countries, however, encouraged a different interpretation of the sacred texts. Many Protestant theologians persuaded themselves that, according to true Christian doctrine, the subjects of a tyrannous prince had a right, indeed a duty, to resist established political authority.[9] The main venue for this notion was sixteenth-century France.

By the early 1560s, the spread of Protestantism in France had resulted in what Franklin describes as "intermittent civil war," with the state favoring the Catholic side (1973, 42). This discord culminated in the infamous massacre of French Protestants on Saint Bartholomew's Day, 1572.[10] True to the adage that spilled blood is a great fertilizer of political theory, these events gave rise to a large body of literature. Bodin's *République* was the outstanding work defending the singularity and absoluteness of sovereign power, while three tracts by converts to Protestantism—François Hotman, Theodore Beza, and Phillipe du Plessis-Mornay—have been identified by historians as the most significant productions attacking the notion that the monarch legitimately possesses such awesome, and potentially destructive, authority.[11]

---

the further technical problems about the distribution of authority within a collegiate sovereign—these are all themes common to medieval canon law, to fifteenth century conciliarism, and to seventeenth century constitutional thought" (Tierney, 1975, 254)

9. On initial Lutheran and Calvinist political doctrine, and the change in it, see Skinner (1978), vol. 2, esp. chs. 1 and 7.

10. Kingdon states that on this day perhaps as many as 10,000 people were murdered in several cities of France by "mobs of Catholic fanatics" (1991, 207). The mobs were apparently encouraged by state authority. As Franklin puts it: "In this fashion a weak and incompetent government finally decided on a criminal solution to its difficulties. The . . . Massacre was designed to accomplish riddance of the Huguenots by assassination of their leaders" (1973, 43).

11. For a more complete discussion of Hotman, Beza, and Mornay than is given here, the reader is referred to Franklin (1969) and Skinner (1978, vol. 2). All references to the original texts are to Franklin's translations (1969).

Hotman

Hotman's *Francogallia* (1573) is Huguenot in that the author's object was to defend the rights of French Protestants, but it is not based in any significant way upon theology.[12] His argument is secular, and historical in its orientation. "Francogallia" is the name he gives to the original French state created by the migration of Frankish tribes from Germany into Gaul in Roman times. There they established certain traditions of government, which, according to Hotman, are the foundations upon which the French state still truly rests.[13] Needless to say, Hotman regarded contemporary monarchs as having violated these ancient traditions.

Hotman's historical research led him to conclude that the concept of the monarch as limited has long been enshrined in French tradition. In ancient times, monarchs did not succeed one another by hereditary right but were elected by the people, who occasionally had even deposed an established king (1969, 57–59). Writing about the deposition of the first king of Francogallia in 469, he observes that "this glorious and remarkable deed of our forefathers is all the more carefully to be noted in that it came at the beginning and, as it were, in the childhood of the kingdom, as though it were a declaration and announcement that they created kings in Francogallia, subject to specific laws, and did not establish tyrants, with powers absolute, unlimited and free" (59).[14] A favorite point with Hotman is that the position of king is established solely for the purpose of serving the needs of the kingdom (that is, the people).[15]

Such propositions (like all versions of the doctrine of "popular sover-

---

12. Nor does Hotman rely upon the *Corpus Juris* or the glosses of it, though he had been a professor of law and a distinguished legal scholar. According to Franklin, his legal research had convinced him "that much of Roman law was irrelevant for understanding European customs" (1969, 48).

13. Hotman's fanciful history of the origin of the French people derived from Tacitus's *Germania*, a notion that we shall meet again in the political literatures of the Dutch Republic and seventeenth-century England.

14. In the third edition of *Francogallia*, published in 1586, Hotman added an appendix in which he specified the most important ways in which the king of France is bound by law (1969, 90–96).

15. "Furthermore, the relationship of king to kingdom is the same as that of father to family, of guardian to orphan, of custodian to minor, of captain to ship at sea, and of general to army. Therefore, as the ward is not created for the sake of the guardian, not the ship for the captain, nor the army for the general, but the latter for the former, so a people is not sought and procured for the sake of a king, but a king for the people . . . And there never was an age that failed to recognize this clear distinction between the kingdom and the king" (Hotman, 1969, 79f.).

eignty") are, however, weightless without specifying how, and by whom, the public good is ascertained. Unlike many other political theorists, Hotman did not simply assert the sovereignty of the people and leave it without ballast. Since the time of "Francogallia," he declares, the interests of the people of France had been represented by the Estates, to whose will the king is subject. The most important of the laws by which kings are bound is that "they must hold the authority of the public council sacred and inviolate and call it into solemn session in their presence as often as the public interest demands" (1969, 90). Similar wise institutions of government, he contends, were present in ancient Greece, and are currently to be found in the organization of the Holy Roman Empire, England, and Spain.[16] In reading Hotman's tract, it is necessary to keep reminding oneself that the author is a sixteenth-century Frenchman, not a seventeenth-century English parliamentarian.

Hotman claimed no originality for his interpretation of the ancient political traditions of France. The same views, he contended, are to be found in the writings of Plato, Aristotle, Polybius, and Cicero, in their analysis of the superiority of "mixed government." Like many others before and since, Hotman believed that political theories, as well as practices, accumulate merit with age.[17]

Beza

Theodore Beza was a close associate of Calvin and, upon the latter's death in 1564, became the leader of the Calvinist movement. After the St. Bar-

16. "In view of all this and since this, I say, has always been the practice of all peoples and nations that have known royal and not tyrannical power, it is completely evident that this splendid liberty of holding public councils is part of the common law of peoples, and that kings who scheme to suppress that sacred liberty are violators of the law of peoples and enemies of human society, and are to be regarded not as kings but as tyrants" (Hotman, 1969, 70).

17. "The constitution [of Francogallia] then is the one which the ancient philosophers— including Plato and Aristotle, whom Polybius followed—declared to be the best and most excellent, a constitution, namely, which is a blend and mixture of all three simple types: the royal, the aristocratic, and the popular; which is the form of commonwealth that Cicero rated above all others" (Hotman, 1969, 66). Hotman quotes "a striking passage" from Cicero, based on Plato's *Republic,* in which the elements of a mixed government are compared to the different instruments and voices of an orchestra that, though dissimilar, together create a pleasing harmony. "What musicians call harmony . . . is called concord in a commonwealth, and it is the best and strongest bond of safety which, without justice, cannot possibly exist." He goes on to add that "as Aristotle very rightly observes . . . kingdoms governed at the discretion and pleasure of the king alone are not governments of men who are free and have the light of reason, but rather of sheep and brute beasts who have no judgment" (66f.).

tholomew Massacre, he wrote *The Rights of Magistrates* (1574), whose main object was to support the proposition that resistance to, indeed even rebellion against, the rule of a tyrannous monarch is justified—by historical experience, by reason, and by the sacred texts.

Despite his Calvinism, and the frequent reference in *The Rights of Magistrates* to biblical illustrations, Beza's basic argumentation is secular. He construes the institution of the state to be founded upon a contract between the government and the people, and uses this notion to make a proposition that clearly anticipates John Locke's celebrated theory of the state. In entering the contract, the people do not give up their freedom entirely, for to do so would deprive them of any remedy against a tyrannous and wicked sovereign. Reason dictates that the people must retain the freedom to determine whether the established political order is just and, if not, to break the contract and rebel (Beza, 1969, 124f.).

This "argument from reason," writes Beza, is supported by historical evidence. Kings have always, "wherever law and equity prevailed," held their authority subject to conditions, and "when kings flagrantly violate these terms, those that have the power to give them their authority [the people] have no less power to deprive them of it." This general assertion, he claims, can be shown to have been "the practice of all the most famous nations of all ages," and he goes on to instance Rome, Athens, Sparta, the Israelites, England, Poland, Venice, Spain, and finally, France (1969, 114f.).[18]

Rebellion against an established ruler should not be undertaken lightly, asserts Beza; nor should it be regarded as a legitimate response to tyranny by individual citizens, for that would bring anarchy. It is the responsibility of the Estates, the lesser magistrates, and other institutional organs to represent "the people" in such circumstances (see 1969, 108f.; 123f.). But a condition warranting rebellion is not a normal state of affairs, and, short of this, the Estates and lesser magistrates have the duty of constraining the excesses of the monarch. This "class of subjects," writes Beza, "includes those who in ordinary matters do not exercise sovereign power but are established to check and bridle the sovereign magistrate" (108).[19]

18. Beza's remarks here on Elizabethan England are especially interesting, foreshadowing the admiration of English government that became common among European intellectuals after the Revolution of 1688: "As for the kingdom of England, it is the happiest in the world today . . . Authority to rule is founded mostly on the consent of Parliament as they call it . . . And . . . shows by experience what happiness and profit there is in moderation of royal power if it is rightly observed" (1969, 118).

19. The original government of the Israelites, "which was given to no other people," writes Beza, was "incomparably the best that ever was, if only they had been content with it." But they were not, and prevailed upon God to abdicate his direct rule over them in favor of a human sovereign. He goes on: "Nevertheless, it is a fact, which neither can nor

Mornay

The authorship of the third great Huguenot work in political theory, the *Vindiciae Contra Tyrannos* (1579) is subject to some uncertainty, but most modern historians attribute it to Phillipe du Plessis-Mornay (Franklin, 1969, 138f.). Unlike Hotman or Beza, he was neither a lawyer nor a cleric, but he became a prominent leader of the Huguenots after the St. Bartholomew Massacre and was a close adviser of Henry of Navarre, before the latter's reconversion to Catholicism upon assuming the French crown in 1589. Mornay repeats many of the propositions that had been stated earlier by Hotman and Beza, but he gives them a somewhat more theological base than they had. The *Vindiciae* is organized in terms of four questions:

1. Are subjects bound to obey princes if their orders contradict the Laws of God?
2. Is it permissible to resist a prince who violates God's Law and desolates His Church? Who may resist, in what manner, and to what extent?
3. May a prince who oppresses or devastates a commonwealth be resisted; and to what extent, by whom, in what fashion, and by what principle of law?
4. Are neighboring princes permitted or obliged to aid the subjects of another prince who are persecuted for the exercise of true religion or are oppressed by manifest tyranny?

Mornay derived his answers to these questions from the fact, which he considered beyond dispute, that political society is founded upon two contracts: the first between God and the members of the polity (including the prince), and the second between the prince and the people. The object of the first contract is to assure that "the people will be God's people" (1969, 143), that is, that God's transcendent fatherhood will be recognized; the second stipulates that the people must obey the prince, but that the prince is obligated to respect their rights and customs, and to rule so as to promote their welfare. The second contract shows, by its very existence, that the people (as a whole) can act as an independent agent, capable of being party to a solemn and legally binding covenant (181f.). The purpose of the agreement is utilitarian; it enables the people to reap the benefits of communal living. If these benefits are denied by reason of a prince's wickedness and tyrannical rule, the covenant may be repudiated and, if necessary, force may be used to place

---

ought to be disguised, that ever since the world began, there has never been a single monarch (even if we take the best) who has not abused his office. And philosophers, relying on natural reason, have also concluded that monarchical government is more often the ruin of a people than its preservation, unless the king is bridled" (1969, 116).

another upon the throne. But, even if we disregard such things as royal oaths and coronation ceremonies that bespeak contract, writes Mornay, "is it not clear, from the very nature of the case, that kings are created by the people on condition that they govern well . . . ? If kings become oppressors, if they commit injustices, if they become the enemy, they are no longer kings and should not be so regarded by the people" (185).

"Only God is to be obeyed absolutely and implicitly," Mornay asserts; a prince, who is a mere mortal, is to be obeyed only conditionally (1969, 142).[20] Any promise that is "against good custom and the law of nature" is void, he declares. "And what," he asks, "is more at war with nature than for a people to promise a prince that it will put chains and fetters on itself, will put its throat beneath the knife, and will do violence to itself (for that is what that promise really means)?" (185). Clearly, therefore, in making the compact with the prince, the people permanently reserve the right to resist and, if need be, rebel.

But here the problem appears that Beza (whom Mornay must have read) had acutely observed. If the individual citizen has the right to determine when the prince is no longer a prince and need not be obeyed, the inevitable result would be anarchy and the destruction of communal peace and plenty. Mornay navigated around this hazard by the same route that Beza had mapped. The right to determine when, and how, to resist authority does not lie with the individual but with the Estates and lesser magistrates. It is their prerogative and, indeed their obligation, for they are the institutional guardians of the people's rights.[21] Resistance, writes Mornay, does not necessarily mean rebellion; each of the lesser magistrates, within his own sphere of jurisdiction, is obligated "on his own initiative" to protect the people from a tyrannous prince so far as he is able (1969, 196f.).[22] It may be, as Franklin observes,

---

20. "How can we doubt that our obedience to God must be implicit and that our obedience to men must always be conditional? Yet there are princes today, professing to be Christians, who brazenly arrogate a power so unlimited that it cannot be from God at all; and they have a swarm of flatterers, who worship them as gods on earth and who, from fear or other pressure, believe, or pretend to believe, that there is no occasion in which princes ought not to be obeyed" (Mornay, 1969, 142).

21. "Do you really mean, it will be said, that the entire multitude, that many-headed monster [a clear reference to the "Leviathan" of the Old Testament], should go rushing into matters of this sort like a raging flood? Can order be expected from the mob? Or wisdom for settling affairs?" asks Mornay. "When we speak of the people collectively, we mean those who receive authority from the people, that is, the magistrates below the king who have been elected by the people or established in some other way . . . And we also mean the assembly of the Estates, which are nothing less than the epitome of a kingdom to which all public matters are referred" (1969, 149).

22. "The officers of the kingdom . . . when all or a good number have agreed, are

that the *Vindiciae* should be read as "an exhortation to rebel" (1969, 39), but its larger theoretical import is not diminished by its immediate intent. Mornay supplied the right to rebel with constitutionalist argumentation more fully and more clearly than anyone before him, and more fully and clearly than anyone was to accomplish in a single document for a long time thereafter.

These Huguenot tracts of the 1570s constitute a remarkable episode in the history of political theory. In stressing the role of the Estates and lesser magistrates in judging, constraining, and if need be organizing rebellion against the monarch, they undermined the defense of absolutism more effectively than Locke later did in his much celebrated *Two Treatises of Government* (1689). Jean Bodin and Thomas Hobbes took the view that the only alternative to government by an absolute prince is anarchy. In the Huguenot presentation, there is a third possibility: a regime in which political power may be controlled by being shared among the monarch, representative institutions, and lesser magistrates. While retaining the language of "sovereignty," the Huguenot support of the right to rebel against a tyrannical prince constituted a rejection in advance of Bodin's doctrine. But more significantly, they extended their argumentation to encompass less extreme conflicts between a prince and his subjects. Rebellion can only be an ultimate constraint upon coercive power, exercised only *in extremis*. More important by far are constraints that operate in ordinary times and bear upon a government that may feel quite secure against insurrection. John Locke's "right of revolution" did not raise this issue, and in that important respect, the Huguenot literature of the sixteenth century addressed the problems of the modern state more trenchantly than he did.

Unfortunately, the works of Hotman, Beza, and Mornay did not initiate a continuing line of constitutionalist political theory in France. The religious repression that had inspired them ended with the promulgation of the Edict of Nantes by Henry IV in 1598. Subsequently, Calvinist political writers tended to support the Bodinian conception of absolute sovereignty, because they regarded the secular authority as the guardian of their religious and civil

---

permitted to use force against a tyrant. And they are not only permitted but obliged, as part of the duty of their office, and they have no excuse if they should fail to act . . . The commonwealth has no doubt been committed and entrusted to the king as its supreme and principal protector, and yet to them also, as its co-protectors . . . to check on the principal guardian . . . and to make sure that he does nothing to the people's detriment . . . The magnates of a kingdom share the prince's guilt if they fail to suppress tyranny, or to prevent it, or to compensate the prince's negligence with energetic activity of their own" (Mornay, 1969, 191f.). This view was not exclusively Calvinist it seems. Miriam Yardeni refers to it as a "Lutheran theory" (1985, 317).

liberties against the continuing threat of Counter-Reformation Catholicism (Yardeni, 1985). It was perhaps naive for a minority that constituted less than 5 percent of the French population to believe that their rights would be protected. At any rate, they were disappointed. Louis XIV summarily revoked the Edict of Nantes, the French state became again an instrument of religious repression, and it remained so until the Revolution more than a century later.

The influence of the Huguenot literature upon the historical development of modern constitutionalism is difficult to assess. Of the three tracts we have examined here, Mornay's *Vindiciae* was by far the best known outside France. It was referred to by the Dutch republicans of the early seventeenth century in defense of their revolt against Spain, and it was brought into the lists in England to justify the trial and execution of Charles I and, later, to support the "Glorious Revolution" of 1688 (Gooch, 1898, 16; see also Franklin, 1969, 45).[23] Such documentary evidence is sparse, however, and it is difficult to assess the importance of Huguenot political theory in the history of Western constitutionalism, but it is evident that it cannot be excluded.

In the next chapter, I return to the domain of practice and examine the Republic of Venice. In the late medieval era, this city-state constructed a political system based firmly on the principle of countervailance—the first significant case of constitutional government since the end of the republican era in ancient Rome.

23. The first English translation of the *Vindiciae* was published in 1589 as *The Defence of Liberty against Tyrants*. It was republished in 1640 and 1689—dates whose correspondence with climactic events in English politics is certainly not accidental.

5

The Republic of Venice

Before the rise of large nation-states, Venice was the wealthiest polity in Europe and the dominant naval power in the Eastern Mediterranean. Today it is only a small and rather unimportant Italian city, known abroad mainly as a mecca for tourists. Venice receives little more than a mention in general European, or even Italian, textbook histories (Zorzi, 1983, 9). Its past eminence and constitutional significance are well appreciated by specialized historians but have almost disappeared from general view. Accordingly, I begin this chapter with a brief sketch of the rise and development of the Venetian Republic, in order to supply some context for an appraisal of its role in the history of Western political theory.

Venice and Europe

The city of Venice is built on more than a hundred small low-lying islands in a lagoon at the northwest end of the Adriatic. A number of rivers drain into the lagoon, offering good transportation routes between the city and the hinterland, but also bringing silt that works steadily to turn the lagoon, bounded on its seaward side by a sandbar, into a marsh. In Roman times, the lagoon extended some seventy miles, from Chioggia to the northernmost tip of the Adriatic. The northern two-thirds of this area has since silted in. The southern part of the original lagoon, where Venice is located, remains open water, but only by virtue of large hydraulic management projects. These, together with the need to protect the city from sea raiders, were the foundations of Venice's beginnings as a social community of lagoon dwellers united by a strong appreciation of their common interests.

In Roman times, there were a few settlements in the lagoon, inhabited by fishermen and salt makers, but there was no Roman governmental or military presence. The Venetians could claim later that they had never been subject to foreign dominion, even that of Rome, but they took umbrage at the taunt that they were descendants of men of low birth. This insult was frequently flung at them by Florentines who took pride in their own city as the "true daughter of

129

Rome." The Venetians claimed that their original inhabitants were nobles from the mainland who had fled to the lagoon when the Lombards invaded Italy (586) because they valued liberty above all else (Contarini, 1599, 104; Gaeta, 1961, 61; Weinstein, 1968, 20). Whether nobles or not, the lagoon dwellers were traders, exchanging their fish, salt—and later, other products—with people on the nearby mainland. Though numerous industries were established as the city grew, trade in commodities produced elsewhere early became, and remained, the main basis of the Venetian economy.

As a Christian community, Venice was initially part of the Byzantine Church. The first cathedral built in the lagoon, at Torcello in the seventh century, was established by the authority of the Byzantine patriarch at Ravenna (Zorzi, 1983, 11). When in the ninth century Venice's trading interests turned toward the sea, its vessels operated under the protection of the Byzantine empire, but the "provincial" status of the city was transitional. By the eleventh century, Venice itself was the dominant power in the Adriatic (Lane, 1973, ch. 3). The Byzantine ports on its eastern shore, as well as the Italian ports on the western, were brought under Venetian dominion, which was then extended to the Ionian Sea and beyond to the Aegean and the eastern Mediterranean, including the islands of Crete and Cyprus. Though Byzantium continued to play an important part in its cultural development, Venice's ecclesiastical orientation turned westward, with the authority of the Eastern Church giving way to the Church of Rome. In 1204 Constantinople itself was sacked by a Venetian fleet and the armies of the Fourth Crusade, giving Venice control of the Black Sea trade and much booty—including the four magnificent bronze stallions from classical antiquity that stood above the central door of the Church of San Marco for six centuries, until Napoleon removed them to Paris.

Venice's command of the Adriatic and mastery of the sea routes to the east were timely acquired, enabling it to take full advantage of the increased demand for eastern goods and the increased supply of European ones generated by the "industrial revolution of the middle ages" (Gimpel, 1976). The city became the most important commercial center and entrepôt for all the varied products that passed through the eastern Mediterranean—from pepper to peacock feathers westbound, from textiles to timber eastbound. Local industries such as sugar refining, glassmaking, fur processing, and textile making (Romano, 1987, 66f.) flourished in the lagoon, thereby adding local products to the trade in both directions. Foreigners from east and west thronged the city, some occupying large buildings that served as offices and warehouses for the trading activities of a particular national group. By the end of the thirteenth century, the buildings on the islets of the lagoon occupied nearly the area on which present-day Venice stands, and the city, though small by modern standards, was one of the largest in Europe during the next four hundred years. At the apex of its history in the sixteenth century, Venice surpassed all other Italian cities in wealth and power (Lane, 1973, 12; Libby, 1973, 7).[1]

The state played an active role in the Venetian economy, through fiscal means as well as by law and administrative regulation. The tax revenues of Renaissance Venice far exceeded those of other Italian cities, and were indeed even larger than those of nation-states such as England and France. Fernand Braudel estimates that the ratio of taxes to income was high in Venice compared to the nation-states (1984, 309f.), but it is clear that only exceptional wealth could enable Venice, with a taxable population (including its possessions in mainland Italy) of less than 2 million, to raise more revenue than Henry VI could from France's 15 million (120).[2] The flow of wealth was, over a long period, sufficient to finance large public works projects, heavy military and naval expenditures, and to leave enough in private hands to permit the construction of scores of magnificent brick and stone palaces, standing on wooden pilings driven into the mud of the lagoon. As elsewhere, the unpredictable and often involuntary expenditures for war occasionally put strains upon the Venetian fiscal system that threatened its political stability (see Finlay, 1980, 163–181), but the city proved itself capable of dealing with all such challenges until Napoleon brought cannon within range and offered destruction as the only alternative to surrender.

Venice's role in the economic history of Europe depended upon its military power at sea. For a long time the republic commanded the strongest naval force in the Mediterranean, indeed in the world, before the mastery of large-vessel sail technology and naval gunnery by nations bordering on the Atlantic. Admiral A. T. Mahan's *The Influence of Sea Power on History* (1890) deals with the period after the beginning of the "age of sail," so it contains no discussion of Venice, but its famous thesis could have been well supported by extending attention back to the era when Venetian galleys, produced by assembly-line methods in the Arsenale, the largest industrial establishment in Europe, dominated the eastern Mediterranean.

Because Venice lived by trade, the main object of its foreign policy had to be the security of its vessels from attack by pirates or by other states. A good deal of Venetian trade traveled in convoys organized by the government,

1. In 1563, the population of Venice was assessed to be 168,627 (Chambers and Pullan, 1992, 6n.).

2. A record of state revenues, compiled in 1469, shows that 60 percent of it was derived from the city itself (including customs and excise taxes), 23 percent from the *terra firma* possessions, and 17 percent from the overseas territories (Chambers and Pullan, 1992, 139f.).

protected by their own readiness for combat, and supported by naval bases that Venice acquired, by treaty and conquest, throughout the eastern Mediterranean. Like Britain later, Venice found that the wealth generated by maritime trade was large, but rendered a nation that might have little fear of invasion vulnerable to strangulation by disruption of the sea routes and blockade. Both also discovered the mutual complementarity of maritime trade and naval power—the navy protected trade, and trade produced a supply of skilled seamen whose services could quickly be drawn upon for military use in time of war. Both adopted a similar policy: the creation of an overseas empire whose colonies served as naval bases as well as centers of commerce.

In addition to possessions overseas, in the fourteenth century Venice began to acquire political control on the contiguous Italian mainland. At its furthest extent, this domain embraced most of the area between the Po river and the Alps, extending eastward as far as Friuli and westward almost to Milan, including important cities such as Padua, Vicenza, Verona, and Bergamo. The population of this area was much larger than that of the city itself. Venetian conquests on the mainland led other Italian states to suspect its leaders of harboring the ambition to achieve political control of the whole peninsula and perhaps even to recreate the ancient hegemony of Rome. But however much the Venetians may at times have regarded themselves as the new Romans, they built no army, not even a militia; instead, they relied on mercenaries for military action on the mainland. Machiavelli held this to be a serious failing and criticized the Venetian political system on the ground that it was constructed for security, not for expansion. But the Venetians were aware, from early times, that the civic tranquility and liberty that they prized could be threatened as much by the presence of indigenous armed forces within the city as by foreign enemies without.

Venice's chief rival for eastern trade was Genoa. On the opposite side of the Italian peninsula, Genoa was similarly well situated to take advantage of trade routes into the European continent. War between the two city-states began in 1257 and was almost continuous until 1381. In that year a Genoese fleet penetrated the lagoon and established itself at Chioggia, awaiting the arrival of allies by land to attack the city. But the timely appearance of a Venetian war fleet from overseas and the adoption of a daring naval strategy trapped the Genoese forces in Chioggia, and forced their surrender. This defeat did not diminish Genoa's role as a Mediterranean trading city, but it was incapable thereafter of challenging Venice's spreading hegemony of the eastern Mediterranean (Cowan, 1986, 19).

The next important threat came from the mainland. The invasion of Italy by France in 1494 introduced a new element into Italian politics: thereafter, the peninsula was dominated by the presence of foreign armies whose concept of land warfare was less genteel than that which had prevailed previously in the many conflicts between Italian states. In 1508, the League of Cambrai, a formidable alliance of France, Spain, the Holy See, the Holy Roman Emperor, Hungary, and some Italian cities, was formed against Venice. The result was a disastrous defeat of its mercenary army and the loss of the entire terra firma. Only the lagoon saved the city itself. But the league was composed of members with little common interest, and less than a decade later, Venice was again in control of most of its mainland territories (Lane, 1973, 242f.). By the early seventeenth century, Venice and the Papal States were the only political entities in Italy that had not become vassals of France or Spain (Pullan, 1974, 448). The recovery of Venice's fortunes from a defeat that, at the time, seemed to have all but annihilated it, and its subsequent maintenance of independence from foreign control made the Venetian Republic greatly admired not only in Italy, but also throughout Europe, and many observers attributed the city's success to its unusual system of government (Logan, 1972, 4f.).

Another threat to Venice developed from the east with the rise of the Ottoman Empire. The Ottoman Turks were in control of all of Asia Minor by the early fifteenth century; then they advanced east to the Caspian Sea and the Persian Gulf, west around the whole coast of North Africa, and north into Europe, bringing Greece, Bulgaria, and Hungary under Ottoman dominion. Constantinople fell in 1453, and the Turkish landward threat to western Europe was not definitively contained until the Battle of Vienna in 1638. Meanwhile, it was Venice that barred the way to Turkish expansion into southern Europe from the sea. The victory over the Turks at Lepanto in 1571, by a combined fleet of Venetian, Spanish, and Papal vessels, broke the momentum of the Turkish maritime advance. But it was left mainly to Venice thereafter to contain Ottoman expansion by way of the north shore of the Mediterranean, through a long series of conflicts that severely weakened both opponents.

In the long run, the most serious challenge to Venice proved to come from the Atlantic, and from developments in commerce rather than foreign armies and navies. The mapping by Portuguese mariners of the route to the east around the Cape of Good Hope soon made it evident that the oriental products that were the staples of Venetian commerce could be obtained more cheaply by an unbroken sea route than by one that required much land transport and transhipment between land and water carriage. The discovery of America and the subsequent maritime development of Spain, Portugal, England, and the Netherlands shifted the lines of commerce, and by the late seventeenth century, Dutch and English ships were even challenging Venice's dominance of the Levant trade (Cowan, 1986, 19). The Dutch East Indies

Company provided northern Europe with direct sea access to the commodities of the orient. Venice did not commence to decline immediately. Its prosperity lasted until well into the seventeenth century, but by the eighteenth it was no longer important in the economic and political affairs of Europe. The "myth of Venice"—its reputation as a model republic—disappeared from the European political literature and was replaced by an "anti-myth" that represented the republic as not only backward, but also decadent, morally and politically corrupt, sinful, and sinister.[3]

Throughout its long history, Venice was a capitalistic society. Its aristocracy, which controlled all the organs of government, was composed of merchants. Feudalism, which had such an immense influence on the economic, social, and political history of Europe, had no effect on Venice. The ownership of land, elsewhere the key to social status, wealth, and power, was of small significance to Venetians. Impervious to the reproaches of patricians elsewhere, the Venetian aristocracy considered itself no less noble because its members invested in commercial and industrial enterprises and personally engaged in their management. Because of the necessities of their occupations, Venetians were an exceptionally literate, and numerate, people (Spufford, 1995). They did not hold the view, common elswhere, that such attainments should be reserved to scholars and "gentlemen." The magnificent palaces that border the Grand Canal were built, like the great houses of Europe, as certificates of social status, but their first floors, at water level, contained warehouses and offices; no effort being made to hide from a visitor's eyes the source of his host's wealth and eminence. Symbolic of Venice in its prime is the building that occupies the most prominent location in the city as one approaches it from the main entrance into the lagoon from the sea: the point of land that lies at the junction of the Grand Canal and the Giudecca Canal is occupied not by a great cathedral, a fort, or an imposing capitol, but a customs house, topped by a weathervane to show which way the wind of commerce blows.

Frederic C. Lane, who pioneered the modern study of Venetian economic history, described the Venetian economy as "communally controlled capitalism" (1973, 1). The convoys of galleys consisted largely of state-owned vessels whose services for each voyage were auctioned off to private traders. There were many privately owned galleys as well, which could, if their owners and captains wished, engage in the more hazardous but potentially more lucrative irregular trade. From the earliest times, overseas voyages were regarded as community enterprises, and even private vessels were subject to extensive regulation aimed at assuring their seaworthiness and preventing

---

3. The best expression of the anti-myth of Venice that I have encountered is by Mark Twain, in chapter 22 of his *Innocents Abroad*.

them from engaging in activities contrary to state policy. The Venetian government saw no harm in monopolies and cartels formed to deal with foreigners, but it discouraged similar organizations that might restrict access by Venetians to trading opportunities, or that could raise the prices paid by its own merchants or consumers (144f.).

Participation in trade was not reserved for the nobility. Following the political reorganization of 1297, noble status was restricted almost exclusively to families of long aristocratic lineage, but Venetian society retained considerable vertical mobility. By engaging in trade and industry, commoners could become rich; and nobles, through misfortune or fecklessness, could become poor. In the sixteenth century, which will be the main focus of our examination of the Venetian political system, most of the patrician families lived in decidedly straitened circumstances (Queller, 1986, 30f.).[4] Many commoners were much richer, and though they could not sit in the Great Council or hold high office in the other organs of state, their role in the governance of Venice was not negligible.

Sixteenth-century Venice offered more than opportunities to become wealthy. It was a haven of refuge for people from other Italian cities and beyond the Alps who sought to escape, not from the Lombards now, but from the religious imbroglio of the Reformation period with its accompanying intellectual repression. Gaetano Cozzi, a leading modern historian of Venice, noting the influx of foreigners into the city in the last decade of the century, observes that they found there "a unique ambiance; a wide circulation of ideas and books which, though often clandestine, was not on that account less stimulating and fruitful; an open style of life, free and easy, with a sense of toleration that was truly exceptional in a Europe still convulsed with religious disputes and enclosed within the defenses of rigid doctrinal beliefs." Cozzi quotes Jean Bodin, no admirer of Venice and one contemptuous of those who idealized its government, as admitting nonetheless that the city attracted "those who aspired to live in the greatest freedom and tranquility; people who wished to engage in trade or industry, or to pursue studies worthy of free men" (1969, 20, my translation; see also Gaeta, 1961, 66, 69; Bergsma, 1995, 209f.).[5]

Consideration of the role of Venice in the history of Europe would be

4. "Girolamo Priuli, the Venetian diarist of the early sixteenth century, reckoned that about three-quarters of [the nobles] could be classed as poor, in so far as they had few or no private resources and depended on jobs given by the government for an income" (Girouard, 1985, 104).

5. The notion that Venice was distinguished for its civic freedom apparently dates from late medieval times. Haitsma Mulier notes that it can be traced back at least as far as the eleventh century (1980, 13).

incomplete, even for the limited purposes of this chapter, without some reference to the contributions to the arts by its own citizens and by others who migrated there. The sixteenth-century development of the neoclassical style of architecture was pioneered in Venice by Andrea di Pietro (Palladio). Composers such as the Gabriellis responded to the acoustic challenges of the Church of San Marco with significant innovations in musical form, followed by Monteverdi, the pioneer of opera. The commedia dell'arte, forerunner of the modern Western drama, was developed in Venice. Carpaccio, Titian, Veronese, Tintoretto, and the Bellinis made Venetian painting second to none in Europe. These achievements, important in themselves, were also influential in advancing the reputation of Venice among the intelligentsia of sixteenth-century Europe.

Venice also contributed to the intellectual development of Renaissance Europe through its outstanding publishing industry. Within two decades of Gutenberg's invention, printing by moveable type was rapidly developing in the city, encouraged by a liberal government, good supplies of paper, and access to the whole European market (Lane, 1973, 3ll; Logan, 1972, 72). By the end of the fifteenth century there were more than a hundred publishers of books in Venice, and over half of the printed books produced in Italy up to that time had come from their presses (Chambers, 1970, 152). The Venetian authorities supervised the activities of the city's publishers, but their censorship was relatively light, and they did not automatically prohibit books that were listed on the indexes issued by the Holy Office. Indeed, there was even a flourishing clandestine industry in Protestant religious works, produced for the trans-alpine trade (Logan, 1972, 76). The famous Aldine Press occupies a permanent place in the intellectual history of the West, not only for its development of good typography and the production of books in cheap editions, but also because of its serious attention to editing and the employment of scholars to sort through and correct the variant and frequently corrupted classical texts.

Among its own native writers, Venetian historians were especially notable in abandoning the humanist style of the Renaissance in favor of narrative that relied on documentary sources. Elegance of language was subordinated to empirical evidence, and flights of fancy that had enabled other writers to reproduce the unrecorded speeches of long-deceased great men, and even their private thoughts, were eschewed. Gasparo Contarini's *De Magistratibus et Republica Venetorum* (1543), which played the leading role in spreading knowledge of the Venetian constitution, and Paolo Sarpi's *History of the Council of Trent* (1619), described by W. J. Bouwsma as "one of the great masterpieces of European historiography," were written in the empirical style (1968, 556; see also Cozzi, 1979, 274).

The Venetian System of Government

Information is sparse about the government of the early settlements in the lagoon, but whatever it was truly like, the Venetians later viewed themselves as having always lived under a government that derived its authority from the citizenry (Lane, 1966, 287). Contarini notes that the first doges were elected by "a general cry and acclamation of the people" (1599, 51). In fact, such a general assembly was convened, as occasion demanded, not to *elect* a doge, but to show its response to the choice of a small group of powerful citizens. These were occasions for public clamor and celebration rather than the exercise of political power, and though they served to impose prudent constraint upon those who did exercise it, political authority in the Venetian state resided, from early times, in the hands of its aristocracy. Before the twelfth century, Venice was no less subject to internal upheaval than were other Italian states. Numerous doges were assassinated or deposed, and on one occasion, rioting culminated in the burning of San Marco and the ducal palace. The stability that the republic later attained through its constitutional structure resulted from attempts, on the part of the aristocracy, to control the power of the doge, and to prevent violent struggles for political preeminence among the leading families—conflicts endemic in Italian cities of the Middle Ages—by sharing political authority broadly among the members of the noble class. Venice was not the only Italian city that sought to achieve stability and order without absolutism. Florence attempted repeatedly to establish a constitutional political order, but Venice was the only city to succeed in constructing a durable one.

In evolving the constitutional structure that accomplished these ends, the Venetians resorted very little, if at all, to the writings of classical or medieval political thinkers (Lane, 1966, ch. 18). Renaissance writers who commented upon the finished constitution of Venice made frequent reference to revered authorities such as Aristotle, but the "wise ancestors" to whom Contarini attributed the merits of Venetian government were not writers on political theory or architects of utopian states; they were practical men of quotidian politics who built the constitution piecemeal, responding to immediate problems as they perceived them.

The year 1297 has been singled out by historians as an important date in Venice's constitutional development. During the preceding two centuries, economic expansion had generated rapid social mobility; the aristocracy, based on wealth rather than feudal rights, had become formally ill-defined and fluid in membership. But in 1297 a closed, hereditary aristocracy was established. The immediate effect of the Serrata (closure), as this came to be called, was to enlarge considerably the number of families recognized as noble, but this class was still a small fraction of the city's population, at its greatest only some 5 percent (Romano, 1987, 28). Membership in the Great Council, reserved to adult males of noble families, increased from about 400 to 1,000 between 1295 and 1311 (Lane, 1966, 525). But thereafter additions were few. Some 2,500 adult males were eligible to attend the Great Council in the early sixteenth century, but the increase over these years was almost wholly due to procreation among the approximately 150 families that constituted the nobility. Fairly rapidly after the Serrata, the rest of the institutional machinery of Venetian government was created, and it lasted, without significant alteration, until the city fell to Napoleon in 1797. The description of the Venetian constitution that follows focuses on the sixteenth century because that era generated the literature that transmitted the image of Venice abroad as a model of good government, but by that time, the Venetian constitution was already famous for its durability.

Venice did not have a written constitution or develop a special body of legislation and jurisprudence that can be distinguished as "constitutional law." Roman law was not recognized by Venetian courts, even after interest in it developed among jurists in the twelfth century (Bouwsma, 1968, 57; Haitsma Mulier, 1980, 14), so there was no authority in the Venetian state that transcended the immediate powers of the ordinary lawmaking bodies. A Venetian court could determine that an official had acted illegally, but it could not declare that a law was invalid on grounds of constitutional principle. A statement of personal rights, acting as a juridically recognized constraint on legislative and executive power, is absent from Venetian law. The guardians of the Venetian state were not unguarded, however. Power was constrained by respect for customary practice and "public opinion" and, more specifically, by the institutional structure of the political system itself.

The governmental organization of Venice was very complex. It would be nearly impossible to describe all of its offices, even if we restricted our attention to those directly administered by members of the nobility, so I will consider only the main ones. Diagrammatic depictions of the relations among these bodies may mislead more than they inform because their membership composition covers the whole range of possible relations—in the language of set theory, they display, in various cases, independence, identity, inclusiveness, and intersection. Unless it were complex to the point of incomprehensibility, a diagram would also fail to capture other essential features of the Venetian system, such as the short, staggered, terms of office of most officials, the complex methods of election, the frequent practice of electing a person to office in a different body upon the conclusion of his service in another one, the restrictions that did not permit more than one member of a family to hold simultaneous office in the smaller councils, and so forth.[6]

The Great Council was initially established in 1170, and the Serrata of 1297 made membership conditional upon noble status. It was not a representative body. All adult noble males age twenty-five or older, with the exception of those who had taken holy orders, had the right to attend its weekly meetings and to vote. The sixteenth-century Venetian diarist Marino Sanuto reported that though 2,500 were eligible, the normal attendance at the Great Council was between 1,000 and 1,400 (Finlay, 1980, 21). The Great Council passed legislation, debated policy, and provided an opportunity for questioning officials similar to Question Time in the modern British Parliament. Most of its work was devoted to the election of persons to serve on the other governmental bodies.[7] There were more than 800 such offices (Davis, 1962, 22; Finlay, 1980, 59; Cowan 1986, 52f.), and the terms of tenure were short, so places were almost continuously becoming vacant. This gave the Great Council considerable power to control the other organs of government by simply refraining from filling vacant places in them (Finlay, 1980, 63), but it is misleading to describe it as the seat of sovereignty in the Venetian state as some have done (e.g., Bouwsma, 1968, 60). "Sovereignty" is a concept that is inapplicable to a political system that, like the Venetian one, is an equilibrium of plural centers of power.[8]

Given the size of the Great Council, and the nature of its functions, one might expect factions or political parties to develop. Venetians had good reason to fear factional politics as the source of conflicts among the nobles that were disturbing the peace of other Italian cities, and had disrupted that of Venice itself in earlier times. Election of officials by a combination of lot and voting by secret ballot was designed to prevent the development of factions. Formal prohibition of campaigning for office did not in fact prevent electioneering and the alignment of members in support of favorite candidates (Lane, 1973, 258–265), but Venice did not develop the hard factionalism that undermined constitutional government in other cities.

The method employed in selecting officials for the various state organs

---

6. See Gleason (1993, app. 2) for a diagram of the structure of the Venetian government that limits itself to showing the composition of its various institutions. Finlay (1980, xv–xvii) provides a useful "Glossary of Governmental Terms," which indicates the compositions and functions of the various official bodies.

7. Most matters considered by the Great Council were determined by simple majority vote, but some, such as altering election procedures, required a much higher proportion of approvals (Finlay, 1980, 60).

8. Finlay describes the Great Council as "a singular combination of electoral assembly, permanent convention, exclusive club, and job market" (1980, 27).

consisted basically of the establishment of nominating committees by lot and subsequent voting on their recommendations in the Great Council (Chambers and Pullan, 1992, 58f.). The election of a new doge was an especially complex mixture of lot and election. In 1268, before the Serrata, the election of Doge Lorenzo Tiepolo was carried out by a process that remained unchanged for the rest of Venice's history as an independent state. A simplified schematic description of the procedure is as follows:

$$30L \rightarrow 9L \rightarrow 40E \rightarrow 12L \rightarrow 25E \rightarrow 9L \rightarrow 45E \rightarrow 11L \rightarrow 41E \rightarrow D$$

L refers here to selection by lot; E to selection by election. In the Great Council, by the drawing of balls from an urn, 30 members of the Council were selected, a further drawing reduced these to 9 who met to elect 40 men. This 40 was reduced by lot to 12 who proceeded to elect 25, and so on until the final election selected 41 nominators, who submitted their choice to the Great Council (for a more detailed description, see Contarini, 1599, 53f.). This procedure clearly was devised to prevent the rigging of doganal elections. It had an important auxiliary effect in that this protracted process, involving many participants, generated a great deal of discussion of the leading candidates for the office within the electoral bodies involved in the process and, generally, among the populace. The result was that the person ultimately nominated was likely to have had broad consensual support and the acceptance of the most influential families.[9]

Having selected the best man for the office, one might expect that the Venetians would allow the doge to wield power. In fact, he was permitted to do nothing alone that concerned state business: two or more members of the Ducal Council were obligatorily present when he received visitors or dealt with memoranda or correspondence. The six persons who made up this council represented the six districts of the city. Each was elected by the Great Council for a term of eight months. The councilors acted as colleagues of the doge in the conduct of various state business, but also as watchdogs who ensured that he obeyed the decisions of the Great Council. The doge presided at meetings of the Great Council and the Senate, but not alone; he shared the podium with the ducal councilors and the three heads of the Quarantia Criminale, the most senior court. This group of ten persons was known collectively as the Signoria.

Until the eleventh century, a Venetian doge had almost unlimited power, but in the changed political organization that was initiated by the Serrata, his authority was subjected to a series of restrictions. By the sixteenth century, little power was attached to the office in itself (Trevor-Roper, 1985, 3; Bo-

9. For a modern historian's appraisal of the doganal election procedure, see Finlay (1980, 141–144).

holm, 1990, 26f.). A new doge was required, upon his election, to swear a *promissio*, which stated in explicit detail the restrictions on his authority.[10] To refresh his memory, it was reread to him every two months. After the death of a doge, as part of the procedure involved in selecting a new one, the Great Council appointed two special committees to look into the late doge's performance and suggest changes that might be required in the *promissio*. If it were concluded that he had acted illegally, a fine might be levied against his estate (Boholm, 1990, 73). Leonardo Loredan, one of the greatest of Venice's doges (known mainly today as the subject of a famous portrait by Giovanni Bellini), received no special consideration on account of his skillful recovery of the the terra firma after the War of the League of Cambrai. The examination of his term of office resulted in a demand upon his heirs for the refund of a large sum considered to have been misappropriated (Zorzi, 1983, 27). Noting that the powers of the doge were negligible, Contarini explained that the office was desired because of the pomp and honor attending it. That reward, he remarked, was in accordance with "prudence and wisdom." (1599, 43). It is not quite true to say that the doge had no political power. He had the very considerable power that accrues to anyone who participates in the deliberations of the highest governmental organs of a state. He had no power *of his own*, but that was true of every official in the Venetian system of multiple counterpoised authorities.[11]

The main policy-making organ of the Venetian state was the Senate. Contarini noted that "the whole manner of the commonwealth's government belongs to the Senate," naming foreign policy and fiscal policy specifically (1599, 68). In periods of crisis, it was the Senate that assumed the special powers deemed necessary to deal with rapidly developing events. The Senate membership was a complex mixture. The Great Council elected sixty senators for overlapping one-year terms; another sixty were chosen by lot for one-year simultaneous terms from nominees furnished by the retiring members of the Senate; and virtually all senior officials, including ambassadors and high naval commanders, were members ex officio. In total, the Senate numbered about 300 members, 230 of whom had the right to vote (Lane, 1973, 254). Senate membership was restricted to nobles thirty-two years of age or older. There was an executive committee of the Senate, the Collegio, composed of the Signoria and sixteen others called the Savii (elected for six-month terms), twenty-six in all. The Collegio, whose presidency rotated every seven days, had the authority to call meetings of the Senate and to prepare their agendas.

10. See Chambers and Pullan (1992, 46f.) for the restrictive obligations that were included in the *promissio* of Christofo Moro, upon his election in 1462.

11. On the regulations to which the doge was subject, and his considerable influence nonetheless, see Finlay (1980, 110f., 113f.).

In fact, no matter could come before the Senate except by way of the Collegio. In the course of the Collegio's performance of its senatorial functions, it exercised general supervision of the executive offices of the state. The Collegio might be compared to the Cabinet, and the Senate to Parliament, in the British constitution—but only loosely, because the Collegio did not control the Senate, and indeed in its formal submissions, it was obliged to furnish not definitive proposals that would be taken as the policy of the inner circle, but an account of the various views held by its several members.

The Venetians feared internal subversion as much as aggression by foreign powers. These two dangers came together in 1310, when during a war with the Holy See, one Baiamonte Tiepolo organized a conspiracy to assassinate the doge and seize power. The coup was defeated largely because timely knowledge of it had been obtained. A permanent new body was established, the Most High Council of Ten, or the Dieci, as it was familiarly known. Its special function was to counter subversion, and it was endowed with special powers to act secretly and quickly without the restraints that were imposed on the other offices of the state. As one might expect, its conception of what was subversive broadened to include many matters not directly connected with any armed threat to established authority. By the sixteenth century, the Dieci was dealing with charges such as sodomy, blasphemy, and counterfeiting (Contarini, 1599, 80; Boholm, 1990, 30). The sinister reputation that Venice acquired in the eighteenth century as a city where citizens were arrested at night and never heard from again was due to the Council of Ten, and the Inquisitors (two of the current Dieci members plus one ducal councilor), established in 1539 to combat disclosure of state secrets. The visitor to modern Venice is sure to be shown the door in the Ten's council chamber through which the condemned were taken, and the "Bridge of Sighs" over which they passed on their way to the prison next to the ducal palace.

In addition to the councils with specific functions, there was an oversight body, the Avvogaria di Comun, which could call any council to account if it violated Venetian law (Haitsma Mulier, 1980, 199). Nevertheless, the power of the Dieci and the Inquisitors posed a great challenge to the system of control. Checking them was not altogether successful, but perhaps not less so than the efforts of modern democratic states to rein in the activities of their security agencies. Members of the Council of Ten were elected by the Great Council for staggered one-year terms from among nobles who met special requirements. It had three chairmen, chosen by lot, jointly serving one-month terms. Its meetings were attended by the doge and his councilors, and also by one of the Senate's attorneys, who could appeal the case under consideration to the Great Council. On especially important matters, up to twenty other officials might be present. So the "Ten" was never less than seventeen, and sometimes as many as thirty-seven. The power of the Dieci should not be dismissed, but it did not wholly deserve the reputation that later became attached to it.[12] Perhaps the greatest disservice it did to the Venetian constitution was that it became a very conservative organization, opposing any change in the structure and practices of Venetian government, thereby restricting the republic's ability to adapt to the new challenges that became ever more pressing as the seventeenth century wore on.

The non-noble citizens of Venice, whether rich or poor, were excluded from membership in the Great Council and could not, therefore, be elected to any of the offices described above. But they were not altogether without place or influence in the government of the city. Artisans and craftsmen exercised a considerable amount of self-government in matters of immediate concern to themselves through their fraternities and guilds (Chambers and Pullan, 1992, 209f.). These were supervised by officials chosen by the Great Council, but they elected their own officers and were able to regulate many aspects of their trades. Service clubs called *scuole*, many of which were created by craft guilds, owned a great deal of property and used the income derived from it and from contributions to promote religious observance and education, succor the needy, and patronize the arts. The six most prominent of these, called *Scuole Grandi*, were especially important as institutions that ministered to the poor (Pullan, 1971, pt. 1; see also Girouard, 1985, 102; Chambers and Pullan, 1992, 297f.).

More important from the standpoint of governmental power is the fact that the bureaucracy of the various organs of the state was recruited from the non-noble class of long-resident citizens known as the *cittadini*, whose numbers approximately equalled those of the nobles (Davis, 1962, 24; Finlay, 1980, 45f.; Finer, 1997, 1012f.). Because the noble officials served short terms, the permanent senior bureaucrats, numbering upward of a hundred, must have had considerable power to determine the routine operations of their agencies, and to influence policy (Bouwsma, 1968, 60; Burke, 1974, 38).[13] Some cases of non-noble political influence were outstanding. Paolo Sarpi, who will soon engage our attention, had more influence on Venetian state policy than any other single person of his time, despite being doubly disqualified from high office as both a commoner and a churchman.

12. See Finer (1997, 1006f.) for a judicious appraisal of the Dieci.

13. "Closely allied [with the nobility] was the Venetian civil service of clerks and secretaries who served in various confidential capacities and enjoyed great influence and power. Secretaryships were life positions and secretarial families served the Republic for generations, forming a kind of subsidiary aristocracy" (Rose, 1974, 483). The topmost post in the bureaucracy, filled by election in the Great Council, was that of Grand chancellor, who Haitsma Mulier describes as "the 'Doge' of the 'cittadini' " (1980, 11).

Of some significance too, perhaps, was the demographic geography of the city. Nobles and commoners lived in the same districts, often in the same buildings, and attended the same churches (Lane, 1973, 11; Cowan, 1986, 51; Romano, 1987, 120f.). There was more daily contact between them than now exists, in democracies, between elected representatives and their electors. One need not resort to the doctrine of "virtual representation" in order to suggest that the members of the Great Council were familiar with the views of the general citizenry, and gave them expression, albeit filtered, in the organs of state.

Venice was not entirely immune from popular disturbances, but the constitutional order that was established following the Serrata was never seriously threatened thereafter. No foreign power, not even the papacy, could count upon the disaffection of Venetians with their rulers to help it attain dominion over the lagoon. Contarini devoted the last chapter of his *Magistratibus* to the fact, which he considered remarkable, that Venetians had been willing to accept with such equanimity the government of a small noble class, making the city free of the "seditions and tumults" that plagued other states. He gave detailed reasons, stressing that not only had the government performed its tasks efficiently, but also that the ordinary citizen was free from arbitrary and unnecessary interference, that his property was safe, that the same laws applied to all, that citizens had control over their own institutions and, moreover, that they were not totally excluded from participation in affairs of state. A "just and temperate manner of ruling," he declared, not "violent force, armed garrisons, or fortified towers," is what had made the city the Serenissima—the most serene of states.[14]

Venetian Constitutionalism

Frederic Lane devoted his 1965 presidential address to the American Historical Association to an examination of the "roots of republicanism" (Lane, 1966, ch. 32). He there construed republicanism as "popular participation in government" and traced its roots to the northern Italian cities of the later

14. The image of Renaissance Venice as Serenissima, assiduously promoted by its own political leaders and by many historians since, has recently been disputed. Guido Ruggiero's study of violence in Venice (1980) shows that crimes such as murder, rape, and assault were prevalent, with the nobility especially prominent as perpetrators. Donald E. Queller (1986) points out that practical politics in Venice was not devoid of tumult, seditious conspiracy, and corruption. Nevertheless, Renaissance Venice was relatively stable and "serene" by contemporary standards. Mark Girouard observes that Venice "was especially a matter of amazement to the other Italian cities as they watched their leading families busily stringing each other out of windows of their Palazzi Publici, massacring or being massacred by their artisans, and finally succumbing to the rule of a despot" (1985, 100f.).

Middle Ages and the Renaissance. Lane considered Venice to have been the only city to succeed in constructing a durable republicanism; all others by the sixteenth century had either lost their independence as self-governing polities or had forfeited their civic liberties to local tyrants. In light of the description of Venetian government given in the preceding section, Lane's thesis is difficult to accept. Popular participation in sixteenth-century Venetian government was not negligible, and it was larger there than elsewhere in Europe, but nonetheless it was much too small to sustain such a general characterization of the political order. If popular participation in government is the criterion of republicanism, Venice had little justification for describing itself as a republic. In fact, Lane seems to have had something else in mind: he speaks of Venice as unique in that it "avoided the dominance of any single family and perfected a system of checks and balances within its ruling class." It was not Venice's republicanism that impressed him, but its constitutionalism.

In terms of the classical categories, Venice was unquestionably an aristocracy. Its noble class was relatively large by comparison with that of other states, but still composed only some 5 percent of the total population. The nobility provided a substantial pool of able men who, by rotating through the various offices, acquired broad training in the arts of government. But the Serenissima did not rely upon the administrative ability, or the civic virtue, of its aristocracy to preserve its liberty. Aware of the sad histories of other states, the Venetians constructed constitutional machinery to assure that the thirst for power, which they feared in every man, would be assuaged for many but sated for none. This was the city's main contribution to the political history of the West.

The notion of Venice as a "mixed government" of the sort described by Aristotle was commonly expressed by Renaissance authors (Haitsma Mulier, 1980, 35f.) and still survives in the writings of modern historians. But in order to understand the Venetian constitution, one must put this idea firmly aside and focus attention on the structure of power relations among the institutions of an aristocratic state. These relations were not ones of status, but function; they were relations of governmental offices, not social classes. There were no grades of nobility in Venice. All nobles had the same status and were addressed by the same title. Some families were more wealthy and/or influential than others, but a man would have great power if, for example, he was a member of the Council of Ten, *because* he was a member of it, and only as long as he was a member. Because of the election system, and the short terms that produced rapid rotation in office, the model of Venetian government consists of the structure of its offices. These were not hierarchically ordered, but neither were they independent of each other. The notion of "separation of powers" does not apply to the Venetian constitution any better than "mixed government" does. It was a system of political authorities that were interdependent due to the overlapping of memberships in the various bodies, the intersection of their jurisdictional areas, and the liability of every official to charges if, in the opinion of other officials, actions were taken without the authority of law.

Clearly at work in the Venetian political system was the principle of checks and balances. Bodin thought that he had achieved an understanding of the Venetian political system by locating its seat of sovereignty in the Great Council. But a more penetrating appraisal of the Venetian system is made possible by recognizing that there was no seat of sovereignty in it. The notion of sovereignty belongs to the hierarchical model. Analysis of how a hierarchy functions must find the linear chain of command and trace it to the top, but the hierarchy model renders no assistance in analyzing the government of Venice.[15]

I might note that the hierarchical model was not restricted to political theory in late medieval and early modern European thought. It was, indeed, one of the most general and influential concepts in the intellectual history of the West, embodied in Christian theology and ecclesiology but, even more broadly, in the metaphysical notion of the "great chain of being," which, as Lovejoy has shown (1936), continued to exert strong influence on Western thought into the eighteenth century. Venetian constitutional theory was one of the earliest departures from this outlook, antedating the development of Newtonian mechanics, which eliminated it from man's conception of the physical world.

The concept of a system of countervailing powers involves the additional ideas of "equilibrium" and "stability." These are not identical concepts. An equilibrium of forces may be in a condition that is "stable," "unstable," or "metastable." If a ball is placed in the bottom of a curved bowl, the gravitation forces acting upon it are in stable equilibrium: any small displacement of the ball will result in its return to the original position. If, on the other hand, one were to balance the ball carefully on the rim of the bowl, it would also be in a condition of gravitation equilibrium, but one that, by the same criterion, is unstable. If the ball is placed on a horizontal surface such as a table, it would be in stable equilibrium there, and if displaced by a small amount, it would still be in stable equilibrium, but in a new position. Such a system is one of metastable equilibrium. Savanarola's brief regime in the Republic of Florence was one of unstable equilibrium. It was unable to deal

---

15. Davis depicts the structure of Venetian government as a pyramid, but quickly goes on to note that power cannot be construed as flowing up or down in a simple fashion (1962, 21).

with the challenges of ongoing events and was replaced by the reestablishment of the Medicean dictatorship. Such unstable conditions characterized most of the city-states of Renaissance Italy that attempted to establish "republican" governments. In Venice, however, the counterpoise of political forces established by the fourteenth-century constitution was a metastable equilibrium, one that could accommodate changes taking place within, and outside, the system without degenerating into a fundamentally different mode of political organization.

In accounting for that stability, one should note in the first place that the topography of Venice made it possible for it to do without a standing army or regular militia. No noble, or commoner, could expect to seize control of the city by commanding an existing body of armed men. In times of crisis, Venice gave extraordinary powers to a special naval official called the captain general, but care was exercised to see that he would not be tempted to use these powers within the lagoon (Contarini, 1599, 137). The defensive capacities of the ducal palace, however, were not sufficient to withstand a well-organized attack by even a small number of men. The Council of Ten no doubt was effective in preventing subversion, but why did it never seize power itself, or even attempt to? The short, and overlapping, terms of office of its members, together with prohibitions against more than one member of the same family holding office simultaneously, must have made conspiracy difficult. These features of the Venetian system are important in explaining its stability, but I think we must look further still, beyond the formal structure of the constitution.

In any system of politics there are, necessarily, both stabilizing and destabilizing elements. As the method through which collective decisions are made concerning "public goods," politics generates the stabilizing social solidarity that derives from commonly shared purposes. Political organization enables people to do collectively much that they cannot do individually. In this aspect, politics is, in modern parlance, a "positive-sum game," generating net gains that can be shared by all. But politics is also a contest for power, and this is, at best, a "zero-sum game" with no such gains. If one person wins an election, another loses; if a coup takes place, one faction is deposed and another installed. The power game of politics is, indeed, likely to have a negative sum, because some ways in which the contest for power takes place are destructive of both public and private goods. This aspect of politics is inherently destabilizing because, in itself, it provides no basis for social solidarity and common purpose. The stability of a social order depends, therefore, on the capacity of its political system to constrain the intensity with which the power game is played.

In other Italian cities, the competition for power was frequently, or continuously in some cases, the dominant aspect of politics. The modern visitor to San Gimignano will see there the remnants of tower fortresses erected in medieval times by factions that warred with one another within the town itself. The skyline of thirteenth-century Florence was dotted with such towers, some over 200 feet high, each attesting the determination of a family to be second to none other in power and prestige. Feuding among such families was almost continuous, destroying public order, lives, and property. During the long struggle in the later Middle Ages between the Holy See and the Holy Roman Emperor, the political factions of Italian cities coalesced into two parties, the Guelphs and the Ghibellines, thus sharpening the contest for power and diverting local politics even further from serving the *salus populi*.

Such factional conflicts were not entirely absent in Venice, but they were much milder there, constituting at most a minor feature of Venetian politics. No fortified towers were erected; no battles took place between feuding families on its streets and waterways; the Great Council did not divide into Guelph and Ghibelline parties. The Venetian aristocracy was notably less fractious than that of other Italian states. Some early admirers were inclined to attribute the merits of Venetian government to the exceptional personal qualities of its aristocrats, reflecting the Platonic notion that the secret of good government consists in the placement of power into the hands of the superior few. That Venetian nobles were exceptionally endowed with civic *virtù* was one of the facets of the "Myth of Venice"—the depiction of the Serenissima as the ideal republic. Noting that this view still persists in modern historiography, Donald Queller (1986) has recently devoted a great deal of effort to its destruction, by cataloguing the crimes and malfeasances of the Venetian patriciate that testify to their lack of restraint in pursuit of personal interests. He concludes that Venetian nobles were no more civic minded than their counterparts elsewhere—which may fail to surprise anyone who adopts a skeptical view of claims, new as well as old, that society's elite are primarily motivated by the desire to render public service. The issue is important only because civic *virtù* continues to be furthered as the main political legacy that the West has derived from Renaissance Italy—with Machiavelli identified as its fountainhead (Pocock, 1975, 1981). An alternative view, which is the theme of this book, is that good government derives from a structure of political institutions that enables power to be controlled and properly directed, without reliance upon the possession of special virtues by those who govern. Renaissance Venice, like classical Athens and republican Rome before, and modern democracies since, exemplify the effectiveness of such constitutional arrangements. Venetian nobles were as motivated by desire for personal power and prestige as other men. Nevertheless, Venice succeeded in controlling the power game of politics, subordinating it to the processes of collective decision-making on matters of common interest.

Church and State

Venice was the most cosmopolitan city in Europe in the sixteenth century, but its many churches were almost entirely Christian and Catholic, and Catholicism was the official religion of the republic. Despite this, Renaissance Venice occupies an important place in the development of religious toleration and the principle of separation between church and state.[16] A secular view of the state developed in Venice mainly as a consequence of conflict between the city and the head of its own religion. The Holy See was not merely a religious authority but also a secular power, sharing territorial borders with Venice. For the Venetians, the pope was head of a foreign state, and his authority over their religious lives was not easily separable from his claim to temporal power—a claim that became more insistent and more comprehensive in the latter half of the sixteenth century. The invasion of Italy by Spain, in its assumed role as the arm of the true faith, added greatly to the Venetian view that the Holy See was a foreign power whose exceptional capacities for internal subversion required special attention.

The doctrine of *separation* of church and state is difficult to maintain, even in twentieth-century America, because the linkage of religion and morality, still widely accepted, appears to give church leaders special authority to render judgment on matters of state policy that are strongly invested with ethical considerations. Separation was much more difficult four centuries ago. Galileo was brought to trial by the Holy Office on a matter that few today would regard as having any relevance to religious faith. Because of the comprehensive scope of religion in those times, and the claim of the papacy to derive its authority from God, through Saint Peter, Venetian policy toward the church

---

16. Sixteenth-century commentators on Venice often noted the remarkable degree of religious freedom allowed to foreigners (McPherson, 1990, 115). Jews were allowed to settle in Venice after their expulsion from Spain in 1492 and, though segregated, enjoyed a high measure of civic liberty and freedom to practice their religion. Pullan refers to Venice's reputation as "a Catholic state where the Protestant could share the security of the Greek and the Jew from persecution" as one of the factors that "helped to quicken English enthusiasm for the Republic and its State" in the early seventeenth century (1974, 450). On foreigners in Venice, see Chambers and Pullan (1992, 323–352).

could not, and was not, based upon a definition of separate spheres of independent authority. Some sixteenth-century Venetians claimed that the state obtained its authority directly from God—and their own state especially so because the apostle Saint Mark had sojourned in the lagoon, and God had appeared to him saying that a great city would be founded there in his name. This legend had at least as much weight with Venetians as the papacy's contention that Christ meant to make the apostolic descendants of Simon the head of his church when he called him Peter ("rock"), or that the "Donation of Constantine" (proved to be a forgery in the early fifteenth century) certified the Holy See's claim as the legitimate successor to the temporal power of ancient Rome. Other Venetians advanced an even more radical notion, following the contention of Marsilius of Padua's *Defensor Pacis* (1324) that all authority is derived not from God above, but from the people below, who had given it to secular rulers, not to the church. Whichever, or whatever, argument served as support, Venice's view of the church was that it was subordinate to the state. This was evident in the Venetian constitution and political practice. Brian Pullan refers to "anticlericalism" as one of the "pillars" supporting the widespread admiration of Venice in the era of the Counter-Reformation. The political history of the West was profoundly influenced thereby, by Venetian writers such as Contarini and Sarpi, and by Florentines such as Machiavelli and Guicciardini, who considered the problems of politics in a thoroughly secular mode.

There was a notable exception to the rule that all adult male Venetian nobles had the right of membership in the Great Council and election to the various high offices of state. By a law passed in 1498, all clerics were debarred. They had even less right to participate in the government than the *cittadini*, for they were not allowed to hold bureaucratic posts either (Bouwsma, 1968, 65). In addition, whenever church matters were discussed in the Great Council or the Senate, the *papalisti*, nobles with family ties to persons holding high office in the church, were excluded. In other Italian cities, the papal cathedral was centrally located and served as the center of its religious and civic life. Not so in Venice. San Marco was the doge's church, not the bishop's, and it was administered by lay officials, the Procurators elected by the Great Council. Nor were the Venetians content to exclude the church from state affairs; they did not refrain from introducing the state into church matters when they considered it desirable to do so. The Holy Inquisition's investigation of heresy, which made powerful princes in other states tremble, was subjected to state supervision in Venice, with three special officials elected to attend its sessions and assure that no Venetian laws were violated. Venice was not the only state that attempted to bring the church under the control of the secular power, but as Lane remarks, "In other Italian cities papal power was not limited as much as it was in Venice, nor was the Church as firmly policed by the state" (1973, 394).[17]

Like Venice, the Papal States bordered on the Adriatic, and from the earliest time of Venice's maritime expansion, the two were commercial and naval rivals. As part of its policy of controlling the sea lanes to the Levant and the east, Venice took possession of a number of cities that had been under papal jurisdiction. Hostility and mutual suspicion never ceased thereafter to characterize relations between the Serenissima and the Holy See. Disputes between them were countless, some even leading to war. In addition to Rome's own military and naval capacities, and those of allied and supporting states, the pope, as head of the church, possessed a special weapon: the power to excommunicate anyone deemed to have violated Christian doctrine or disobeyed his authority. Innocent III was so angered by Venice's diversion of the armies of the Fourth Crusade to attack Zara in 1202 that he invoked this power in the form of a general Interdict, denying the sacraments to all Venetians and refusing sanctification of their civic functions and personal contracts. Venice was placed under Interdict on a number of occasions thereafter, without much distinction between religious and secular offenses (Libby, 1973, 39f.). The most important occasion was in 1606, in a dispute that began over minor matters and quickly escalated into a bitter conflict. Although the dispute never came to war, it nevertheless resulted in a defeat for the papacy that ended, for all practical purposes, its claim to exercise authority over the temporal rulers of Christian states. The Interdict of 1606 generated a large literature in political theory, written by the most able scholars of the time, in which the question of the relation between church and state was thoroughly debated. The dispute between Venice and the Holy See was followed closely by other European powers, and the arguments presented by the protagonists were widely read and discussed. The effects were strongest in Protestant states; there the Venetian Interdict of 1606 played a significant part in the development of the modern view of church and state, and in the evolution of constitutionalism.[18]

The immediate causes of the Interdict were the arrest, on criminal charges, of two priests whom the Venetian authorities refused to hand over to the church for trial, and the Senate's rejection of the Holy See's demand that

17. Galileo was advised by his friend Paolo Sarpi not to leave his post at the University of Padua because it provided him with security against his enemies in the church who regarded Copernican cosmology as heretical. Nevertheless, Galileo went to Florence, where he was forced by the Inquisition to abjure his views.

18. "The first major episode in the history of seventeenth-century absolutist thought was the controversy over church-state relations that resulted from the Interdict of Venice" (Sommerville, 1991, 350).

laws recently passed restricting church construction and acquisition of property be rescinded.[19] The deeper source of the dispute, however, was the adoption by the Holy See of a militant policy toward the Reformation, and its choice of Venice as the locus for a battle that it hoped would halt, and reverse, both the spread of Protestantism and the tendency in Catholic states for civil authorities to assert their independence from the church. The Council of Trent, convened in 1545 to consider the threat of Protestantism, rejected the contention of reformers that the church must cleanse itself in order to perform its holy mission. Thomas Aquinas's view that the authority of the church extended to all aspects of life was adopted by the council as Christian doctrine. But even if the decrees of the council had sought only to deal with spiritual matters, the implementation of them on such issues as book censorship, the conduct of the Holy Inquisition, and even charitable activities necessarily introduced the church into areas that the Venetians regarded as belonging to the secular domain (Wright, 1974). An active center of the ecclesiastical reform movement, Venice proposed in 1562 that the council be reconvened to consider this alternative policy in response to Protestantism, but to no avail. The election to the papacy of Pius V in 1566 confirmed the hard stance of the church: no concession was made to the reformers; indeed the Holy See increasingly insisted that obedience to papal authority was the first duty of all Christians, including those who held secular power in independent states. Outside Italy, this policy was not easy to implement; within the peninsula the main stumbling block was Venice. This was the state that the Holy See had to tame if the policy of Counter-Reformation was to succeed (Cozzi, 1979, 250). In 1605, the papacy and the dogeship of Venice both fell vacant. The church elected Paul V, a hard-liner, and Venice named as its new doge Leonardo Donà, a leader of the church reformers who had already distinguished himself as one who advocated firm resistance to the extension of papal power. The stage was set for confrontation. In April 1606, the Holy See placed Venice under a general Interdict (Chambers and Pullan, 1992, 225).

The republic viewed this Interdict as an immediate threat to its liberty and, more broadly, as a challenge to the political philosophy embodied in the Venetian constitution. An alternative to the hierarchical model of order had been found, and the Venetians did not regard religion, whatever its value in people's spiritual lives, as an essential element in government. A battle of words ensued, with Paolo Sarpi leading the Venetian forces and Cardinal Bellarmine, the leading scholar of the Curia, the papal ones. The defeat of the Holy See on the immediate issues was complete. The Interdict was re-

19. See Cozzi (1969, 113f.) for a summary of other matters that also soured church-state relations at the time.

scinded without Venice granting any of the concessions that had been demanded. The church did not undertake to reform itself, as Sarpi and others continued to advise, but it began the pragmatic accommodation to secular power that became, and remains, its political policy. The Thirty Years' War of 1618–1648 determined the division of Europe between Catholicism and Protestantism, but it was the Venetian victory in the Interdict dispute that foreshadowed what was to become in time the accepted view of church-state relations in the West.

According to an old adage, nothing succeeds like success. Just as Venice's quick recovery from the War of the League of Cambrai engendered wide admiration of its political capacity and interest in its political system, so its victory in the Interdict dispute drew favorable attention to the political philosophy that had been advanced by its defenders. The chief of these, Paolo Sarpi, was a man of extraordinary talent and learning. A priest of the Servite order, he had great interest not only in theology and canon law, but also in the secular domains of science and mathematics. He made some significant contributions to physiology and was instrumental in encouraging Galileo's use of the recently invented telescope. His philosophy of science was materialist in its metaphysical outlook and empiricist in epistemology, viewpoints that carried over to his thinking about history, religion, and politics (Wooton, 1983, 15). Though he was a priest, he did not regard religious belief as necessary to moral conduct, and he viewed the Catholic Church in sociological rather than theological terms.

While yet a young man, Sarpi became a senior officer in the Servite order, and spent some four or five years in Rome, during which time he formed, or fixed, his view that the church had become corrupted by wealth and temporal power. Returning to the Veneto, he became clearly identified with those who argued that the church could not combat Protestantism until it had reformed itself as an institution and once again concerned itself exclusively with man's spiritual life. When Paul V gave the Serenissima an ultimatum—to meet his demands or be placed under Interdict—the Senate turned to Sarpi, creating for him a special post as councilor of the republic. Sarpi drafted Venice's response to the Holy See and subsequently played a leading role in the dispute, as adviser to the Senate and as author and impresario of many writings that sought not so much to convince the Holy See as to defend Venice against it in the eyes of Europeans north of the Alps. Hitherto well known among scientists in Europe, Sarpi now became an important figure in the political thought of the era, and especially those aspects of it that concerned the relations of church and state.

As a political philosopher, Sarpi cannot be described as an advocate of the constitutional theory of checks and balances. He leaned more to Bodin's view that there must be a central seat of sovereignty in a state. His main significance lies in his thoroughly secular view of politics and his insistence that the state is not subordinate to the church. In the era of the Counter-Reformation, the protection of the citizen from the powers of the state had to take second place to the independence of the state itself from the church's claim to universal authority. In fact, Sarpi used the doctrine of undivided sovereignty to argue that the state was not merely independent of the church but superior to it. Perhaps influenced by Montaigne, whose writings he admired, he viewed the church in a sociological fashion as an institution that may play a utilitarian role in various aspects of civic life, a perspective that was far cry from the Holy See's demand that the decrees of the pope must be obeyed without question as the commands of God. Sarpi sometimes spoke of the state as deriving its authority directly from God, but his essential view was that the state is a utilitarian artifact, designed to serve mundane human purposes. State and church could work together for common ends, but a state like Venice, whose goal was the welfare and freedom of its citizenry, could not work with a church whose aim was to subject them to the absolute dominion of a foreign bishop.

Sarpi regarded the Interdict dispute not only as a defense of Venice, but as a struggle for the future of Christianity. That struggle was of course taking place throughout Europe in the rival claims of Protestantism and Catholicism.[20] Venice was the only city south of the Alps where it seemed possible that Protestantism might gain a foothold.[21] The English ambassador reported in 1608 that had the Interdict continued for a while longer, Venice would have broken permanently with the papacy (Cozzi, 1969, 238). England worked hard to detach Venice from the Church of Rome, officially siding with the republic during the Interdict and promising military aid if needed. Sarpi's *History of the Council of Trent* was first published (1619) in England, under the imprimatur of James I. During the following century, it went through many editions and numerous translations. It was mainly read in Protestant countries as an anti-papal tract, not appreciated at first for its significance as a work of empirical historiography. Though Cardinal Bellarmine strove hard to undermine Sarpi's position in Venice by accusing him of Protestantism, there was nothing particularly Lutheran or Calvinist in his theol-

20. A. D. Wright (1974) points out that Venice was not the only state that was engaged in jurisdictional disputes with the papacy in the early seventeenth century. The Interdict, he contends, must be viewed in a wider context in which the relations between Spain and Rome were especially important because many, especially the Venetians, were inclined to see a Spanish threat behind every move of the papacy.

21. Martin (1993) shows that Protestantism had spread significantly among the Venetian populace, especially in the artisan class.

ogy. Anglicanism attracted him, and other Venetians, at least in part because it represented a separation from the *organization* of the church, not from its theological doctrine; and the declaration of the English king as head of the church *in* England was in accord with Sarpi's views on church and state.[22]

Venice did not become Protestant, nor did its ecclesiastical reformers succeed in persuading the republic to insist upon radical constitutional change in the Holy See. During the seventeenth century, beset by many difficulties, Venice could not afford such a stance. Its foreign policy was one of prudence, of seeking to maintain good relations with the church and the big powers like Spain with which it could no longer compete militarily. The great Interdict dispute is mainly significant not for its immediate effects, but for its long-term influence on the political thought of England and northern Europe. Bouwsma remarks that the Interdict was "one of the earliest in the long series of seventeenth century disputes over sovereignty" (1968, 435). But the contest was between two parties that represented more than different opinions as to where sovereignty should lie. The Counter-Reformation papacy both exemplified and advocated in extreme form the model of hierarchical order; the Venetian Republic, a profoundly different one—a network of mutually controlling powers.

The Myth of Venice

In their comprehensive history *Utopian Thought in the Western World*, Manuel and Manuel (1979, 153) note that sixteenth-century Italian writers like Gasparo Contarini played a special role in the history of political ideas by idealizing an existing state, instead of writing frankly fictional accounts of imaginary ones or advocating the creation of a wholly new society that would meet the author's philosophic notion of perfection. Sir Thomas More named his own imaginary society *Utopia* (1516), meaning "nowhere," but Contarini's Venice was located in real space and time, and his *De Magistratibus et Republica Venetorum* (1543) was presented to the reader as an empirical description of a functioning political system of long standing. That Contarini idealized the Venetian constitution and its history has been made clear by

22. "His works reedited and carefully examined, his links with advanced scientific currents uncovered, his position in broader devotional movements noted with precision and sympathy, his reputation as historian and controversialist firmly established, Sarpi has taken his place among the leading European figures of his day. At the same time Sarpi emerges as quintessentially Venetian, apologist and embodiment of the finest in specifically Venetian culture" (Grubb, 1986, 54f.). One of the very few statues of Venetian worthies in the city today is that of Paolo Sarpi, standing on the former site of the Servite monastery. It was erected in the nineteenth century.

modern historical research on Renaissance Venice (see, e.g., Cozzi, 1973), but it would be going much too far to classify the *Magistratibus,* and other similar writings of the time, as belonging to the utopian genre of political literature. In fact, despite their deficiencies by the standards of modern historiography and political science, they were well in advance of their time in bringing to the study of political organization an empirical and analytical outlook that focused attention on the *machinery* of government rather than its philosophical and theological foundations, which had been the absorbing interest of medieval thinkers. Moreover, even if Contarini, Giannotti, Guicciardini, and Paruta had written purely utopian texts, they would not thereby merit exclusion from the history of political theory. That history is the history of *ideas,* and intellectual historians admit that even the most impractical doctrines have influenced Western politics. In evaluating the role of Venice in the political history of the West, we have to focus on the *interpretation* of its political system that formed part of the intellectual world of sixteenth- and seventeenth-century Europe. What historians have come to call "the myth of Venice" refers to the conception of Venice as an *ideal republic* that in itself influenced Western political theory and constitutional development.[23]

The notion that Venice represented a model to be admired and emulated can be traced back perhaps at least as far as Marsilius of Padua in the fourteenth century (Lane, 1966, 303), but it was during the sixteenth century that it became a prominent feature of Italian political thought. Venice's remarkable recovery from the War of the League of Cambrai (1508–1509), without the internal disorders that under similar circumstances would have convulsed other states, drew special attention to the capacities of its governmental system (Gaeta, 1961). In the 1520s Donato Giannotti, a Florentine, wrote his *Libro della Republica di Venezia* and Contarini, a Venetian, his *Magistratibus,* which, when published in the 1540s, became the classical studies of the Venetian constitution and the main sources for its idealization by foreign writers (Bouwsma, 1968, 154; Gaeta, 1961). But Giannotti and Con-

---

23. "A huge historical and political literature has tried to explain why Venice preserved its republican independence, and taken together the explanations make up what historians have called 'the myth of Venice.' Some writings ascribe Venice's good fortune to its form of government. Those who lived in a republic enjoyed a degree of freedom and political influence that kept them obedient and contented. Other writings praise the constitutional arrangements through which the classical notion of mixed government had been kept alive in Western Europe . . . Venice also served as the perfect example for the advocates of an aristocratic form of government . . . In later times, from the seventeenth century on, this view prevailed. The miracle of Venetian stability was seen in its being ruled by patricians who served unselfishly the well-being of society and state" (Gilbert, 1987, 37). Grubb's survey of Venetian historiography (1986) contains a review of the history of the myth of Venice, and the anti-myth.

tarini did not create the "myth of Venice"; they provided texts for, and thereby accelerated, a view of Venice that was already widespread, even before the War of the League of Cambrai.[24]

In the development of the "myth of Venice," its rival city-state, Florence, played an important role. There was some tradition of republican government in Florence, as there had been in other Italian cities going back to medieval times. In 1434, the Medici family assumed power, beginning a reign that lasted, with some significant interruptions, until the eighteenth century. From early in the Medici period, Florentines cast their eyes toward Venice as the great living example of a state that was a republic in more than name.[25] Poggio Bracciolini, a papal secretary, was scornful of the low origins of the Venetians, but wrote a book *In Praise of the Venetian Republic* (ca. 1450), seeing it as a realization of the ideal mixture of monarchy and aristocracy expressed by Aristotle (Chambers, 1970, 25; Skinner, 1978, 1:171). The expulsion of the Medici in 1494 began a thirty-six-year period of alternating republican and Medicean rule, which generated some of the richest political literature of the Renaissance (Bondanella, 1976, 42). In this literature, and in Florentine practice during the city's brief republican periods, the Venetian constitution was looked to as the ideal model to emulate (Gilbert, 1968). Even Savonarola, whose main object was the religious regeneration of Florentines, viewed the Venetian system of government with favor and, during his brief tenure of office, established a Florentine Great Council in imitation of Venice (Pocock, 1975, 103f.; Rubinstein, 1991, 61). Especially noteworthy is Francesco Guicciardini's *Dialogue on the Government of Florence*. Written in the early 1520s as a guide for the reconstruction of Florentine government, it presents Venice as a model, not to be copied exactly, but to be used as a general guide for any society in which "one of the principal fruits to be derived from good government is security for one's person and one's possessions, and the ability to dispose of them as one wants." Guicciardini clearly recognizes as necessary to this end the establishment of a constitutional structure that will control the exercise of political power (1994, 85, 110f. and *passim*).[26] Florence did not succeed in establishing a lasting republic on the Venetian model, but the Florentine political literature of this period was widely read in Europe and

24. Libby (1973) suggests that the near disaster of that war stimulated admirers of Venice to make a more thoughtful, and less complacent, examination of the Venetian political system than theretofore.

25. On the admiration of Venice by Florentine writers, see Muir (1981, 45f.).

26. Rubinstein (1991) provides a useful brief account of Guicciardini's political theory as well as that of his fellow contemporary Florentine, Donato Giannotti. See also Bondanella (1976).

played a substantial role in introducing to European political thinkers the notion of a checks and balances constitution.

As we have seen, there were good reasons for sixteenth century Florentines, and others, to admire the Venetian constitution. It had by then been operative for more than two centuries in a city that had achieved civic liberty and tranquillity as well as wealth and security from foreign enemies. Even Machiavelli, who did not have a high opinion of Venetians and regarded their constitution as an inadequate model for a state that aimed at territorial expansion, grudgingly admitted its success in achieving what he considered to be lesser objectives. But neither the Venetian writers nor the Florentine ones were inclined to praise the constitution of Venice simply because it worked, without asking *why* it did. Political science began in this period because the best of these writers practiced analysis as well as description. In examining the analytical content of this literature, modern scholars have placed excessive weight on its use of the language of "mixed government" and its frequent references to Aristotle, while inadequately appreciating that a very different notion of constitutional structure was closer to the essential arguments it contained.[27] Giannotti, in fact, did not use the concept of mixed government at all; instead he wrote of the Venetian constitution as like an organic system whose parts function interdendently (Gilbert, 1968; Pocock, 1975, 307).[28] We cannot here examine all of these writers, but Gasparo Contarini is worth some special attention because his *Magistratibus* (1543) established the paradigmatic interpretation of the Venetian constitution that was adopted by later writers and, more than any other document, was responsible for promoting the image of Venice as the ideal republic that was so prominent in the political literature of the seventeenth century (Gilbert, 1967, 183; Chambers, 1970, 434f.; Finlay, 1980, 31, 222). It went through some twenty different editions, in four languages, during the century after its original publication (Lindenbaum, 1991, 129).[29]

The oldest child of one of the foremost noble families of Venice, Gasparo Contarini was, from early youth, a devoted Christian. In early writings he expressed the view that man's primary imperative is to lead a life that will

27. A notable exception is S. E. Finer, who emphasizes the error of interpreting Venice in terms of mixed government (1997, 1021).

28. Haitsma Mulier writes of Giannotti's discussion of Venice that "he never quite succeeded in identifying where the core of power lay," but two paragraphs later, he describes Giannotti as depicting Venice as "a society equipped with an ingenious system of checks and balances" (1980, 23f.).

29. "Gasparo Contarini's *On the Venetian Republic* quickly became famous all over Europe and remained a primary source for knowledge about Venice in the following centuries" (Gilbert, 1987, 37). Gleason notes that even today it is "the best known treatise on Venetian government" (1993, 110).

secure the salvation of his soul. Nevertheless, he did not follow his friends of like views who decided to withdraw from the world of practical affairs and devote themselves to prayer and meditation. He became active in Venetian politics and occupied a succession of important posts in Venetian government.[30] A leader in the movement for church reform, he was apparently quite surprised when, at the age of fifty-two, he was appointed by Pope Paul III to the College of Cardinals (Gilbert, 1977, 267). One would not surmise, from the pages of the *Magistratibus*, that the author had a religious vocation. Contarini does not argue that the Venetian constitution is in accord with divine will or intention; he does not resort to the legend of Saint Mark to explain why Venice became the ideal republic; he does not claim that the Venetians succeeded where others failed because of their devotion to the true faith or their great virtue. He writes of the Venetian constitution as having been constructed by "our wise and prudent ancestors," ascribing to them mundane political acumen rather than mystical revelation or metaphysical insight.

In the opening pages of the *Magistratibus*, Contarini advances a utilitarian view of the purposes of civil society: men bind themselves together in this fashion "so they might live happily and commodiously." He also makes a special point of rejecting the notion that the purpose of the state is to enable men to earn honors and glorify their state in warfare. "There have been many commonwealths," he writes, "which have far exceeded Venice as well in empire and in greatness of estate, as in military discipline and glory of the wars: yet have there not been any, that may be paragoned with this of ours, for institutions and laws prudently decreed to establish unto the inhabitants a happy and prosperous felicity" (1599, 5f.).

Contarini was a utilitarian in the psychological, ethical, and political intentions of that term. He believed that men are by nature motivated to seek their material welfare, that this is a morally worthy objective, and that the purpose of the state is to serve it. Jeremy Bentham could have lifted whole passages from Contarini and could have referred to him as anticipating his view that the main problem of governance is the establishment of machinery that directs state policy toward "the greatest happiness of the greatest number" in a community composed of self-interested individuals. Unlike the beasts, writes Contarini, man is a rational creature, and Venice has demonstrated that it is possible to devise means of effective governance that are not dependent upon the altruism of governors. In analyzing the working of the Venetian constitution, he praises its capacity to select men of ability and civic

---

30. See Gleason (1993, ch. 1) for an account of Contarini's family origins and youth, and his career in Venetian government.

virtue to fill its various offices, but he lays much more emphasis on its ability to generate good laws rather than good governors.[31]

Contarini stresses that the purposes of government cannot be served without political stability. The upheavals that have punctuated the histories of other Italian states are not mere occasional nuisances that temporarily dislocate the operation of civic functions; they place the lives, liberties, and welfare of the citizenry at hazard. Venice is noted, above all, for its stability, which is desirable in itself but is also an essential precondition for the operation of rational processes of collective decision-making. Venice's ancestors had clearly perceived "that there was not anything so much to be doubted and feared, as an intestine enemy, or civil strife and sedition among the citizens" (78). The constitution they had constructed, by reserving power to men of noble lineage, had avoided both the tumults of the multitude and the "seditions and great troubles" that inevitably arise when wealth alone determines access to power (16f.). But the establishment of a hereditary aristocracy would not have been sufficient. More was necessary: the aristocracy must be large; access to office must be open to all nobles; power must be prevented from concentrating in a few families; and the various offices of the state must act as guardians over each other. He views Venice as a perfect republic because its constitution meets these requirements.

Contarini was no democrat in the modern sense of the term. He favored the Serrata of 1297 as an act of wise statesmanship that had assured the Great Council would not be diluted with men of low quality. But he did not regard noblemen as having such great civic virtue that they could be entrusted with uncontrolled authority. The desire for personal power and distinction is in every man, even the Venetian noble. The genius of the constitution, in Contarini's judgment, lay in recognizing, and in prudently accommodating, this human passion. By its methods of election to office, short terms, and various

31. I should note that this interpretation of the *Magistratibus* is sharply at variance with that of some prominent modern historians. Felix Gilbert regards Contarini's political thought as dominated by the metaphysical conception that the universe is hierarchically ordered as a great chain of being, and by a religious conviction that social organization has an essentially moral purpose—the promotion of virtue: "social life was meant to serve man's development towards the spiritual world" (1977, 265). According to Gilbert, Contarini adopted the notion that "a society must be organized in such a way that it places the right ruler in control" (261). The *Magistratibus* is an idealization "because it emphasizes only those aspects of political life that help to explain how governments can lead people to perfection" (264). Pocock advances a similar interpretation of Contarini's political thought as dominated by the need to promote *virtù* (1975, 320f.). Such views, it seems to me, are not supported either by the general tone or the specific content of the *Magistratibus*. A recent biography of Contarini, by Elisabeth G. Gleason, presents it as depicting the government of Venice in mundane utilitarian terms (1993, 110–128).

other features, the Venetian constitution both fed and controlled the desire for power. It was structured "with great reason and discretion, to the end that the preeminence of public authorities might pertain to many, and not be engrossed up among the few: lest thereby through too much greatness of power might become disturbers or oppressors of the commonwealth: and on the other side, those that do find themselves void and hopeless of honor and government, might grow into dislike and hatred of the same" (1599, 33). Contarini does not argue that all nobles have a moral *right*, derived from God or natural law, to participate in the government of the state; he views this simply as a prudential matter, a requirement of stability.

In terms of the later history of constitutional theory, the most important feature of Contarini's analysis of the Venetian constitution is his view of how the various organs of the state are related to each other. He does not use a hierarchical model at all. From his account, one could not draw a diagram showing the power pyramid in the Venetian state. He stresses instead the intersection of offices and its function of mutual control. Contarini sometimes employs the language of "mixed government," but this concept does not serve him as an analytical model any more than hierarchy does. He writes of the doge as bearing the "show" of monarchy, the Senate and other offices as carrying "a certain show" of aristocracy, and the method of election of officials as having a "popular show" (1599, 18f., 35); he is obviously not anxious to press the institutions of the Venetian state into the traditional Aristotelian taxonomy. His analysis is carried out in terms of a different conception—the notion of checks and balances. Some modern commentators on Contarini have noted the checks and balances character of his analytical model (e.g., Gilmore, 1973; Bouwsma, 1973; McPherson, 1988), but its significance for the history of constitutional theory has yet to be fully appreciated.[32]

In recent years, numerous historians of Renaissance political thought have emphasized the importance of Machiavelli. As part of an attempt to rescue him from the evil reputation that has clung to his name for four centuries, they claim for him a significant role in the development of a theoretically coherent, and greatly influential, approach to politics (see esp. Pocock, 1975). Of Machiavelli's voluminous writings, *The Prince* (1517), written as a manual of political advice for the Medici, became by far the best known. Its insistence

32. Robey and Law point out that the notion of Venice as the "ideal republic" in the earlier literature was strongly bound to the Aristotelian categories and interpreted Venice as a "mixed government," squeezing its various political institutions into the tripartite classification of monarchical, aristocratic, and democratic "elements" (1975, 9f.). They fail to note that Contarini's analysis of Venetian government constituted a significant departure from the Aristotelian model. Pocock perceives the distinction, but rejects the notion that Contarini entertained a Polybian theory of checks and balances (1975, 326).

that a successful ruler must be totally unscrupulous, devious, and amoral, recognizing no loyalties or obligations that will not assist him to sustain and extend his power, is responsible for the pejorative adjective "Machiavellian." There is indeed nothing in *The Prince* that requires a modern reader to revise this view. In his *Discourses* Machiavelli presents larger views, revealing himself to be at heart a republican and suggesting that civil society is founded upon a social contract. Nevertheless, the contention that Machiavelli deserves a leading place in the history of political science or political theory is questionable. He does adopt a secular view of the state and insists on construing man as a self-interested creature—ideas that English thinkers of the seventeenth century were to absorb from *The Prince* itself, while reading it with revulsion (Rabb, 1964). But this notion virtually exhausts Machiavelli's contribution to the modern study of politics. He does not examine the *organization* of government as a means for making collective decisions, and despite his republicanism, he does not consider how the liberty of the citizen may be preserved, or how the self-interest of the governors may be directed to the service of the general welfare.[33]

Contarini is as secular as Machiavelli in his view of the state, and as realistic in his view of human nature, but he goes much further, examining in detail the machinery of Venetian government and analyzing its dynamics. His main object may have been to praise the Serenissima, but he does so by empirical description and analysis. That the mechanism he describes is somewhat idealized renders his account no less instructive to the student of politics. The *Magistratibus* did for political science what Adam Smith's model of the marketplace later did for economics: it showed how a stable social order can be achieved without a hierarchical structure of authority, and demonstrated that personal liberty is harmonious with social order in a pluralist system of countervailing powers.

Venice, Mixed Government, and Jean Bodin

In commenting upon the provenance and development of the myth of Venice, numerous scholars have pointed out that many of the Renaissance writers who promoted this image of the Serenissima as the ideal republic attributed it to its adoption of classical "mixed government." Quentin Skinner names Pier Paolo Vergerio, a Florentine, as the first (1394) of those who explained the excellence of the Venetian state as due to its fusion of monarchic, aristocratic, and democratic elements (1978, 1:140). Vergerio's identification of the doge, the Senate, and the Great Council as respectively representing these

---

33. See Hulliung (1983) for a salutary reappraisal of Machiavelli that contradicts the exalted depiction of him in much of the modern literature.

elements became the standard depiction of the Venetian constitution in the subsequent literature. Gianturco names fourteen Renaissance Italian authors who expressed support of the principle of mixed government and notes that it was customary among them to point to Venice as living proof of its merits (1938, 685f.). Well into the seventeenth century, and spreading beyond the confines of Italy to countries such as England and Holland, Venice was celebrated as exemplifying the benefits of mixed government (see, e.g., Fink, 1940 and 1945; Haitsma Mulier, 1980; Lindenbaum, 1991).[34]

The concept of mixed government makes no appearance today in the literature of political science. The notion that the political systems of countries such as the United States or Great Britain can be construed as mixtures of the Aristotelian pure forms would be summarily dismissed by modern scholars as bizarre. Nonetheless, some modern historians still use it in discussing the political system of Renaissance Venice (for example, Lane, Bouwsma, Fink, Pocock, and Panagopoulos), thereby evading or eliding the distinction between the concept of mixed government as formulated by Plato and Aristotle and modern denominative terms such as cultural and social pluralism and the pluralistic organization of political power.

The earliest writer to levy a major frontal attack on the notion that the Venetian Republic was a working example of the classical fourth form was Jean Bodin, whose important role in establishing the theory of sovereignty was examined earlier. Bodin regarded the notion of a mixed government as the most important challenge to his thesis that every viable polity must have a unified locus of absolute political power. At the end of the first book of his *Six Livres de la République* (1576), Bodin writes that "since the form of a commonwealth depends on who holds the sovereignty, let us see how many sorts of commonwealth there are" (1992, 88). This sentence introduces the first chapter of Book 2, entitled "Of the kinds of state in general and whether there are more than three," which is devoted to attacking the notion of mixed government.

Bodin was entirely familiar with the classical and contemporary writings on mixed government. He cites Herodotus (fifth century B.C.) as having been the first to refer to an idea that is usually attributed to Aristotle or Polybius. He observes that the notion of a compound of monarchical, aristocratic, and democratic elements in the constitution of a state had also been advanced in ancient times by Cicero and Dionysius of Halicarnassus (a Greek historian and philosopher of the first century B.C.), and more recently by Thomas

---

34. "Several generations of writers from and on Venice devoted themselves to promoting a view of the Venetian state as a republican Sparta or Rome, and in fact better than those of earlier mixed polities because dedicated to peace and civil ends rather than war" (Lindenbaum, 1991, 128f.).

More, Machiavelli, Contarini, "and many others" (1992, 90). The basic weakness of any mixed government is that it violates the most fundamental principle of political organization, the necessity of undivided sovereignty. "Mixture then," he writes, "is not a state but a corruption of a state." Polybius and others were in error in calling republican Rome a mixed government. It was a really a democracy, in which the people delegated their sovereignty only temporarily (95f.). Sparta was, and the German Empire is, an aristocracy (94f.). The Swiss States are either democracies or aristocracies. France has been called a compound state, but "it is a pure monarchy, unmixed with democratic power, and still less with aristocracy. . . . We shall conclude, then, [he goes on to write] that there is not now, and never was, a state compounded of aristocracy and democracy, much less of the three forms of state but that there are only three kinds of state" (100–103).

Bodin seems to have been fully aware that he must devote special consideration to the case of Venice, which by his time had become the most often cited example of mixed government. Bodin agreed with those who depicted Venice as a state of unprecedented stability in which the citizenry enjoyed an exceptional degree of personal liberty and the benefits of impartial law, but he disagreed with the mixed government interpretation of its political system. Noting that Contarini and Giannotti disagree on Venice's constitutional history, he comments, "However this may be, it is certain that at present it is a true aristocracy" (98).

It was not difficult for Bodin to deflate the notion that there are monarchical and democratic elements in the Venetian government. The doge, he points out, is not only elected, but has very little power; no significant monarchical element can be construed as characterizing his office. There is no democratic element either, for commoners are excluded from the Great Council and other state institutions. All political power in the Venetian state is in the hands of the noble class, and the Great Council is, unquestionably, the seat of sovereignty in the state. That the Great Council might delegate its authority to other bodies for administrative purposes does not gainsay the fact that it is the sovereign political authority. For Bodin, the acid test of sovereignty was the power to make law, and in Venice the Great Council was clearly the lawmaking body.[35]

As a critique of the notion that the Venetian system of government can be construed as a compound of monarchy, aristocracy, and democracy, Bodin's argumentation is compelling. It is thereby a successful critique of the theoretical notion of mixed government, but only to the degree that the concept

---

35. Gianturco (1938) examines in detail Bodin's interpretation of the Venetian system of government. See also Haitsma Mulier (1980).

of *stato misto* in the writings of Renaissance Italians was the same as the concept of *mikte* in Aristotle's taxonomy of state forms. Many sixteenth-century writers adopted such an identification, but some, such as Gasparo Contarini, were beginning to develop a different notion. In his *Magistratibus* the locution of "mixed government" is employed, but it refers to a pluralist conception of the Venetian constitution. For Bodin, the most fundamental property of government was indivisibility, and in order to maintain this view, it was necessary for him to regard the Venetian patriciate as a singular political entity. Contarini saw the Venetian system of government as one in which power was divided among its many councils. All political power resided in the noble class, but *within* that class it was institutionally dispersed, forming a complex of mutually controlling centers.

Bodin formulated his theory of sovereignty much more clearly than Contarini (or any other Renaissance writer) stated the principle of countervailing powers. It is impossible to say how much influence Bodin's theory had on the political history of Europe, but it certainly provided intellectual support for the trend toward absolutism that dominated European governance for the next three centuries. The outstanding exceptions to this trend were the Dutch Republic and England, where pluralist forms of political organization took root and developed. In the next two chapters, I will endeavor to trace the transformation of the idea of mixed government into the conception of a system of countervailing powers in those countries.

6

The Dutch Republic

At the middle of the sixteenth century, the Low Countries of northwest Europe were minor possessions of the Habsburg dynasty, prized mainly for their strategic value in the contest for maritime supremacy of the Atlantic seabord. A century later, the northern part of this region had successfully rebelled against Habsburg rule and had created an independent state that became a major player in the military, economic, intellectual, religious, and cultural developments of the early modern West. In terms of political organization, the "United Provinces of the Netherlands," as the new nation called itself, deviated significantly from the trend that dominated the rest of Europe. While nation-state development elsewhere was characterized by the centralization of political power and the establishment of absolutist regimes, the Dutch constructed their union upon pluralist principles, with local and regional governments playing the leading roles in the making of state policy.

It is evident from the case studies presented so far that the pluralist model admits of diverse specific realizations. The political systems of the states we have examined in the preceding chapters bear little structural resemblance to each other. The Dutch Republic created yet another new variant of pluralistic political organization that, in retrospect, appears to have been at least as important in the development of Western constitutionalism as any of its predecessors. The exercise of sovereign power requires a hierarchical system of political organization, but a system of plural and countervailing powers can be embodied in many architectural styles. Tolstoy's famous remark about families might be adapted to polities: all despotisms are alike, whereas every constitutional state is constitutional in its own way.

The Golden Age of the Dutch Republic

Prior to the Dutch Revolt, virtually all the states of Europe, great and small, were organized as monarchical absolutisms, exemplifying the principles that Jean Bodin declared to be essential to political stability. The only exceptions were Venice and Switzerland. The latter was a confederacy of semiautonomous political entities. The Dutch Republic was also organized on federalist principles, and well before the independence of the United Provinces was secure, it had replaced Switzerland as a center of attention by writers interested in alternative forms of political organization (Davids, 1995, 8). The United Provinces shared with the Republic of Venice the admiration of early modern observers who believed that governmental effectiveness and civic liberty were not incompatible political objectives.[1]

Economic Development

In the discussion of republican Rome in Chapter 2, I noted that the roadways built by the Roman legions to serve their logistical needs had a significant impact upon the economic structure and development of the Italian peninsula. After the fall of Rome, the roads they had built throughout Europe fell into disrepair, and until the construction of canals and railways in the nineteenth century, overland trade was dependent upon roadways so poor that only commodities of great value in relation to their bulk or weight could bear the cost of long-distance carriage. Even today, with the great technological developments of the twentieth century in modes of transport by road, rail, and air, shipment by water is the cheapest, and in the "world economy" that has come into being since World War II, communities that have close access to navigable water enjoy a considerable advantage over those that do not. This economic advantage was much greater in earlier times, and played an important part in all aspects of the development not only of the Netherlands, but the whole of the Western ecumene.

The Low Countries might well have been designed by a benevolent deity to enable their inhabitants to enrich themselves through the possession of such an advantage. The contours of the coastline provided many safe anchorages for vessels that ventured into the Atlantic, and rivers that were navigable for considerable distances into the hinterland debouched into these waters.[2] A limited supply of arable land led the Dutch to build dikes and drain swampy areas to provide additional tracts. This was an expensive way to acquire farmland, but it also yielded what economists call "external benefits" in the form of advanced technical knowledge. Sophisticated engineering, initially developed in order to improve waterways and harness wind power for

1. The Dutch Republic is largely ignored in standard works on the history of political theory (see Gelderen, 1992, preface) as well as in general histories of Western political development. Except for a small number of specialist historians, knowledge of the republic's history, and its significance in Western political development, is virtually nonexistent.

2. This region today handles a larger tonnage of shipping than any other harbor complex in the world.

the purpose of drainage, could also be applied to serve the energy requirements of milling and other industrial activities (Wilson, 1968, ch. 5; Huizinga, 1968, 15f.; Davids, 1995, 338).[3]

The rich herring stocks of the North Sea were an early interest of communities strategically situated to exploit them. The herring fishery of Holland
and Zeeland grew into a large industry; at the beginning of the seventeenth
century, 450 boats were engaged in it, and 80 percent of their catch was
processed in their home ports for export (Haak, 1984, 162). The shipbuild-
ing and seafaring skills required for fishing were not dissimilar from those
needed to participate in the coastal trade between the Baltic and ports in
Britain, France, and Spain as well as among the Low Countries themselves.
The invention of a vessel specifically designed for bulk carriage at the end of
the sixteenth century enabled the Dutch to dominate the transport of low-
value goods such as Russian grain, Norwegian timber, and Swedish iron and
steel (Wilson, 1968, 23). The coastal regions of the United Provinces became
"the warehouse of the western world" (Rowen, 1972, 143). As early as 1596,
the city of Amsterdam boasted in a report to the States General of the republic
that Dutch trade and shipping had surpassed that of England and France
(Huizinga, 1968, 21). As of 1670, "the Dutch owned . . . more than the
tonnage of England, France, Portugal, Spain, and the Germanies combined,
[and] the percentage of Dutch-*built* ships was even larger" (Hart, 1993, 16).

By the early seventeenth century, the naval power of the United Provinces
had grown to rival that of any other European state, and like the other leading
maritime nations, the republic began to accumulate an overseas empire in
America and the East Indies. Many of the colonial possessions were subsequently lost in the wars with other European nations that punctuated the
latter half of the seventeenth century, but the Dutch East Indies and West
Indies Companies succeeded in retaining a network of bases in both hemispheres that supported a large and lucrative overseas trade well into the eighteenth century (Israel, 1995, 934f.).[4] Dutch ships began to enter the Mediterranean trade in large numbers in the early seventeenth century. Supplied

3. Wilson notes that Dutch engineers were sought after throughout Europe for the
construction of drainage projects, canals, and other hydraulic works (1968, 74).

4. The East and West Indies Companies were chartered in 1602 and 1621, respectively,
with monopolies of Dutch trade in the two hemispheres. Though subject to the supervision
of the States General of the Republic, they had, in practice, powers that one normally
regards as reserved to a national state, such as the ability to negotiate treaties, to wage war
if attacked, and to build fortresses as well as trading posts. Marjolein 't Hart says that they
"constituted, in fact, extra-territorial states within the Dutch Republic" (1993, 23).

with oriental commodities by the East India Company, they were able to compete effectively with Venice and Genoa because the long voyage around the Cape of Good Hope (settled by Dutch "Boers" [farmers] in 1652) proved to be cheaper than the overland route to the Levant on which the Italian cities depended (Geyl, 1961, 160).

As with Venice and, in our own time, communities such as Hong Kong and Singapore, exploitation of the republic's maritime advantage provided a catalyst for other economic activities. Founded in 1609 to finance trade, the Bank of Amsterdam helped to make that city not only Europe's leading merchandise entrepôt but its dominant financial center as well. In that role it quickly outstripped Venice and Genoa, and despite the rise of London, retained its leadership until the end of the eighteenth century (Geyl, 1961, 161). The textile industry of Leiden became the largest in Europe (Hart, 1989, 668). Access to markets stimulated the growth of manufacturing in the inland provinces as well as in the coastal towns and cities. The Dutch became leaders in the industrial application of scientific knowledge, which added to their geographical position another potent source of competitive advantage in foreign markets.[5] The impact of these developments differed among the provinces, but generally the Netherlands experienced an "industrial revolution" well before the date commonly given in history textbooks, which locate its beginnings in later eighteenth-century England.[6]

Throughout this period, the United Provinces operated with a political system that seems almost deliberately designed to render effective governance impossible. But the facts are plain: the Dutch not only succeeded in winning their political independence from Spain, but also fought England and France to a standstill on land and at sea while becoming the wealthiest nation in Europe. Sir William Temple, who had served as the English ambassador to The Hague, observed in 1673 that the Dutch were "the Envy of some, the Fear of others, and the Wonder of all their Neighbours." He identified "the form of this government," which he proceeded to describe, as "the chief ingredient" of their remarkable accomplishment (1972, 1, 5).

5. Karel Davids contends, "This advanced position in technological development was a key element in the economic primacy of the Dutch Republic. Economic expansion in the United Provinces between around 1580 and 1680 would have been far less impressive than it was, if there had not appeared a wide array of new artifacts and new techniques for making things" (Davids, 1995, 338).

6. Jacob and Mijnhardt refer to the Dutch Republic in the mid-seventeenth century as "probably, per capita, the richest nation in the world and the most influential in international politics" (1992, 2). Angus Maddison's comparative estimates of per capita gross national products show the Netherlands in first place from at least as early as 1700 until 1785, when England took the lead (1982, 29f.).

Population and Urbanization

By comparison with England, France, and Spain, the Dutch Republic was a small country in both area and population. At the time of the Revolt, the population was less than 1.5 million. It grew during the succeeding century, but barely touched 2 million by 1750 (De Vries, 1985, 662). Much more important, however, was that this population was urbanized to an exceptional degree for the time. Amsterdam contained fewer than 15,000 people in 1514. By 1622, its population exceeded 100,000, and by 1675, 200,000, making it one of the largest cities in Europe. The other towns were much smaller than Amsterdam, but they were also important as economic, political, and cultural centers. In 1550, a quarter of the population lived in towns of more than 10,000 inhabitants, and by 1675, a quarter were in towns of more than 20,000 (De Vries, 1985, 662; Hart, 1989, 665).[7]

The population history of the Golden Age largely reflected the growth of an urban populace, with urban economic interests and "bourgeois" cultural values. Moreover, the towns were concentrated within a small area and were linked by waterways that afforded not only cheap transport of goods but also the easy and rapid movement of people among them. Elsewhere in Europe, cities and towns were typically insular communities, often deliberately built on hilltops or other places that hindered access, with walls that made them into fortresses capable of resisting the ever-present danger of raiding parties from neighboring towns. This medieval urban design did not characterize the towns of the Low Countries. They were open to each other, and though each was highly sensitive to its own particular interests, they composed an interactive complex of urban centers whose common interests were evident. The political system that developed in the republic was based upon the governments of the towns. The urban population never constituted a numerical majority in the United Provinces, but it was the part of the population that was politically organized, and for that reason it dominated the whole. In England and France, London and Paris were singular centers of national politics. Amsterdam never achieved a similar status; even within the province of Holland, it had to share political power with sixteen other urban centers that sent representatives to the provincial assembly, or "States." Though the degree of urbanization was much greater in the United Provinces than in England or France, political power was much more dispersed. It was largely be-

---

7. By comparison with other European areas, the Low Countries were exceptionally urbanized. As of 1650, the proportion of the population that was urban was 32 percent in the northern seven provinces and 21 percent in the ten southern ones. In Portugal, the next highest, it was 17 percent, in Italy 14 percent, and in Spain and in England and Wales it was a mere 9 percent (De Vries, 1984, 39).

cause of the pattern of urbanization that had developed in the Low Countries from late medieval times that the Dutch Republic adopted a pluralist form of political organization. Except for Switzerland, it was the first nation to construct a federal form of government.

Social Structure

Describing the province of Holland in the 1670s, Temple identified five classes in the population: (1) farmers, (2) mariners, (3) merchants, (4) *Renteeners,* whom he defined as "men that live . . . in all their chief cities upon the rents or interest of estates formerly acquired in their families," and (5) "Gentlemen or Nobles." This last class, he went on to note, were few in number and were "prideful of their noble status" (1972, 82f.).

Elsewhere in Europe, except in a small number of commercial city-states such as Venice, Florence, and Genoa, political power and personal wealth, as a consequence of feudalism, derived from the ownership of land. The experience of the Low Countries was significantly different. A great deal of its area consisted of swamps and shallow submarine regions until they were converted into arable territory by drainage and diking projects, which had begun as early as the eleventh century. As these new lands were created, they were not organized into feudal fiefs belonging to the noble class, but were divided into family farms whose possessors enjoyed full property rights in the fields they cultivated and in the crops and herds they raised on them. Moreover, much of the land that had been feudal in the inland areas was gradually transformed into freeholds. By the seventeenth century, there was little that remained of a feudal past in the northern provinces of the Low Countries. In sum, land in the Dutch Republic was simply a species of private property, and the noble class lacked any significant economic base to support a claim to high social status. A Dutch nobility continued to exist as a distinct social class, numbering some 200 families, and though their political power was greatly inferior to that of the merchants, it was not altogether negligible (Griffiths, 1959–1960, 453; De Vries, 1973; Israel, 1994; Speck, 1995, 189).

In assessing the Dutch social structure in terms of its political role, it is somewhat misleading, however, to refer generally to the "merchant class," because the town governments were monopolized by an elite echelon of merchant families that constituted a small, closed, subclass. This governing elite, or "Regents" as they were called, continued to retain their business interests, but as the seventeenth century wore on, they devoted an increasing proportion of their time to governmental activities, and their sons were educated to play roles in public service (Rowen, 1972, 143). In the Dutch Republic, political power was not derived from land, but the possession of great wealth was an essential precondition of it. The town governments of the Republic—the base of its federal political system—were oligarchies (Price, 1994, 34). The republic was not a "democracy," if that term is meant to denote a polity in which there is wide participation of the general populace in the affairs of state. Like Renaissance Venice, the Dutch Republic anticipated the modern world, not in the development of democracy, but in constructing a pluralist system of political organization in which political power, despite its social class exclusivity, was dispersed and controlled.

The Dutch Republic was a "bourgeois" state—the first nation in Europe, according to Jan De Vries, "to throw off a monarchical regime and bring a bourgeois social class to full political power" (1973, 191). In addition to its role in the history of constitutionalism, the republic was important in the early development of the essential features of modern capitalism: private property, production for sale in general markets, and the dominance of the profit motive in the behavior of producers and traders. Sir William Temple was impressed by the rationality and pragmatism of the Dutch, remarking that "Appetites and Passions seem to run lower and cooler" in the United Provinces than in other countries that he had observed—with the exception of "Avarice." He was, apparently, not the only foreign observer to note that the Dutch exhibited extraordinary dedication to the pursuit of material wealth.[8] Unlike most others, however, Temple did not regard avarice as necessarily evil. He went on to note that where this passion "feeds only upon Industry and Parsimony [as, presumably, it did in the Republic] it is less violent" than "where it breaks into Fraud, Rapine, and Oppression" (1972, 88). The cupidity of the Dutch was channeled in directions that were socially constructive. In writing this, Temple anticipated the notion advanced by Bernard Mandeville, a Hollander who had migrated to England, that "private vices" may be the engine of "public benefits." Mandeville's *The Grumbling Hive* (1705) and *The Fable of the Bees* (1714), which when published were reviled as morally repugnant, have frequently been noted by historians of economic theory as foreshadowing Adam Smith's famous remark that in seeking his own gain, the businessman may be led "as if by an invisible hand" to serve the public interest. Even today, after more than two centuries of economic analysis of the market economy, most people disagree, believing apparently that avarice is a moral defect in any person and an unambiguous social evil. But whatever might be said of economic theory, the Dutch Republic, like Venice, demonstrated empirically that a society dominated by so-

8. Pieter Geyl notes, "Numerous witnesses hailing from the Catholic countries of Europe were shocked to find that greed of gain seemed the prime motive power not only of the leading class, but of the entire community" (1961, 248).

called bourgeois values may yet be capable of great political, intellectual, and cultural achievements.

Religion and Civic Liberty

The toleration of minority religious views, and the institutional separation of church and state, are widely accepted in the West today as fundamental constitutional principles. These principles have been established longer, and more firmly, in Protestant countries than Catholic ones, but not because the political theories of the major early Protestant theologians supported such views. Martin Luther held his own theology with complete conviction, regarded all others (including other Protestant ones) as heretical, and expected that a wise and godly state would use its powers without stint to promote the one true religion and stamp out all others. The same was true of John Calvin, whose theology was embraced by most of the Dutch who rejected the Catholic Church.

The rebellion of the Low Countries against Habsburg rule culminated in the creation of a nation by the union of the seven northern provinces that were officially Calvinist, while the southern provinces that remained under Spanish rule continued to be Catholic. From the standpoint of political theory, the significance of this split was not that the Dutch Republic was Protestant, but that it became the first nation in Europe to tolerate a plurality of religious confessions and to adopt, in practice, the separation of church and state.

From the birth of the republic, the Dutch Reformed Church was the official state church, but it was then, and remained, a minority confession. Modern historical research has shown that the notion that the Dutch quickly and almost universally embraced Calvinism is erroneous. Defection from the Catholic Church was a long and gradual process. Fully reliable data on the religious demography of the republic is not available, but it appears that, as at the beginning of the seventeenth century, Catholics constituted about half of the population and at its end they still composed more than a third. Moreover, not all who rejected Catholicism embraced Calvinism: in various places there were substantial numbers of Baptists, Lutherans, and Mennonites. In Amsterdam, a large Jewish community existed. The Catholic and Calvinist groups were the largest, but neither was unified in its profession of faith: Catholics were divided over the issue of Jansenism, and Calvinists split into Arminian and orthodox factions (Duke, 1985, 111; Price, 1994, 260f.; Israel, 1995, 649f.).

The dominant faction in the Reformed Church insisted on strict adherence to Calvinist doctrine, and persistently urged that the power and authority of the state be employed to suppress heresy. Article 36 of the church's "Confession of Faith" declared that the state is a divinely ordained institution that is obligated to promote the "true" religion (Gelderen, 1992, 229). This mandate was at variance with the Treaty of Utrecht (1579) through which the northern seven provinces of the Netherlands had become a political union, which provided that "each person shall remain free in his religion and no one shall be investigated or persecuted because of his religion" (Bergsma, 1995, 203). The reference to persecution here was undoubtedly to the Spanish Inquisition, which had played a large part in motivating Netherlanders to rebel. In the opinions of some Calvinists, the general rejection of pressure to conform to a state religion applied also to the United Provinces, in which their own Reformed Church was accorded official status. But other Calvinists were of a very different opinion. During the second decade of the seventeenth century, the Reformed Church split into two irreconcilable factions: the Remonstrants, who advocated a general policy of religious toleration, and the Counter-Remonstrants, who insisted that Calvinists were under a divine obligation to destroy religious heresy in all of its forms.

The liberal viewpoint was expressed as early as 1564 by William of Orange, who though still an official in Philip's government, boldly attacked the policy of persecution. The doctrine of religious toleration was forcefully advanced by Caspar Coolhaes, who held that the Revolt was essentially motivated by the desire for religious freedom: he advocated a tolerant and open church that would recognize no group as possessing a monopoly of religious truth (Gelderen, 1992, 235). Coolhaes was excommunicated, but his view was restated as a philosophical principle by the powerful voice of Jacobus Arminius (1560–1609), professor of theology at the University of Leiden. The eponymous term "Arminianism" entered the language as referring to liberal theological views and, especially, to political toleration of religious diversity.[9]

A national synod was convened at Dordrecht in 1618 to consider the issue. The views of the Counter-Remonstrants prevailed, and the Reformed Church fell under their complete domination. The document issued by the synod upon its conclusion indicates that the victors regarded themselves as mandated to

9. The "Remonstrants" took their name from a "Remonstrance" drawn up by Simon Episcopus, a disciple of Arminius. In Jonathan Israel's view, Episcopus deserves a more prominent place in the history of political theory than Arminius, because "only Episcopus . . . developed a fully fledged doctrine of toleration, breaking with the premises of the past, arguing for unrestricted freedom of practice, as well as conscience, for all Churches and individuals . . . According to Episcopus . . . a wide variety of views may legitimately be derived from Scripture, which means that diversity of belief is not harmful, and indeed has a certain validity, in God's eyes, each strand comprising fragments of truth . . . Disparity in interpreting Scripture Episcopus thus elevates to a positive good, where for . . . the Counter-Remonstrants such diversity is a plague" (1995, 502f.).

purge the Church of Remonstrants, and to insist that the power of the state be used to eliminate all other religious institutions.[10] Liberal Calvinist clerics were driven from their pulpits, and some of the provincial and local authorities were persuaded to institute repressive measures against other Protestants, Catholics, and Jews (Price, 1994, 271f.; Israel, 1995, 460f., 476).

The Counter-Remonstrants won the battle of Dordrecht, but they failed to win the war. The brand of Calvinism they insisted upon prescribed severe restraints upon personal behavior and strict doctrinal tests for church membership that, had they been imposed, would have been deeply resented, even by many who professed the Calvinist faith. Rioting by Remonstrant supporters broke out in a number of towns, and it was apparent that the very existence of the Union was threatened by the religious policies espoused by church authorities. The key factor in the situation was the regency. Without the support of the town magistracies that the regents monopolized, the policy of repression could not be implemented, let alone succeed. The insistence of the Counter-Remonstrants forced the regents, in effect, to choose between religious toleration and the high probability of civil war. Such an event would have threatened the ability of the republic to defend itself against foreign enemies, so for the merchant class, whose prosperity depended upon the uninterrupted flow of trade, it was hardly an option. The economic interests of the regents were identified with those of the merchants, and their roles as town governors led them to resent interference by the church in political matters. The fundamentalists in the Dutch Reformed Church did not abandon their aim to create a Calvinist nation, however. As late as the 1690s they made concerted efforts to enlist the state as an active weapon against their theological opponents (Geyl, 1956, 202f.; Price, 1994, 86; Israel, 1995, 468f., 929).

Unwittingly, the orthodox Calvinists helped to establish religious toleration as the actual, if not the official, policy of the republic. At the time, this was a novelty that most political observers would have rejected as depriving the nation of the "unity" that was generally regarded to be an essential ingredient of a stable polity. Writing in the mid-eighteenth century, David Hume observed, "Before the United Provinces set the example, toleration was deemed incompatible with good government; and it was thought impossible that a number of religious sects could live together in harmony and peace . . . England [he continued] has set a like example of civil liberty" (1953, 6).

The republic was not by any means a society of complete civic or religious freedom during its Golden Age. Catholics, Jews, and Protestant noncon-

---

10. The document is printed, in English translation, in Rowen (1972, 138–142).

formists were excluded from the governing class and had to be circumspect in practicing their religion; censorship of printed matter was comprehensive, barring the expression of extremely radical ideas such as atheism and Arianism, and the Dutch populace at large remained doubtful that any state could afford to permit unlimited freedom of expression. The Dutch valued civic order as well as personal freedom, and they had limited tolerance of behavior and ideas that were regarded as undermining the foundations of social stability (Israel, 1995, 637f., 676f., 915f.). Baruch Spinoza, whose political philosophy was well in advance of his time, was expelled by the Jewish congregation of Amsterdam on its own initiative, and his *Tractatus Theologico-Politicus* (1670) was banned by the civic authorities as seditious. Practical politics in the republic was characterized by strong factional dispute and could be an exceedingly hazardous activity. Johan van Oldenbarnevelt, who as advocate general of Holland played an important role in the government of the republic during a critical period, earned the bitter enmity of the stadholder, Prince Maurice, who seized the opportunity presented by Oldenbarnevelt's support of the losing side in the Remonstrant affair to have him summarily tried and executed. Hugo Grotius, as pensionary of Rotterdam, became entangled in the same events and was sentenced to life imprisonment. He escaped and wrote his celebrated treatise on international law, *De Jure Belli ac Pacis* (1625), as an exile in France. The notion that tolerance and personal freedom in the seventeenth-century Dutch Republic was firmly established on the basis of widely accepted philosophic principles, not merely pragmatic necessity, is an exaggeration of an overenthusiastic earlier historiography, which modern scholars have been at pains to correct.

Nevertheless the Dutch Republic was, in comparative terms, the freest nation in Europe. This was not only due to its policy of religious toleration. The pluralist nature of its federal political organization was unique on a continent where centralization of political power and its exercise by absolute monarchs was almost everywhere ascendant. Only in the rather insignificant "Generality Lands," administered directly by the States General at The Hague, were the people ruled by a single government. Other rural folk were subject to two governments and their bureaucracies, town dwellers to three. The lines of jurisdiction between these authorities were unclear, and the power of each was constrained by the others. Some contemporary observers appreciated the connection between the republic's constitution and its reputation for freedom. Sir William Temple, remarking upon the great number of foreigners who migrated to the Dutch towns in search of "quiet in their lives, and safety in their Possessions and Trades," noted that there was good reason for their choice because, by virtue of the Dutch "Constitution . . . , neither the States-General nor the Prince have any Power to invade any man's

Person or Property within the precincts of their Cities. Nor could it be fear'd that the Senate of any Town should conspire to any such violence; nor if they did, could they possibly execute it, having no Soldiers in their pay, and the Burgers only being employed in the defence of their Towns, and execution of all Civic Justice among them" (1972, 112; see also Wilson, 1968, 165f.).

Temple was not alone in remarking upon the migration of foreigners into the republic. It was too conspicuous a phenomenon to escape notice. Flemings came in large numbers, fleeing from religious persecution in the southern provinces; Huguenots from France arrived for the same reason; and Sephardic Jews, who had failed to find a satisfactory lodgment after their religion had been proscribed in Spain and Portugal at the end of the fifteenth century. Many of these immigrants had skills that were in high demand in the developing economy of the United Provinces (Wilson, 1968, 165f.; Haley, 1972, 166f.; De Vries, 1985, 667; Davids, 1995, 342). Deserving special notice in any history of political ideas is John Locke, who fled to Holland in 1683 with his patron Lord Shaftesbury to escape charges of treason in Restoration England. During his exile there, Locke wrote his famous treatises *Of Civil Government* and his essay *Concerning Toleration*, which were published upon his return to England with the Revolution of 1688.

Cultural and Intellectual Development

The Dutch Republic not only attracted foreigners of talent, but also released within its own people an efflorescence of achievement that made it, for a brief but significant period, a widely acknowledged center of European scholarship, science, and art.[11] This development was undoubtedly due in some measure to the fact that the Dutch escaped from the thought control of the papacy while evading that of its own Reformed Church. It also reflects the need, in a commercial society, for the services of literate and numerate people whose skills, though initially acquired for narrow vocational purposes, opened broader intellectual and cultural vistas. Compared to other nations, an exceptionally high proportion of the Dutch population was literate, and it has been estimated that as much as a third of Amsterdam's upper-class males attended university (Burke, 1994, 91). Their favored subject was law, the study of which was not only of immediate practical value for merchants, but also had great potential to awaken interest in political philosophy and ethics. A large publishing industry flourished, serving a market that was growing in both demand and supply as the numbers of readers and writers, domestic and

11. "If we consider all aspects of intellectual achievement, the United Provinces rank, together with France and England, as one of the three chief centers of European thought from the end of the sixteenth down to the early eighteenth century" (Israel, 1995, 899).

foreign, continued to increase. It has been estimated that during the seventeenth century, the average production of Dutch publishers amounted to more than a thousand titles per year. Many English works were first published in Holland (Wilson, 1968, 155f.; Spufford, 1995, 278n.).

The excellence of Dutch education antedates the Revolt and provided a foundation for one of the most notable developments of the early Revolt period: the creation of universities. The first of these was the University of Leiden, established by the provincial government of Holland in 1575. By the middle of the seventeenth century, four more provincial universities had been founded, at Franeker, Groningen, Utrecht, and Harderwijk. During its Golden Age, the Dutch Republic could boast the largest national complex of universities in Europe, each independent of the others and all protected by their provincial sponsors from interference by the Reformed Church. By the 1640s, the University of Leiden was the largest in the Protestant world, with an extensive library. It offered instruction not only in theology and law, but also in classical studies, history, mathematics, and medicine. Many students came from foreign lands. The effect of the Dutch universities on the early modern mind exceeded that of academic institutions in England or France (Geyl, 1966, 287f.; Kossmann, 1991, 295; Cook, 1992, 116, 120; Israel, 1995, 569–575, 899–902).[12]

To the seventeenth-century European, the great philosophical schism of the period was the conflict between Protestantism and Catholicism, but from the vantage point of today, a more fundamental debate was that which followed the publication, in 1637, of René Decartes's *Discourse on Method*. This debate ended the long intellectual dominance of Aristotelianism and Thomism, detached natural philosophy from theology, and established the foundations for what historians now call the Scientific Revolution. The Dutch Republic was the initial venue of this quantum leap in the development of the modern age.

In 1617, at the age of twenty-one, Descartes visited the Netherlands for the purpose of studying the innovations in military tactics that had brought widespread fame to the Dutch stadholder Maurice of Nassau. While there, he met Isaac Beeckman, a Middelburg candlemaker whose interest in natural

12. Israel gives data on Dutch and foreign students at the University of Leiden, 1575–1794. During the last quarter of the seventeenth century, foreigners constituted 44 percent of the enrollment (1995, 901). Charles Wilson notes that, in 1700, one-third of Leiden's students were English or Scottish (1968, 183). One of the main themes of Wilson's book is the close contact that pertained between England and the Netherlands during the seventeenth century, at all levels—scholarly, artistic, scientific, and economic. Despite their commercial rivalry and the series of Anglo-Dutch wars, the affinity felt by the English for the Dutch was greater than for any other people of Europe. (See also Hill, 1965, 283f.).

phenomena was both broad and profound. Beeckman resurrected the ancient notion of atomism, and, in his work on mechanics and hydrodynamics utilized the experimental procedures and the application of mathematics that Galileo had pioneered. It was apparently Beeckman who persuaded Descartes that natural phenomena provided more interesting material for study than did warfare. When Descartes went back to France, he studied medicine, chemistry, and optics, and began to develop his ideas for a new philosophical system. Aware that his philosophy was distinctly at variance with Christian doctrine, he returned to the more tolerant climate of the Netherlands in 1628 and lived there for the next twenty years. His major works, including the momentous *Discourse on Method,* were written and published in the Netherlands. "The Dutch Republic," writes a modern historian of science, "did not just provide a series of places for Descartes to live and write: his encounters with Dutch intellectual colleagues helped shape the development of his philosophy, both for him and for his interpreters" (Cook, 1992, 130). It is doubtful that an open debate on Descartes's mechanistic view of nature could have taken place in any other place in Europe during the mid-seventeenth century. In Catholic countries the book was quickly declared heretical by the church, which was fully supported by the power of the state. In the republic, the Reformed Church was equally hostile but lacked the ability to suppress it.[13]

Galileo had painfully discovered that a scientist could not defend himself from a charge of religious heresy by arguing that the study of nature was independent of theology, and the patronage of even as powerful a prince as Cosimo de Medici proved incapable of protecting him from the enmity of the church. The Holy Office forced Galileo to abjure Copernican cosmology in 1633—an event that must have had a chilling effect on Italian science, which until the Golden Age of the Dutch Republic was the most highly developed in Europe. Dutch scientists were not entirely immune from similar hazards, but the relatively high degree of intellectual freedom in the republic permitted the uninhibited investigation of natural phenomena.[14] The number of Dutch scientists was large, and their contributions were important in the development of modern scientific knowledge and its investigative technology. For example, Christiaan Huygens married mathematics to science, formulated the wave theory of light, discovered the laws of reflection and refraction, and applied Galileo's discovery of the isochronal behavior of the pendulum to the construction of the first reliable clock. Cornelis Drebbel invented the microscope and the thermometer, which greatly extended the observational

13. On the development of the mechanistic philosophy in the Dutch Republic, see Cook (1992) and Israel (1995, 581–587, 889–899).

14. The manuscript of Galileo's *Two New Sciences* was smuggled out of Italy to the Dutch Republic and published in Leiden.

capacities of scientists. Jan Swammerdam applied the technique of microscopy to make pioneering observations in human anatomy and entomology. Anthony van Leeuwenhoek greatly improved the microscope and used it to discover bacteria, thus revealing a domain of organic life whose existence had not previously been suspected (Geyl, 1964, 227f.; Haley, 1972, 147f.; Cook, 1992, 133; Israel, 1995, 903–909).[15]

Dutch science remained vigorous well into the eighteenth century. The great botanical garden of the University of Leiden, furnished with many exotic species supplied by the ships of the East and West Indies Companies, attracted the attention of the Swedish botanist Carolus Linnaeus, who spent several years in the republic completing his monumental work in taxonomy, the *Systema Natura,* which was published in Leiden in 1735. Relations between Dutch and English scientists were especially close, from early in the seventeenth century. The Royal Society, founded in London in 1660 for the promotion of science, was a latecomer by Dutch standards, but several Dutch scientists were pleased to become members of it. Many of Huygens's and Leeuwenhoek's important discoveries were communicated to the Royal Society and first saw publication in its *Transactions.* When Isaac Newton's great *Principia* was published in 1687, Dutch scientists were quick to appreciate its significance and played an important role in transmitting Newtonian mechanics to the rest of Europe (Wilson, 1968, 100f.; Cook, 1992, 120; Snelders, 1992, 308f.; Israel, 1995, 1043).

The rise of science in other European states, especially in England, eventually undermined the republic's position of leadership. The replacement of Latin as a universal vehicle of scholarly communication by the various vernacular languages created a barrier between Dutch scientists and their foreign counterparts, because there were few people outside the Netherlands who could read Dutch. Not until the later twentieth century did Dutch scholars and scientists accept the fact that if they expected their work to receive more than domestic notice, they would have to publish in English—which had become the new lingua franca. In the interim, the productivity and repute of Dutch science declined to a low level. Until quite recently, the role that the Dutch Republic had played in the development of modern science was little appreciated, even by historians.

Much better known, and more widely, is the place of the Dutch Republic in the history of art. Indeed the term "Golden Age" is sometimes used specifically to denote the efflorescence of Dutch painting in the seventeenth

15. Cook (1992) deserves special note as a brief, but comprehensive, examination of the role of the Netherlands in the early development of modern science. He emphasizes the importance of Dutch scientists in investigating the details of natural phenomena, rather than in the construction of a grand philosophical system. See also Snelders (1992).

century. This was a remarkable development, during which a distinctive Dutch School emerged that became second only to the Renaissance contributions of northern Italy in the artistic development of the modern West.

In their treatments of the Dutch School, comprehensive modern surveys of the history of art such as H. W. Janson's (1986) usually concentrate on three outstanding master painters: Rembrandt van Rijn, Frans Hals, and Jan Vermeer. But if one turns to books devoted specifically to the Dutch School, an enormous community of lesser, but nevertheless excellent, artists appears. Haak's recent survey of the period from 1560 to 1680 contains the names of more than 400 artists whose works merit modern notice (1984). Quantitative researchers have estimated that, as of the middle of the seventeenth century, some 700 painters were active, mostly in the province of Holland, producing at the rate of more than 60,000 works a year (North, 1995, 285). The pictorial arts constituted a major industry, which supplied, and created, a growing market for art works in the republic and abroad.[16]

Though they made important innovations of their own, Dutch artists were initially inspired by the work of Italian painters, especially Caravaggio, whose realistic style appealed to the Dutch preference for empiricism over classical symbolism (Janson, 1986, 526, 528). The overland trade route from northern Italy to the Low Countries was as important in facilitating an exchange of artistic and intellectual ideas as it was in commerce. But there was a striking difference between Italian and Dutch art in the themes depicted. Modern visitors to a large art gallery will find, in the rooms containing Italian works, a seemingly endless procession of scenes from the Garden of Eden, the life and death of Christ, the martyrdoms of saints, and other stories from the Old and New Testaments. When they move on to the Dutch School, however, the walls are filled with landscapes; tavern scenes; group portraits of civic guards; paintings of carousing soldiers, town burgomasters, the governing boards of charitable institutions, and artisans at work; as well as kitchen scenes depicting in exquisitely realistic detail food items, cooking utensils, busy housewives, and other renderings of commonplace contemporary life. Secular themes are present in the Italian gallery, and religious ones in the Dutch, but the difference in predominant weight is striking. The Dutch Revolt began with anti-Catholic rioting that vented itself in the destruction of religious "images," foreshadowing a growing secularism that was reflected in the tastes of Dutch painters and their customers.[17]

16. By the last decade of the sixteenth century, writes Jonathan Israel, "an abundance of artistic talent of stunning sophistication was already in place, making possible an outpouring of art, the like of which, in terms of quantity, quality, and variety, has never been equalled by any other society or age" (1995, 549f.).

17. Michael North observes that the popularity of secular themes in European art gen-

Like other people in a division-of-labor economy, artists cannot live without customers. The Italian painters of the high Renaissance worked for clients on a "made-to-order" basis. Churches and other institutions (like the great *scuole* of Venice) commissioned artists to provide canvases or frescoes on contractually specified themes. City governments commissioned similarly specified works to adorn public buildings. Wealthy individuals contracted for portraits of themselves and their families and sponsored other works. In the Netherlands, many works of art were also commissioned, but there developed as well a general market in which both new and old works could be bought and sold. Painters sent most of their canvases to art dealers, who offered them for sale like any other commodity. The large size of the market permitted artists to specialize in particular genres, such as seascapes or still lifes, which enabled craftsmen of less than magisterial talent to produce paintings of acceptable technical quality and artistic value, and to turn them out more quickly, at lower cost. The great Rembrandt was not too proud to use the technique of copperplate etching for original works, which distributed their initial cost of production over multiple copies (Janson, 1986, 531f.). Middle-class Dutchmen, even of modest means, could buy works of art for their own homes, for speculative resale, or for longer-term investment. For a time, art collection in the republic amounted to a mania, though it never attained the level of the famous tulip mania of the 1630s. Export sales of paintings were considerable, and Amsterdam added the art trade to the other activities in which it was the commercial center of Europe.

Some of the great artists of the Italian Renaissance may have regarded themselves as exceptional individuals, selected by God to celebrate his glory and to fortify the Christian faith, but most of them had the social status of craftsmen, without any more pretension to lofty rank than the masters of other skilled trades.[18] The Dutch artists of the Golden Age were equally, or even more, pedestrian in their pretensions. Their singleminded focus on the commercial value of their work is only surprising if one fails to recognize that the view of the artist as a philosopher, endowed with special power to grasp and reveal the human condition, is a modern conceit that did not enter the

erally was increased by the Reformation, which "inspired a fundamental change in the function of paintings . . . This development reached its climax, however, in the seventeenth-century Dutch Republic, where the proportion of [secular] paintings rose from 65 percent at the beginning of the century to 90 percent at the end" (1995, 297f.).

18. This was especially true of Venice, which, unlike Florence and Rome, had no prince-sponsored "academies" of artists. Venetian painters "were registered together with other artisans in a guild, the Scuola dei Depentori, and were regarded as craftsmen in the social class of the *popolano*" (North, 1995, 298).

mentalité of the West until Romanticism began to infect European literature, art, and political theory in the nineteenth century.

The Political History of the Republic, 1566–1814

As we have already seen, the Golden Age marked important developments in Western science and art, and in the religious controversies of the early Reformation period that laid the foundation for toleration of diversity and the separation of church and state. In regard to the history of constitutionalism the republic also deserves recognition, and study, as the first nation-state in history to adopt a pluralist structure of political organization. The object of this section is to provide the reader who is unfamiliar with the history of the republic with a sketch of the main events that constitute the background for the developments in political organization and theory that will soon engage our attention.[19]

The Revolt

The region of northwest Europe, where the waters of the Rhine, Meuse, and Schelde flow into the sea, form an extended delta that, together with contiguous inland areas, came into the possession of the dukes of Burgundy in the late fourteenth century. Through a series of marriages, the seventeen provinces that constituted the Low Countries became part of the sprawling Habsburg empire in the late fifteenth century. Charles V, elected Holy Roman Emperor in 1519, inherited suzerainty over them from his father and, from his mother, the crown of Spain. Charles abdicated in 1555, and his vast empire was divided between his brother, who succeeded him as emperor, and his son, who became Philip II of Spain. The seventeen provinces, which came under Philip's rule, had never constituted a united political entity, and Philip was installed separately as Count of Holland and Zeeland, Lord of Friesland, Duke of Brabant, and so forth. The unification of the seven northern provinces into a distinct political entity was the result of their success in rebelling against Spain (Haak, 1984, 14f.; Gelderen, 1992, 1f.).

Philip resided briefly in Brussels, but had been born and raised in Spain and was "a Spaniard to his finger tips" (Rowen, 1972, xviii). In 1559, he took up permanent residence in Spain, leaving behind his half-sister, Margaret of Parma, as regent in the Low Countries. Seven years later, wide-

19. For a comprehensive history of the Dutch Republic, see Israel (1995). Though Rowen (1988) focuses primarily on the roles of the princes of Orange in the Dutch Republic, it is an excellent brief political history.

spread disorders broke out that historians have labeled the "Dutch Revolt." Sixty years of the eighty-two between the onset of the Revolt and Spain's acknowledgment of Dutch independence in 1648 were wracked by warfare, with high costs in lives and property (Parker, 1976, 53), but the period was nevertheless one of great social, economic, and cultural progress.

The ten southern provinces—now Belgium—remained under Spain. The disorders that initiated the Revolt reflected the growing spread of Calvinism in the Low Countries and the attempts of the authorities to suppress it. Long before Martin Luther and John Calvin came upon the scene, the Church of Rome had adopted a militant and uncompromising stance toward Christian sects that were deemed heretical. The papal office of the Inquisition was established in the early thirteenth century as the primary instrument of this policy.[20] In 1478 a separate inquisitorial institution was created in Spain, under the direct control of the monarch, whose intial object was to investigate covert Judaism among Jews who had formally converted to Catholicism. With the Reformation, both of these offices faced new challenges to the spiritual hegemony of the church. For the Spanish Inquisition, the chief locus of concern was the Netherlands, where Calvinism was making great inroads. Charles V regarded himself as "God's deputy on earth" with special responsibility as "protector of the true Catholic religion" (Gelderen, 1992, 30). He issued a series of edicts prescribing draconian punishment of heretics. In 1522, he ordered his inquisitorial office to pay special attention to the growth of Protestantism in the Low Country provinces. Philip II shared his father's view of monarchy and continued his campaign against heresy in the Netherlands. This, as well as his decree of new taxes, engendered widespread opposition, even on the part of Catholic burgomasters, who perceived his religious and fiscal policies as threatening their long-standing local autonomy (Geyl, 1966, 55f.; Gelderen, 1992, 36f.).[21]

The nature of the Revolt, and of the protracted war that followed, was evident from the beginning of the conflict—which most historians date at the summer of 1566, when widespread rioting broke out in Flanders and quickly spread throughout the Low Countries. This uprising has been called the

---

20. See Davies (1996, 361f.) for a brief account of the Albigensian Crusade, which initiated the church's attack on heresy with actions of unrestrained ferocity.

21. Most historians have treated Spanish behavior in the Netherlands as exceedingly barbaric. This view has been contested by Swart (1975) who contends that the traditional depiction is exaggerated to the point of myth, and that it ignores the tangible benefits that the Netherlands derived from their connection with Spain. Dutch historiography, in Swart's view, has contributed greatly to the undeserved "Black Legend" of sixteenth- and seventeenth-century Spain, which originated earlier in Italy, with the Spanish invasion of the peninsula.

"Iconoclastic Fury" because the rioters focused their attention on religious statues and other items of church property that zealous Protestants regarded as idolatrous images. The town authorities, who were mainly Catholic, did little to restrain the mobs, however, and in some places, assisted them in the destruction and effacement of church property (Gelderen, 1992, 82; Israel, 1995, 148–152). Despite the fact that their houses of worship were being defiled and their personal safety threatened, many Catholics of the Low Country provinces regarded Philip's policies as negatively as did Protestants. As early as December 1564, William of Orange, an official representative of the king as stadholder in three of the provinces, declared in the Council of State, "The king goes astray if he thinks that the Netherlands, in the midst of lands where freedom of religion exists, can continue to endure the blood-stained edicts . . . No matter how strongly I am attached to the Catholic faith, I cannot approve of princes who wish to govern the souls of their subjects and to deprive them of their liberty in matters of conscience and religion" (Haak, 1984, 17). But what appeared on the surface as a religious conflict was a rebellion of Netherlanders at large against the governance of a foreign power that refused to respect the rights and privileges, secular as well as religious, that they regarded as traditional.[22]

In April 1566, a petition signed by some 300 nobles was presented to the regent condemning the Inquisition as "the mother and cause of all disorder and iniquity" in the provinces and demanding that it be ended (Gelderen, 1992, 111).[23] Margaret announced that the policy of religious repression would be moderated, but the outbreak of the Iconoclastic Fury led Philip to dispatch troops under the command of the Duke of Alva to quell the disorders by force and to root out all opposition to his policies.[24] The Netherlanders had little ability to combat the invasion, and Alva's army swept through the country, initiating a bloody repression in its wake. The wholesale massacre of

22. "Alva's tyranny had exasperated the whole nation. The Spanish government, which had trampled under foot the liberties of all the provinces, was hardly less hateful to the catholic majority than the protestant minority" (Pirenne, 1963, 227). From the beginning of the revolt, writes Kossmann, "the religious problem was associated with the constitutional problem," that is, the demand that indigenous political institutions play a part in the governance of the Netherlands (1991, 285).

23. "The three main headings under which their grievances were grouped were that this essentially foreign prince had infringed the liberties and privileges to which he and his predecessors had sworn, that he had gone beyond the invasion of legal and political privileges in the excess of religious persecution, and that he had compounded all these abuses of his feudal and reciprocal obligations to his subjects by taxing them beyond right or reason" (Leeb, 1973, 14f.).

24. According to Gelderen, Alva aimed "to establish a new order in which there was no place for heresy. privileges, and local autonomy" (1992, 40; see also Pirenne, 1963, 226f.).

the population of Naarden by Alva's troops drew Catholic Netherlanders to the support of the rebellion (Parker, 1976, 54). William of Orange hurriedly attempted to organize a military defense, but it was quickly disposed of by Alva. William fled to his ancestral estates in Germany, resigned his stadholderships, and commenced to raise an army. Between 1568 and 1573, he made three attempts to invade the Netherlands, but his armies were no match for the forces under Alva's skillful command (Rowen, 1988, 12f.).[25]

The rebels were more successful at sea. Operating under letters of marque formally issued by William in his capacity as sovereign monarch of the independent principality of Orange, a group of seafaring Calvinists began to attack Spanish shipping in the English Channel and North Sea. In 1572, expelled by Queen Elizabeth from their bases in England, these "Sea Beggars" sailed across the Channel, captured the seacoast town of Brill, and in short order wrested most of Holland and Zeeland from Spanish control. Encouraged by their success, William issued a call for a general revolt in the Low Countries. It had little military effect, but it was a notable political document, serving almost as a manifesto of the Revolt. William recited the sufferings and torments that had been imposed on the people in the name of the Philip II "without his knowledge [sic], in violation of his oath, and contrary to the liberties and privileges of the country . . . With [God's] blessing [he declared] after expelling the tyrannical oppressors together we shall see the Netherlands in their ancient freedom, governed again without any violence, with proper obedience to King and security for your consciences, and according to the advice of the States General."[26] The prominent notion here and in other political documents of the Revolt period—that rebellion against established political authority is justified by the ruler's violation of his oath of office, and by disregard of long-standing privileges—punctuated the radical political thought of the West during the following two centuries.

Spain's campaign in the Netherlands was distracted by events elsewhere, and its forces there, deprived of Alva's leadership in 1573 and disheartened by the death of his successor three years later, fell into disorder. Meanwhile, the ability of the Dutch to mount an effective military opposition increased, especially after 1579 when, by the Union of Utrecht, the northern provinces formed an alliance to pursue a unified defense strategy. Under the command of William's successor, his son Maurice of Nassau, the armed forces grew pro-

25. William, Prince of Orange and Count of Nassau, inaccurately called "the Silent," was one of the richest members of the Dutch nobility, having inherited large properties in the Netherlands and Germany. His title as "Prince of Orange" was derived from his inheritance, from a cousin, of a small principality in the south of France, which is notable today only as the location of an exceptionally well-preserved Roman theater.

26. The full text of the document is printed in Rowen (1972, 40–42).

digiously in size and effectiveness—to the point where, by the end of the century, the republic was one of the major military and naval powers in Europe, capable of meeting the forces of Spain on equal terms (Israel, 1995, 253).[27] In the event, Spain succeeded in maintaining its authority in the provinces south of the rivers, but the seven northern ones won their independence.

The Adoption of Republicanism

The Dutch did not undertake to establish a new constitution. The political system that emerged consisted almost entirely of institutions that long antedated the Revolt. The political theory of the period was centrally concerned with justifying the Revolt, with virtually no attention to the issue of political organization. Prince William's declaration of 1572 focused upon the conditions under which it was legitimate for a people to rebel against their established government. The same is true of the Act of Abjuration declared by the States General in 1581, which rescinded the sovereignty of Philip II.[28] The Union of Utrecht of 1579, which formally created "The United Provinces of the Netherlands," was more like a treaty of alliance between independent states than the foundational document of a new political entity, and there is no indication in it that its signatories favored a republican form of government (Temple, 1972, 32f., 49, 52; Huizinga, 1968, 28; Rowen, 1972, 67; Haak, 1984, 24; Rowen, 1988, 23; Kossmann, 1991, 293; Israel, 1995, 209).

When the Dutch formally deposed Philip II, monarchy was generally regarded as the only viable form of government. Up to this point, and for some time afterward, few suggested that the union should be a republic. "In monarchical Europe" writes Pieter Geyl, "the Northern Netherlands was generally looked upon with scoffing unbelief" (1964, 19). The Dutch themselves regarded the acquisition of a new monarch to be essential.[29] In the mid-

---

27. Maurice was an exceptionally able commander, much admired in European military circles. Together with his Nassau cousins, he occupies a place in military history for introducing important innovations in field tactics and military training (Keegan, 1994, 327f., 342f.). Maurice successfully attacked the fortified towns on the southern and eastern borders of the United Provinces, which effectuated the stabilization of its frontiers (Rowen, 1988, 40). For a recent assessment of Maurice's place in military history, see Eltis (1995).

28. The full text of the Act of Abjuration is given in Rowen (1972, 92–105). Rowen observes in his introduction that it is "important in the history of political thought as the most explicit statement of the doctrine of the right of a people to throw off a tyrant and establish government by their own authority until the American Declaration of Independence in 1776."

29. Long after the renunciation of Philip II, writes Haitsma Mulier, "Political Theory in the United provinces continued to focus on the advantages and disadvantages of mon-

1570s, negotiations were initiated with the Duke of Anjou, brother of Henry III of France, to become monarch of the Netherlands. Anjou soon realized that he was expected to share power with the stadholder and be bound to act with the advice of the States General, which did not accord with his conception of sovereign status. In January 1583, he attempted to force the issue by a military coup and attacked Antwerp. The attempt was unsuccessful, and Anjou forthwith retired from the scene (Rowen, 1988, 24f.).

William had strongly supported the efforts to install the Duke of Anjou as monarch, but his main object in doing so was to enlist the military assistance of France in the contest with Spain. He had no intention of giving up his own power as stadholder and commander of the Dutch forces. With the abjuration of Philip, it was inevitable that he himself would be considered as a potential replacement. William was the ranking member of the Dutch nobility, he belonged to the wealthy and powerful House of Orange-Nassau, and he already possessed the royal title of "prince." More important perhaps for the ordinary Dutch citizen was the fact that he had opposed Philip's repressive policies from an early date, had organized the initial military defense against the Spanish armies, and despite disheartening defeats, had persisted in spearheading the political and military drive for independence. But he was assassinated by Spanish agents in July 1584, at the age of fifty-one. William was thoroughly familiar with the political traditions of the Netherlands and fully approved of its pluralistic structure. Had he lived, he might have inaugurated the first *constitutional* monarchy in history. Eventually, the United Provinces became such a monarchy, with the House of Orange as its hereditary royal family, but not until 1814. In the intervening two centuries, the princes of Orange played a leading role in the Dutch Republic and stood ready in the wings, so to say, to provide it with a monarch.

Arguments in favor of a republican form of government first began to be voiced in the Netherlands after the Anjou affair, but the notion that monarchy is necessary to political stability was still widely held as an axiom of political science. In February 1585, Henry III was invited to add the Netherlands to his royal possessions, but France was at this time embroiled in civil war, and Henry's position as a Catholic monarch who favored a moderate policy toward Protestantism was insecure. He declined the offer. The search for a new monarch next focused on Queen Elizabeth of England, a staunch Protestant who had supported the Dutch Revolt from its beginning. Elizabeth also declined, but offered to send an army, under the command of Robert Dudley,

---

archy. A republican theory began to be formulated only with the greatest reluctance and it took to the second half of the seventeenth century before it came to be seen as a real alternative" (1987, 179).

Earl of Leicester, to assist the Dutch in their struggle against Spain. The States General appointed Leicester "Governor and Captain General" in January 1586. He apparently assumed that he had been given absolute power, but as Herbert Rowen puts it, "Two years' time was enough for Leicester to display such military ineptitude and such political folly that he returned home a total failure" (1988, 36). For their part, the Dutch decided to abandon the search for a new sovereign and to proceed as they were, a de facto independent republic.

The forty years during which Maurice occupied his offices of state were ones of progress for the republic, but they were fraught with political strife that to a considerable degree reflected the ambiguous, quasi-monarchical status of the House of Orange-Nassau. As the Leicester regime was coming to its unlamented end, Johan van Oldenbarnevelt emerged as a political figure of outstanding competence and influence. He was appointed advocate of Holland in 1587, and for the next three decades, which were crucial in the shaping of the union as a republic, he dominated the government of the province, and the domestic and foreign policies of the States General.[30]

It was perhaps inevitable that Oldenbarnevelt and Maurice should come into conflict in a polity where the powers of the various governmental offices, and the spheres of jurisdiction between the provinces and the States General, were ambiguous. The tensions between them came to a head in 1617 over Oldenbarnevelt's attempt to form new military units in the towns to deal with sectarian rioting that the local authorities were unable, or unwilling, to control. Maurice perceived this as a dilution of his authority as army commander. In what some historians describe as a coup d'état and others call a "revolution," he arrested the leaders of what had now become identified as the "anti-Orangist" party. Oldenbarnevelt was quickly tried and executed; others, including Hugo Grotius, were sentenced to long prison terms, and Maurice quickly proceeded to replace hostile town governors with men who could be relied upon to support him in the States General. The danger of civil war was averted, but the United Provinces had moved a considerable step toward establishing a monarchy under the House of Orange.[31]

30. "Forty years of age in 1587, [Oldenbarnevelt] was at the height of his powers of mind and will, ready . . . to prove himself the equal of any statesman anywhere in his time. Although there were no such offices or titles, he became in practice both the prime minister and the foreign minister of the Dutch Republic . . . He was the true creator of the Dutch Republic, adapting the institutions inherited from the past for the work of republican government" (Rowen, 1988, 37; see also Price, 1994, 3f.; and Israel, 1995, 959).

31. Maurice succeeded to the title of "Prince of Orange" in 1618, upon the death of his older brother, who had remained Catholic and loyal to Spain. After the "revolution of 1618–19" observes Geyl, Maurice was "all powerful; so long as he lived, the Republic was in fact a monarchy" (1961, 77).

Maurice died in 1625 without heirs; his half-brother Frederick Henry became prince of Orange and was appointed stadholder of six of the provinces. He harbored monarchical ambitions and sought to strengthen the role of the House of Orange as a Dutch dynasty with hereditary claims to positions of state.[32] But a direct challenge to the republican form of government did not develop during his lifetime. The defining crisis took place within a few years of his death (in 1647), when his son William assumed the title of Prince of Orange and became stadholder.

William II was an energetic youth of twenty-one when Frederick Henry died. He had a "haughty and irascible temperament" (Israel, 1995, 596) and regarded his position as hereditary heir of the House of Orange as endowing him with autonomous political power not subject to modification or control by any of the governmental organs of the republic. Like his uncle forty years before, William passionately opposed any settlement with Spain that would leave the southern provinces under Spanish dominion, supported by ardent Calvinists who considered it their sacred duty to liberate the south from the grip of the papacy. Their opposition could not prevent the conclusion of peace with Spain in 1648, but William continued to hope that the war would be resumed and insisted that the republic maintain a large army in readiness for the conquest of the southern provinces. This policy led him into conflict with the province of Holland, which shouldered two-thirds of the financial burden of the republic's army. In 1650, William arrested six of the deputies of the Holland States and ordered the army to attack Amsterdam. Historians differ as to whether this affair should be regarded as a successful coup d'état, but there is general agreement that it placed William in a position to make himself the dominant power in the state. He contracted smallpox and died the following November, however, leaving no heir capable of effectively consolidating his political authority. A son, born eight days after his death, eventually became one of the most important figures in Dutch (and English) history, but he was a minor during the crucial phase in the constitutional development of the republic that followed the death of his father (Rowen, 1988, 84–94; Israel, 1995, 603–609).

The brief rule of William II convinced many that concentration of domestic power posed as much a threat to the constitution—and thereby the safety of the republic—as foreign enemies. After William's death, five of the seven provinces, including Holland and Zeeland, decided to leave the office of stadholder vacant. This state of affairs, called by historians the "First Stad-

32. In the early 1630s, Frederick Henry persuaded the States General to name his infant son William as general of the cavalry and to assure that he would succeed him as stadholder. With dynastic motives, he arranged a marriage between William and Mary Stuart, the daughter of Charles I of England.

holderless Period," lasted for twenty-two years. During it, the republic found itself engaged in wars with its former supporters, England (in 1652–1654 and 1665–1667) and France (1667). Most of the colonial possessions were lost, but the republic succeeded in maintaining its land borders, and the Golden Age of economic, intellectual, and cultural achievement continued. The First Stadholderless Period demonstrated that a nation did not need a monarch, or even a quasi-monarch, in order to be stable and prosperous. Renaissance Venice had shown that a city-state could be a republic, but not until the First Stadholderless Period in the United Provinces was it demonstrated empirically that the republican form can be successfully used in a polity with multiple population centers and more than one level of governmental administration. This was a step in the development of pluralistic constitutionalism that deserves much more recognition than it has received.

The stadholderless era was brought to an end in 1672 by a simultaneous attack on the union by France and England, and by German states on its northern borders. Initially, the invaders met with little opposition; their advance was only halted by opening the dikes and flooding the land below sea level. Popular clamor for a more effective defense led to the appointment of William III as stadholder and commander of the Union's land and sea forces.[33] He proved to be an able military strategist and tactician, as well as an astute and pragmatic politician. A French-English attempt at a seaborne invasion was thwarted, England withdrew from the war, and Louis XIV recalled his troops. By the spring of 1674, the Dutch Republic, which had been facing virtual extinction only a year and a half earlier, had reestablished itself as an independent state (Rowen, 1988, 131f.; Israel, 1995, 796–824).

These dramatic events greatly increased the prestige and popularity of the Prince of Orange. A movement arose to elevate William's noble rank in the United Provinces closer to that which would be enjoyed by a hereditary monarch. But the general opposition to monarchy, and the more specific anti-Orangism of the stadholderless period, had not been extinguished. William had acted during the war to increase the influence of his supporters in the town governments and provincial assemblies in order to quiet the domestic scene while he attended to the French and English. He was equally pragmatic in declining an offer to make him Duke of Gelderland in 1675, and he discouraged the Orangists from similar efforts on his behalf elsewhere. By this date, it appears that majority opinion in the United Provinces (among the regents at least) favored remaining a republic and identified this form of gov-

---

33. William's mother died in 1661, when he was eleven years of age. In her will she had named her brother, the newly restored Charles II of England, as his sole guardian. The Dutch disapproved, and Mary's wishes were disregarded. He was educated in Holland and throughout his life regarded himself as a Netherlander.

ernment with the maintenance of economic prosperity and civic freedom (Kossmann, 1991, 291f.).

As it turned out, William III became a king—but of England, not the United Provinces. He conceived the bold strategy of invading England in order to eliminate it as a potential threat to the republic. The opportunity to do so was provided by the growing opposition in England to the rule of James II, a firm believer in the Bodinian principles of monarchical absolutism and a deeply committed Catholic. The Dutch, having recently been almost conquered by a coordinated land and sea attack by England and France, seized the opportunity to prevent a repetition of it. The invasion of England in the fall of 1688 was successful. James II fled the country, and William and his wife Mary (James's daughter) assumed the English crown as joint monarchs.[34]

In English historiography, the Dutch invasion is celebrated as a "Glorious Revolution" that proved to be a climactic event in England's constitutional development. So far as the Dutch Republic was concerned, it removed the Prince of Orange from the quotidian play of Dutch politics because he had to remain in England to tend to affairs there. He retained the office of stadholder, but delegated his authority in the Netherlands to the councillor-pensionary of Holland. "William's trust in him," writes Rowen, "was such that the government in the Netherlands, as distinct from his authority, slipped from the hands of the stadholder-king. It was becoming a government that did not need him" (1988, 146).

The Republic in the Eighteenth Century

At the end of the seventeenth century, the Dutch people were the most prosperous in Europe; their political system had shown itself capable of providing efficient domestic administration and defense against foreign attack; and the Union was recognized as one of the world's great powers. In all these respects the eighteenth century was an era of decline. Military and diplomatic status are matters of relative power, and it was probably inevitable that a nation as

34. The Dutch fleet and invasion force was much larger than the Spanish Armada of a century earlier, but it was smaller than the English fleet that might have engaged it in battle. The first attempt to sail for England had to be abandoned because of the weather. In the second attempt, a favorable "Protestant wind" prevailed that enabled the Dutch to proceed to a landing in Devon, while keeping the English ships bottled up in their ports. "The States General, the States of Holland, and Stadholder," observes Jonathan Israel, "took an immense risk in sending across all the best regiments of the Dutch army, together with the pick of the Republic's field artillery . . . and much of the war fleet to British shores amid the stormy weather to be expected in late autumn" (Israel, 1995, 850f; see also Israel and Parker, 1991). Jones calls the Dutch strategy "preposterously rash" (1972, 281).

small as the Dutch Republic would experience a decline. But domestic affairs also degenerated. The political system began to display significant deficiencies in dealing with factional conflict, and the economy deteriorated in its capacity to supply the material wealth that had supported the remarkable achievements of the Golden Age.[35]

When he died in 1702, William III left no son to succeed him as stadholder of Holland. He had been grooming Johan Willem Friso, the son of a cousin, as his political successor for some time and had tried to persuade the States of Holland to name him as its future stadholder. But Holland, along with Zeeland and some other provinces, decided to leave the stadholderate vacant. A Second Stadholderless Period ensued, which lasted until almost the mid-point of the century. It was during this period that the political defects of the republic's constitution became manifest, especially in its incapacity to resolve the problem created by the quasi-monarchical status of the House of Orange and the ambiguity of the political relationship between the provincial states (Holland in particular) and the States General.

By this time there was a strong Orangist faction in the republic that was, in effect, a monarchist party. It supported Friso's claims as William's successor, and was only temporarily deflated in the pursuit of its basic objective by Friso's accidental death by drowning in 1711. An anti-Orangist faction had also become an established feature of the Dutch political scene, and conflict between the two groups, sometimes punctuated by violence, was prevalent during the Second Stadholderless Period.

Like the First Stadholderless Period, the Second was brought to an end by a foreign threat to the republic's independence. France invaded the Netherlands again in 1747, the Orangist party won popular support for its contention that concentration of political power was what the Union needed. The then head of the House of Orange, Friso's son William, was appointed stadholder of all seven of the provinces. This "Orangist Revolution," as Dutch historians have called it, "turned the Republic into what was really more of a constitutional monarchy without a crowned monarch" (Israel, 1995, 1077f.). But the new stadholder, William IV, died unexpectedly in 1751, before he could consolidate his political power, leaving an infant son as head of the House of Orange.

---

35. Angus Maddison's calculations of productivity (GDP per hour) show the Netherlands as declining absolutely over the whole of the period from 1700 to 1785. He notes that "the economy did not collapse . . . It simply entered on a long period of decadence." He attributes this mainly to a change in the Union's position in international trade, on which its economy was crucially dependent; specifically, "the destruction of monopolistic trading privileges in conflicts with France and the UK." (1982, 31f.). See Israel (1995, ch. 37) for a general discussion of the economic decline and its consequences.

After a regency period of fifteen years, the stadholderate, now effectively hereditary, was bestowed upon William V. Though amiable and intelligent, William was politically inept and irresolute. He was urged by his advisers to adopt a monarchist stance and insist upon his possession of prerogative powers. The anti-Orangist opposition tightened, and during William's reign Dutch politics was dominated by a continuous struggle between the Orangists and the "Patriots" (as their opponents now called themselves) that, in the early 1780s, came close to civil war. William was unable to deal with the crisis and announced that he would go into retirement. This only exacerbated the factional conflict, however. In support of the Orangists, Prussian troops (sent by William's brother-in-law) invaded the republic in 1787. In a few weeks, they overcame all Patriot resistance and occupied the whole country. The United Provinces thereupon became a joint protectorate of Prussia and England (Kossmann, 1971, 162; Rowen, 1988, 195–204, 215f., 220–229; Prak, 1991, 88).

In the meantime, Bourbon France had been transformed, first into a republic and then into a dictatorship under Napoleon Bonaparte. He invaded the United Provinces in 1793 and quickly occupied most of the country, while William V fled to England. Some historians consider this event as marking the end of the republic, but it had really ceased to be an independent nation in 1787. If we date the birth of the republic from Maurice of Nassau's military successes against Spain in the 1590s, it had endured for almost two hundred years.

Napoleon allowed a measure of political autonomy in the Netherlands before tightening his rule and establishing his brother, Louis Bonaparte, as monarch. In the general European settlement that took place after Waterloo, the original seventeen provinces of the Low Countries were united as a monarchy under the head of the House of Orange. The southern provinces, however, were staunchly Catholic. In 1830 they broke away with little resistance from the north, thus creating the two nations of Belgium and Holland that exist today.

The Republican Political System

Whoever it was who said that "God is in the details" could have had pluralist political systems in mind. The governmental institutions of polities based upon undivided sovereignty can be described simply in terms of their hierarchical ordering, but the countervailance model permits such a variety of applications that no specific case can be adequately understood without attention to the details of its organizational structure.[36] This is particularly so

---

36. Until quite recently, the material available on the organization of the Dutch political system in English or, apparently, in Dutch, was meager. No systematic account had been

of the Dutch Republic, a three-tiered federal system composed of sixty-five governmental entities: A States General, seven provincial states, and fifty-seven town governments.[37] In the description that follows I shall simplify, as other writers have, by restricting an account of the two lower tiers of government to the province of Holland. The institutions we shall examine were not created by a discrete act of construction ab initio, and we cannot consult any constitutional document that defines their several structures and powers. Moreover, all of the republic's political institutions were in existence before the Revolt, and their sense of having traditions and privileges long antedating it was an important factor in the politics of the republican era.

The following passage from Sir William Temple's book on the republic has frequently been quoted by modern Dutch historians as epitomizing its political system:

> This state . . . cannot properly be styled a Commonwealth, but is rather a Confederacy of Seven Sovereign Provinces united together for their common and mutual defence, without any dependance, one upon the other. But to discover the nature of their Government from the first springs and motions, It must be taken yet into smaller pieces, by which it will appear, that each of these Provinces is likewise composed of many little States or Cities, which have several marks of Sovereign Power within themselves, and are not subject to the Sovereignty of their Province; Not being concluded in many things by the majority, but only by the universal concurrence of Voices in the Provincial-States. For as the States-General cannot make War or Peace, or any new Alliance, or Levies of Money, without the consent of every Province; so cannot the States-Provincial conclude any of those points without the consent of each of the Cities, that by their Constitution has a voice in that Assembly . . . By this a certain Sovereignty in each City is discerned, the chief marks whereof are, the power of exercising Judicature, levying of Money, and making of War and Peace. (1972, 52)

Sir William was typical of his age in focusing his attention on sovereignty, but he obviously did not harbor any Bodinian compulsion to find that, despite appearances, undivided and unlimited sovereign authority resided somewhere

---

published since Sir William Temple's *Observations on the United Provinces of the Netherlands,* which was written more than three centuries ago. The gap has now been appreciably repaired by recent research; J. L. Price's *Holland and the Dutch Republic in the Seventeenth Century* (1994) is especially valuable.

37. In addition, the herring fisheries were regulated by a special board composed of deputies from the main seaside towns; there were five quasi-independent "Admiralties' governing the navy; and the responsibility for building, maintaining, and administering the large network of water control facilities was in the hands of scores of independent local boards.

in the Dutch state. He unperturbedly treated the republic's political system as essentially pluralist and acutely perceived that a coherent description of it must begin with the powers and institutions of the local communities.

The Dutch Towns

Though increased urbanization of the Dutch population was a notable feature of the republican period, most of the towns existed before the Revolt, and many had histories that went back well into medieval times.[38] Dutch urban dwellers identified with their local community so far as their material interests and political loyalties were concerned. Even their affiliation to the Christian community was institutionally second to their town citizenship. Such divided loyalties that they may have had between secular and religious communities before the Reformation were largely eliminated by the adoption of local autonomy in the organization of Protestant churches.[39] While town governments in most of the rest of Europe were steadily subordinated to the authority of larger political entities during the seventeenth century, the towns of the Netherlands continued to enjoy autonomous powers. In effect, Dutch government during the republican era was unaffected by the most significant development in European political organization since the fall of Rome, the emergence of the nation-state (Cooper, 1960, 83f.; Pirenne, 1963, 51f.; Wansink, 1971, 136.f; Haley, 1972, 194.f; Gelderen, 1992, 27.f; Price, 1994, 3; Boone and Prak, 1995; Davids and Lucassen, 1995, 445).

Popular political action in the days before the development of mass media was necessarily an urban phenomenon; it could only occur where numbers of people were in direct contact with each other and were able to organize effectively for a common purpose. The Dutch Revolt, as a popular rebellion against the governance of Spain, took place in the towns. The "liberties and privileges" that the rebels referred to as threatened by the policies of Philip II were rights that they had long enjoyed as citizens of self-governing towns. The success of the Revolt and the organization of the northern provinces into a comprehensive union did not lead to any diminution in the role of the

38. The urban centers of the republic differed enormously in size. At the zenith of the Golden Age, the population of Amsterdam was three times that of Leiden, five times that of Rotterdam, and much larger still than the other sixteen towns that had voting rights in the States of Holland (Hart, 1989, 665). In the following description I shall refer to all urban centers, large and small, as "towns." For a detailed description of typical town government, see Price (1994, chs. 2 and 3) and Speck (1995, 185f.).

39. Some Protestant sects were strictly congregational. The Dutch Reformed Church had a hierarchical structure, with national and provincial synods, but the fundamental institutional entity was the local consistory, dominated by laymen, which supervised the activities of clerics as well as parishioners (Israel, 1995, 367f.).

towns in Dutch politics, and it was not until the nineteenth century, after the republic had ceased to exist, that the Netherlands followed the rest of Europe in subordinating local authorities to the national government (Haley, 1972, 71; Price, 1994, 7f., 12f.).

The town governments were the most important fiscal agencies of the Dutch Republic; they levied most of the taxes and most of the (nonmilitary) public funds. Agencies financed and controlled by a town government were responsible for its defense installations, the maintenance of public order, the operation of a judicial system, and the provision of welfare services, which were much more highly developed in the Union than elsewhere in Europe. Policies enacted by the provincial states depended upon town officials for their translation into action; they could be, and not infrequently were, rendered inoperative locally by the opposition of local authorities (Wansink, 1971, 138f.; Haak, 1984, 52f.; Hart, 1989, 677; Price, 1994, 177–182; Israel, 1995, 353–360).

Town government in the United Provinces was oligarchic. Political power was exercised exclusively by the members of a small number of the richest families, collectively called the regents. Typically, there was a governing council (varying, in Holland towns, from fewer than twenty to sometimes more than forty members), which was the policy-determining organ, and a number of magistrates (burgomasters) who, generally speaking, constituted the executive and judicial branches of government. Members of the council held office for life, and when a vacancy occurred, it was filled by the council itself selecting a replacement from among the regency class families. The burgomasters were elected annually by the council, usually from its own ranks. In some provinces, a strong stadholder played a role in the selection of town burgomasters and, on occasions of great political turmoil, such as occurred in 1618 and 1672, unilaterally determined them. In general, however, the town governments were self-perpetuating. The councilors and burgomasters regarded themselves as "representing" the citizenry (Prak, 1991, 77), but this claim was as false as the contention that an absolute monarch represents his subjects. Historians have found evidence of factional and family conflict within the regency, but the council meetings were held in camera and its decisions announced as a unanimous consensus. There was thus at least the appearance of solidarity, which helped to insulate the regents from public criticism.[40]

40. "A central problem was that the whole system of administration was open to corruption because there were so very few checks and controls over what the regents did, certainly within their own towns . . . where their authority was practically absolute" (Price, 1994, 50f.). On the other hand, Haley contends that the town citizenry were willing to tolerate the rule of the regents not only because it was traditional but because "their rule

Though the oligarchic nature of town government cannot be denied, its power was tempered by another institution: the local militias, or civic guards. Ordinary police work was handled by a small force commanded by a sheriff, but this agency was incapable of dealing with large disturbances, which were not rare events in the Dutch towns. The civic guards, consisting of a large number of heavily armed and well-trained men organized into military-style units, were responsible for dealing with such local emergencies. All adult male citizens were formally obligated to enroll in a militia company, but each person was required to supply his own equipment and contribute to the company's finances. In practice only the richer citizens actually served (Prak, 1991, 84; Rowen, 1988, 47; Price, 1994, 93f.). Being an officer in a civic guard company was valued highly as a mark of prestige, and the various companies constituted social institutions with a considerable degree of communal solidarity.[41] Though the guards were formally bound to obey the orders of their town councils and were commanded by members of regent families, many commanding officers regarded themselves as free to make independent policy judgments. The regents were aware, through hard experience, that they could not always count upon the support of the town's organized policing institutions.

In all societies, including modern democratic ones, civic rioting constitutes a potential, and at times an actual, part of the political system in operation. Through rioting, the lowest socioeconomic classes can exercise a tangible, and at times determining, degree of influence over political decision-making. From the days of the Iconoclastic Fury that initiated the Revolt against Spain, rioting was from time to time an important feature of Dutch civic politics. The fact that the guards could, and sometimes did, refuse to quell local disturbances increased the political power of the lower classes, as did the fact that the regents, being town dwellers themselves, were aware that highly unpopular actions could place their persons and property at risk. In sum, the oligarchic town governments were subject to some countervailing power in practice, if not in formal constitution. One of the major deficiencies of the Dutch political system was that the republic never found a way of checking the power of the town governors by more orderly procedures.[42]

---

was on the whole successful, providing conditions for growing prosperity . . . even for the lowest classes . . . The regents [he notes], continuing to live in their city houses, were in touch with the interests and sentiments of their citizens and took care not to outrage them" (1972, 61).

41. The social nature of the militia organizations is displayed in the many group portraits of their officers commissioned from Dutch artists, including Rembrandt's famous painting now called *The Night Watch* (Haak, 1984, 104–108).

42. Price (1994, chap. 7) is an excellent extended discussion of the role of rioting in

The Provincial States

The origin of the Dutch provincial assemblies, or states, has been traced to the late Middle Ages.[43] By the time of the Revolt, they had acquired a governmental status not unlike that which the English Parliament enjoyed under the Tudor monarchs (Gelderen, 1992, 22f.). The membership of a provincial state was essentially determined by its urban centers, which had the status of voting towns. In Holland, the largest of the provinces, there were eighteen such towns. In addition, the Holland nobility as a whole had one vote. In Zeeland there were six voting towns plus one vote for the nobility. A town could appoint more than one person, and usually did, but it was the town that was regarded as the voting entity, and every town, regardless of size, cast one vote. Decisions of the states were made by general consensus. But in practice, Amsterdam had much greater weight than the other towns in the states of Holland, just as Holland had much greater weight than the other provinces in the States General of the Union.

In the preceding paragraph I avoided referring to the members of the provincial assemblies either as "representatives" or "delegates" (as historians have variously done) because their powers were a fluid mixture of both. In Holland, the "assemblymen," as we might call them, were chosen from among the members of the town councils. They were given specific instructions before going to a meeting of the states, and on matters of importance, they were obligated to refer back to their towns. Nevertheless, true discussion and free negotiation, not merely vote-casting, took place at the states' meetings. When a matter of general importance, or one engaging the interests of a particular town, was before the states, assemblymen traveled frequently back and forth between The Hague (where the Holland states met) and the voting towns. Procedures in the other provinces were substantially the same (Temple, 1972, 58–61; Haley, 1972, 64f.; Burke, 1994, 44; Price, 1994, 14f., 122–133).

The provincial states had a variety of governmental responsibilities, the most important of which were military. Data for the first half of the seventeenth century show that the proportion of the Holland States's total expenditure that was for military purposes varied from a low of 62 percent to a high of 84 percent. Provincial expenditures were financed by various taxes

---

Dutch politics and the inability of the regents to rely upon the civic guards to control it. See also Rowen (1988, 47, 103).

43. The term "states" is not a plural noun that refers to the provinces in general, but to each one's governing organ. It is an awkward term in English, and especially so for the American reader, but "estates," which some historians have used, is no better because it inappropriately suggests similarity to the three status classes of France during the ancien régime.

and, upon some occasions, the flotation of loans. Needless to say, the town councils had a strong interest in the fiscal policies of their states (Haley, 1972, 69f.; Hart, 1989, 674–678; Hart, 1993, 207).

The most important officials of a provincial government were its pensionary and stadholder. Because Holland carried exceptional weight in the Union, its own pensionary and stadholder were powerful national as well as provincial figures. As I noted earlier in sketching the history of the republic, there was constant tension between them, which sometimes culminated in violent confrontation. Anti-Orangist sentiment was strong in Amsterdam; nevertheless, the head of the House of Orange-Nassau was always appointed as Holland's stadholder, except during the two stadholderless periods. Because of the special influence of Amsterdam in the provincial government, there were occasions on which the states of Holland was in sharp conflict with its own stadholder.

The States General

The history of the States General goes back to the mid-fifteenth century when the Burgundian dukes, in attempting to deal with the restraints on their powers that the provincial states of the Low Countries constantly sought to maintain, created a central institution with which they could deal more conveniently and, they hoped, to greater effect. With the onset of the Revolt, the necessity for coordinated military action by the provinces led to the retention of this institution as a States *General,* which met regularly in The Hague (Hart, 1989, 667, Gelderen, 1992, 22f.; 1993, x).[44]

In establishing a central governmental entity, the provinces had no intention of giving up what they regarded as their "sovereign" status. Nevertheless, the need to deal with the immediate, and what turned out to be long-lasting, problems of foreign conflict and competition resulted in the assumption by the States General of large responsibilities: the conduct of warfare and diplomacy, the regulation of commercial policy and foreign trade, and the administration of colonial possessions. It would be reasonable to assume that these functions would, over time, lead to a significant concentration of political power in The Hague. But in fact, this did not occur. The composition of the States General, its procedures of decision-making, and the means by which it was financed prevented it from developing into the dominant political entity of the union. Even after two centuries, it had a very small bureaucracy of its own, and most of its executive functions were carried out by a council of state, composed of the stadholders and twelve other appointees of the provincial states (Temple, 1972, 65f.; Hart, 1993, 209, 215–217; Price, 1994, 215f.).

44. Grever (1982) provides a detailed account of the structure and functions of the States General, together with specific cases that illustrate its role in Dutch government.

The sources of revenue for the States General clearly display its weakness as an organ for governmental policy and administration. It had, indeed, no substantial revenues of its own. Its ability to levy domestic taxes was severely limited, and the colonies yielded little net revenue. Its funding came mainly from an (unenforceable) schedule of provincial assessments with Holland liable for more than half of the total. It could borrow by selling bonds in the general market, but all loan flotations required the approval of the states. Its finances were closely monitored by a chamber of accounts composed of two representatives from each province (Haley, 1972, 69; Rowen, 1988, 84; Hart, 1989, 678; 1993, 112f., 201; Price, 1994, 217f., 235).

The members of the States General were, in actuality, the provincial states. The seven provincial delegations (here that term is more clearly appropriate) were not uniform in size or composition, but their remits were the same: to do what their states wanted them to do. Each province had one vote in the States General. All proposals had to have unanimous approval for passage into law. This principle was disregarded at times, but Holland could never be denied veto power because its cooperation was absolutely necessary for any meaningful action. Every province sent an official of its own to serve on the secretariat of the States General so that it could be kept informed and furnished with copies of relevant documents. The agendas for the States General's daily meetings was prepared by its president, who functioned as the chairman or speaker. The presidency rotated weekly among the seven provincial delegations.

The discussions that took place in the States General were not general; one member of each provincial delegation spoke for the whole, stating in effect the position that his states had decided to adopt. Committees were established on specific issues, a policy that reconciled divergent views, but not without constant reference back to the provincial states. After examining the procedure employed in some concrete cases during the first stadholderless period, Grever comes to the conclusion that the system was "a form of government based upon persuasion" (1982, 151), but it was the provincial states (with Holland taking the lead) that had to be persuaded to compromise, not the individuals who composed their delegations.

The Stadholderate and the House of Orange

Intersecting with all three levels of government was the stadholder—a provincial appointee, but one whose political status was such that the stadholderate must be recognized as one of the primary institutions of the republic's political system.[45] The stadholderate had its roots in the Habsburg era when

---

45. The institution of the stadholderate and the special status of the House of Orange is prominent in all of the modern literature on the Dutch Republic. Rowen (1988) is

the monarch, whose attention could not be directed exclusively, or even mainly, to the Low Countries, appointed a high local noble to act as governor in each of the provinces.[46] At the start of the Eighty Years' War in 1568, William the Silent, Prince of Orange and Count of Nassau, had occupied this post in the provinces of Holland, Zeeland, and Utrecht for almost a decade. William resigned his offices when he took up arms against Spain, but he was shortly reappointed stadholder by the provincial states. During the following two centuries, except for the periods when the office was left vacant, the Holland stadholderate was occupied by the head of the House of Orange. The special position of that House in the history of the republic is another of the institutions of the republic that was taken over from the monarchical era.[47]

The stadholder of Holland was invariably made commander-in-chief of the Union's land and sea forces, thus combining a high position in provincial government with that of a civil servant of the generality. The role of the stadholder in Dutch politics was further enlarged by other positions and conventional practices. He was ex officio president of the court of Holland, had the authority to pardon convicted criminals, and was generally responsible for the administration of justice in the province. His influence extended into the sphere of local government as well because (Amsterdam noteworthily excepted) he had the right to select town burgomasters from lists of acceptable candidates compiled by the regents.[48] At the level of the generality, the Holland stadholder served on many of the working committees of the States General and was, ex officio, a member of the Council of State. He played a prominent role in determining the policies of the States General, at times taking foreign policy into his own hands. The principal check upon him was

noteworthy as a chronological history of the republic that focuses on the changing role played in it by the princes of Orange.

46. "They [the stadholders] were on the spot, the eyes, ears and the enforcing arms of the Emperor" (Rowen, 1988, 5). Speck describes the stadholder as the king's "viceroy or lieutenant" (1995, 174).

47. From 1589 on, all of the provinces appointed members of the House of Orange-Nassau as their stadholders, but it was not until 1747 that, with the end of the Second Stadholderless Period, the same person (William IV) held all seven stadholderships.

48. "It is difficult to assess how important such powers [of local appointment] were . . . [but this was] clearly one of the ways in which the stadholders were able to build up their support among the ruling groups in the voting towns . . . [From about 1618 onward] there were Orangist parties (or factions . . .) among the regents of most of the *stemhebbende* [voting] towns" (Price, 1994, 140f.; see also Israel, 1995, 450f.). The power to make such appointments was only part of a widespread patronage system that made many important figures in Dutch government, at all levels, beholding to the prince of Orange (see Price, 1994, 252).

the anti-Orangist sentiment of Amsterdam, which assured that he could not exercise dominating influence over the States of Holland to the degree that he was able to do in other states. There was constant hostility, and occasional overt conflict, between Holland and its stadholder. Holland's domination of the Union's finances gave it the power to determine the size of the army, and accordingly, it wielded considerable control over its stadholder. But the political role of the stadholder varied with the exigencies of the times, and with his abilities, ambitions, and personality. The House of Orange was one of the central political institutions of the Dutch state.[49]

The history of the Dutch Republic with respect to the constitutional status of the House of Orange and the stadholderate conspicuously lacks any consistent line of development. When William the Silent undertook to support the Revolt, he apparently regarded himself as having resumed the position of high authority that he had enjoyed under Philip II, with the right to hold that status until a new monarch should be appointed. The failure of efforts to find an acceptable foreign prince to fill the vacancy moved the House of Orange itself toward monarchical status. The coup d'état executed by Prince Maurice in 1617 was another step in the same direction, a trend that continued during the terms of office of the next two stadholders. In the 1630s the monarchical status of the House of Orange became virtually recognized by the provinces, including Holland, when they passed Acts of Survivance that made the succession to their stadholderships hereditary (Israel, 1995, 539).

The direction of constitutional development swung sharply in the opposite direction when, after the death of William II, Holland and four other provinces declined to fill the office of stadholder and kept it vacant for twenty-two years. The Prince of Orange was replaced as the republic's leading political officer by Johan de Witt, the pensionary of Holland. During this period the Holland States passed an "Act of Seclusion" (1654) that barred members of the House of Orange from any future stadholdership in Holland.[50] In 1667 it passed an "Eternal Edict . . . for the Preservation of Freedom," which abolished the stadholderate in Holland and declared illegal its combination,

49. "The Dutch Stadholderate was a unique institution. In its everyday workings it corresponded to no other political structure of the time, and political theory has no category into which it readily fitted" (Rowen, 1985, 3). "The princes derived their peculiar place within the Republic's political system from a complex and sometimes even bizarre combination of specific powers and offices, together with an indispensable charismatic element . . . They enjoyed a special status within the Dutch state, almost mystical . . . in its nature, as symbols of Dutch unity and common purpose" (Price, 1994, 247).

50. This action was urged upon the States of Holland by Oliver Cromwell, lord protector of England, as a condition for ending the First Anglo-Dutch War, in order to reduce any claims that the House of Orange might have to the English throne by virtue of William II's marriage to the daughter of Charles I (Rowen, 1972, 191).

in any province, with the position of captain-general (Price, 1994, 22, 148, 168f.; Israel, 1995, 791f.).

This eclipse of Orange power in the Republic proved only transitory. With the English-French invasions of 1672, the acts of 1654 and 1667 were negated, and the Prince of Orange again became stadholder and captain-general. Holland and Zeeland formally made their stadholderates hereditary offices of the House of Orange. But William III's absence from the country after 1688 diminished the importance of the stadholderate, and when he died in 1702 without a direct heir, the office was left vacant again and remained so for forty-five years.

Modern historiography on the Dutch Republic focuses tightly on that element in its political system that came near to achieving the status of monarchy and exercising its prerogative powers—the Orangist stadholder cum captain-general. Although concentration on the stadholderate may be unavoidable in narrating the history of the Republic, such a narrow focus is insufficient, and to a degree misleading, if one's object is to assess the republic's role in the evolution of Western constitutionalism. The political system of the republic operated effectively for nearly half of its existence without a stadholder, if we add to the two stadholderless periods William III's absence in England and the fifteen-year regency during the minority of William V. Even when a stadholder was firmly in place, he never had powers that were remotely comparable to those of the monarchs of Spain and France, or even the Parliament-constrained Stuart monarchs of England. The Orangist stadholderate was unquestionably an important element of the Dutch political system, but it constituted just one of several centers of power in a state that was formally pluralist in its federalist organization and functionally pluralist in the manner in which public policy was determined.

Assessment of the Dutch Constitution

Blair Worden describes the Dutch constitution as "a bizarre and improvised solution to the needs of war" (1991, 446). It was indeed "improvised." With the outbreak of the Revolt, the Dutch used the political institutions that were immediately at hand for the singular objective of effective defense. Though I have not found it described elsewhere as "bizarre," terms such as "cumbersome," "sclerotic," "designed for deadlock," and "unworkable" are common in the modern historiography. Nevertheless, with this political system, the Dutch not only fought Spain and France to a standstill and invaded England, but also made their little collection of swamps and polders into the richest, most civilized, nation in the early modern world.

In terms of the history of constitutionalism, the most obvious significance of the Dutch Republic is that it blatantly defied the principles of political organization classically expressed by Jean Bodin—principles that had become conventional in European political thought. As monarchical absolutism spread almost everywhere, the Union remained an aberrant island in which a pluralist system of governance was maintained.[51] Many modern historians have stressed the inability of the Dutch constitution to adapt to new problems after the Golden Age was over and its economic and cultural leadership was challenged by other European states.[52] Nevertheless, the simple fact is that the Union did not disintegrate. Whatever the centrifugal tendencies might have been, it remained intact until it was overwhelmed, as was the rest of Europe, by the military forces of Napoleonic France.

Numerous modern historians have assessed the political system of the republic as critically lacking a centralizing element capable of supplying the requisites of effective governance and the unifying *mentalité* of nationalism (e.g., Rowen, 1988, 229; Hart, 1989; 1993, 18f.).[53] Others, however, have appraised it as a system that worked effectively despite, or even because of, its dispersion of political power (e.g., Wansink, 1971; Price, 1994). A wider angle of vision, one that includes the histories of other nations besides the Netherlands, appears to support the second of these assessments. We now have available to us the empirical experiences of many more polities that have operated with pluralist political systems, as well as numerous modern examples of centralized ones to add to those of times past. The advantage of a centralized system seems to be that public policy can be determined and executed expeditiously toward the achievement of clearly defined, coherent, national objectives. But the evidence fails to indicate that the *quality* of public

51. "The marked weakness of central government in the Dutch Republic was an apparent anomaly in seventeenth-century Europe, when centralizing, absolutist governments tended to be seen as the sine qua non of efficient rule, and provincial and local rights and privileges were regarded as incompatible with a strong state . . . The Republic was a living refutation of conventional wisdom regarding the necessity of both strong central direction and monarchical leadership, just as its unusually tolerant religious policies proved, in despite of contemporary assumptions, that religious diversity was compatible with a stable social and political system . . . Not only did the decentralized system work remarkably well, but . . . such a system was the only way in which the Union could have been able to work at all" (Price, 1994, 278).

52. In the later eighteenth century, writes Barbara Tuchman, Dutch government was "a paralytic system that would not have been tolerated by a primitive island of the Pacific" (1988, 23). Although other historians might reject such a comparison, the notion that the political system of the late republic was incapable of making effective public policy is frequently expressed in the modern literature. Leeb, for example, in his study of the Republic in the second half of the eighteenth century, declares that, by the 1770s, "the failure of political arrangements in the Netherlands was apparent to all but the most myopic" (1973, 9).

53. See Price's remarks on this feature of Dutch historiography (1994, 289f.).

policy in centralized states, evaluated in terms of the welfare of its citizenry at large, is superior to that achieved in states where public policies reflect a discordant and time-consuming process of widespread discussion, sectional competition, negotiation, and compromise. Moreover, in certain domains, it may well be that a lack of state policy is the best social policy. Laissez-faire, in the domains of religion, science, scholarship, and art, was a better stance for the Dutch state to take than any conceivable policy it might have adopted. In the domain of economics, the republic did better to leave a large scope for individual initiative than to copy the detailed mercantilist regulatory policies of England and France (Huizinga, 1968, 22f.). Even if the passivity of the Dutch state in these areas was due to political inanition, such a stance was not necessarily a defect in itself. A good public policy is better than doing nothing, but a bad policy, as Adam Smith argued in his critique of mercantilism, is inferior to no policy at all.

Any appraisal of the republic's political system that focuses upon its lack of a central locus of dominating power is misdirected in that, at bottom, it criticizes the union for not adopting the hierarchical model. The union was, indeed, cobbled together from extant institutional materials for the immediate purpose of defense, but after its borders were secure, the Dutch could have reorganized their political system if they had wished to do so. Various attempts were made to promote a more centralized constitutional design, but all were firmly rejected. To construe the failures of these efforts as an inherent weakness in the Dutch polity, an inability to overcome the "particularism" of the provinces and towns, fails to recognize that the Dutch placed positive value on their system of dispersed political authority. They had no desire to establish a centralized state, even when they thought it necessary to find a monarch to replace Philip II. The Dutch did not deliberately set out to establish a federal union either, but their retention of the political institutions of the Habsburg era, and their insistence on maintaining the independence and privileges of the towns, clearly show that they desired a union in which political power was shared among several independent institutional entities.

In the era of the Dutch Republic, the countervailance model of political organization was a concept that very few could grasp intellectually. Nevertheless, it was the guiding principle of the Dutch political system in practice. Amsterdam was the dominant urban entity in the province of Holland, and Holland was the dominant province in the Union, but the regents of Amsterdam did not determine the public policy of the republic. The other towns of Holland recognized the necessity of accommodating the views and interests of Amsterdam, and the other provinces did likewise with respect to Holland, but Amsterdam and Holland were fully aware that their own wishes could not be forced upon the other towns and provinces without costly consequences.[54] The stadholder's position in the republic's political system was similarly constrained. Even when he was "dominant," he could not rule without the cooperation—or at least the passive acquiescence—of the other political institutions. Like all countervailance systems, determinant power in the republic was denied to any single institution, and the political weights of the mutually "checking and balancing" entities were in constant flux.

The regents constituted an oligarchic ruling class in the Netherlands, but they were not a unified one. Altogether, the members of the town councils numbered some 2,000 persons of differing economic and political interests, living in more than fifty independent towns. They never formed, or apparently even attempted to form, an organized nationwide political entity. Within the regency itself, there operated the checks and balances of differentiated interest and competition for social and political status. Like other Dutchmen, the regents identified themselves more with their towns and provinces than with their social class. The town councils and magistracies were monopolized by the local regents, but their formal authority was constrained by the ever-present possibility of civic disturbance. Rioting, however, was not the only means through which other social classes could express their disapproval of regency governance. Literacy in the Dutch Republic was exceptionally widespread, and the weight of censureship exceptionally light. As a consequence, the press was an institution of political significance. These factors do not justify any significant modification in categorizing the republic as an oligarchy, but its ruling elite did not possess powers that can be described as "sovereign" in anything like the Bodinian sense of the term (Haley, 1972, 72–74; Grever, 1981, 13; Mörke, 1995, 168f.).

Although I have referred to the Dutch Republic as a "federation," such a generic label is questionable. Political scientists differentiate between "federal" and "confederal" political systems, in order to distinguish, respectively, those that constitute fully unified national entities (such as the United States of America today) from those that form much looser ones (such as the European Union, or the American union from the mid-1770s to the adoption

---

54. "To oversimplify for the sake of clarity," writes Peter Burke, "the councillors ruled Amsterdam, Amsterdam ruled Holland and Holland ruled the United Provinces . . . In practice . . . the Amsterdam elite had ways of getting what they wanted" (1994, 44). This is a misleading simplification. Hart points out that "no single city constituted a centralizing force . . . Even Amsterdam was prevented from assuming a leading position because of combined opposition from other towns . . . The province of Holland dominated national politics . . . However, despite the gravitation towards the maritime west of the nation, Holland could not do without the support of the inland provinces. Also, within Holland itself, no single economic or urban elite emerged as rulers, owing to the wide differentiation in commercialization and the constant bickering of factions" (1993, 18; see also Hart 1989, 672).

of the Constitution). Three centuries ago, Sir William Temple wrote that the republic was not a "Commonwealth" but a "Confederacy of Seven Soveraign Provinces" (1972, 52). Modern Dutch historians echo Temple's appraisal (e.g., Price, 1994, 149; Speck, 1995, 174). As a nation-state, the Dutch Republic derived from an alliance of independent provinces that was formed for the purpose of fighting the armies of Spain more effectively. The Union of Utrecht in 1579 did not significantly alter the nature of their association, and all subsequent efforts to construct a tighter organization came to nought. In sum, the place of the Dutch Republic in the history of federalism is much less significant than its role in the evolution of pluralistic constitutionalism. As we shall see in the following section, however, the confederal nature of the Union had a strong influence on Dutch political *theory*, much of which was driven by a perceived necessity to establish the locus of "sovereignty" in a polity that had multiple governmental entities.

Dutch Political Theory

The Dutch Republic does not usually appear as a significant venue of political theory in modern histories of the subject. Erasmus of Rotterdam (who ante-dated the Republic) is frequently mentioned as one of the great humanist scholars of the Renaissance whose defense of doctrinal toleration in religion anticipated the development of liberal political thought in the Netherlands.[55] Baruch Spinoza receives attention for undermining the theological founda-tions of ecclesiastical authority by espousing a rationalist interpretation of the Judaeo-Christian sacred texts. Hugo Grotius is generally recognized as the founder of the subject of international law. These alone were important ben-efactions to Western political theory in its infancy, but they fall far short of exhausting the significant contributions of Dutch thinkers. Recent scholar-ship has revealed that the political literature of the republican era in the Neth-erlands, though oriented to specific immediate issues, deserves recognition for its broader philosophical content. In some important respects, Dutch writers anticipated the literature of seventeenth-century England, which is usually credited with originating the principles of modern political liberalism. On the other hand, Dutch political theorists of the republican era are also

---

55. "Through his struggle against religious obscurantism, through his humanism, through his own vivid, fastidious personality, [Erasmus] helped to prolong and preserve his own ideals through a period when they came under ferocious attack by bigots on both sides of the religious fence. They were ideals well suited to the new bourgeois state of the Republic which they helped to inspire . . . In the mind and spirit of Erasmus lies the key to the understanding of much later Dutch history" (Wilson, 1968, 18).

noteworthy as having failed to grasp the principle of countervailance, despite the fact that it was embodied in their own political system.[56]

Freedom and Privileges

The concept of "liberty" or "freedom" occupies a place in the history of Western political philosophy that is second to none other. The meaning of this concept is, however, fraught with ambiguities that must be clarified in order to understand the argumentation contained in the Dutch literature of the republican era. The first distinction I should note is between the personal freedom of the individual, and the freedom of his community as a collective whole from the dominance of any other political entity. Though different, these two domains of liberty are not necessarily disjunct, and in specific cases personal freedom may be dependent upon the political independence of the collectivity. Early Dutch political thought is somewhat tangled on this point. On the one hand, achieving collective freedom from Spain was regarded as essential to personal freedom, especially, but not exclusively, with respect to religion. On the other hand, the Dutch could not have believed that the political independence of the Netherlands was vital in itself, because they tried hard to attach the northern provinces to another foreign nation after announcing the abjuration of Philip of Spain.[57]

In attempting to disentangle the complex weave of Dutch political theory, we have to begin with the notion of collective or community freedom. The key to Dutch thinking here lies in identifying the community that was the primary locus of concern. The tendency of political science to focus intently upon nation-states, supported by the history of warfare over the three or four centuries before World War II, is sometimes misplaced, as is evident from even a cursory survey of the world's trouble spots at the end of the twentieth

56. Gelderen (1992) is an indispensable study of the political theory of the Revolt period. Gelderen (1993) edits and reprints in English translation the most important documents of the 1570s and 1580s, and its introduction summarizes the main findings of the earlier work. Rowen (1972) provides English reprints of selected documents, from before the Revolt to the end of the republic. Leeb (1973) is a detailed survey of Dutch political thought towards the end of the republican era. In his introductory chapter, Leeb discusses the main lines of political theory that had been developed during the sixteenth and seventeenth centuries. Kossmann (1960) and Worst (1992) are also valuable on seventeenth- and eighteenth-century Dutch political thought, respectively. In his comprehensive history of the republic, Israel (1995) includes informative commentaries on the contemporary literatures of philosophy and political theory.

57. Gelderen asserts that in the early Revolt period "liberty was seen as the political value *par excellence* . . . the source of prosperity and justice, and the intrinsic connection between the liberty of the country and the personal liberty and welfare of the inhabitants was emphasized time and again" (1993, xxxii).

century.[58] In the era when the nation-state was in its infancy, this angle of vision was less appropriate, and especially so with respect to the Netherlands of early republican times. As we have noted, the Low Countries were an exceptionally urbanized region of Europe. The politically articulate part of the Dutch population consisted almost entirely of urban dwellers, who identified their interests and loyalties with their towns. Until well into the eighteenth century, the liberties that Dutch writers spoke of were connected in their consciousness with the independence of the towns, not with the Netherlands as a whole or with the northern seven provinces that succeeded in separating themselves from Spain.[59]

The political literature of the Revolt period was punctuated repeatedly by references to established "privileges" as having been threatened by the policies of Philip II. That term referred to a variety of rights that the towns had acquired as dispensations from their political masters. Some of these privileges had histories that stretched back to medieval times; some were even embodied in formal documents that specified contractual obligations between the town and its lord or prince. The privileges varied from town to town. Most common was the general right to self-government in local affairs without outside interference. Some dispensations were of considerable economic value, providing a town with a privileged status in a branch of trade or manufacture. It is not surprising that the town regents, and the population generally, had a strong desire to maintain these rights, even at the cost of insurrection.

In protecting its liberties, the individual town could generate little power or influence. The organization of larger geographic areas into provinces supplied a means through which towns could cooperate in mutual defense of them. The provincial states, composed of them, were not unified centers of citizen identification, but pragmatic instruments for the achievement of diverse urban objectives. In his study of the political thought of the Revolt period, Martin van Gelderen repeatedly stresses the trinitarian foci of the literature on "Liberty, Privileges, and States."[60]

---

58. For example, conflict between ethnic, not national, communities in the Balkans; between tribes in Africa; between religious communities in the Middle East and Ireland; and between linguistic communities in Canada and Belguim.

59. This view was clearly enunciated in the Dutch literature of the Revolt period and reiterated subsequently. Leeb singles out P. de la Court as contending that the independence of the Netherlands as a polity was rooted in the ancient independence of the towns: "every city its own polis." De la Court's most important book, *Demonstrations of the Salutary Political Foundations and Maxims of the Republic of Holland and West-Friesland* (1669), writes Leeb, "served as the chief repository of republican wisdom down to the end of the Republic" (1973, 34f.).

60. On the relation between these, Gelderen refers to a publication of 1570 as "a powerful reformulation of views which had been articulated during the 1560s claiming that the

The Dutch were undoubtedly concerned with their personal liberties as well as their communal ones. The initial cause of the Revolt was the attempt by Philip of Spain to suppress "heretical" religious belief. In the sixteenth century, religious homogeneity was commonly regarded as a vital precondition of political stability. A corollary of this belief was that the established political authorities had the right, as a matter of prudence, to suppress nonconformist preaching and worship. Arguments to the contrary were sparse, and except for the French Huguenot writers of the 1570s, were exclusively advanced by Dutch thinkers.

On the plane of grand political theory, the most influential work of the period was Jean Bodin's *République* (1576), which rejected any notion of personal liberty, religious or secular, beyond that which the absolute sovereign might be willing to grant. Henry IV's Edict of Nantes (1598) established religious toleration in France only as a monarchical dispensation that, as Louis XIV later demonstrated, could be summarily revoked at will. Philip II entertained no doubt that he acted as God's chosen agent when he directed the Spanish Inquisition against the Netherlands. But the orthodox Dutch Calvinists demonstrated in the Remonstrant controversy that religious liberty in the republic was no more secure if a Protestant state church were empowered to determine the boundaries of permissible worship. The Dutch partisans of toleration recognized early that their views were anathema not only to Catholics, but also to the Calvinists who dominated the Reformed Church.

Luther and Calvin were strongly averse to the free expression of divergent views, because they believed it would dilute "true" Christianity. But their theologies inadvertently provided a foundation for such toleration in stressing the individualistic nature of the relation between man and God. A number of sixteenth-century Dutch writers seized upon this tenet to develop a theoretical defense of toleration. There is no assurance, they contended, that any single person, or group of persons, can infallibly discover the truth in matters of religion. Any interpretation of the sacred texts may be in error. The most secure route to truth, therefore, is to allow free expression of all views and unconstrained public discussion. An imposed uniformity of religion was not necessary to communal solidarity; that could be better achieved by mutual toleration and peaceful debate. This argument can easily be extended beyond religion to support the general contention that a public policy of intellectual freedom assists the discovery of truth in all domains of human experience. The

---

foundation of the Dutch political order was a trinity of liberty as the crucial political value, with privileges as the constitutional guarantees of liberty, and the States as the guardians of the privileges" (1992, 125).

achievements of Dutch science in the Golden Age owed much to the struggle for religious freedom that took place in the early years of the republic.[61]

In such terms, Dutch political theorists, and even some theologians, defended intellectual freedom on utilitarian grounds. But other arguments in defense of personal freedom also appear in the Dutch republican literature. Two of these, which were quite independent of the demand for religious liberty, should be noted: the general notion that the freedom of the individual, even vis-à-vis the governance of domestic authorities, is a "natural right"; and the appeal to long-standing tradition with the contention that the Dutch had enjoyed an exceptional degree of personal freedom for almost two millennia, since the dawn of their history as a distinct people.

The notion that freedom of thought and expression belongs to all persons (or, at least, to all adult male citizens) as a "natural right" that no government or other institutional authority may abrogate, appears in the early Dutch literature (Gelderen, 1992, 228). In contrast to the utilitarian defense of intellectual liberty, this idea cannot be provided with a persuasive philosophical foundation. Since becoming prominent in the English political literature of the seventeenth century in documents such as John Milton's *Areopagitica* (1644), it has been the object of sustained and close attention by philosophers and political theorists, but it remains today what it was when the Dutch writers of the Revolt era enunciated it: an assertion *tout court*.

The Dutch of the republican era regarded themselves as heirs to a tradition of liberty that extended back to pre-Christian times. The source of this notion was *Germania*, by the Roman historian Cornelius Tacitus. Tacitus glorified the culture of the Germans (as compared with that of his own first century Rome) and stressed in particular the large degree of personal freedom enjoyed by members of the German tribes. The accuracy of this claim is dubious, but its influence on European humanists in the later fifteenth century was enormous.[62] It became especially popular in the Netherlands with the onset of the Revolt (Schöffer, 1975, 80, 87f.). Many of the Revolt's protagonists contended that the "Batavi," the German tribes that had migrated into the Low Countries in ancient times, were the progenitors of the Dutch. Thus arose what became known as the "Batavian Myth" in Dutch history.[63]

61. The defense of intellectual freedom is stressed repeatedly by Martin van Gelderen in his survey of Dutch political theory (1992 and 1993). See, especially, his examination of the work of Franciscus Junius and D. V. Coornhert during the early Revolt period (1992, 83f., 243f.). Jonathan Israel's summary of the writings of Simon Episcopus in the Remonstrant debate (1995, 503) indicates an anticipation of many of the arguments for intellectual freedom made later by John Milton, John Locke, and J. S. Mill.

62. Blair Worden writes of "the rage of Tacitism in the Europe of the later sixteenth and earlier seventeenth centuries" (1982, 186).

63. "The two Characters that are left by the old Roman Writers, of the ancient Batavi, or Hollanders, are, That they were both the bravest among the German Nations, and the

Hugo Grotius was the most prominent of the early writers to use the Batavian Myth as a political argument. During the seventeenth century, writes Leeb, "the theme of Batavian liberty became a commonplace . . . and pervaded the cultural life of the Republic in many forms" (1973, 28). In 1795, Napoleon allowed his Dutch supporters to establish a new regime, called the "Batavian Republic," which formally existed until 1806 when the Netherlands was made into a monarchy, with Louis Bonaparte as its king. But the myth lived on and even survived the German invasion of Holland in 1940. When the country was liberated toward the end of World War II, references to the Batavian history of the Dutch were prominent in the celebrations (Schöffer, 1975, 78f.).

This feature of Dutch intellectual history attests to the power of a myth that claims an ancient lineage for a political principle, but like the notion of natural rights, it supplies no weighty philosophical support for the doctrine of civic liberty. It does little, if anything, to explain why the Dutch valued personal freedom or to reveal the intellectual grounds for their doing so, but it serves to show the great intensity of their libertarian political outlook.

The Contract Theory of the State

The American Declaration of Independence opens with an acknowledgment that when a people decide to dissolve their established political connection and form an independent state, "the opinions of mankind require that they should declare the causes which impel them" to do so. The Dutch political thinkers of two centuries earlier felt at least as much obligated to justify such a rare and questionable action (Leeb, 1973, 17). The defense of civic rebellion swiftly engages the gears of political philosophy, and in the process of justifying the Revolt, Dutch political writers revealed what they held to be the essential nature of the state as a social institution.

Like other monarchs of the mid-sixteenth century, Philip II regarded his political authority as derived from his status as the representative of God. To rebel against one's monarch was therefore equivalent to rejecting divine will. Many Dutch writers appear to have been much more troubled by the idea of violating this mandate than they had been in denying the authority of the papacy. The Revolt was not universally supported by Protestants. Numerous writers expressed unconditional opposition to the use of force against the Spanish armies, often quoting the Gospel of Matthew and Paul's Epistle to

---

most obstinate lovers and defenders of their Liberty [reference here to Tacitus] . . . The last disposition seems to have continued constant and National among them ever since that time" (Temple, 1972, 91f.). As pointed out in Chapter 4, François Hotman had used a similar notion in his *Francogallia* in attempting to support religious toleration for the Protestant minority of a predominantly Catholic nation.

the Romans as commanding passivity and, if need be, the acceptance of martyrdom as the price that Christians might occasionally have to pay.[64] Members of the Dutch Reformed Church could perhaps be swayed by some passages in Calvin's writings that might be interpreted as legitimizing opposition to unjust monarchs, but Lutherans were adamant that opposition to established political authority was never justified (Gelderen, 1992, 67f., 80f., 87f.).

When organizing rebellion in the Netherlands, William the Silent was fully aware of the theological argument against it and "mounted a carefully orchestrated propaganda campaign to justify . . . armed resistance" (Gelderen, 1992, 102). In the call for a general revolt that he issued in 1572 (see Rowen, 1972, 40–42), William tried to make an end run around the doctrine of divine monarchical authority by suggesting that it was not Philip but his officials that were at fault in implementing, without his knowledge and consent, a repressive policy in the Netherlands. But the Revolt could not be justified by such patently casuistical reasoning. Within a decade, Dutch revolutionaries had adopted a bolder tack. The Act of Abjuration of 1581, which deposed Philip II as monarch of the Netherlands, admitted it to be "common knowledge that the prince of a country is established by God" but went on to assert that he has been appointed for the purpose of serving the interests of his people and, if he oppresses them instead, "he may be renounced and another chosen in his stead" (Rowen, 1972, 92f.). In making this assertion and supporting it with many writings, the Dutch, contemporaneously with the French Huguenots, opened the issue of the foundations, and limits, of civic obedience to established authority—an issue that dominated Western political thought until the American and French revolutions of the later eighteenth century.[65]

As noted earlier, the Dutch regarded the communal liberties and privileges of the towns as based upon agreements that had been made over the years between the towns and their lords or princes. Little ingenuity was required to move from this notion to the contention that all governing authority is

64. In the King James version, Matthew 5:10 reads: "Blessed are they which are persecuted for righteousness' sake; for theirs is the kingdom of heaven." Paul's Epistle to the Romans 13:1 and 2 reads: "Let every soul be subject unto the higher powers. For there is no power but of God: the powers that be are ordained by God. Whosoever therefore resisteth the power, resisteth the ordinance of God: and they that resist shall receive to themselves damnation."

65. E. H. Kossmann observes that "we have good reason to be amazed at the untiring exertions of the men of the sixteenth and seventeenth centuries . . . to speculate on the grounds and limits of obedience . . . filling entire libraries with their writings." Kossmann attributes this to the fact that "they lived in a period when the state, which is now so all-pervasive, was still under construction, only recently established and extremely unstable" (1981, 27).

based upon a contract between the people and their governors. With the adoption of such a view of the state, it was easy to justify the Revolt as a response to breach of contract on the part of the prince. Dutch political theorists abandoned the effort to find a theological justification for rebellion and developed a secular theory of the state based upon the legal notion of contract.

In the standard modern textbook treatment of political theory, Thomas Hobbes and John Locke are usually presented as the originators of the contract theory of the state. This is misleading on two grounds: they were, in fact, latecomers in advancing such a theory, and they construed the contract as an agreement among the members of a polity to establish a government. The older literature was both historically more realistic and politically more trenchant in regarding the contracting parties to be the government of a community and its citizens. The latter sense of contract can be traced back to the biblical texts of Judaism and Christianity, if one construes God in the role of governor.[66] The idea was at least latent in ancient Greek political theory and both definite and prominent in the medieval era; it reflected the system of mutual rights and obligations that characterized the feudal system of political organization (Sabine, 1937, 430; Gough, 1957, 12f., 33; Lessnoff, 1986, 15). Manegold von Lautenbach (later eleventh century) is the writer most frequently cited by historians as the first to provide a clear and explicit statement of contract theory and to associate it with the notion that the citizenry possessed rights that could not be arbitrarily abrogated (Sabine, 1937, 430; Gough, 1957, 12f., 29, 32f.; Lessnoff, 1986, 15).

The Dutch of the sixteenth century did not have to depend upon such sources for the notion of contract. There were numerous concrete examples in the history of the Low Countries of a ruling prince and a town making a contract that specified mutual rights and duties. One of the most famous of these was the "Joyous Entry of Brabant," which from the mid-fourteenth century each successive Duke of Brabant solemnly swore to uphold. This document asserted the liberties of the citizenry, confined the duke's authority in various ways, and stated that Brabanters had the right to disobey any orders of the duke that violated the entry's provisions. Charles V took the customary oath to uphold it when he came of age in 1515. A reading of this document

---

66. See, e.g., the use of the term "Covenant" to denote mutual promises between God and the Israelites in Genesis 9 and 17; Exodus 19 and 24:8; and Deuteronomy 4:13, 4:23, 7:9, 7:12. "Testament" is the King James version's translation of a Greek word meaning contract or promise. The term "New Testament" seems to refer to the prophecy of Jeremiah 31 that the old covenant between God and Israel through Moses will be replaced by a new one. "Covenant" appears in the New Testament in the Gospel of Matthew in describing the eucharist, and several times in the epistles of Saint Paul.

(see excerpts in Rowen, 1972, 12–16) leaves no doubt that the relation between the monarch and the people of Brabant was construed as based upon a binding contract.

The Dutch, therefore, were quite accustomed to the political notion of contract before the Revolt. When it occurred, that concept was pressed into service to justify the Revolt in numerous official documents, such as the Act of Abjuration, and by many writers, including William I, Hugo Grotius, and Johannes Althusius. The last of these has received special notice from intellectual historians because he broadened the concept of contract into a general sociological theory, contending that *all* human associations, whether economic, social, or political, are contractual in nature.[67]

The use of the contract theory of the state by Dutch republican writers, by John Locke in the late Stuart era, and by defenders of the American Revolution in the 1770s made it into one of the most influential concepts in the history of political thought. The recent revival of it in the American political and philosophical literatures suggests that it is perdurable as well.[68] The articulation of contract theory with the notions of law and tradition as fundamental parts of the social fabric explains a good deal of the favor it found with seventeenth-century political philosophers, but its remarkable popularity in the domain of practical politics has a simpler cause: it provided an effective vehicle for attacking a policy of the state as *morally* offensive. A contract is a promise, and promises ought to be kept. In the Dutch literature of the Revolt period, the argument repeatedly appears that in failing to keep his tacit and explicit promises, Philip had offended against an accepted principle of morality. In the Dutch Republic, a country that was becoming increasingly secular in its cultural and intellectual worldview, this argument could carry much heavier political freight than Philip's contention that to rebel against his rule was to deny the will of God.

In embracing the contract theory of the state, the Dutch contributed significantly to the development of Western political philosophy. This conception effectively undermined the notion that the state has a transcendental

67. Althusius was a German jurist, but his writings in political theory have usually been treated by historians as part of the Dutch literature because he greatly admired the political system of the republic and his writings in political theory seem to have been inspired by it. His chief work in political theory was his *Politica Methodice Digesta,* first published in 1603 and greatly enlarged in 1610. According to G. H. Sabine, Althusius "reduced the whole range of political and social relationships to the one principle of consent or contract. The compact, express or tacit, was made to account for society itself, or rather for a whole series of societies, of which the state was one" (1937, 419). Lessnoff (1990) contains selections, in English translation, from Althusius's writings germane to the theory of contract.

68. On John Rawls, Robert Nozick, and James M. Buchanan as contract theorists, see Gordon (1976).

status, that it represents on earth the ultimate sovereign authority of God over all mankind. In the Dutch republican literature, one finds repeated expression of the very different view that the state is a social artifact, established to serve the mundane utilitarian purposes of the citizenry. It is an instrument not for executing divine will, but for enabling individuals to cooperate for the achievement of objectives that require an organized coercive authority.

Nevertheless, despite its argumentative value, the contract theory of the state has been largely abandoned by empirical political scientists. Its chief deficiency is that it cannot be effectively employed as a heuristic instrument in the analysis of the day-to-day operation of a political system. It fails to focus on the central issue: the structure and dynamics of political power. With respect to a pluralist constitutional order, it provides no insight into the shifting distribution of power or the mechanics of power control. The Dutch political writers embraced the contract theory in justifying the Revolt, but could make no use of it in analyzing the political system of their union.

The Concept of Sovereignty

The concepts of sovereignty and liberty in political thought suffer from analogous ambiguities. On the one hand they may refer to the relationship of a community to other political entities, while on the other, they may refer to the organization of political power within a community. The first of these notions of sovereignty is in common use in modern political discourse—the United Nations, for example, is described as an association of "sovereign nations," which are represented by their governments. The second referent of the term still persists in the modern political literature, but its meaning has been greatly attenuated from its use in the seventeenth century. The classic doctrine of sovereignty can be reduced to two propositions: (1) in every stable polity there must be a singular center of ultimate political power, and (2) that power must be absolute. The Dutch political thinkers were familiar with Jean Bodin's *République*, Thomas Hobbes's *Leviathan*, and the other contemporary literature on sovereignty.[69] Their writings indicate that, except for the ardent Orangists, they were strongly disinclined to accept the second of these propositions, but they seem to have had no doubt as to the validity, and importance, of the first. Though the union they constructed was deliberately

---

69. In his *Politica* (1603), Johannes Althusius was especially concerned to deal with the Bodinian theory of the state. "It could hardly be otherwise," writes Kossmann, because Bodin's *République* "had become an authority whose political implications could no longer be ignored" (1981, 12). Hobbes's *Leviathan* (1651) did not appear in Dutch translation until 1667, but when it did, according to Israel, it caused "a considerable stir" (1995, 787).

designed as a polity of dispersed power, the concept of sovereignty was central in the political debates of the republic during the whole of its existence.

The hesitation of the Dutch to accept the full doctrine of sovereignty became clearly evident in their negotiations with the Duke of Anjou in 1580 to replace Philip of Spain as the monarch of the Netherlands. The States General offered to accept him as "prince et seigneur," but the duke insisted on being called "prince et seigneur souverain," which the Dutch delegation rejected (Kossmann, 1981, 11). That Jean Bodin was one of the duke's advisers at this time may have alerted the delegates to beware of using a term that might have connotations for the duke that they had no intention of accepting. It was plain that the Dutch wanted no absolute political authority, but their belief that nonetheless every state must have a definite locus of sovereignty resulted in a persistent debate over the constitutional nature of the union.

The House of Orange aside, there were three contenders for sovereign status in Dutch political theory: the States General of the union, the several provincial states, and "the people." The last of these was prominent in the early Revolt period literature and was essentially a part of the propaganda justifying the Revolt. But a number of able writers, including Johannes Althusius, undertook to provide such propaganda with philosophical foundations that would render it applicable to the pluralist structure of the Dutch political system. The central notion was that "the people," as a collectivity, can be construed as a singular ontological entity. In such terms, Althusius argued, sovereignty in the Netherlands is indivisible and inalienable, while the day-to-day acts of governance are performed by the town, provincial, and national institutions.

From its first expression in the early years of the Revolt until the end of the republic, the notion of popular sovereignty punctuated the Dutch political literature.[70] Its main function was negative: to deny a claim to supremacy on the part of a political entity whose authority the particular writer desired to attenuate. In the early Revolt period, the idea was used to undermine the authority of Philip II. Later, a different locus of sovereignty was argued, as the struggle for political hegemony became strongly focused as a contest between the States General and the province of Holland.

The constitutional status of the States General was never formulated in clear terms during the history of the republic. The division of jurisdiction between it and the provincial states was a tendentious issue from the beginning of the Revolt. With Prince Maurice's coup d'état in 1618, and the subsequent trials of Johan van Oldenbarnevelt and Hugo Grotius, this division

---

70. Kossmann (1981) is a good discussion of the concept of popular sovereignty in the Dutch literature, which focuses upon the ambiguity of its key concepts.

was identified as a matter that demanded clear recognition of the locus of sovereignty in the union. It was under the authority of the States General that Oldenbarnevelt and Grotius were arrested, and they were tried by a court constituted ad hoc by the States General. In his defense, Oldenbarnevelt contended that the trial was illegal because the provinces, not the generality, had jurisdictional authority. He failed to convince the court and was condemned. Most Dutch political writers, however, were sympathetic to his argument, which was perceived as soundly based on the principle that sovereignty in the union resided with the provincial states, where it had always been, long before the Revolt. In the literature of the seventeenth and eighteenth centuries, this idea was frequently reiterated as a fundamental political principle of the union.[71]

Hugo Grotius was only one of many who embraced the doctrine of provincial sovereignty, but his stature as a political theorist by far surpassed that of any other Netherlander during the Golden Age of the Republic, or indeed since then. After his escape from prison, he was forced to spend most of his life abroad, but his writings were read widely in the Netherlands. Grotius was a classical scholar, historian, philologist, poet, and dramatist—but above all, he was a jurist. The basis of all social arrangements in his view was "natural law," which he interpreted in secular terms as imperatives derived by human reason. In 1622, he published his *Justification of the Lawful Government of Holland*. There he strongly defended the sovereign authority of the provinces as a matter of fundamental principle, one that could not be set aside on the ground that a centralized authority in the republic could provide more effective governance. The book was banned by the States General but circulated freely in the Netherlands nonetheless. During the following years, a copious stream of writings issued from his pen in which he reiterated the principle of provincial sovereignty and, despite his own treatment by the Republic, compared it favorably with the great civilizations of Athens and Rome, as well as that of the ancient progenitors of the Dutch, the "Batavi" (Sabine, 1937,

---

71. Rowen (1972, 105f.) reprints a declaration issued by the States of Holland in 1587 that firmly rejected the Duke of Leicester's contention that sovereign authority in the Netherlands resided in the States General and the Council of State, through which he expected to exercise monarchical powers. This was, writes Rowen, "the first in a long line of affirmations of provincial sovereignty in the history of the Dutch Republic." Price regards the assertion of sovereign authority by Maurice and the States General in 1618 as purely opportunistic. "It is a striking fact," he observes, "that this discovery of sovereign authorities in the Generality was discarded as soon as the immediate problem had been dealt with" (1994, 284). Jonathan Israel refers to a three volume work published in 1663–64 by Johan de Wit as using "every conceivable argument to demonstrate that sovereignty, in Holland, resided in the States of Holland" (1995, 763).

420–425; Geyl, 1961, 73f.; Friedmann, 1967; Kossmann, 1968; Haitsma Mulier, 1985).

The theoretical import of the proposition that the provincial states were sovereign governmental bodies was that sovereignty in the republic as a whole was construed to be divided. None of the Dutch political theorists expanded this notion into a searching examination of the constitutional nature of a polity in which political power is dispersed. They thought of the union as something more than an alliance of independent states, but they lacked the conceptual equipment to analyze a pluralistic political system. At bottom, the Dutch discussion of the locus of sovereignty was driven by the practical necessity of recognizing the special importance of Holland in the Union without allowing it hegemony over the whole. Such a discussion served that purpose poorly. What was really required was an understanding of how a pluralistic system works with countervailing centers of power.

The Notion of Mixed Government

The idea that the union was a "mixed" political system was suggested by many writers during the republican era. Baruch Spinoza, Johannes Althusius, Johan de Witt, and numerous others depicted, and defended, the Dutch political system in such terms. In the universities, mixed government was the predominant concept used by professors who lectured on the country's political system. But this literature made no advance from, or even equalled, Erasmus's observation that the best form of government was a "limited monarchy, checked and lessened by aristocracy and democracy." The notion of mixed government was ubiquitous in the European political literature of the seventeenth century. It did not go unchallenged by Dutch writers, however. Hugo Grotius and the de la Court brothers were prominent critics of it in general, and rejected its applicability to the United Provinces (Weston, 1965, 11f.; Leeb, 1973, 24; Haitsma Mulier, 1980; Haitsma Mulier, 1987, 187; Rowen, 1988, 67; Kossmann, 1991, 290; Worst, 1992, 152; Speck, 1995, 181f.).[72]

From the standpoint of the history of constitutional theory, the fact that many Dutch writers embraced the notion of mixed government is, in itself, a matter of secondary interest. The main issue is: Were they able to use it as

72. Grotius's position is somewhat ambiguous. Haitsma Mulier points out that in his book on the ancient Batavian Republic, he used the notion of mixed government (1980, 69). He was an admirer of Venice and regarded its governmental system as resembling that of the Dutch Republic, but it is unclear whether he perceived the resemblance to reside in the fact that they were both oligarchies (of which he strongly approved) or that they both had "mixed" political systems.

an effective instrument in understanding the dynamics of their political system? Or, because some modern historians appear to regard mixed government as a viable concept of the state, can we today make use of it in attempting to understand the Dutch Republic and account for its remarkable contributions to Western civilization? We saw in our examination of the Venetian Republic that the attempt to classify its political institutions according to whether they constituted monarchical, aristocratic, or democratic elements serves no analytical purpose. The same judgment must hold for the Dutch Republic. Even if one could perform the taxonomic feat, it would render no analytical assistance. What understanding would be gained if we were to claim that popular rioting in the Dutch towns constituted the "democratic element" in the Dutch polity, or if we were to describe Prince Maurice's coup d'état as an increase in the weight of the "monarchical element" in the state?[73]

The notion that the republic was a mixed government of the Aristotelian sort is fundamentally misleading because the whole power of the Dutch state, as in Venice, was in the hands of the regent aristocracy. Recognition of this fact is a necessary preliminary to any empirical examination of how the various political institutions worked in coping with the mundane quotidian problems, as well as the occasional great crises, that were the agenda of Dutch public policy. No insight into how the republic succeeded in combining effective government with an exceptional degree of personal liberty is provided by simply classifying its political institutions in terms of the classical triad.

The notion of mixed government did not, of itself, denote a system of dispersed power. In its classical Greek formulation, the basic idea was that each of the pure forms of government had certain inherent properties that could be preserved in a mixed polity: the unity of the one, the wisdom of the few, and the liberty of the many. It is not a large step from this perspective to view these properties as associated with different political institutions, representing the three "elements." It is a much greater step to construe these institutions as competing or mutually controlling centers of political power. Indeed, the grafting of this notion onto the concept of mixed government had no logical foundation. Nevertheless, it is clear from Gasparo Contarini's book on the government of Venice that, by the mid-sixteenth century, this interpretation of mixed government had begun to appear. By the eighteenth

---

73. William Speck notes, "For much of the seventeenth century . . . discussion focused round the question of whether the Stadholder represented the monarchical element in a mixed constitution of monarchy, aristocracy, and democracy; or whether the Princes of Orange were using it as the Habsburgs had done, to upset the balance in favour of the monarch" (1995, 181). It seems obvious that the mixed government schema could only serve to turn the important question of the changing power of the stadholder into an arid semantic debate.

century, it was the standard interpretation. Did the Dutch political theorists contribute significantly to this transformation? I think we must admit that they did not.

In the republican literature there are references here and there to the desirability of "balance" in political power, or to the need to "check" those who exercise it.[74] But, so far as I have been able to ascertain, no one produced a systematic theoretical discussion of the countervailance model of the state, or a sustained empirical examination of Dutch government in terms of such a conception. On this matter, the most interesting idea contained in the literature is the view that while the common citizen is obligated without qualification to obey the established lawmaking authorities, the "lesser magistrates" may disobey them and indeed are morally obligated to do so if the protection of the citizenry from unjust laws requires it (see Gelderen, 1992, 73f., 99f., 108, 269). This idea was expressed earlier by the Theodore Beza and Phillipe du Plessis-Mornay (see Chapter 4). It contained the seed of the countervailance model of a constitutional polity and, given the structure and dynamics of the Republic's political system, could have taken root in Dutch political theory—but in fact, it did not.[75]

74. Althusius is, once again, noteworthy as having clearly expressed the idea of checks and balances (see Kossmann, 1981, 16; Lloyd, 1991, 290f.).

75. It would serve no purpose here to examine the influence of Venice on Dutch political thought. Admiring references to the Venetian Republic were prevalent in the Dutch political literature, but Dutch political writers failed to grasp the checks and balances nature of the Venetian political system. The predominant interpretation was that Venice exemplified the principle of mixed government. The impact of Venice on Dutch political thought has been intensively examined by Haitsma Mulier (1980); see also Burke's comparative study of Venice and Amsterdam (1994).

7

The Development of Constitutional Government and Countervailance Theory in Seventeenth-Century England

According to standard histories of modern Europe, the seventeenth century was the century of France. Not only was France the most powerful nation-state on the continent, but its cultural influence was also more widespread and profound than any hegemonic center had exercised since Roman times. French replaced Latin as the common language of diplomacy and was adopted by the educated classes of Europe as the proper medium of sophisticated conversation. French literature was unrivaled in popularity. The Comédie Française, subsidized by the state and nourished by the genius of Molière, became the paragon theater of Europe. The brilliant court of Versailles was emulated in far-off capitals, where men and women of high society dressed themselves in the latest French fashions, gathered at salons, danced the minuet, displayed their mastery of flamboyant bowing and curtseying, drank tea and coffee, and, in their private ablutions, employed a dainty silver-backed brush for cleaning the teeth. When Charles II was called back to England after his fourteen years of exile in France, he and his "Cavaliers" introduced French culture and manners into London society—to the mortification of the Puritans, who regarded them as ungodly.

In political organization, seventeenth-century France represented the ultimate in monarchical absolutism. Louis XIV destroyed what remained of independent local and regional governments, concentrated all political power at his Court of Versailles, and ruled without calling the Estates General into session. "L'état, c'est moi," a statement attributed to him, has come to epitomize the theory of absolute sovereignty. In the United Provinces of the Netherlands, a pluralist system of political organization was fully established, and in England, one was in development. These nations, however, were small compared to France and lacked the influence that French language and culture exerted on the politically active sectors of other European states.

As of even the end of the seventeenth century, an observer of the European scene would have had good reason to believe that concentrated power was to become the universal model of political organization for nation-states, and that the French language and culture would play a special role in furthering it. From the vantage point of the present day, such a view might well illustrate the perilous nature of historical prediction. Absolutism has not disappeared from the modern world, but constitutional government is clearly the ascendant political doctrine of our time. In this development, it is England that has played the dominant role. A remarkable proportion of today's democracies have derived their political systems directly, or indirectly via the United States, from England. Even in countries whose peoples differ greatly from the English, such as India and Pakistan, the period of British colonial rule seems to have been sufficient to establish constitutionalism as a widely accepted political ideology. That ideology has not proved to be nearly so robust in regions that were colonies of France, Spain, or even the Netherlands.

In this development, events in North America played a crucial role. In 1664 the Dutch colony of New Amsterdam became the English colony of New York. A century later, at the insistence of the American colonists, English forces attacked and took Louisburg and Quebec, thus completing the English dominance of the eastern seaboard of North America and control of the St. Lawrence river, the great highway into the heart of the continent. Otto von Bismark, who assembled the diverse German states of central Europe into a unified nation, is reported to have said (apparently with some regret) that the most important political fact of the twentieth century will prove to be that America speaks English. The importance of American support of Britain in the European conflicts of the past century sustains Bismark's opinion, but the "special relationship" between Britain and America is more than a matter of language. English political forms and principles were also transplanted to America, creating a large transatlantic communion of political philosophy that has led the development of constitutionalism in the modern world.

France, Spain, and Portugal established their colonial governments on the same principles of hierarchy and absolutism that prevailed at home. The political system of the United Provinces of the Netherlands was pluralist, but it would have been very difficult to install it elsewhere; at any rate, the Dutch made no attempt to do so in their colonial possessions. The English system of government could travel across salt water, and it did. Britain's colonial history is not a story of beneficent government—far from it—but the transmission to the colonies of British constitutional forms and principles endowed these colonies with social and intellectual capital that proved of inestimable value when they came to set up national housekeeping on their own.

It is evident in retrospect that modern constitutionalism, in both practice and theory, had its main origins in seventeenth-century England, but for England itself, that period was one of political upheaval. Tendentious disagreements between the king and Parliament appeared soon after James VI of Scotland became James I of England in 1603. These conflicts were greatly exacerbated during the reign of Charles I, and culminated in a long civil war in the 1640s. The completeness of Parliament's military victory was marked by its trial of the king for treason, and his execution in 1649. But its supremacy was short-lived, giving way to a "Protectorate" in which Oliver Cromwell held the full powers of a Bodinian sovereign. The Stuart monarchy was restored in 1660, but the conflict between king and Parliament resumed pretty much where it had left off two decades earlier, and when James II succeeded to the throne in 1685, it sharply increased in intensity. The invasion of England by William of Orange in 1688 ended the Stuart monarchy, but his own reign was punctuated by disputes with Parliament. Not until the eighteenth century was well advanced did English politics cease to be dominated by friction between king and Parliament. English constitutionalism developed out of the political conflicts of the seventeenth century. Much of the literature of political *theory* that this period produced in large quantity (and high quality) was framed in terms of abstract philosophical principle, but it was inspired by contemporary practical problems.

During this same century, England was transforming itself from an island of minor importance in European affairs into a world power, outpacing Spain, France, and the Netherlands in the acquisition of colonies and in the crucial dominance of the sea. On the intellectual plane, the century also witnessed the emergence of England to a position of prominence in philosophy and science.[1] In the intellectual historiography of the West, few English names appear before the seventeenth century, but during it, to mention only the stellar figures, there were Francis Bacon, the contra-Aristotelian advocate of inductive epistemology; Thomas Hobbes, the promoter of Cartesian metaphysical materialism; and John Locke, whose *Essay Concerning Human Understanding* (1690) was a philosophic foundation of modern empiricism. In the domain of natural science, there were William Harvey, who initiated the materialist empirical study of physiology with its revolutionary impact on the practice of medicine; Robert Boyle, who began the detachment of scientific chemistry from the mysticism of alchemy; Robert Hooke, who made important discoveries in biology, physics, and astronomy; and above all, the great Isaac Newton, whose *Mathematical Principles of Natural Philosophy* (1687) was arguably the most important scientific book of all time. State support of scientific discovery and its practical application was signaled by the establishment of the Royal Society in 1660, and the Royal Observatory at Greenwich

1. "Before 1660 England had been culturally dependent on Italy, France, and Spain. No Englishman had any serious reputation on the continent, with the possible exception of Sir Thomas More . . . In the scientific revolution especially England lagged behind Italy and France" (Hill, 1990, 17).

in 1665.[2] As in the Dutch Republic during the same century, disturbed political conditions did not hamper intellectual progress.

The establishment of a causal connection, though surely not impossible as David Hume contended, is especially difficult with respect to the relationship between the domain of ideas and that of material events. I shall not undertake to argue that large issue here; it is sufficient for our purposes at the moment to observe that seventeenth-century England demands special recognition in an account of the history of modern constitutionalism in both practice and theory. The protracted struggle for power between king and Parliament was accompanied by an efflorescence of political ideas in which the concept of a polity composed of countervailing powers was clearly defined.

Seventeenth-century England contained a complex of governmental authorities. In addition to the national government in London, a heterogeneous array of regional and local institutions had evolved since the Norman Conquest. For most of the 4 million or so inhabitants of England and Wales, daily life was regulated by county, parish, village, and church authorities, whose respective domains of jurisdiction varied from place to place (Hughes, 1995, 255). Though these local governments sometimes played a role in great affairs of state, London was the almost exclusive venue for the constitutional developments examined in this chapter. London was not only the seat of the royal court and the meeting place of Parliament, it was the only urban center of substantial size.[3]

In the Dutch Republic, with its highly urbanized population, political organization was dominated by the town regents. The system of government that developed there after the Revolt was necessarily federalist in nature, in order to accommodate the diverse economic and political interests of the towns and provinces. In England no such necessity existed. The geographical concentration of governmental power that characterized absolute monarchies was continued in England as it developed the institutional structure of a pluralist system. England also differed from the Netherlands in another respect of great significance—the role of military power in politics. The importance of the stadholder in the history of the Dutch Republic derived from the fact that he was commander of its armed forces. The persistence of the

2. The practical value of science, and the role of the state in furthering it, was graphically evidenced by the Longitude Act of 1714, which offered an enormous prize for an effective method of locating a ship's position at sea. This incentive led to the development of the first reliable marine chronometer by John Harrison (see Sobel, 1996).

3. As of the accession of Charles I in 1625, "London, with about half a million, remained the only sizeable town . . . Of the other towns the greatest, such as Bristol and Norwich, were no more than fair-sized villages, while the overwhelming majority of people farmed their living from the land as they had done since time out of mind" (Falkus, 1992, 20).

republic's pluralistic system of government was, on occasion, threatened as much by its own Orangist faction as by Spain and France. Because of its insular geography, England did not need a standing army to defend itself against foreign enemies, and until the outbreak of the Civil War, it had none. The ability of Parliament to defy the early Stuart monarchs rested, at bottom, on this elementary fact of power politics. After the Restoration the king had a standing army of considerable size at his disposal, and it is doubtful that a rebellion could have succeeded without armed intervention from abroad.[4]

England and the United Provinces were, however, alike in that they were both aristocracies; the role of governance was reserved exclusively to a very small segment of the population. The modern concept of democratic government is absent from the Dutch literature of the seventeenth century, and surfaced in England for only a brief period in the Leveller writings of the late 1640s. Two centuries more were to pass before the idea took hold that the populace at large could be safely permitted to share in the exercise of state power.

Seventeenth-century England was the Golden Age of Western political philosophy. The literature of this era gave expression to an extraordinarily wide range of ideas, from the theory of the "divine right of kings" and the patriarchal concept of governance to the advocacy of popular participation in government, the right of rebellion, and, most importantly for the history of constitutionalism, the clearest expressions since Polybius of the countervailance model of the state.

Given the wealth of primary materials, it is not surprising that intellectual historians have devoted a great deal of attention to the political literature of seventeenth-century England. The stream of commentary on this topic began in the mid-eighteenth century and has since become a flood that shows no sign of diminishing. In the early twentieth century, revisionist historians attacked the standard Whig historiography, which had projected an idyllic, almost teleological, appraisal of seventeenth-century England.[5] This criticism was clearly justified, but only to a degree. The Act of Settlement of 1701 did not establish a finished constitutional order; it served only as a base-point for further constitutional development, which continues to the present day (see Chapter 9). Nor was the outcome of the century of troubles as inevitable as the Whig doctrine of progress appeared to imply. If Richard Cromwell had

4. "In the period 1603–40 the number of fighting men whom the king could count upon in an emergency could be counted in the scores rather than the thousands." At the height of the civil war, 150,000 men were in arms. Cromwell retained a standing army that, after the Restoration, contained some 3,000 men (Morrill, 1984, 299f.; Hart, 1993, 33).

5. See Kenyon (1990, 11–18) for a brief but balanced discussion of Whig historiography and its critics.

inherited his father's personality, if the "Protestant Wind" of November 5, 1688, had shifted, or if any of a score of other particulars had been otherwise, the constitutional history of Britain might well have been very different. But the events of the seventeenth century did in fact establish the principle of constitutional government in the nation that was the leading world power during much of the following two centuries, and one does not have to embrace a Whiggish ideology in order to recognize the great importance of this fact in the political history of the modern world.

Religious Toleration and Civic Freedom

Seventeenth-century England may be depicted in terms of a contest for power between the Crown and Parliament, but religion played such a large role in the political controversies of the period that it could also be treated as part of the pan-European struggle between Catholicism and Protestantism. Religion was at the forefront of English politics, and the constitutional contest between king and Parliament was greatly exacerbated by the fears of Protestants that the king could not be trusted to defend their faith against the growing force of the Counter-Reformation in Europe.[6] Suspicion that Charles I secretly harbored a desire to restore the Catholic faith and the authority of the papacy was an important factor in the events that led to civil war in the 1640s. William of Orange projected the invasion of England in 1688 as a strategy for the military defense of the Dutch Republic, but the main aim of the English parliamentarians who urged him to undertake it was to defend Protestantism in England against the Counter-Reformation intentions of James II.

In the Netherlands, Protestantism had won the allegiance of a substantial part of the population of the northern provinces by the time of the outbreak of the Revolt against Spain. In England, however, the Reformation had made little headway by that date. Henry VIII was a strong supporter of the church. He was awarded the title of "Defender of the Faith" by Pope Clement VII for his services in contesting the heretical doctrines of Martin Luther. England joined the Protestant camp in the 1530s as a consequence of Clement's rejection of Henry's petition for the annulment of his marriage to Catherine

6. At the middle of the sixteenth century, half of Europe was Protestant. During the ensuing century, this proportion declined to a fifth (Ozment, 1991, 28). According to McIlwain, the Counter-Reformation was the most important fact of the early seventeenth century, and "England was universally recognized then as the one corner of Christendom in which there was still hope of checking the onward moving tide of the Catholic reaction" (1918, l, lvi).

of Aragon. Henry defied the pope, married Anne Boleyn, and was excommunicated from the church. He acted quickly to crush any domestic opposition, including the dissolution of the monasteries, which in much of rural England were the most powerful institutions of local government. By the Act of Supremacy of 1534, the monarch was declared to be the supreme head of the Church of England, thus officially uniting church and state.[7] In Catholic countries, political power was shared between the secular monarch and the church authorities, who owed their appointments, and their primary allegiances, to the papacy. In England this degree of pluralism was swept away in the 1530s. Until Parliament began to assert its independence after James I came to the throne, political power in England was institutionally more concentrated than in any other nation in Europe.

Protestantism was brought under vicious attack during the brief reign of Mary Tudor (1553–1558), the ardently Catholic daughter of Catherine of Aragon. The long reign of Elizabeth I (1558–1603) secured the consolidation of the Church of England, but more significant politically was that during this period other Protestant communions spread. By the beginning of the Stuart era, the religious profile of England was characterized by diversity. A large proportion of the population adhered to the official state church, but there were also substantial numbers of continuing Catholics, Presbyterians, and a variety of "Independents" who eschewed any ecclesiastical organization beyond that of the individual congregation (Haller, 1955, ch. 4; Williams, 1965, 13–23).

The various Protestant churches were all fiercely hostile to Catholicism and the power of the papacy, but that was virtually all that united them. They differed sharply on theological issues, and each regarded itself as the exclusive repository of "true Christianity," duty-bound to spread its own vision throughout the land. Religious toleration was not on the agenda of the Protestant churches in England. As in the Dutch Republic, it derived not from philosophical or theological principles, but from the fact that all religious groupings were minorities. In such a state of affairs, toleration was a policy that was "second best" for all parties. England did not adopt such a policy officially until after the Revolution of 1688, but the foundations for it had been laid during the Elizabethan period, when the ecclesiastical structure of Protestantism had become pluralist. During the eighteenth century, and de-

---

7. "On the whole, English men and women did not want the Reformation and most of them were slow to accept it when it came . . . The religious changes of the sixteenth century were acquiesced in and accepted by the English laity rather than initiated or promoted by them. Of course these changes could not have carried through without some cooperation from 'below.' But the drive, timing, and organization came primarily from above" (Scarisbrick, 1985, 1, 61).

spite the existence of an official state church, England's repute as a land of religious freedom surpassed even that of the Netherlands.[8]

Of all human beliefs, religious doctrine is the least amenable to compromise, for rejection of theological truth is not merely an error in reasoning; it is heresy, an offense against God. At the same time, the adoption of religious toleration as state policy has great consequences for the general exercise of political influence. The toleration of an aberrant religion means that its adherents are left free to preach, publish, and organize. Where such freedoms exist for religious groups, they cannot be effectively denied to citizens who have other agendas. Intellectual freedom, and the freedom to associate with others who have like interests and ideas, are the essential foundations of civic liberty and support the development of institutions that may exercise control over the power of the state. The toleration of diverse religious views in England was a salutary political achievement in itself, but it also served as a catalyst for the development of personal freedom in the secular domains of civic life.

This argument, however, is one of sufficiency, not necessity, and in fact the history of English liberty did not begin with the establishment of religious diversity in the sixteenth century. Historians commonly depict it as originating with Magna Carta a full four centuries earlier. William the Conqueror had completely dismantled the old political order and established a new regime in which the territorial barons held their fiefs as his personal gifts. But the passage of time eroded whatever debt of gratitude the original barons may have entertained, and after a few generations, their successors regarded themselves as holding prescriptive rights that the king was bound to sustain. The barons drafted Magna Carta in order to secure their own interests, but it was written in such broad terms that subsequent generations could construe it as a general charter of civic liberty. Magna Carta was not the only document of the feudal era that constrained the power of the king, and in practical terms it was less effective in this respect than the royal charters establishing incorporated boroughs, which usually contained specific promises by the king not to interfere in local affairs. But over time Magna Carta became the iconic symbol of the principle that the authority of the monarch was subordinate to what came to be called England's "ancient constitution" (Barlow, 1967, 120; Holt, 1972, 49–55).

There are, however, features of Magna Carta that have more than symbolic significance for the history of constitutionalism. Most notable among these is its implicit assumption of the dependence of freedom on the secure pos-

---

8. Voltaire captured the essence of the matter when he remarked: "If there were only one religion in England, we should have to fear despotism; if there were two, they would cut each other's throats; but there are thirty, and live in peace and happiness" (Wood, 1992, 14).

session of property, and the dependence of this, in turn, on control of the royal power to levy taxes. The barons of the early thirteenth century could easily appreciate that what they referred to as their "liberties" derived from their status as owners of landed property, and that this could be undermined or subverted if there were no restraints upon the taxing power of the king. The principle that taxation required the assent of the Great Council, that is, the taxpayers, actually antedates Magna Carta by a century, but that document conferred canonic status upon it (Burke, 1991, 82f.). By the seventeenth century, property had become more diverse in form and more widely distributed, but the prominence of the issue of taxation in the conflict between king and Parliament (composed entirely of property owners) reflects a continuation of the view that without security of property there can be no liberty. Two centuries later, "taxation without representation" was again a central issue in the conflict between Britain and its American colonies. Taxation is still a highly sensitive issue in modern democratic politics, but it does not have the intimate connection with liberty that it once had in the minds of those who opposed the unbridled sovereignty of monarchs.

An innovation in governmental administration that was included in Magna Carta also deserves notice; the creation of courts of "Common Pleas." Prior to this, the courts of England were parts of the king's administrative bureaucracy and accompanied him on his travels to adjudicate pending cases. The establishment of permanent local courts was probably not regarded as more than a matter of convenience at the time, but it led to the development of a judicial system separate from the prerogative courts of the monarch. The complete independence of the courts from the Crown was not achieved until the end of the eighteenth century, but its notable development in the seventeenth was an outcome of the court system that had been established by Magna Carta.[9]

In considering the constitutional significance of Magna Carta, it is also important to note that King John did not sign it willingly. He was forced to do so by men who commanded military power. Statements of general principle, such as those contained in Magna Carta, deploy no compelling power by themselves. Like ordinary laws, they must be *enforced*. Magna Carta was condemned by Pope Innocent III, but this did nothing to release John from its provisions, for the barons had coercive powers in England that were more tangible and immediate than those of the church. With the emergence of the

9. Edmund Burke described the creation of courts of common pleas as a "great revolution. A tribunal, a creation of mere law, independent of personal power was established; and this separation of the king's authority from his person was a matter of vast consequence towards introducing ideas of freedom, and confirming the sacredness and majesty of laws" (1991, 84).

nation-state as the primary instrument of political organization, the power of the local feudal lords was greatly attenuated, but by then another institution of the feudal era had emerged as part of the system of national government in England—Parliament. It became the self-appointed guardian of the English constitution and the protector of English liberty.[10]

The Roles of Parliament

The Great Council called by Edward I in 1295 has been enshrined in history as the first of England's parliaments. Later dubbed the "Model Parliament," it included representatives from the lesser aristocracy, the clergy, and the urban boroughs.[11] From that time on, Parliament has been composed of two groups: those entitled to membership by virtue of their aristocratic status, and those who attend in their capacities as *representatives* of other classes. From early on, these met separately as a House of Lords and a House of Commons, each of which thereafter developed its own traditions and rules of procedure. Bicameralism was thereby entrenched in the English system of government, dividing the authority of Parliament between two independent bodies with the power to check one another as well as the monarch. Bicameralism is an almost universal feature of modern constitutional governments, even in countries such as the United States where there is no aristocracy and both houses are selected by the same set of electors. In modern Britain the House of Lords is widely viewed as an anachronism, but all proposals to abolish it have failed so far because a bicameral Parliament is generally valued as an important component of a checks and balances system of government.

In the typical introductory textbook in political science, governments are often described in terms of a tripartite classification of "functions"—legislative, executive, and judicial—with institutions such as the British Parliament and the American Congress classified as performing the first of these. The doctrine of "separation of powers" between the institutions charged with these several functions continues to be favored by American lawyers, but as an in-

---

10. "Modern liberty, as inhabitants of Western democracies enjoy it . . . [is] perhaps *the* superordinate political good. Without it many other human goods and all other political goods become uncertain, precarious and insecure . . . An Inquiry into its origins is not an exercise in a sterile antiquarianism but an effort to know the ultimate terms for the well-being of modern society . . . In view of the historical geography of liberty, it is therefore of highest consequence . . . that we understand what went on in England and especially in English parliaments between 1529 and 1688" (Hexter, 1983, 51).

11. The council assembled earlier by Simon de Montfort during his brief authority as leader of the Barons' Rebellion against Henry III included persons who were not lords and, consequently, has some claim of priority as England's first Parliament.

strument of political analysis it quickly shatters when applied to modern American, or modern British, government. That Parliament plays a central role in lawmaking is indisputable, and even when Jean Bodin was writing the *République,* the power to make laws, which he regarded as the fundamental mark of "sovereignty," was pluralist across the Channel. But Parliament played other, more important roles in the evolution of modern constitutionalism.[12]

Except for its insistence on having veto power over taxation, the status of the Great Council in King John's time was that of an advisory body to the monarch, in whose hands alone lay the authority to make state policy. But the council did not restrict itself to this role. Its meetings also provided a venue for the venting of general or local complaints against the policies of the Crown or the behavior of its officers. By at least as early as the fourteenth century, it was common for members of Parliament to introduce "petitions" reflecting the grievances of their constituents (Morgan, 1989, 223f.). During the reign of Elizabeth, this was one of the main roles that members of the House of Commons perceived themselves as empowered, and indeed *obligated,* to perform.

The venting of complaints is of little moment in itself, but in the early seventeenth century it was joined to the fiscal authority of Parliament, and a powerful political weapon was forged thereby. The House of Commons made its assent to taxation conditional upon the monarch's favorable response to a petition for "redress of grievances" (Lockyer, 1989, 129–133). Other than acceding to the demands of the Commons, the only response open to the king was to exercise his authority as convener of Parliament. When Charles I's relations with Parliament reached an impasse in the spring of 1629, he dissolved it and ruled without calling another for eleven years. But he was only able to do so because England was at peace during this period and the royal treasury was not stressed by heavy military expenditures. A rebellion in Scotland in 1639 changed the situation; the Crown needed new revenues that only Parliament could furnish. Charles was forced to call a new Parliament and to face again its demands for redress of grievances (Lockyer, 1989, 249).[13]

12. L. L. Peck points out that Parliament passed little legislation between 1603 and 1640 (1993, 94). The contest over the constitutional status of Parliament during this period did not center on an attempt to play a larger role in lawmaking.

13. "The power of the purse was effective only because the king was impoverished and the kingdom secure from foreign invasion. These two circumstances, more than any others, explain why responsible government came to England rather than on the continent" (Roberts, 1966, 62). France also had a parliament of ancient lineage, but it had not acquired the same degree of authority or constitutional entrenchment. When the Estates General became troublesome in 1614, Louis XIII dissolved it, and he and his successors ruled comfortably without it—until 1789. According to A. P. Monahan, the English Parliament and the French Estates General began to diverge significantly in their political roles during the fourteenth century (1987, 251f.).

Some historians have argued that the concept of monarchical sovereignty was significantly attenuated in early Stuart England by the notion that the power of the king was limited by "law."[14] This idea was indeed frequently stated, but there is little reason to regard it as more than a convenient dissimulation of royalist supporters. In itself, the "law" disposes no political power, and so far as the monarch is concerned, it is deprived even of prescriptive weight by the legal doctrine that he cannot be charged before a court of law. That doctrine was widely accepted, even by opponents of James I and Charles I. Nevertheless, the House of Commons established itself during their reigns as a judicial organ of state, with the authority, not possessed by any other court of the land, to render judgments on charges against the conduct of the Crown and, in 1649, against the king in person.

The political power of the House of Lords remains considerable today, but it is not what it once was. Viewed in the context of the long history of aristocratic rule, the decline of the Lords is one of the more striking constitutional developments of modern times. The ascendancy of the House of Commons over the House of Lords was in process during the Tudor era, but it greatly accelerated during the early seventeenth century. The role of the Lords in the momentous political developments of that period was largely passive; it acquiesced in actions by the Commons that challenged the king's power, but it initiated none of its own. An unbroken decline in the political significance of the Lords has continued since. Today, when writers on British politics refers to "Parliament," they often have only the House of Commons in mind.

The political ascendancy of the Commons over the Lords reflected changes in the economic and social organization of England as feudalism gave way to capitalism. But from the standpoint of constitutional *theory,* the most important factor was that the House of Commons was a *representative* institution. The device of representation extenuates the ancient distinction between government by the few and government by the many, and provides a means by which the virtues that Aristotle had ascribed to aristocracies and democracies may be combined. The franchise in seventeenth-century England was severely restricted, and remained so until the latter part of the nineteenth century, so the few that sat in the House of Commons were the elected representatives of only a somewhat larger few. But this did not prevent those who opposed the king from claiming that they held a mandate from "the people."

14. See especially Burgess (1996) who argues, at length, that the view that the king was constrained by law was widely held at the time to be the central constitutional principle of English government.

There are still some who claim that "democracy" requires that the people at large directly determine the laws by which they are governed, and this view is sometimes supported by reference to what is supposed to have been the political system of Periclean Athens (see, e.g., Dunn, 1992, 239–266). The town governments of early New England are notable examples of direct democracy, but no political entity with a large population and/or geographic extent can function in this manner. The difficulties encountered by the Roman Republic in operating its system of popular assemblies and effectively subordinating them to the aristocracy illustrate the point. The modern nation-state could only have been built upon the hierarchical model if it were not for the practice of representation. For the development of a constitutional political order, that device was vital.

In England the principle of representation has had an almost continuous constitutional history since the thirteenth century. It spread widely in the following century and became a common feature of government in late medieval Europe, but the tide changed, and by the seventeenth century, it had virtually disappeared from the continent. In England, by contrast, it was strengthened by the contest between king and Parliament in the early Stuart era and survived the dictatorship of Oliver Cromwell and the Stuart Restoration. With the Revolution of 1688, an elected House of Commons, construed as representing "the people," was firmly established as a fundamental feature of the constitution.[15] The principle of representation was institutionalized in the colonial governments of British America, and was adopted by them for their state and national governments after they became independent. Today, the existence of an elected representative assembly is generally regarded as a litmus test of "democratic government."[16]

The principle of representation, however, does not necessarily require that representatives be selected by election. The members of a legislative assembly could be chosen by lot, or they could be named by the monarch or by other

15. "The shape of the historical geography of free representative institutions is like an hour-glass. From its beginnings in the thirteenth century it spreads within 100 years across the map of Europe. And then it narrows and narrows until by the end of the sixteenth century only England, and perhaps the Netherlands, still had representative institutions committed to the preservation of the liberties of the subject or citizen . . . For more than a century the stream flowed only through that narrow channel" (Hexter, 1983, 51; see also Plumb, 1969, 90).

16. So far as I know, no general *theory* of representation appeared in the political literature of seventeenth century England. Edmund Burke's famous "Letter to the Sheriffs of Bristol," in which he asserted that an elected representative is a free agent, not bound by the wishes of his electors, was written in 1777. The first comprehensive discussion of representation in the history of political theory occurred in the American Constitutional Convention of 1787, which was continued in the subsequent ratifying debates (see Rakove, 1997, ch. 8).

governmental institutions—as were, for example, the members of the provincial states and the States General in the Dutch Republic, and until 1913 the members of the Senate of the United States. The establishment of an *elected* House of Commons in England was especially significant in supplying a new foundation for the claim that the state exercises coercive power legitimately. William the Conqueror ruled England by "right of conquest." From that time until the accession of James I, only a bare majority of the monarchs of England arrived at the throne through the established rules of hereditary succession, and there were periods during which there were more "usurpers" of the Crown than legitimate heirs (Morrill, 1991, 82f.). Nevertheless, the principle was generally accepted that the English monarch, and the members of the House of Lords, legitimately enjoyed their status by virtue of birth.

The question of the legitimacy of state power was a prominent topic in seventeenth-century political thought. It was tactically useful for members of the House of Commons to claim that they held a mandate to rule that had been legitimized by "popular election." When preparing the ground for the trial of Charles I, the House of Commons passed resolutions declaring that "the people were the source of all just power, that it was exercised for them by the House of Commons, and that whatsoever was enacted for law by the House bound all the people of England even though the King and the House of Lords had not consented" (Weston, 1965, 58).[17] The members of the Commons knew full well that they had been elected by a very small fraction of the citizenry. Their claim to special status in exercising "just power" was patently self-serving, supported in the following century by the contention that the disenfranchised were represented "virtually" by the elected MPs. Nevertheless, the principle that the coercive authority of the state is legitimized (only) by election became standard constitutional doctrine two centuries before the Reform Act of 1832, which took the first small step in the enlargement of the English electorate. Even Thomas Hobbes, the great defender of monarchical absolutism, embraced it in tracing the foundations of the state to a contractual agreement by the people to submit to its authority.

"Constitutionalism," as I have been using that term, refers to a political system that imposes constraints upon the exercise of political power. As I have frequently emphasized, it is not identical with "democracy," which I take to refer to a polity in which the opportunity to participate in political

17. When sentencing the king to death in 1649, the Commons asserted that a king had "a limited power to govern" and that "all redress and remedy of misgovernment [were] by the fundamental Constitution of this Kingdom . . . reserved on the People's behalf in the Right and Power of frequent and successive Parliaments or national Meetings in Council." Charles Stuart, it declared, "hath traitorously and maliciously levyed War against the present Parliament and People therein represented" (Blakeley and Collins, 1975, 189).

processes is open to the citizenry at large, without significant restriction. According to such definitions, even a direct democracy would not be a constitutional order if there were no constraints upon what the majority of the people can do in exercising the coercive power of the state. In such terms, the concept of a "constitutional aristocracy" is perfectly intelligible: a polity in which all political power is reserved to a small part of the citizenry, but is distributed among a number of institutions in such a fashion that they mutually constrain each other. Republican Rome, Renaissance Venice, and the Dutch Republic were constitutional aristocracies. So was England at the end of the seventeenth century. England remained a constitutional aristocracy for a long time thereafter, but during that century it developed political procedures that serviced its evolution into a constitutional democracy.

Mixed Government and the Countervailance Model

A great deal of the political discourse of the seventeenth century focused on the issue of sovereignty. Jean Bodin's *République* (1576) was widely read in England,[18] and Thomas Hobbes's *Leviathan* (1651) renewed attention to the matter at a moment in history when it seemed that the ancient traditions had been swept aside and many English political thinkers were resorting to basic philosophical principles for guidance in the construction of a new political order.[19]

Some modern historians embrace the view that the struggle over sovereignty is the key to understanding the role of seventeenth-century England in early modern political thought.[20] This is, in my opinion a profitless ap-

18. "Quite quickly the book came to be treated as an authority on political matters and an enormous resource of information and argument" (Burgess, 1996, 65).

19. As noted in Chapter 1, Hobbes regarded the social contract as authorizing the monarch to exercise coercive power over the citizenry, whereas Bodin identified sovereignty with the authority to make law. In England, there had not been for centuries a singular center of lawmaking authority, and Hobbes's presentation of the issue was more germane than Bodin's.

20. Weston and Comstock construe seventeenth-century England in terms of a "Grand Controversy over Legal Sovereignty," the ideological contestants being the theory of absolute monarchy on the one hand and, on the other, the theory that although the power of the king flowed from God, it could be exercised only with the people's consent. The latter theory, which in their view brought about "the radicalization of Stuart political thought" is described as an "order theory of kingship" and a "community-centred view of government" that stressed "legal sovereignty" and construed the monarch and the two houses of Parliament as "co-ordinate powers" (1981, 1f., 17f., 32f.). J. G. A. Pocock regards the conflicts of seventeenth century England as bearing upon the issue of sovereignty, and expresses the view that what was in process of development was a coalescence of Crown, Parliament, and church into a "unified sovereignty" (1993, 257f.; see also Nenner, 1993,

proach. Admittedly, the language of sovereignty was ubiquitous in the political literature of the period, and that era is certainly notable as one in which the theory of sovereignty, as such, was renewed and elaborated. But the significance of seventeenth-century England for constitutional theory was that during this period the concept of sovereignty was *replaced* by the concept of checks and balances. This transformation in theory paralleled the evolution of political practice. No significant alterations in the political system's institutional structure took place prior to Walpole's establishment of the cabinet system, but during the seventeenth century, the operational dynamics of the system developed in accordance with the countervailance model of government. The trend in this direction was reversed during the Cromwellian period, and was unable to resume during the era of the later Stuarts. These periods together constituted four-tenths of the years from 1603 to 1688, so the development of a countervailance system of government in England was by no means continuous. Nor was it secure until the "Glorious Revolution" firmly established the principles of dispersed power and checks and balances as the central pillars of English constitutionalism.

During the eighteenth century, the countervailance model of British government was embraced by all the major writers on the subject. It appears to have been generally accepted until Walter Bagehot and A. V. Dicey initiated in the nineteenth century a reinterpretation of the English constitution in terms of the doctrine of parliamentary sovereignty.

The Early Stuart Era

In the four decades between the accession of James I and the Civil War, England became the most important venue in Western history for the development of the theory of constitutional government. The doctrines of sovereignty and countervailance confronted one another in a protracted dispute between the king and Parliament over specific issues of state policy, over the

---

194). Glenn Burgess contends that although the doctrine of sovereignty was the centerpiece of contemporary political theory, it was construed only by marginal writers such as Filmer as supporting the proposition that the king held absolute power. Burgess views the notion that the king was generally regarded as bound to act according to law as the significant meaning of "sovereignty" in early Stuart England. He sees widespread agreement on three propositions: that the king was accountable only to God; that he was bound to govern "according to the laws of the land"; and that he had absolute power only in certain specific matters (1996, 209). On this basis Burgess argues, at length, that "the early Stuart political nation was held together by an *anti*-absolutist consensus" (19). I cannot see either the logic or the operational significance of such a conception of "limited" monarchical sovereignty. As a window upon early seventeenth-century political thought, it is as opaque as the wall in which it is set.

distribution of political power, and, in the theoretical domain, over the interpretation of the English constitution. Though these three matters are analytically disjunct, they were intimately related in the political contest of the Early Stuart period. If the members of the House of Commons had had no objection to the policies of the king, they would have had little reason to insist upon an enlargement of the powers of Parliament at the expense of the prerogative authority of the Crown. And because they were clearly pressing for a novel arrangement of political power, one that was hitherto unknown in England and the other monarchical nations of Europe, a philosophical defense, or at least a rationalization, was required. Over this period, the notion that England was, or should be, a pluralist political system in which the several institutions of the state could check each other, was stated repeatedly in parliamentary speeches and political publications. It was finally acknowledged by the king himself, on the eve of the Civil War, as the meaning of England's "mixed government."[21]

Conflict over Policy and Power

Because the House of Commons was an elected institution, its members could claim that they represented the people of England. The electorate, restricted by property qualifications, was only a small fraction of the population, but it had been growing. In the seventeenth century, the franchise was exercised by most of the country gentry, and by the wealthier merchants and craftsmen of the towns, who were inclined to elect men of their own socioeconomic class (Plumb, 1969; see also Judson, 1964, 218f.; Manning, 1976, 1f., 153f.). The exercise of the royal prerogative impinged directly upon the economic interests of a larger segment of the English populace. Queen Elizabeth had done most of the things that inflamed Parliament during the Stuart era (Allen, 1967, 14f.), but the exercise of the royal prerogative was now more broadly seen to infringe on the rights of property.

Direct taxation of property, which normally furnished the greater part of the national revenue, had been under the control of Parliament long since. But the yield of these taxes was insufficient to satisfy James I, who, in coming to the throne of England from the impoverished throne of Scotland, expected to reign with lavish magnificence equal to that of the French and Spanish monarchs. Charles I was less profligate, but when in 1629 he decided to rule without Parliament, he also was impelled to seek other sources of revenue.

21. Revisionist historians who trace the Civil War to socioeconomic conditions have contended that the early Stuart period was not such a period of continuous conflict between king and Parliament, nor so important in constitutional development and theory, as this paragraph depicts. For a spirited reassertion of the older, "Whig" view, see Hexter (1978).

During this era, the Crown lands were sold, monopoly privileges were granted and new peerages created in exchange for ready money.[22] New tariffs were levied on the ground that regulating imports was part of the exclusive royal authority in foreign affairs, and, without any comparable rationalization, wealthy citizens were compelled to subscribe to loans with little prospect of repayment. Charles's levy of a special assessment of "ship money" to support the navy might have been quietly accepted as necessary to the nation's defense, if not for the fact that, by this time, many Englishmen were determined to oppose all of the king's efforts to by-pass Parliament's authority over taxation and to defend their property rights against what they regarded as nothing less than arbitrary confiscation. As it was, the ship money policy engendered an acrimonious dispute. (Judson, 1964, 229f.; Lockyer, 1989, chs. 4 and 10; Hulme, 1960, 99, 110f.; North and Weingast, 1989; Kenyon, 1990, 46–50; Sharpe, 1992, 552–558).

Stuart fiscal policies were deeply resented, and opposed, by Englishmen of property, but another policy issue engaged the interests of a much broader segment of the populace and generated unremitting hostility to the Stuarts: suspicion that they were secretly pressing to restore England to the Catholic fold. James's personal commitment to Protestantism impressed his coreligionists less than did his clear leaning toward a policy of Catholic toleration at a time when the Counter-Reformation movement was militant, and successful, on the continent. His Catholic queen was an object of suspicion, as was the Spanish ambassador, Count Gondomar, who became James's close adviser on foreign policy. Intense efforts to forge a marital alliance between the heir to the throne and the Spanish royal house deepened the suspicion that James was preparing to bring England under the dominance of Spain and the papacy. The Spanish negotiations came to nought, but the marriage of the Prince of Wales to Henrietta Maria, sister of Louis XIII of France, renewed the fears of Protestants, for she was strong-willed and an ardent Catholic, and had the effrontery to bring a cadre of Catholic priests, including a bishop, to her English household. In the marriage contract, Charles agreed that any children of the union would be baptized and reared by their mother in the Catholic faith, thus opening a clear prospect that the next king of England would be Catholic. Charles was compelled to renege on this prom-

---

22. James I had elevated a large number of his fellow Scotsman to the peerage. At the beginning of his reign, the membership of the House of Lords numbered 55. By 1628 it was 126 (Kenyon, 1986, 412). This undoubtedly assured that the House would contain loyal supporters of the king, but it also generated animosity among the older peers, whose social status had been depreciated by inflated numbers. On the issue of monopolies and its checkered history during the early Stuart era, see James (1930, 131f., 342); Foster (1960, 77); Hulme (1960, 109); Kenyon (1986, 47f.); Lockyer (1989, 190f.).

ise, but his own hostility to Protestantism deepened as his conflict with Parliament grew in intensity. He envied the unalloyed sovereignty of Europe's Catholic monarchs. By 1640, claims J. P. Kenyon, it appeared evident to many that Charles aimed at "a total subversion of Church and state to bring them into line with the Church of Rome and with the continental autocracies of France and Spain" (1986, 177). English Protestants were deeply divided among themselves on issues of theology and on the principles of ecclesiastical organization, but they were united in their hatred and fear of Catholicism. The Calvinist "Puritans" were as deeply convinced of the evil of the papacy as they were of their own righteousness. This view was reflected in Parliament and was expressed in continuously more strident language as the conflict with the king developed. The evils of Catholicism and the existence of a "popish plot" to subvert the constitution were dominant themes in the speeches of John Pym, the leader of Charles's critics in the House of Commons (McIlwain, 1918, l–lvii; Judson, 1964, 222f.; Jones, 1968; Fletcher, 1981, xx, xxii; Kenyon, 1986, 36, 78, 96f.; Lockyer, 1989, 13f., ch. 12).

Viewed as a struggle over the authority to exercise the coercive power of the state, the early Stuart era was significant in English constitutional history in a number of ways. One of the most important was that firm foundations were laid for the development of the judiciary into an independent center of power that could act as a check upon both the Crown and Parliament. At the beginning of the Stuart era, the Crown's authority over the judicial system remained unchallenged. The king appointed all superior court judges, and the prerogative courts such as the Court of Star Chamber operated under his immediate direction. The abuse of these powers was a prominent focal point of parliamentary hostility, and in the latter part of his reign, Charles was forced to dissolve Star Chamber and other prerogative courts and to recognize that the judges of the ordinary courts, unlike other officials of the Crown, should not be subject to arbitrary dismissal at the pleasure of the king. Security of tenure for judges was not enshrined in statute law until after the Revolution of 1688, but the early Stuart era began the process by which the judiciary came to be recognized as an institution of independent status in the English constitution. The courts could not justify their judgments by referring to a specific constitutional document, but the case law tradition of English jurisprudence was made to serve a similar purpose. Not since ancient Athens had the courts of a nation been placed in such a strong position to act independently of the other agencies of the state, and to restrict their exercise of power.

The parliamentarians of the early seventeenth century did not limit their demands to judicial reform; they also wanted to increase their own powers and reduce the Crown's. As a center of political power *in se*, Parliament suffered from severe disabilities. Only the king could command an election of members to the House of Commons, and only he had the authority to call Parliament into session. At any time, he could adjourn a meeting of Parliament, prorogue it, or dissolve it altogether. At first, James I called Parliament meetings almost every year, but he found the House of Commons unfriendly and uncooperative, determined to set its own agenda instead of dealing immediately with the matters that the king had placed before it. He decided to dispense with its services as much as possible. From 1611 to 1621 (except for the two-month session of the so-called Addled Parliament of 1614), Parliament did not meet. This lapse represented a sharp departure from Elizabethan practice (and his own as king of Scotland) of calling it into session every three or four years. Under the Stuart monarchy, parliamentarians learned early that when they were called into session, they should make the most of it while it lasted.

Seventeenth-century members of Parliament did not enjoy the freedom of speech of their modern successors. They could be, and were, arrested for expressing views that displeased the king. James I held that Parliament only had the authority to discuss topics that lay within its jurisdiction, as he construed it, which excluded many of the policy issues that lay at the heart of the conflict between them. As the opening of the 1621 Parliament approached, James warned it to eschew "lavish speech on matters of state." Nevertheless, the Commons engaged in an intense and critical discussion of the king's foreign policy and issued a "Protestation," stating in plain terms that it had "an ancient and undoubted birthright" to discuss any and all matters. Moreover, it contended, members of Parliament should enjoy "freedom from all impeachment, imprisonment, and molestation . . . for or concerning any speaking, reasoning, or declaring of any matter or matters touching the Parliament or Parliamentary business" (Kenyon, 1986, 47).

Charles I apparently hoped to have more satisfactory relations with Parliament than did his father, but he warned it early that "Parliaments are altogether in my power for their calling, sitting, and dissolution; therefore as I find the fruits of them good or evil they are to continue or not to be" (Kenyon, 1986, 52). He was as good as his word, on this matter at least, and finding the evil outweighing the good, he dissolved the Parliament of 1629 and did not issue writs for new elections until 1640.

Charles's precipitate dissolution of this Parliament may have reflected some regret that he had not acted more quickly in dissolving its predecessor. The Parliament of 1628 had not only defied his requests, but had attempted to make its role in English government explicit by issuing a Petition of Right.[23]

___

23. In principle, a "Petition of Right" demanded recognition of rights that already

Claiming that Parliament possessed certain rights by long-established tradition, the petition asserted that these had been violated by recent royal policies and actions, such as forced loans, imprisonment without charge, declaration of martial law, and so forth (Kenyon, 1986, 82–85). In David Hume's view, the Petition was founded on the belief "that the English have ever been free, and had ever been governed by law and a limited constitution" (1983, 5:192).[24]

Parliament's trump card was its authority over taxation. The imposition of taxes without the sanction of Parliament was generally regarded, even by royalists, as illegal. Charles was eventually forced to call a new Parliament after eleven years of "personal rule" because of the financial demands of warfare. This Parliament also proved intransigent, however: it drew up a list of grievances and demanded that the king agree to a statutory restriction of his prerogative powers before dealing with the financial crisis. Appropriately called the "Short Parliament," it was dissolved after three weeks. But the military situation deteriorated, and Charles was forced to issue writs for new elections within the year.

The ensuing Parliament, dominated by opponents of the king, quickly moved to strip his prerogative powers. Star Chamber and other prerogative courts were abolished, ship money was declared illegal, the Triennial Act was passed (which provided that Parliament must meet at least once in every three years, whether summoned by the monarch or not), and the king's power to dismiss a sitting Parliament was curbed. In addition, a series of impeachments was lodged against the King's chief ministers.[25]

Relations between the king and Parliament continued to deteriorate, and Charles finally decided to resort to arms.[26] The Civil War that ensued cul-

---

belonged to Parliament, in contrast to a "Petition of Grace," which requested the king to grant it some of his own powers, which he could refuse if he wished (Judson, 1964, 59).

24. "It may be affirmed without exaggeration," Hume concluded, "that the king's assent to the petition of right produced such a change in the government, as was almost equivalent to a revolution: and by circumscribing, in so many articles, the royal prerogative, gave additional security to the liberties of the subject" (1983, 5:200). For a good account of the debates in Parliament that led to the petition, see Judson (1964, 250–269).

25. In Judson's view, "The speed and thoroughness with which the parliamentary opposition swept away the personnel and institutions of prerogative government is one of the most remarkable achievements in English constitutional history" (1964, 351). J. H. Hexter describes it as marking "a revolution in politics" which witnessed the birth of a new conception of the English constitution: "No longer reflecting a harmonious balance of authority and liberty under law, it represented an adversary sort of balance, the restrictions of power imposed on one another by three bodies with independent foundations in law: in terms still current in politics today, a system of checks and balances" (1978, 46f.).

26. Charles's first attempt to employ force against Parliament occurred on January 4, 1642, when he suddenly appeared in the chamber of the Commons with a body of armed

minated in the king's defeat and capture by the forces of the "Long Parliament." The House of Commons constituted itself as a high court of justice, tried him for treason, and ordered his execution in 1649. Charles contended that Parliament's assumption of judicial powers was unconstitutional, but in fact it was an extension of Parliament's authority to impeach officers of the Crown for having illegally misused their authority. This authority had fallen into disuse during the Tudor era, but had been revived in the 1620s when the House of Commons undertook impeachment proceedings against seven of the king's high officers, including Francis Bacon, the lord chancellor, and Lionel Cranfield, the lord treasurer (Roberts, 1966, 8; Peck, 1993, 101). Additional impeachments followed, establishing the principle that Parliament had the authority to hold officers of the Crown to account for their actions and, if found wanting, to punish or condemn them.[27]

The importance of this principle in terms of the theory of countervailing powers is self-evident, but its future constitutional significance could not have been predicted. The pathmaking event in this respect was the attempt of the Commons to impeach the Duke of Buckingham in 1626. Charles Villiers, scion of a minor gentry family, attracted the attention of King James; in 1616 they became lovers, and within a few years, Villiers had been promoted from a courtier of no distinction to the king's most trusted political adviser and the possessor of a great title. Buckingham's political talent was meager and his administrative ability dismal, but when Charles I came to the throne upon his father's death in 1625, he retained Buckingham as his own chief adviser. The duke had earned the enmity of Parliament by his role in James's government, and the first Parliament that Charles called into session demanded his dismissal. Charles refused and dissolved the Parliament. The issue continued

---

men to arrest his leading critics—who, forewarned, had escaped. Thousands of Londoners armed themselves with whatever weapons they could find, and others in the nearby countryside prepared to march on London in support of Parliament. The king fled from the city and began to raise an army in the north (Manning, 1976, 95f.; Lockyer, 1989, 386).

27. Parliament's claim to impeachment authority was supported by highly tendentious reasoning. The ancient doctrine that "the King can do no wrong" was interpreted to signify that any wrongdoing that did occur was attributable to others, who must bear responsibility for it, even if the king's signature could be produced to show that they were following his direct orders. In this way, high officials of state were brought under the "rule of law," with little more immunity from prosecution than the ordinary citizen enjoyed. The principle that the king himself was immune was, of course, discarded in 1649. The argumentation of the 1620s was probably as disingenuous as it was ingenious. The pamphlet warfare of the 1840s, says Roberts, "taught a whole generation of Englishmen that since the King can do no wrong his ministers must answer for whatever wrong was done" (1966, 121; see also Morgan, 1989, 25–34).

to fracture king-Parliament relations until Buckingham was removed in 1628, not by Charles or Parliament, but by an assassin.[28]

The special significance of the Buckingham case derives from the fact that his enemies in the Commons were unable to find any evidence of criminal misconduct. Determined nonetheless to end his influence on the king, they demanded his dismissal on grounds of "common fame," that is to say, his widespread bad reputation. This introduced a new constitutional principle—that Parliament's disapproval is sufficient to debar anyone from holding a high position in councils of state.[29] This principle reappeared in 1648 when the Commons undertook impeachment proceedings against Charles II's chief minister, the earl of Danby. It was unsuccessful, as were a number of similar actions during the following decade, but the notion that the approval of the Commons was necessary to the holding of ministerial office became widely, and in time universally, accepted. The exposure of ministers to impeachment without actually having done anything illegal meant, in effect, that they could not escape being held *personally* accountable for the policies of the Crown. In the early 1690s, two of William III's ministers who were opposed to certain of his policies resigned, a prudent action in view of their presumptive culpability if they had not. Thus, the twin pillars of "responsible government"—ministerial solidarity and the confidence of the Commons—were established well before Robert Walpole introduced the modern system of cabinet government (Behrens, 1941, 57f.; Roberts, 1966, 222f., 268).

The Theories of Monarchical Sovereignty and Countervailing Power

In 1598, when he was King James VI of Scotland and Elizabeth still reigned in England, James wrote and published anonymously a brief essay entitled *The Trew Law of Free Monarchies*. In it, he projected a conception of monarchical sovereignty that was essentially Bodinian. It is highly probable that he had read the *République* and found its advocacy of absolute and undivided sovereignty congenial (Chew, 1949, 111, 127). The modern reader is likely to be disinclined to accept the substantive arguments of James's essay, but he was an able disputant and developed a coherent case for the position he wished to advance. In view of the subsequent conflict between king and Parliament, anything he might have written about the nature and locus of sov-

28. For a full account of the Buckingham affair, see Roberts (1966).

29. During the discussion of the proceedings against Buckingham in the Commons, John Pym stated that Parliament's impeachment powers "are not limited by either civil or common laws, but matters are judged according as they stand in opposition or conformity with that which is *suprema lex, salus populi*" (Peck, 1993, 101).

ereignty would have been important, but the *Trew Law* would be a significant document in the history of political theory even if its author had been less eminent.

In the *Trew Law*, James clearly intends his arguments to be general, but they are stated as applying only to "free monarchies," that is, polities in which the monarch has attained the throne by hereditary right.[30] In claiming absolute power for such a monarch, James relies heavily upon scriptural authority (especially the account in the First Book of Samuel of God's permitting the Israelites to have a king) and upon the analogical contentions that a king is to the people as a father is to his children, or as an individual's head is to his body (1918, 57, 65). From these propositions it follows directly, or so James contends, that monarchs occupy their office by virtue of God's will and the natural order of things, that they are the uncontestable source of all law, and that their subjects must endure their rule with patient submission, no matter how hard that rule might be. Even the Roman emperor Nero, he writes, despite his being a "bloody tyrant" and an "idolatrous persecutor," could not be legitimately opposed, for "as Christ saith," God had commanded the "giving to *Caesar* that which was *Caesar's*, and to God that which was God's" (1918, 60f.). It is evident that in a "Free Monarchy" as James conceived it, policies of state derive solely from the will of the monarch.[31]

The subtitle of the *Trew Law* is *The Reciprock and Mutual Dutie Betwixt a Free King, and His Naturall Subjects,* and James begins by noting the duties that a monarch owes to his subjects to serve their well-being, but it quickly becomes plain that he, and he alone, has the authority to determine how these obligations are to be met. Though a good king will respect established traditions, he is the source of all law and is himself "above the law." He has no obligation to conform to previous laws or to established customs (1918, 63). If a king swears an oath upon his coronation, James declares, it is not binding upon him as a proper contract would be, for who but God would have the authority to judge whether or not the king had fulfilled the terms of the contract? If there were a true contract between the monarch and the

30. "I mean always of such free monarchies as our king is, and not of elective kings, and much less of such sort of governors, as the dukes of *Venice* are, whose Aristocratic, and limited government is nothing like to free monarchies; although the malice of some writers hath not been ashamed to mis-know any difference betwixt them" (James I, 1918, 64; here, and in other quotations from the *Trew Law*, I have modernized the spelling).

31. James was fully aware of the contrary view because, from the age of three, his tutor had been the Calvinist George Buchanan, whose political writings resemble those of the French Huguenots. (See Skinner, 1978, 2:338f. for a review of Buchanan's ideas). Upon attaining his majority, James firmly rejected his teacher's political theories and, at his behest, the Scottish Parliament issued a formal condemnation of them in 1584 (Chew, 1949, 110f.).

people, and the people were authorized to determine if the king had broken it, they would be acting as judge in their own case, which is "absurd" (68).

Upon his accession to the throne of England in 1603, James quickly discovered that his view of sovereignty did not sit well with Parliament. Nevertheless, he persisted. In a speech to the Lords and Commons in 1610, he reiterated the contentions of the *Trew Law* and, to make the matter clear beyond any possibility of misunderstanding, asserted that "The State of MON-ARCHY is the supremest thing upon earth: For Kings are not only God's Lieutenants upon earth, and sit upon God's throne, but even by God himself they are called Gods" (McIlwain, 1918, 307; Williams, 1965, 39).[32] Small wonder that James's doctrine came to be called the "divine right of kings." The Roman law principle of *plenitudo potestatis,* used by Pope Innocent III in the thirteenth century to elevate himself to divine status as head of the church, bespeaks a similar transcendent eminence for a secular ruler, for in James's view, to be endowed with "fullness of power" means the possession of God-like authority. During the twenty-two years of his reign in England, James never altered the doctrine of sovereignty he had expressed in the first of his numerous writings in political theory, the *Trew Law.* C. H. McIlwain, the modern editor of James's political works, observes that "In James' political theory there is no place at all for an independent Parliament. The King may do whatever he likes, with Parliament of without it. . . . The stubbornness, with which, throughout all the vicissitudes of his later struggles with the English Parliament, James held to the doctrine there laid down indeed explains much" (1918, xxxvii, xli).[33]

To the literate person of the early seventeenth century, James's political theory would not have appeared as wrongheaded as it may to the modern reader. His doctrine was in fact the regnant political theory in most other

32. "Nimble-witted James," writes Williams, "was too clever by half. He told Parliament too often and in too much detail how similar he was to a god" (1965, 39). On James's attitude to Parliament, see also McIlwain (1918, 307, Introduction); Lockyer (1989, 125f.); and Peck (1993).

33. Christopher Hill makes an interesting point: "Why did James make such a song and dance about monarchy being the divinest thing on earth? Surely because men were now denying what Henry VIII and Elizabeth had never needed to emphasize" (1990, 27). James's doctrine was, at any rate, tenaciously supported by many of the Church of England clergy (Judson, 1964, ch. 5). In 1640, as the rift between king and Parliament was widening rapidly, the Convocation of Canterbury passed a series of canons, which it ordered to be read from the pulpit four times a year. Inter alia, these stated that "the most high and sacred Order of Kings is of Divine Right, being the ordinance of God himself . . . The power to call and dissolve Councils . . . is the true right of all Christian kings within their own realms and territories" Attempts to set up "any independent coactive power" is treason against God as well as against the king (Kenyon, 1986, 136, 150f.).

European nations, had been supplied with a basis of secular philosophic reasoning by Jean Bodin, and was in accord with the widely held belief that all social organization must, of necessity, be hierarchical. The most important English writers who subsequently attempted to sustain the doctrine of monarchical authority in as uncompromising a form as James I had done were Robert Filmer and Thomas Hobbes. Hobbes's political theory belongs to a later period in English constitutional history, and we have already examined it in reviewing the doctrine of sovereignty (see Chapter 1). Filmer deserves some attention here as a political theorist responding to the constitutional disputes of the early Stuart era.

Filmer's defense of unlimited monarchical authority is based squarely upon the analogy, which James had employed, that a king is to his subjects as a father is to his family. Hence the title of his most comprehensive political work: *Patriarcha*. The history of the patriarchal conception of the state extends back to the ancient Greek philosophical literature. Aristotle embraced a naturalistic view of the state, regarding the polis as having evolved spontaneously from other social organizations, the most elementary of which was the biological family. An offshoot of this line of thought is that, despite this long evolution, certain fundamental affinities remain between the family and the state as social institutions. From the standpoint of political theory, the most important of these is that the relation between the head of the state and his subjects is analogous to the relation between a father and his family. Political argumentation based on this analogy regards it as virtually axiomatic that it is the responsibility of the father to protect the members of the family and promote their welfare, and in order to carry out these responsibilities, the authority of the father must be unlimited—the members of the family are bound, without reserve, to obey him. Similarly, it is claimed, the duty of the monarch is to promote the *salus populi,* and he must have absolute authority to do whatever he considers serviceable to that end.[34]

34. The provenance of this argument can be traced back, at least, to classical times. In Cicero's *Republic,* for example, he contends that one of the advantages of monarchy is that "the name of king seems like that of a father to us, since the king provides for the citizens as if they were his own children" (1988, 83). The analogy loses much of its force unless one notes that the authority of the Roman father was much greater than it is today. Every family was under the rule of a single dominant male who was recognized as *pater familias* (a phrase meaning "master of the household"; the original meaning of *familia* referred to the household slaves). Though his power was constrained, as much as his personal sensitivity to custom and public opinion allowed, it was not otherwise limited. Legally, he had absolute authority over the members of his household. "He was the judge of the household, and his rulings could not be set aside by any external authority, even though he might kill, mutilate, expel, or give into bondage his sons, or housemates, and though he might break or dispose of the household property" (Heichelheim et al., 1984, 37–38, 362). Filmer and

In the history of political theory, the most important figure to pursue this line of thought was Sir Robert Filmer, who resorted to political theory in order to find a path through the thicket of troubles that was growing fast in early-seventeenth-century England.[35] Filmer is known today by college students of the history of political theory solely as the foil of John Locke's criticism in the first of his *Two Essays of Government,* but he deserves more notice than that, for it was he who provided the most sustained and coherent argument in the literature of the period in support of monarchical absolutism.[36]

Filmer pays special attention to the contract theory of the state, and rejects it as empirically false and logically untenable. He ridicules the notion that the mass of the people could meet spontaneously, without prior organization, to form a society and create a state. He points out that such a process, if it occurred, must embrace the whole world because, if it is already subdivided into nations, then states already exist. He notes that the contract theory must presume unanimous agreement not only of the persons who are construed as making it, but of all members of all subsequent generations. He is particularly critical of the notion that a state of nature is characterized by personal liberty because, as Hobbes later argued, every man is there exposed to the uncontrolled violence of his fellows. Order is produced by the institution of government, Filmer explains, and it is essential to recognize that government is inherently incompatible with freedom: "to be governed," he perceptively observes, "is nothing else but to be obedient or subject to the will or command of another" (Laslett, 1949, 205). The notion that government originates from the people is valueless, for the people at large cannot wield this power, and political philosophers who contend that the people may choose

---

other Englishmen educated in the classics would have been perfectly familiar with the authority of the Roman *pater familias.*

35. Filmer died in 1653; the *Patriarcha* was first published in 1680, probably as part of the political "cold war" that punctuated the reign of Charles II. It was written during the later 1630s and was possibly first sketched out as much as thirty years earlier (Laslett, 1949, 3; Burgess, 1996, 218). I include Filmer as an "early Stuart" political theorist because he was first motivated to write on political theory in support of their conception of monarchical authority.

36. Filmer wrote a number of brief political essays in addition to the *Patriarca.* Their neglect by scholars is unfortunate because the quality of some of them is superior to the *Patriarcha,* and they were widely read during the 1680s, when England was again drifting toward a major political upheaval. Peter Laslett has provided a reliable edition of Filmer's *Patriarcha* and other political works. They are listed in the bibliography at the end of this book under Laslett (1949). Laslett notes that it was not just the *Patriarcha* that made Filmer's political thought "an organic part of the cult of monarchical legitimism, and . . . a major obstacle to the Whig theory of the Glorious Revolution" (1949, 34).

"representatives" to exercise power in their behalf do not understand the nature of government. The idea that a king is bound by contract is equally useless, for what worldly authority is set above the king to judge and enforce a contract? Moreover, if the *salus populi* requires the king to break a promise, his malfeasance, if any, lies in having made it, not in breaking it.[37]

Filmer also rejects the notion that a monarch is bound by custom and, in particular, attacks the view that had been advanced by the great jurist Sir Edward Coke, that the rights of Parliament are part of the "ancient constitution" of England that, though unwritten, is enshrined in legal tradition. The powers and privileges of Parliament, Filmer contends, are only those that the king chooses to grant to it. A close attendance to the wording of statutes shows that Parliament merely *petitions;* it is the monarch who actually *makes* the law. Parliament originated from the need that the monarch felt for advice and counsel, and this remains its sole role, he asserts, pointing to the wording of writs summoning Parliament as late as the reign of Charles I.[38]

In his various works Filmer criticizes (effectively one must fairly grant) a wide range of writers, including Aristotle, the Jesuit liberal Cardinal Bellarmine, Hugo Grotius, Edward Coke, Philip Hunton, John Milton, and Thomas Hobbes; but these critiques are merely buttresses for the central pillar of his political thought: the necessity, and desirability, of a form of government in which power is concentrated, indivisible, and absolute.[39] Of earlier political writers, he found Jean Bodin the most congenial and went to the trouble of compiling extended passages from Bodin's *République,* which he published under the title of *The Necessity of the Absolute Power of All Kings, and in Particular of the King of England* (Laslett, 1949, 317–326). In Filmer's view, all stable governments are hierarchical, with ultimate power in the hands of a single sovereign. He could not conceive of a pluralistic governmental structure, and dismissed cases such as Republican Rome, Venice, and the Netherlands, which appeared to have operated effectively with pluralist systems (Laslett, 1949, 86–88, 208–222). He was especially critical of

37. The views outlined in this paragraph are expressed repeatedly in Filmer's works, but especially in the *Patriarca,* his *Observations upon Aristotle's Politiques,* and *The Anarchy of a Limited or Mixed Monarchy.* For some specific references, see Laslett (1949, 71, 81, 188, 223–225, 243, 256, 285–288, 293–295).

38. See especially Filmer's *The Freeholder's Grand Inquest Touching the King and His Parliament* (Laslett, 1949).

39. "How is it possible," Filmer writes in his essay on Milton, "for any government at all to be in the world without an arbitrary power; it is not power except it be arbitrary" (Laslett, 1949, 254). And in his essay on Aristotle: "If God ordained that supremacy should be, then that supremacy must of necessity be unlimited, for the power that limits must be above that power which is limited; if it be limited, it cannot be supreme . . . because a supreme limited power is a contradiction" (284).

the doctrine of "mixed government" or "mixed monarchy," which in his era was the main conceptual vehicle of political theorists who were beginning to construct a pluralist model of governance.[40]

Although it appears that Filmer would have been prepared to defend absolutism solely on the ground that it was practically indispensable to effective government, he sought to provide it with more than utilitarian foundations. This is the aspect of his political thought that locates him as an exponent—indeed the prime exponent in the literature of political theory—of a "patriarchal" theory of the state. In the domain of *orbis mundi,* he contends, there can be no authority above the sovereign, but the Divine Being is superior to all humans and has expressed His will in the Bible. Filmer points out that the Book of Genesis tells us that Adam was given absolute dominion over his family, from which descended, as the race of men grew, the authority of the monarch over the people. This authority was divided after the Deluge, when God gave supreme authority over their several families to the three sons of Noah. After a few generations, "true fatherhood" having become "extinct," monarchs succeeded to this "natural" right of fatherly dominion (Laslett, 1949, 61). Other writers, notes Filmer, have claimed that the authority of government comes from God, but scripture only supports this in giving Adam "fatherly power, and therefore we find the commandment that enjoins obedience to superiors, given in the terms of honor thy father" (289). This biblical reference is, however, quite sufficient to support the claim of monarchs to absolute power. There is no scriptural authority at all, Filmer emphasizes, for the notion that governmental authority is derived from the people.[41]

Recognizing that many extant princes have achieved their station by usurpation, Filmer remains undaunted; God works His will in mysterious ways, and in such cases "doth but use and turn men's unrighteous acts to the performance of His righteous decrees." Regardless of the means by which a prince may have obtained his Crown, he has the "right and natural authority of a supreme Father. There is, and always shall be continued to the end of the world, a natural right of a supreme Father over every multitude, although,

40. See his essay *The Anarchy of a Limited or Mixed Monarchy* (Laslett, 1949, 277–313).

41. Filmer declares: "I cannot find any one place, or text in the Bible, where any power or commission is given to a people either to govern themselves, or to choose themselves governors, or to alter the manner of government at their pleasure; the power of government is settled and fixed by the commandment of 'honor thy Father'; if there were a higher power than the fatherly, then this commandment could not stand" (Laslett, 1949, 188). Filmer criticizes those of his fellow Protestants who, having rejected the authority of the pope, slip into the error of contending that political power derives from the people: "It is a shame and scandal for us Christians to seek the original of government from the inventions or fictions of poets, orators, philosophers and heathen historians . . . and to neglect the scriptures" (278).

by the secret will of God, many at first do most unjustly obtain the exercise of it" (Laslett, 1949, 62; see also 231–232). In this way Filmer sought to counter the argument, often made against the notion of the divine right of kings, that most kings owe their station, directly or indirectly, to the dethronement of a previous monarch by rebellion or conquest.

At the end of his essay on Aristotle, Filmer attributes to him views (which, clearly, are his own) in the form of six crisp propositions:

1. That there is no form of government, but monarchy only.
2. That there is no monarchy, but paternal.
3. That there is no paternal monarchy, but absolute, or arbitrary.
4. That there is no such thing as an aristocracy or democracy.
5. That there is no such form of government as a tyranny.
6. That the people are not born free by nature. (Laslett, 1949, 229)

Given the direction taken by subsequent political thought, especially in English-speaking countries, it is not surprising that, as Laslett put it, Filmer's was "the most refuted theory of politics in the language" (1949, 20). It needs to be noted, however, that dictatorial government has not been extirpated from the world, and though it is unlikely that modern tyrants have read Filmer, it is clear from their own statements that many regard themselves as wise parents of an immature people who must be coerced for their own good. Moreover, the patriarchal view of the state is not entirely absent from constitutional polities, where it has supported state encroachments on personal freedom that are difficult to justify on any other grounds. Filmer gave voice to a doctrine that has in fact been one of the most durable in the history of political thought.[42]

The view that England is a pluralist polity in which political authority is shared by a number of independent institutions was the main alternative line of political theory that emerged during this period. This idea was expressed in general terms by many, but the credit for first stating it systematically and for contributing significantly to its development must go to Sir Edward Coke, who not only played a prominent part in asserting Parliament's right to participate in English governance, but supported that demand with strong intellectual foundations. Coke's most important contribution was the establishment of the English judiciary as a distinct center of political authority, independent of both the Crown and Parliament. In modern democracies, the theory of constitutionalism recognizes multiple centers of political power and influence: the mass media, political parties, churches, labor unions, trade associations, sectoral pressure groups, and so forth. It pictures the political

---

42. For a larger study of patriarchialism, and its articulation with other strands of seventeenth-century English political theory, see Schochet (1975).

system very differently from the tripartite model of Aristotelian "mixed government." The English political system of the seventeenth century could more easily be accommodated to that model than any other pluralist polity that had ever existed—with king, House of Lords, and House of Commons conceived as representing, respectively, the classical monarchical, aristocratic, and democratic elements. The recognition of the common law courts as a fourth primary entity was practically important in itself, but it was also significant in the history of constitutional theory as marking the liberation of pluralist doctrine from the intellectual straightjacket of the classical triadic model.

Edward Coke (1552–1634) achieved an early reputation as a practicing lawyer and legal scholar. He became solicitor general during the reign of Elizabeth, and was appointed to high positions in the judiciary and councils of state by James I. He fell out of royal favor, however, and was dismissed from his offices in 1616. He was elected to the Commons in 1621 and quickly became a leading critic of Crown policy and the king's pretension to a large domain of prerogative power. His unequalled mastery of English legal history, and his pugnacious temperament, were an ideal combination of qualities for that role.[43] In the 1621 and subsequent Parliaments, he played a leading role in the attack on the royal grant of monopoly privileges, the drafting of the Petition of Grievances in 1624 and the Petition of Right in 1628, the demand that Parliament should meet annually, the defense of free speech by members of Parliament, numerous specific pieces of reformist legislation, and the revival of the Commons's authority to impeach high governmental officials. As a consequence of his role in the Parliament of 1621, he was accused of treason and imprisoned in the Tower, but he avoided condemnation and returned to the Commons with little change in his determination to diminish the power of the Crown (Williams, 1965, 40; White, 1979, 44, 166f.; Lockyer, 1989, 67).[44]

While Coke's role as a parliamentary activist is an essential part of the history of the early Stuart era, his work as a legal scholar predominates in the larger picture of English constitutionalism. Before the accession of James I,

---

43. In his Selden Society Lecture of 1952, a prominent American legal scholar said: "We meet this afternoon to pay our respects, on the 400th anniversary of his birth, to an extraordinarily able lawyer, a great judge, and a remarkable parliamentary leader. He was, as well, an unpleasant, hard, grasping, arrogant, and thoroughly difficult man, of whom his widow, after thirty-six years of married life, could write, not without more than sufficient cause, 'We shall never see his like again, praises be to God' " (Thorne, 1957, 4).

44. "Edward Coke, by the sheer force of his personality and the prestige of his learning, was probably the most formidable of all the government's enemies in the early years of Charles I" (Allen, 1967, 31).

he began a comprehensive compilation of English case law and interpretive commentaries that engaged his attention until his death more than a half-century later. The publication of his multivolumed *Law Reports* and *Institutes of the Laws of England* (between 1600 and 1659) had a profound impact upon English legal thought. As Edmund Burke put it, Coke became "the oracle of the English law" (1991, 189). For two centuries, and even after the publication of William Blackstone's *Commentaries on the Laws of England* (1765–1769), Coke's *Reports* and *Institutes* served as primary texts for English legal education and jurisprudence (White, 1979, 3, 10f.; Kenyon, 1990, 90, 116; Weston, 1991, 375).

In surveying the "Intellectual Origins of the English Revolution" of the 1640s, Christopher Hill called attention to the increased interest in history as a factor of great importance (1965, ch. 4). In the Tudor era, historical scholarship began to replace theology as the methodology for the discovery of the determinants of social phenomena, and as the foundation of political legitimacy. James I's contention that his worldly authority derived from divine grace resonated strongly with the early-seventeenth-century mentality, but among educated Englishmen at least, it was giving way to the secular claims of historical tradition. The English system of case law, in contrast to the continental system of code law, was historical in its basic orientation. Judgments rendered by the courts were not merely applications of law, but constituted law in themselves in that they were regarded by the judiciary as precedents for subsequent similar cases. By constructing his *Reports* and *Institutes,* Sir William Coke profoundly strengthened the historical orientation of English law. As a practicing lawyer, he had undoubtedly found the lack of a systematic compilation of past cases and judgments vexatious, but he was also moved to repair this deficiency by a profound conviction that the body of common law reflected the accumulated wisdom of centuries of English jurists. When he became engaged in Parliament's opposition to the king, Coke carried over his antiquarian reverence to the domain of contemporary politics. He was the leading exponent of the doctrine that England possessed an "ancient constitution," which if properly consulted showed clearly that by long-established tradition English monarchs have been restricted in their exercise of state power. The Stuart kings, in Coke's view, had violated these restrictions in disregarding the rights of Parliament as a branch of government, and by sanctioning actions by officers of the Crown that negated the personal liberties of the citizenry and the security of their property.

The doctrine of the ancient constitution traced the origin of parliamentary government and the liberty of Englishmen back beyond Magna Carta, beyond the Norman Conquest, to the sixth and seventh centuries, when, it was contended, the freedom-loving and democratically governed Germanic tribes that Tacitus described had migrated to England (Judson, 1964, 399).[45] As we have seen, the same notion was employed by François Hotman as the origin of the French nation, and by Dutch political theorists who traced the freedom of the Netherlands to the ancient "Batavi." In France and the Dutch Republic the idea had little influence on contemporary politics, but in early Stuart England it became one of the two main pillars of Parliament's claim to independent political authority.[46] It is striking how frequently the Parliamentary documents of the early Stuart period (including the Protestation of 1621 and the Petition of Right of 1628) referred to the ancient constitution of England. As early as 1604, in an address to the king, Parliament blithely disregarded the practices of the Tudor monarchs and minced no words in claiming substantial *rights* for the commons, which it defended as ancient. Throughout the remainder of the century, the doctrine of the ancient constitution punctuated the recurrent conflicts between Parliament and the king (Allen, 1967, 28f.; Kenyon, 1990, 37f.).

Edward Coke's reputation as a historical authority provided the notion of England's ancient constitution with support that parliamentarians welcomed uncritically. Modern historians have pointed out that it is totally devoid of empirical foundations (see, e.g., Hulme, 1960; Skinner, 1965), but Coke's treatment of the idea became, in itself, an important fact of English constitutional history. In his view, the ancient constitution was contained in the English common law, which remained alive, and continued to develop, in contemporary England. Thus England was argued to have a tangible constitution, embodied in the judgments of the common law courts. With the abandonment of the royal prerogative courts, and the development of secure tenure for judges, the judiciary began to emerge as an independent center of

45. The notion that England had derived its tradition of liberty from the ancient Germanic tribes persisted for a long time in the political literature. David Hume and the Baron de Montesquieu were among those who continued to embrace it in the later eighteenth century. "Despite occasional references to Polybius and the classical cult of liberty," writes Wormuth, "eighteenth century England looked to the Germany of Tacitus for its antecedents" (1949, 173). This line of thought continued to be expressed throughout the following century. Writing in 1940, the distinguished constitutional historian Charles McIlwain observed that "a generation or two ago, it was the fashion to trace all our constitutional liberties back to the institutions of the Germanic tribes as described by Tacitus" (1940, 43). It finally met its demise as one of the many casualties of World War I.

46. The other pillar was that because the House of Commons was elected, it represented "the people," a proposition that Coke also firmly embraced. Addressing a joint committee of the Lords and Commons, when the House of Lords was resisting the impeachment of Cranfield in 1624, Coke is reported to have pointed out "that your Highness and my Lords do enjoy your places by blood and descent . . . but the members of the House of Commons by free election . . . They are the representative body of the realm, for all the people are present in Parliament by person representative" (Kenyon, 1986, 101).

power in English government.[47] As I have frequently emphasized, the notion that the Crown is constrained by divine will, or by natural law, or by the obligation to serve the *salus populi*, is of no account if there is no institution that can effectively challenge the monarch's interpretation of such constraints.[48] During the seventeenth century not only did Parliament become established as a powerful political institution; the foundation was also laid for the role of the judiciary as a protective buffer between the government and the citizenry, a role that it plays in all modern constitutional polities.[49]

Jean Bodin's thesis that there must be in every state a singular seat of sovereign power was widely held by political thinkers in the early seventeenth century, including English ones. As the dispute between the king and Parliament developed on matters of policy, this theoretical issue engaged attention. Most of the king's supporters, and at least some of his opponents in the House of Commons, viewed the contest as hinging on the fundamental issue of the locus of sovereignty in the English state. Bodin's thesis had, and still has, a special appeal to lawyers, engaged as they are in proceedings that, for pragmatic reasons, require the existence of an authority that can issue a final, incontestable, ruling. Despite his being a lawyer, however, Coke had no truck with the concept of sovereignty, and denied its applicability either to the king or to Parliament (Sabine, 1937, 450; Hinton, 1957, 124; Mosse, 1968, 171). The notion of sovereign power, he contended, is meaningless in England's political system, where Parliament shares political authority with the monarch and the coercive power of the state is exercised through law.[50] So far as I

47. Until the Civil War, the general stance of the courts was to support the king's exercise of prerogative powers. Parliament's ire was aroused especially by judicial acquiescence to the levying of ship money, which threatened to undermine its authority over taxation (Judson, 1964, 143f.). In the political context of the time, an independent judiciary would have seemed to be the only viable alternative to one dominated by the Crown.

48. The notion that a political power can be constrained by an abstraction is as difficult to destroy as the legendary Phoenix. In a recent study of the English political literature of the 1640s, David L. Smith (1994) claims to find that the political doctrine that then emerged was "constitutional royalism," which he construes as the contention that the power of the English monarch is limited by "the rule of law." It seems to me that the writers he cites in support of this theory simply lacked the imagination to conceive of any political order that was not strictly hierarchical, and were engaged in attempting to save the doctrine of sovereignty from Charles I's fatal admission in his *Answer to the Nineteen Propositions*.

49. The independence of the judiciary can be viewed as beginning in 1641, when Charles I agreed to make the appointments of judges subject to "good behaviour" rather than the king's "pleasure." David Hume referred to this as "a circumstance of the greatest moment towards securing their independence, and barring the entrance of arbitrary power into the ordinary courts of judicature" (1983, 5:330).

50. In the debate on the Petition of Right in 1628, the Lords objected to the Commons's

know, Coke never explicitly expressed a doctrine of checks and balances, but his rejection of the notion of a singular locus of sovereign authority was a long stride in that direction.

The doctrine of the ancient constitution was a potent instrument of argumentation for those who sought to diminish the power of the Crown and to increase that of Parliament. But if Coke's role had been merely to support the side of Parliament, his stature in English constitutional history and theory would be much smaller than it is. In effect, Coke made the myth of the ancient constitution into a reality by identifying it with the common law, which was a living institution in the English polity. This elevated the judiciary, the authoritative interpreter of common law, to an autonomous political status equal to that of Parliament and the Crown.[51]

The view that the various institutions of English government constituted a system of countervailing powers can be identified as implicit in many of the speeches and writings of those who supported Parliament in its struggle with the king. The notion of "mixed government" was commonplace, and many commentators upon it, such as Robert Filmer, construed it as inherently denoting that the power of the monarch was "limited" (Laslett, 1949, 279).

A clear statement of countervailance theory was contained in a document issued by Charles I himself. It was prepared by his close advisers in response to a series of *Nineteen Propositions* addressed to him by Parliament on June 1, 1642.[52] With a complete breakdown of relations imminent (Charles had already left London with his family and court), the *Nineteen Propositions* began with the statement that Charles's acceptance of the propositions would resolve the conflict between them. It demanded that all the king's advisers and certain high officials should be approved by Parliament, that judges should have security of tenure, that members of Parliament should be im-

---

attempt to deprive the king of his prerogative power to imprison without explicit cause, and asserted as a general principle that "the entire sovereign power" of the nation must remain with the king. Coke responded: "I know the prerogative is part of the law, but *sovereign power* is no Parliamentary word in my opinion. It weakens Magna Carta and all other statutes, for they are absolute without any saving of *sovereign power,* and shall we now add it we shall weaken the foundations of law, and then the building must needs fall" (Lockyer, 1989, 342; Lockyer's italics). Coke did not seek to destroy prerogative power altogether. Like Parliament, it was part of the ancient constitution in his view, and with appropriate constraints, should be preserved (Mosse, 1950, 165f.).

51. In his study of John Cowell, another distinguished legal scholar of the early seventeenth century, S. B. Chrimes, writes of him as embracing the "medieval tradition of co-existent authorities within the state," which were construed to be "the king, the parliament, and the common law" (1949, 475).

52. The important sections of the *Nineteen Propositions* and Charles's *Answer* are reprinted in Kenyon (1986, 244–247, 21–23).

mune from arrest, that the king's prerogative should not include personal command of any armed forces, and that various measures be taken to defend Protestantism in England, including treaties for that purpose with the Dutch Republic and other Protestant states. As Kenyon puts it, the document constituted "terms of unconditional surrender" (1990, 151).[53]

Charles's *Answer* rejected the specific demands of the *Nineteen Propositions,* contending that to do so would reduce the power of the monarch to nothing, which would "make us despicable both at home and abroad." But as a last-ditch attempt to mollify Parliament, and to save what he could of the royal prerogative, Charles seized the opportunity to state what he construed to be the fundamental theory of the English constitution. He prudently made no reference to divine right. Following Aristotle, he recognized three primary forms of government, noted their inherent "conveniences and inconveniences," and declared England to be a compound of all three with the king, Lords, and Commons embodying, respectively, the basic elements of monarchy, aristocracy, and democracy. Up to this point in the *Answer,* Charles's constitutional theory was commonplace, and in some passages he used it to claim for the monarch a domain of entrenched power, secure from invasion by Parliament. But he went on to assure his opponents that Parliament's existing authority was "sufficient to prevent and restrain the power of tyranny" and pointed out specifically that "the Lords, being trusted with a judicatory power, are an excellent screen and bank between the prince and the people, to assist each against the encroachments of the other."

The purist might wish that Charles's adoption of the countervailance principle had been less guarded, but as it stood, the *Answer* contained the clearest statement of that principle to be found in any language since Polybius's account of the government of republican Rome. The king's *Answer* was widely regarded as containing a definitive statement of the essential nature of the English political system, and it was embraced (with varying emphases) by both parliamentarians and royalists (Weston, 1960; Weston and Greenberg, 1981, 35f.). During the Cromwellian era, the doctrine it enunciated receded into the background, but it was revived as anti-royalist ammunition during the Restoration. After the Revolution of 1688, it was virtually uncontested as the standard theory of the English constitution.[54]

53. "The terms offered to Charles were such as might be imposed on a completely defeated enemy. There can hardly have been, at Westminster, any but the faintest hope that he would accept them" (Allen, 1967, 400).

54. Referring to the *Answer* and other statements of the king in 1642, David Hume writes that they contain "the first regular definition of the constitution, according to our present idea of it, that occurs in any English composition, at least any published by authority" (1983, 5:572f.). Following Weston's (1965) and Allen's (1967) detailed studies,

The effect of Charles's *Answer* was to divert attention from the specific issues in dispute between him and Parliament toward a more abstract and general question: the fundamental nature of English government. This query immediately engaged the interest of numerous able writers on both sides. Royalists (such as Henry Ferne, the king's chaplain during the Civil War) maintained that, despite the king's admissions, the principle of unified sovereignty remained intact. The opposite view was expressed most powerfully by Henry Parker, Philip Hunton, and an anonymous writer whose identity has not yet been determined. The importance of their contributions to the war of words in 1642–1643 has only recently begun to be recognized by historians, but they deserve to be ranked alongside Edward Coke as early modern promoters of the countervailance doctrine.

Henry Parker, Parliament's leading propagandist, responded to Charles's *Answer to the Nineteen Propositions* by composing his *Observations upon Some of His Majesties Late Answers and Expresses,* which was published, anonymously, in July 1642. It was primarily a polemic against the king, who was then engaged in raising an army, and a defense of Parliament's decision to do likewise, but Parker undertook to base his judgment of these matters on some general propositions in political theory.

In Parker's view, the welfare of the people is the dominant, indeed the sole, purpose of civil society. The authority of the state to wield coercive power is derived from the people, but it is only legitimate when exercised through the established processes of legal enactment and adjudication. This means that Parliament and the courts are essential institutions in the English system of governance. The main object of this arrangement is to protect the people's liberties from arbitrary power. Its merit has been certified, Parker notes, by the "conditionate" political systems of ancient Rome and the contemporary republics of Venice and the Netherlands. But Parker does not advocate republicanism for England: "I am as jealously addicted to Monarchy," he writes, "as any man can, without dotage." Since the king has abandoned the seat of government, he argues, Parliament is now the sole authority in the land, but this is an unusual circumstance. In normal times, England has a government in which power is shared among the king, the two houses of Parliament, and the independent judiciary.

Philip Hunton was a Puritan divine who allied himself to the side of Parliament. His *Treatise of Monarchy* (May 1643) is a remarkable document in its

---

most historians regard the impact of the *Answer* as introducing the countervailance doctrine as a constitutional principle. J. G. A. Pocock argues likewise (in 1992, 189) but elsewhere construes it as advancing the notion of a "conjoint" but nonetheless "undivided" sovereignty (1965, 568; Pocock and Schochet, 1993, 150f.).

tone, structure, and content. Written after the opening shots of the Civil War had been fired and the war of words had degenerated into passionate recriminations, calumnies, and threats, it is a model of calm and detached, yet nevertheless trenchant, argument. Hunton treats the contest between king and Parliament as if he were a Law Lord assigned to consider and adjudicate their differences on the basis of evidence and argumentation placed before him by able barristers on both sides.[55] The *Treatise* begins by consulting what sacred scripture has to offer on the issue of rebellion against an established monarch, and throughout Hunton resorts occasionally to that source of enlightenment. But the principle that he relies upon most is secular: governments are instituted among men in order to serve their mundane interests while protecting their liberties against the arbitrary or excessive application of state power.

Hunton's procedure is first, to establish the fundamental principles of all monarchies, and then to apply these to England's particular monarchy. In the first part his main object is to distinguish between monarchies that are "absolute" and those that are "limited" or "mixed." In an absolute monarchy, the monarch's power is unlimited, because there is no other institution that is independently authorized to share it. England is, indeed, a monarchy: the power of the king to call and dissolve Parliament and the Crown's responsibility for public administration mean that he has a large share of power. But he does not have the whole of it, for no legislation can be enacted and no taxes collected without the houses of Parliament. "The Sovereignty of our Kings," declares Hunton, is "radically and fundamentally limited." If there is an unlimited sovereign authority in England, it consists of the king, Lords, and Commons. "All three together," he writes, "are absolute and equivalent to the power of the most absolute Monarch" (1689, 48).

Hunton draws attention to the fact that the king himself had described the English monarchy as "limited" and its system of government as "mixed," but he does not rely on this to make his point. These properties are inherent in any monarchy where the creation of law requires the assent of more than one independent institution. Like Jean Bodin, Hunton regards lawmaking as the fundamental power, but he inverts the epistemic thrust of the argument. Bodin regarded the indivisibility of sovereignty as proving that Rome and Venice could not be true examples of mixed government; Hunton construed

55. Historians differ greatly in their appraisal of Hunton; compare, e.g., Judson (1964, 397–409) and Allen (1967, 449–455). Judson regards Hunton as meriting recognition on three counts: for providing the period's keenest analysis of England's government as a "mixed monarchy"; for clearly explicating the central issues of the contemporary controversy; and for resolving it by argumentation that John Locke employed four decades later. Allen, however, regards Hunton's *Treatise* as superficial, and unsuccessful in supporting the Parliamentary cause.

the palpable existence of mixed governments as falsifying the proposition that sovereignty is inherently indivisible.

Hunton admits that the critics of mixed government would be on solid ground if it were construed to denote a regime in which the several independent authorities were *completely* independent. But this need not be so, he argues, and is not so in England. Hunton would have rejected the concept of "separation of powers" if it were taken to mean that the several institutions of government possessed distinct and nonintersecting domains of jurisdiction. He emphasizes that the nature of England's mixed government is that the king and the houses of Parliament all participate in performing the lawmaking function of the state; they constitute, he claims, "three concurrent Powers" in legislating, none of which is subordinate to another, and each one having the authority to negate the public policy decisions of the other two.

What is the purpose of this form of government? Hunton asserts that the preservation of the people's liberties is one of the primary objectives of political organization. Absolute power, lodged in the monarch or any other estate, inevitably threatens that liberty. It can only be secured by a mixed polity. "Why is this mixture framed, but that they [the three estates] might confine each other from exorbitance? . . . That Monarchy, in which three Estates are constituted, to the end that the power of one should moderate and refrain from excess the power of the other, is mixed in the root and essence of it." Hunton recognizes that the determination of state policy in England requires that the three estates *cooperate* with each other, but the main thrust of his argument is to defend their authority to *oppose* each other as essential to the preservation of the people's liberty. For this end, oaths of office and statements of principle will not serve. Nor can the doctrine of popular sovereignty effectuate it; the contention that the authority of the state is derived from the "governing power originally in the people," he observes, is "but built upon foundations laid in the Air." The desired end can only be attained by a constitutional structure that permits each estate to act as a buffer against the excesses of another. In Hunton's reasoning, the theory of checks and balances is argued with the language of mixed government, but it emerges in the *Treatise* with exceptional clarity.

Another pamphlet, published at the same time as Hunton's *Treatise*, also deserves attention. Entitled *A Political Catechism; or, Certain Questions Concerning the Government of This Land, Answered in His Majesties Own words*, it was printed at the order of the House of Commons. Its authorship is uncertain, but it was a major document in the political theory controversy of the period.[56]

---

56. Earlier researchers attributed it to Henry Parker, but this is rejected by Mendle (1995, 195). It is reprinted in Weston (1965).

Some of its argumentation is obviously aimed at justifying Parliament's decision to take up arms against the king, but its main focus is upon the theoretical foundations of the English political system. It systematically and tenaciously examines Charles's characterization of English government as a "regulated monarchy" in which all three of the classical pure forms are "mixed." The main import of this system, the writer contends, is that "the House of Commons, the Representative Body of the People, must needs be allowed a share in Government (some at least) which is yet denied [by the king]," and that the king is "accountable to the Law, and not to God only, as men would make us believe." This "Excellent Constitution" was created by "the Experience and Wisdom of your Ancestors," and rests upon the authority of the people, not divine right or the right of conquest. The source of its excellence lies not in "the Greatnesse of the King's Power over his People, but the Restraint of that Power . . . It is safer to Restrain the King of some Power to do us Good, than to grant him too much opportunity to do us hurt."

"In this Kingdom [the *Catechism* continues] the Lawes are joyntly made by a King, by a house of Peers, and by a house of Commons, chosen by the People . . . It is the Priviledges of the two Houses of Parliament that makes the mixture, and so they must Regulate and Interpret the Priviledges of the King, and not the Priviledges of the King Regulate or Interpret theirs . . . The Good of the Subjects is ever to be preferred before the Monarchicall Greatnesse of the King . . . Salus Populi is suprema Lex." The House of Commons is "an Excellent conserver of Liberty . . . [and] is presumed to be more careful of the Subjects Liberties, than either the King, or the House of Peers." To this end, Parliament's authority to impeach the king's advisers must be secure. Its two houses together "are supreme Judges of all matters in Difference between the King and the People." In claiming that sufficient power to restrain tyranny exists, "what ever Power is Necessary to Prevent or Restrain the Power of Tyrannie is confessed [by the king] to be Legally placed in both Houses."

Nowhere in the text of the *Catechism* is the doctrine of countervailing powers explicitly stated, but as the foregoing précis indicates, it construes the relationship between king, Lords, and Commons in such terms. The Commons, being an elected body, is regarded as the primary institution, but the author stops well short of contending that it is the locus of sovereignty in the English state. As an item in the "cold war" between Parliament and the king, before the conflict was submitted to the test of battle, the *Catechism* was a brilliant piece of propaganda, but it also deserves recognition as containing a statement of basic constitutional theory. Long after the end of the Civil War, and even after the accession of William and Mary, it was frequently reprinted. Designed as it was for popular consumption, it became, in Weston's judgment, "a main channel through which the discourse on the constitution . . . passed into English political thought" (1965, 37f.).

The principle of pluralistic constitutionalism that Parker, Hunton, and the author of the *Catechism* espoused was not established by the Civil War. The Long Parliament did away with the monarchy and the House of Lords, thereby reducing the basic institutions of government from three to one. Coercive power was effectively concentrated in the victorious army, which Cromwell employed to decimate the House of Commons and make himself a sovereign monarch in all but name. The Restoration of 1660 reestablished the traditional triad, with the Commons retaining a good deal of the power that it had had under the early Stuarts. Charles II was a popular monarch despite his administrative incompetence and a lifestyle that suggested a desire to equal the status of Louis XIV, at whose court he had spent his early manhood. When his brother James, a militant Catholic, succeeded him in 1685, opposition to monarchical absolutism revived, exacerbated by fear that the new king, now having a standing army at his command, would resume the task of cleansing England of religious heresy that had been in suspension since the death of Mary Tudor.[57] Another contest of arms was to take place before a pluralistic constitution was firmly established in England and the doctrine of countervailance became generally accepted as the central principle of England's political system.

Some modern historians have taken to referring to the Civil War as a "revolution," but if that term is meant to denote a political climacteric—as it clearly does when applied, for example, to events in America in the 1770s, France in 1789, and Russia in 1917—it does not seem appropriate. No lasting change in the institutional structure of government, or in the distribution of political power, resulted from it. In the domain of ideas, the emergence of the principle of countervailance was indeed revolutionary, but as we have seen, that principle had been clearly formulated before the Civil War. The early Stuart era was the seminal period in which the hierarchical model of the state and the concept of sovereignty gave way to the countervailance model and the concept of checks and balances in English political thought. Never-

---

57. That this fear was well founded is certified by the "Bloody Assizes" that took place after the suppression of the Monmouth rebellion (Zee and Zee, 1988, 23). James's policies generally "suggested to many people that he aimed to Catholicize the nation, destroy Parliament, violate ancient law and custom, weaken local government . . . and create a centralized government backed by a standing army and allied to Catholic France" (Schwoerer, 1981, 109).

theless, we cannot disregard subsequent events altogether. Although they did not modify the central core of countervailance theory, they contributed to its amplification and widespread acceptance.

From the Civil War to the Revolution of 1688

After the appearance of Charles I's *Answer to the Nineteen Propositions,* the concept of mixed government became nearly ubiquitous in English political literature. The adoption of the classical triad was unproblematic because the main institutions of government were the king and the two houses of Parliament, which appeared to correspond well to Aristotle's classification of monarchical, aristocratic, and democratic elements. Its applicability was attenuated, however, by the development of additional institutions that demanded recognition as fundamental parts of the English political system: the judiciary, which I have already noted in discussing Sir Edward Coke's contributions to political theory and practice, and the uncensored press, which emerged in the 1640s.

The invention of mechanical printing in the fifteenth century, which made possible the production of multiple copies quickly and at low cost, was one of the most important contributions of the Renaissance era to Western civilization and, in terms of political development, the most momentous one. Even today, innovations in publication technology such as photocopying machines and electronic web sites continue to influence the quotidian play of politics, and to frustrate the efforts of established authorities to control its intellectual substrate. In absolutist states on the continent, religious and secular authorities succeeded in controlling the press for a long time; in England, the Tudor monarchs claimed jurisdiction over printing as within the prerogative powers of the Crown, but as the conflict between king and Parliament grew in the early Stuart era, the ability of the Crown to impose effective censorship was greatly attenuated. The Puritans argued for complete freedom of the press as a matter of principle. The Long Parliament, dominated by more control-minded Presbyterians, never embraced this idea as public policy, but during the 1640s relaxed supervision resulted in a phenomenal output of publications of all sorts including, for the first time in England, regularly published newspapers. Censorship was reinstituted with the Stuart Restoration, but once unfettered, the inky Prometheus could not be bound again without the aid of a tyrannous despot (Haller, 1955, 134f.; Hill, 1975, 17f.; Lindley, 1986, 112–116; Richardson and Ridden, 1986, 3).[58]

The half-century from the beginning of the Civil War to the Revolution

58. The censorship of publications was not immediately suspended after the accession of William and Mary, but when it was in 1695, "to the great displeasure of the king, and

of 1688 has never been equalled in production of political theory. In addition to the authors already discussed as important in the contest between the doctrines of sovereignty and countervailance, numerous others—such as John Milton, James Harrington, Gerrard Winstanley, Algernon Sidney, and John Locke—were to demand attention in a broader history of political thought. Most remarkable of all were the Levellers and the proposals they advanced for the reconstitution of the English political system. In 1647, Cromwell's victorious army made camp at Putney, near London, adopted in effect the role of a constitutional convention, and for more than a week its officers and representatives of the rank and file discussed England's political future. In these debates, John Lilburne and other leaders of the Levellers advocated principles of political organization that anticipated modern views of popular participation in governance by more than two centuries. "For a few wild months," writes Kenyon, "it seemed that England might even topple into democracy" (1986, 2).[59] This literature, however, is only tangential to the history I am tracing. The theory of countervailance was not developed beyond the ideas proposed by Henry Parker, Philip Hunton, and the author of the *Catechism*. The same is true of the political literature of the Restoration period and that which accompanied and followed the Revolution of 1688.

The Revolution was labeled "Glorious" by later Whig historians, who construed it as the singular crucial event in the development of English constitutionalism. Modern revisionists appear to be intent upon negating its significance altogether. The truth of the matter, it seems to me, lies somewhere in between, but closer to the Whig than the revisionist view. The Revolution resulted in the statutory establishment of a secure judiciary, the firm adoption of the principle of press freedom, and the beginning of the separation of church and state. It also repeated a motif that had been silent for almost fifty years, since Charles I's *Answer to the Nineteen Propositions*—the clear acceptance by a reigning monarch that the Crown was only one of several institutions that shared political power in England.

After James II had fled to the continent, William of Orange commanded the only significant armed force in the country. He could have adopted the role of conqueror, but he had not exposed the cream of the Dutch army to the hazards of a Channel crossing in late Autumn for that purpose. Nor was his main object to respond to the request of English parliamentarians that he should rescue their nation from Stuart absolutism and the threat of popery.

---

his ministers" (Hume, 1983, 6:540), "independent newspapers then appeared again, and thereafter multiplied rapidly, until by 1700 the reading of newspapers had become a settled habit in England" (Gibbs, 1969, 73).

59. The "Putney Debates" are reprinted in Woodhouse (1992). On the political theory of the Levellers, and the Marxist interpretation of them, see Hampsher-Monk (1976).

The invasion of England was for him, and for the Dutch Estates General that had permitted him to undertake it, a strategic move in Dutch foreign policy: to eliminate the danger of an English-French alliance against the United Provinces. To achieve this objective, William had not only to invade England successfully, but also to pacify her sufficiently to allow the speedy return of his army to the continent. A disaffected English populace and a rebellious Parliament would have endangered this. For Dutch *raison d'état,* if for no other reason, he was prepared to be an accommodating monarch.[60]

William did not take the view that his defeat of James had made him king of England; he wished to be invited by Parliament to assume the Crown. William waited, with growing impatience, while the "Convention Parliament" discussed at length the terms on which such an invitation should be tendered. These were embodied in a "Bill of Rights," presented to William and his wife for acceptance simultaneously with a request that they become joint monarchs. In itself, this procedure was constitutionally significant. Mary was James II's daughter, and William his nephew, but it was the invitation of Parliament, not hereditary claims, that was construed as the legitimizing foundation of their monarchical status. The provisions of the Bill of Rights clearly embodied the principle of *limited* royal authority, but more significant was the fact that William and Mary accepted it as a binding specification of the conditions of their rule.[61]

Once the euphoria that attended James's defeat had subsided, many parliamentarians became suspicious of William's domestic intentions and foreign policy, and sought to supplement the Bill of Rights with statutes that embodied further restrictions on the royal power. The House of Commons adopted the same tactic that it had employed against the Stuarts, using its authority over taxation to keep William in short supply of funds in order to induce him to assent to legislation of which he disapproved (Miller, 1983, 50). William could have purged Parliament, as Cromwell had done, or refrained from calling it into session as had Charles I and James II, but he did neither. It sat frequently, and for long sessions, passing legislation of great constitutional significance, to which William, often reluctantly, gave royal assent. In 1679, the Habeas Corpus Amendment Act was passed, and the

---

60. William also hoped to enlist the military resources of England in the defense of the Dutch Republic. In his opening address to the Convention Parliament in January 1689, he stated that the most urgent matter they should address was the sending of immediate and large-scale military assistance to the Dutch (Israel, 1991).

61. Parliament was far from unanimous on the matter. The proposal to offer the Crown to William and Mary passed the Commons by a vote of 251 in favor and 183 against, and the Lords by 74 in favor and 38 against (Zee and Zee, 1988, 229). See Schwoerer (1981) for a detailed discussion of the the Bill of Rights.

(press) Licensure Act of 1662 was repealed. The Triennial Act of 1694 provided that elections for a new Parliament should be held every three years. The Act of Settlement of 1701, entitled "An Act for the further Limitation of the Crown and better securing the Rights and Liberties of the Subject," increased the accountability of ministers to the Commons and provided terms of appointment for judges that secured their independence from the Crown.

These legislative initiatives of Parliament during the reign of William and Mary did not provide England with a legally entrenched constitution, but they substantially reduced the powers of the Crown. When the Convention Parliament was debating the terms of the Bill of Rights, William remarked testily that he had not come to England to be a "Doge of Venice," but he accepted the restrictions placed upon his powers. On a later occasion he is reported as observing that though he was Holland's stadholder and England's king, he was more like a stadholder in England and a king in the Netherlands (Speck, 1995, 183f.).

A statute of Parliament that had William's full support was the Toleration Act of 1689. Charles II's efforts to establish religious toleration in England had been aimed at removing the disabilities of Catholics, a tactic that only fed the paranoia of the radical Protestants and added to the growing suspicion that he was an agent of France and the papacy (Falkus, 1992, 145, 153f.). James II bypassed Parliament and issued a royal "Edict of Toleration" in 1687, with no effort to disguise the fact that his intention was eventually to restore England to the Catholic fold (Zee and Zee, 1988, 29). For a long time after the Revolution of 1688, Catholic emancipation was politically impossible.[62] The Toleration Act of 1689 did nothing to moderate the severe disabilities of Catholics, Jews, or Protestants who rejected the doctrine of the Trinity, and did very little for trinitarian Protestants who eschewed membership in the Church of England. In itself, the Toleration Act hardly seems to deserve its grand title, but in a longer focus of vision it can fairly be viewed as initiating a trend that eventually resulted in religious freedom for all Englishmen (Israel, 1991, 152f.; Trevor-Roper, 1991, 389f.).

William was strongly committed to religious toleration. He did not entertain any systematic body of philosophical principles, but he was well aware of the role that toleration had played in the history of his native land.[63] He used

---

62. Parliament's repeal of repressive statutes in 1778 led to a widespread display of anti-Catholic fervor culminating in the Gordon riots. The legal disabilities of Catholics were not finally abolished until 1829.

63. Lossky's survey of William's "Political Ideas" (1985) shows that he really had none if that term is meant to denote a coherent political philosophy or a systematic theory of politics. His Calvinist upbringing did not instill in him any deep religious conviction. He had strong opinions, but they were those of a pragmatist whose main interest was the preservation of the Dutch Republic (Israel, 1991, 129–131).

the Toleration Act as a statutory warrant for pursuing a liberal religious policy within his sphere of administrative authority. The harassment of dissenters by officers of the state, and by the Church of England, was sharply curtailed, and in the new environment the dissenting Protestant churches experienced substantial growth (Holmes, 1969, 25; Israel, 1991, 153f.). There was a reversal during the reign of Queen Anne (1707–1714); the authority of the Church of England was reasserted, and its dominance in Parliament resulted in the passage of legislation to curtail dissenters. Following her death, however, these measures were repealed, and the desire of the Anglican bishops to exercise religious hegemony in England was permanently negated (Israel, 1991, 165f.; Trevor-Roper, 1991, 393).

Modern scholars hold differing views not only about the Toleration Act but also, more generally, about the historical impact of the Revolution of 1688. [64] In one respect it was clearly no "revolution" at all because it left untouched the reservation of parliamentary authority to a small propertied class. The "lower orders" could influence politics through demonstrations and riots—not a negligible power, as seen in the early 1640s and the reign of James II—but the ending of press censorship permitted their literate members to exercise a more continuous as well as a more peaceful influence on state policy, and the Toleration Act accented the political profiles of their religious leaders. The great majority of the English citizens were excluded from the franchise until the later nineteenth century, but they had begun to play a regular role in the nation's politics in the more liberal environment that followed the accession of William and Mary. However it pleases one to label the events of 1688 and the years following, it cannot be denied that the course of England's political development during the eighteenth century was radically different from that which took place on the continent. To insist on

---

64. The papers contained in Grell, Israel, and Tyacke (1991) illustrate the widely different appraisals of the Toleration Act by historians. In Schwoerer's view, the revolution "accomplished more of lasting importance than any other revolution in England or Europe in the early modern era" (1981, 3). Jones sees it in even larger terms: it "delivered the first decisive blow to . . . the principles and institutions of the *ancien régime*—legitimate monarchy, divine right, an authority demanding unconditional obedience in every sphere of life" (1972, 330). North and Weingast (1989) narrow the focus of appraisal to the Revolution's economic impact, but without diminishing its importance. In their view, it laid the foundations for the development of the modern capitalistic economy by transforming the state from being the main threat to private property to its protector. On the other hand, some historians express a radically contrary view. "The more we examine the Glorious Revolution," writes Kenyon, "the more it appears as an aristocratic coup . . . with the gentry . . . accepting the leadership of their seigneurial lords" (1986, 419); see also Clark (1986, 75) and Zee and Zee (1988, 240).

maintaining that the era of William and Mary had little to do with this contrast would seem to have no foundation other than a determination to be "revisionist," no matter what.

The Provenance of English Countervailance Theory

Literate seventeenth-century Englishmen would have been knowledgeable about the long-defunct countervailance polities of Periclean Athens and Republican Rome. The standard curriculum of English education at that time was still dominated by the study of Greek and Roman history and literature that the monastic pedagogues had established. Many students would have read Polybius's interpretation of the Roman Republic as a system of checks and balances, but even without his assistance, it would not have been difficult for them to perceive that the ancient world had contained examples of admirable states in which the exercise of power was controlled, in contrast to the absolute monarchies that pertained in most of contemporary Europe. Educated Englishmen of the period would also have known something about the Conciliar Movement in the church during the Great Schism, and its failure to modify the absolute power of the papacy. The French Protestant political theorists of the later sixteenth century were also familiar to many Englishmen who had a practical or philosophical interest in politics. The opponents of what James I called "Free Monarchy" ransacked history for support and made frequent reference to classical Athens and Rome, but it would serve little purpose to examine these connections. The cases that demand attention here are the contemporaneaous republics of Venice and the Netherlands.

The place of Venice in the provenance of English constitutionalism was neglected by intellectual historians before Zera Fink's examination of the subject (1940, 1945).[65] During the last two decades or so, it has become a distinct theme in the historiography of early modern constitutionalism. Venice was greatly admired in northern Europe, and nowhere was there more interest in its system of government than in England, where it had become

65. "The reputation of Venice in seventeenth-century England appears to have been almost totally neglected by English writers," observes Fink, and the few writers who have noted the connection are unreliable (1940, 155; see also 1945, 42n). Christopher Hill was apparently unaware of the Venetian connection when writing his detailed study of *The Intellectual Origins of the English Revolution* (1965). He makes no reference to it until the concluding chapter, where a brief acknowledgment of the importance of Venice (and of the Dutch Republic) is included as an afterthought. Fink did not emphasize sufficiently, in my view, that the notion of checks and balances was the living flesh and bone that lay beneath the locutional garment of "mixed government," but neither do many of the historians who have addressed the issue more recently.

prominent in popular political discourse well before the beginning of the Stuart era.

Englishmen traveled to Italy in substantial numbers from at least as early as the eighth century, and with the Renaissance introduction of classical humanism, Italy attracted visitors who had historical and intellectual interests as well as the desire to escape the English winter. As a consequence, writes Felix Rabb, "ideological links between England and Italy were forged and strengthened" (1964, 28). William Thomas's *Historie of Italie,* appeared in 1549 and was soon followed by other accounts that spread knowledge of Italy widely in England. These books provided advice for travelers and described the climate, landscape, and the splendid works of art and architecture of Italy, but when they came to Venice other topics were frequently added: the city-state's ambience of civic liberty and its unusual form of government.[66]

English admiration for Venice was increased by the republic's remarkable recovery after it had been almost overwhelmed by an alliance of the great powers of Europe in the War of the League of Cambrai (1509) and by its role in checking the Turkish maritime expansion into Europe (see, e.g., Howell, 1651, 2). With the Reformation, Venice emerged as the only state south of the Alps that resisted the church's efforts to consolidate its authority in Catholic countries. Its defiance of the general interdict placed upon the city in 1606 by Pope Paul V added to its repute as a bastion of religious liberty. Venetian critics of the Holy See, most prominently Paolo Sarpi, sent their writings to England, to be published there and widely distributed, in an effort to defend Venice by displaying the malfeasances of the church to all of Europe. Formal diplomatic relations between England and Venice were established in 1604, and the first two English ambassadors, Henry Wooton and Dudley Carleton, encouraged Anglo-Venetian friendship and promoted the view that they shared similar civic philosophies. Many references to the excellence of Venice and the merits of its unusual system of government are present in the literature of early seventeenth-century England (see Chapter 5; Perkinson, 1940, 13; Pullan, 1974, 449f.).[67]

66. According to Muir, the earliest English book on Italy appeared in the early fourteenth century, but Thomas's *Historie* contained "the first English eulogy of Venice's political traditions" (1981, 51f.).

67. The repute of Venice in England was employed to great effect by the two greatest dramatists of the age. The city is the mise-en-scène for Shakespeare's *Merchant of Venice,* and the title character in his *Othello* is the governor of a Venetian colony. Ben Jonson chose Venice as the locus for his *Volpone.* These plays are especially noteworthy not merely on account of the eminence of their authors, but also because they display a detailed knowledge of Venice's customs and institutions. All three were introduced to English audiences during the first decade of the seventeenth century. Several scholars have commented upon their significance as a window on contemporary English political thought. The most comprehensive studies are Poss (1986) and McPherson (1990).

There was a large body of literature on the government of Venice available to the English during the late Tudor and early Stuart eras, but the leading source in use was undoubtedly Lewes Lewkenor's translation of Gasparo Contarini's *Magistratibus* as *The Commonwealth and Government of Venice* (1599).[68] In addition to presenting Contarini's book in full, Lewkenor added forty-eight pages of "Divers Observations upon the Venetian Commonwealth," among which he included excerpts from five other published works and brief biographies of the Venetian doges from 697 to 1578, which amplified the information contained in the main text.[69] As noted earlier, Contarini did not restrict himself to pure description. He tried to explain to his readers how the Venetian system provided political stability, controlled the exercise of state power, and serviced the desire of the populace to be prosperous and free. He employed the language of "mixed government" to depict Venice as a pluralist system of mutual checks and balances.

Francesco Guicciardini's *History of Italy* was another prominent source. Guicciardini expressed great admiration of Venetian government, which he referred to as a mixture of the classic Aristotelian forms and interpreted as a system of checks and balances. Venice is clearly the model for Guicciardini's proposals for the reform of Florentine government. He favored a regime in which governmental functions are reserved to a severely restricted aristocratic class, but because all men have an insatiable thirst for power, in his view, and a government that preserves the liberty of the citizenry must be one designed to constrain the aristocracy by having its members control each other (Bondanella, 1976).[70]

Guicciardini's *History* was was widely read in England, where the first English translation, dedicated to Queen Elizabeth, appeared in 1579. This version

---

68. "Sir Politic Would-be," a character in *Volpone,* declares that he has read Bodin, and Contarini's book on Venice. Jonson must have felt that at least some of the audience would recognize the references. See Boughner (1962) for an analysis of Jonson's use of Lewkwnor's translation of Contarini, and Whitfield (1964) for Shakespeare's.

69. Lewkenor introduced his "Sundry Notes" as material "which I have gathered as well by reading and observation, as also by conference with Venetian Gentlemen, skillful in the state of their countrey, for the better understanding of sundry points eyther not at all touched in the former discourse, or else so obscurely that the reader being a stranger cannot thereby rest fully satisfied, especially if he have a curious desire to know every particular of their government." McPherson describes Lewkenor's translation of Contarinini's *Magistratibus* as "clear, complete, and workmanlike" (1988, 462).

70. "Venice is consciously copied [by Guicciardini] as the best example ever to have existed of a constitution uniting the three forms of government" (Pocock, 1975, 241). Pocock goes on to note that Guicciardini did not advocate a "mechanical" system of checks and balances because he believed that political power must be in the hands of men of high quality (262).

was republished in 1599 and 1618 to meet continuing demand. Although it did not deal directly with the Venetian system of government, it served as a source through which its principle of countervailing powers came to the attention of English readers (Rabb, 1964, 95; Bondanella, 1976, 127; see also Luciani, 1947; McPherson, 1988, 461f.).

In 1651 another book on the government of Venice appeared, written by an Englishman: James Howell's *Survay of the Signorie of Venice*. Some historians have noted it as promoting the idea of mixed government and as urging England to emulate Venice (Fink, 1940, 159f.; Haitsma Mulier, 1980, 47). Published at a time when the constitutional future of England was a matter of intense debate, it would seem to be a prime candidate for inclusion in the early history of English countervailance theory, but this expectation is damped by reading it. It is an ill-organized and badly written collection of facts that includes, in addition to a dense description of Venetian government, a chronological account of all the Venetian doges since the city's founding, with digressions on such things as Venetian marriage and baptismal customs, the course of the Battle of Lepanto, and the instructions of a papal mission to Venice. Howell's admiration for Venice was unbounded, but it derived from the city's extraordinary durability and its role in the European defense against Ottoman expansion.[71] His book is totally lacking in any political analysis aimed at discovering the basic principles of the Venetian constitution. In the final pages of the book, it appears that Howell's main purpose in writing it was to persuade England, and other nations, that they should come to the aid of Venice in its struggle against the Turks. It was never reprinted, and I have not encountered any reference to it in the later seventeenth-century literature. It is unlikely that the *Survay* had any role in transmitting the notion of countervailance to any English readers who might have had the tenacity to read it.[72]

71. Opposite the first page of the text, Howell placed a poem of his own composition in which he praised Venice's "virginity," i.e., that it had never been invaded by a foreign power:

> Could any State on Earth Immortall be,
> Venice by Her Rare Government is she;
> . . .
> These following Leaves display, if well observd,
> How She so long her Maydenhead preservd,
> How for sound Prudence She still bore the Bell;
> Whence may be drawn this high-fetched parallel,
> Venus and Venice are Great Queens in their degree,
> Venus is Queen of Love, Venice of Policie.

72. Howell uses the term "counterpoise" once (1651, 180), but he is there referring to the Venetian foreign policy of keeping foreign states in a balance of power against each other.

For the historian of political ideas, Howell's *Survay* should warn against indiscriminately including everyone who expressed admiration for Venice and its government as evidence of support for the principle of checks and balances. The significant test demands that the writer in question admired the republic for its notable degree of civic liberty, *and* that he or she attributed this liberty to a political system of mutually controlling multiple centers of power. Between the end of the Civil War and the Revolution of 1688, numerous Englishmen expressed admiration for the Venetian Republic, but no one, so far as I am aware, coupled this with advocacy of such a constitutional order. John Milton is the most famous of the seventeenth-century Englishmen who held Venice in high esteem, but an examination of the essays in which he expressed this reveals that his appraisal of its government focused on its Great Council as a unified and all-powerful institution that, in Milton's view, realized his own preference for a Platonic government by the superior few (e.g., Milton, 1915, editor's introduction, *passim;* Sabine, 1937, 508–512; Gooch, 1959, 314f.; Lindenbaum, 1991; and Worden, 1991). Similar caveats can be registered against James Harrington, Algernon Sidney, and others whom some historians have included as deserving recognition in an account of the provenance of English political theory.

The role of the Dutch Republic in English political thought is a more complex story. On the one hand, the two countries were intense commercial and colonial rivals. The first of the English Navigation Acts (1651) was aimed at excluding Dutch shipping from the maritime trade between England and its colonies. This ignited a series of Anglo-Dutch wars during the ensuing two decades. On the other hand, the English felt great sympathy for the Dutch in their struggle to free themselves from Spanish dominion. To assist them, Queen Elizabeth sent a large military contingent, which remained in the United Provinces for more than a century (Zee and Zee, 1988, 42). As the "Golden Age" progressed, admiration of the republic was frequently expressed in England on account of the republic's remarkable wealth, its cultural and scientific achievements, and the personal liberty and security of property that pertained there. Sir William Temple's laudatory account of Dutch society and government, first published in 1673, was widely read, with six editions printed before the end of the century.

The marriage of William II of Orange to Charles I's daughter led the Dutch to support the royalist side in the English Civil War, but the fact that William III was both nephew and son-in-law to James II did not appear to exercise any constraint upon him in deciding to invade England in support of Parliament. Much had transpired between 1640 and 1688, not the least significant of which was that the English and the Dutch people came increasingly to recognize each other as having similar political ideals, ones that were in sharp contrast to the monarchical absolutism of other European states. If the armies of any other nation had invaded in 1688, Englishmen of all parties would have united in support of their king. That no such patriotic reaction occurred reflects the confidence of the English that a Dutch prince could be relied upon to foster their liberties and to restore Parliament to a major role in the governance of their land. A foreign invasion was transmuted, by the alchemy of politics, into a "Glorious Revolution" that later historians celebrated as the signal event in the development of English constitutionalism.

It must have been obvious that the institutional structure of the Dutch Republic could not be introduced into England, and no admirer of it advocated the adoption of Dutch federalism or any of its specific political institutions. It was clearly the liberal ambience of Dutch society and the effectiveness of its government that impressed the English. By 1688, these principles had been tested empirically across the Channel for more than a century—adding one more example to the still small roster of cases exemplifying the countervailance model of political organization. Nonetheless, the precise nature of this influence upon English constitutional thought remains problematic. As noted earlier, none of the Dutch political writers interpreted their nation's political system in terms of the countervailance model, and among English observers, only Sir William Temple did so.

Finally, we must consider pre-seventeenth-century domestic sources of political theory. Before the efflorescence of the Stuart era, Englishmen do not appear to have had much interest in the subject. Two writers, however— Thomas More and Thomas Starkey—deserve brief notice as having expressed the idea of a countervailance system of political organization in the early sixteenth century. More constructed such a system of government for the imaginary state called "Utopia" that he depicted in his famous book with that title. One cannot be certain that this fictional government reflected More's own political philosophy, but no matter; the notion of countervailance was expressed in a book that was widely read, and supplied the generic term for a large body of political literature.[73]

---

73. In titling his book, More resorted to a pun that would not have been missed by his educated contemporaries. In classical Greek, "utopia" means "nowhere" and "eutopia" means "the perfect place." On the composition and content of *Utopia*, see Trevor-Roper (1985, ch. 3). More began to write his book during a visit to the Netherlands before the Revolt. Trevor-Roper observes that, even then, More "discovered a new society, more highly developed and sophisticated than any he had seen before: A society of prosperous well-ordered urban republics, loosely federated under the rule of a young and, as yet, merely titular prince. This was very different from the Tudor monarchy in England. Was it not

The political organization of Utopia was not described with perfect clarity by More, but its main features are evident. Utopia was a loose federation of fifty-four city states, each of which had three organs of government: a prince, a senate, and an assembly. The senate and assembly apparently met daily. The prince was a lifetime officer who was elected by the assembly from a list of candidates nominated by the four districts of the city. The assembly consisted of 200 members elected by the populace. The senate, which performed judicial as well as legislative functions, was much smaller: it had twenty members, two of whom were seconded to it each day by the assembly. The prince was the chief executive officer of the city, but he was obliged to consult every few days with the senate. All important matters were referred to the assembly. Every city assembly annually chose three of its members to sit on a national senate. This body apparently dealt with matters of general concern, but its powers were left unspecified by the author. It seems evident that More intended to describe a countervailance system of institutional organization, and the popularity of *Utopia* would have served to familiarize many Englishmen with this basic idea.[74]

Thomas Starkey was, like More, a member of Henry VIII's court circle. He spent some years in Italy and studied at Venice's university at Padua, from which he received a doctor's degree in civil law. According to a modern editor of his *Dialogue between Cardinal Pole and Thomas Lupset,* he was greatly impressed by "the flourishing oligarchical humanism of Venice" (Mayer, 1989, vii). His *Dialogue,* written in the early 1530s, is a remarkable document for that period. Starkey advocates an elected monarchy instead of the traditional hereditary one, and argues that if England persists with the traditional monarchy, it is especially important that its authority be constrained. He expresses regret that the office of constable of England, which had sufficient "power to counterpaise the authority of the prince and to temper the same," had been abandoned. It should be reestablished, he recommends, together with an elected council of ten persons which, headed by the king, should determine all important matters of state policy. "The most wise men," he

---

also a better, and better organized society? So almost every Englishman thought who visited the Netherlands in the years of their prosperity" (1985, 39).

74. R. J. Schoeck writes that, "More, it is clear, thought in terms of an equilibrium of powers and forces" (1973, 411). He treats More as an early modern era supporter of the contention that "mixed government" is the best political form, and discusses the possibility that Jean Bodin might have had *Utopia* in mind when formulating the critique of that notion in his *République*. In his comprehensive study of the provenance of "classical republicanism," Zera Fink refers to More's *Utopia* as having had an important role in the emergence of the countervailance interpretation of the ancient concept of mixed government in England (1945, 21f.).

writes, "considering the nature of princes, yea, and the nature of man as it is indeed, affirm a mixed state to be of all other the best and most convenient to conserve the whole out of tyranny" (1948, 165).

Remarkable though it is, the position of the *Dialogue* in the history of countervailance theory is problematic. It was left unpublished (until 1871!), and only a handful of Starkey's personal acquaintances could have read it in manuscript. It stimulated no publication of responding commentary. In his preface to the 1948 edition of the *Dialogue*, Tillyard claims that it may be viewed as representing the views of contemporary "moderate English reformers," but I do not know that this contention can be supported.

Literate Englishmen of the early seventeenth century were familiar with the notion of a political system of countervailing powers, as an alternative to the Bodinian doctrine of sovereignty. But on the whole, I doubt that the development of countervailance theory (and practice) in seventeenth-century England owes much to earlier English or foreign writers, or to foreign empirical models. The dominant forces, it seems to me, were contemporaneous and indigenous. The concept of mixed government had become commonplace in English political thought before the end of the Tudor era. During the reign of James I and Charles I, the identification of the classical triad with England's king, Lords, and Commons was firmly established, and the Aristotelian notion of their essential properties—unity, wisdom, and liberty—was modified in parliamentary debate into an almost exclusive focus upon liberty. In that venue, the so-called Myth of Venice had less impact than the truly mythical notion of an "ancient English constitution." Contarini had less influence than Tacitus. Whether English constitutionalism was a native plant or an imported one is a historical problem that cannot be definitively settled, but it is beyond dispute that, once it was well established there, it was exported and took root in many parts of the modern world.

The Eighteenth Century, and Montesquieu

In 1735, James Thomson published a long poem in which the "Goddess of Liberty" describes the history of her dominion from ancient times to the present. After the defeat of Athens and the downfall of the Roman Republic, she says, it survived only among the German tribes. Their migration into England established the ethos of liberty there, where it flourished for many centuries, until it was suppressed by the Norman Conquest.

> But this so dead so vile Submission, long
> Endured not. Gathering Force, My gradual Flame
> Shook off the Mountain of tyrannic Sway.

Unus'd to Bend, impatient to Controul,
Tyrants themselves the *common Tyrant* check'd.

. . .

The *Barons* next a nobler League began,
Both those of *English* and of *Norman* Race,
In one fraternal Nation blended now,
The Nation of the Free!

. . .

           on Britannia's Shore
Now present, I to raise My Reign began
By raising the *Democracy,* the third
And broadest Bulwark of the guarded State.
Then was the full the perfect Plan disclos'd
Of Britain's matchless *Constitution,* mixt
Of mutual checking and supporting Powers,
King, Lords, and Commons. (1986, 112–114)

Thompson's work is still reprinted in anthologies of English verse; he was a better poet than these lines suggest. He earned no status as a political philosopher, but the banal hyperbole of his celebration of British liberty should not blind one to the fact that, in the brief passage quoted here, he captured virtually all of the elements of English constitutional theory that had been developed in the seventeenth century and continued throughout the eighteenth: the notion of an ancient tradition of freedom inherited from the German tribes (as Tacitus had described them); the Norman Conquest as a temporary suspension of the "ancient constitution"; the baronial opposition to King John resulting in Magna Carta; the House of Commons, representing "the people," as the democratic element in English governance; the continued use of the concept of mixed government; and the countervailance principle as the essential import of that concept.

During the eighteenth century, the English political system continued to develop in the direction it had taken during the early Stuart era. When Robert Walpole became first lord of the treasury and chancellor of the exchequer in 1721, he chose to remain in the House of Commons, which initiated the practice that the prime minister, and other high officers of the crown, be selected (mainly) from the elected membership of the Commons and remain there to participate directly in parliamentary debate. The power of the House of Lords was reduced by both statute and practice, and by the reign of George IV, the role of the monarch had become largely ceremonial.

In the light of these developments, which made the House of Commons the dominant institution in English government, it is perhaps surprising that the doctrine of sovereignty was not effectively revived until Bagehot and Dicey reassessed the English constitution in the later nineteenth century. The leading political thinkers of the eighteenth century viewed the political system as pluralistic, with independent institutions that had power to constrain each other (Weston, 1965, ch. 4).[75] In its fundamentals, English political theory in the eighteenth century was merely an epilogue to that of the seventeenth. In pursuing the history of the countervailance doctrine, it is not necessary for us to examine the works of David Hume, William Blackstone, Edmund Burke, and other eighteenth century writers. But as preliminary to the next chapter on late-eighteenth-century political thought in America, we must take note of a Frenchman, the Baron de Montesquieu, whose comments on the English system of government in his *Spirit of the Laws* were closely studied by Americans who, after the Revolutionary War had been won, faced the task of constructing a constitution that would bind the thirteen former colonies into one nation.

Montesquieu was trained as a lawyer at the University of Bordeaux but after his graduation devoted most of his attention to the natural sciences. He possessed great literary gifts, and the publication in 1721 of his amusing *Persian Letters* catapulted him to fame. He was elected to the French Academy in 1727. In the following year, he embarked on an extended tour of Europe, which included visits to Venice and the Dutch Republic and ended with a long stay in England. His political sentiments leaned strongly toward republicanism, but he was not much impressed by the Venetian and Dutch political systems. His observation of the Dutch Republic, however, initiated in him the idea that personal liberty could be protected by a system of dispersed power, which he later found to be superbly realized in England (Fletcher, 1939, 18f.). Upon his return to France, he devoted himself to the study of history and politics. His *De L'Esprit des Lois,* the book on which his lasting fame as a great figure in the development of social and political theory rests, was published in 1748 in Geneva. An immediate success, it was frequently reprinted, translated into many languages, and condemned by the Holy Office.

Although it appears that Montesquieu's political theory was inspired by his study of the English system of government, the discussion of it only occupies a dozen pages in the more than six hundred of the *Laws*. Nonetheless, it was

75. According to Pocock, "The doctrine that the king, lords, and commons together constituted a marvelously equilibrated and gloriously successful distribution of powers was . . . endlessly celebrated throughout the eighteenth century" (Pocock, 1975, 364). Wood contends, "Through its expression in the eighteenth-century British constitution this theory of balanced government attained a vitality and prominence it had not had since antiquity" (1992, 94).

this brief section that secured his place in history as a describer, and advocate, of the countervailance model of political organization. Montesquieu emphasizes that the English system of governance is notable as one of the few in history that have effectively secured the liberty of the citizenry. Referring to Tacitus's description of the ancient German tribes, he observes that "it is from that nation the English have borrowed the idea of their political government, this beautiful system was invented first in the woods" (1966, 161). As we have seen, this notion was employed by Sir Edward Coke and other early-seventeenth-century parliamentarians to support the view that England possessed an ancient tradition of liberty, and it continued to appear in the English political literature of the eighteenth century. But Montesquieu does not make much of this point. In his view, the English had developed their admirable political system by their own efforts, and owed little, if anything, to foreign examples.[76]

The brevity of Montesquieu's discussion of the English system of government indicates that it was not his major intent in writing the *Laws*. It is introduced in support of a general thesis that in today's terminology we would classify as "sociology" rather than "political science."[77] In Montesquieu's view, the political institutions of a nation must be considered in relation to its broader social environment; they cannot be properly analyzed or evaluated in themselves because their articulation with the cultural and social-psychological characteristics of the society is vital to any understanding of how they function. Chronologically, Montesquieu lies between Giambattista Vico (1668–1744) and Johann Gottfried von Herder (1744–1803), who were enormously influential in introducing the concept of culture into Western social thought. Philosophically, however, he belongs to a very different tradition. Vico and Herder inspired the development of romantic political philosophy and the metaphysical conception of the nation-state as an ontological entity. Montesquieu embraced both a utilitarian view of political institutions and an epistemic outlook that derived from the scientific revolution.

In Montesquieu's view, communities differ greatly in their cultural characteristics, and a political system suitable for one may not serve for another. The specific laws of a community must conform to the "spirit" that animates it and

76. The *Laws* contains extended discussions of Rome, Sparta, and other ancient states, but Montesquieu does not construe them as constitutional precursors of England.

77. Montesquieu, writes Raymond Aron, "was still a classical philosopher to the extent that he believed a society is essentially defined by its political regime and that his theory culminated in a conception of liberty. But, in another sense, one can indeed say that he was the first of the sociologists, for he reinterpreted classical political thought in terms of a total conception of society and he sought to explain all aspects of collectivities in a sociological mode" (1965, 1:56).

provides purpose for its organization as a social collectivity. "The government most conformable to nature," he writes, "is that which best agrees with the humor and disposition of the people in whose favor it is established" (1966, 6). Under the heading "Of Laws in Relation to the Principles which form the General Spirit, the Morals, and Customs of a Nation" (bk. 19), he enlarges on this theme. "Mankind," he writes, "are influenced by various causes: by the climate, by the religion, by the laws, by the maxims of government, by precedents, morals, and customs; whence is formed a general spirit of nations." Even in a despotism, where there are no laws ("that is, none that can properly be called so"), there are "manners and customs; and if you overturn these you overturn all," for all people "are in general very tenacious of their customs" and are deeply disturbed if they are violently altered (293, 297f.).

Montesquieu considers the English system of government to be admirable for two reasons: because it conforms to the fundamental spirit of English society, and because that spirit is worthy of admiration in itself. Some nations, he explains, have been animated by religion, desire for conquest, or tranquility, but "one nation there is also in the world that has for the direct end of its constitution political liberty." That nation is England; there liberty has attained "its highest perfection" (1966, 151). Montesquieu notes that the word "liberty" has various meanings, denoting different conceptions of freedom in different cultures. In order to understand the English constitution, one must recognize that what the English desire is not the anarchistic "natural liberty . . . of the Savages," each person being free to do whatever he pleases, but a system of "political liberty," under which the citizen is constrained by laws, yet the authorities who make and administer the laws are also constrained. The genius of the English constitution lies in its having solved the problem of power. The hand of the state, necessary to protect members of society from each other and from foreign enemies, is strong in England; the citizens are protected *by* the state; but they are also protected *from* the state: they have *political* liberty.[78]

How has this remarkable result been achieved? Montesquieu does not claim that the culture of England endows its governmental authorities with a high sense of civic virtue, or that they are constrained in their exercise of power by their religious beliefs. Plato would have it that the ideal republic would be governed by guardians of such merit that they need not themselves be guarded. The absolute sovereign of Jean Bodin's political order would rule justly because he feared God's punishment if he did not. In Montesquieu's

---

78. It is quite clear in the opening pages of the *Laws*, where Montesquieu discusses the various forms of government, that he considers the main problematic of political organization to be the control of state power.

analysis of the English political system, arguments of this sort make no appearance. Good government, suitable to the English spirit of liberty, is provided by a contrivance, a constitutional mechanism that functions with governors who are ordinary men, each motivated mainly by the desire to serve his own mundane interests.

In describing this constitutional machinery and explaining how it functions, Montesquieu makes no use of the doctrine of "mixed government." He mentions the combination of monarchy, aristocracy, and democracy only as an early and transitory form of "Gothic government" (1966, 163). For general political analysis, he classifies governments as being "monarchies," "republics," or "despotisms" and describes the characteristics and tendencies of each of these as pure types, but he does not consider a combination of them to be a realistic practical possibility (see, e.g., his discussion of China in bk. 7, ch. 21). England, in his view, "may be justly called a republic, disguised under the form of monarchy" (68).[79]

The notion of a *functional* separation of powers occupies a prominent place in Montesquieu's general political theory and in his analysis of the English constitution. Montesquieu did not originate this idea, but the *Laws*, more than any other document, was responsible for the importance it attained in later-eighteenth-century constitutional theory.[80] Through the development of the countervailance theory of political organization, followed by the English classical economists' construction of a model of economic organization based upon functional specialization and competitive markets, the long-standing belief that social order requires a comprehensive hierarchical form of organization was effectively contested. But the role of the separation of powers in that development is problematic, and has led to a great deal of confusion in political analysis to the present day. The idea that the different functions of the state should be performed by different institutional organs is not, in itself, a countervailance doctrine. If each of the separate institutions were endowed with absolute authority in its own specific domain, they could not limit the powers of each other within those jurisdictional boundaries.

79. Carrithers writes of Montesquieu as presenting the English political system as a "combination of democracy, aristocracy, and monarchy" (Montesquieu, 1977, 57); but there is no justification in the text for this view. Roche (1968) erroneously construes Montesquieu as advocating a mixed government in the sense that the different state functions would be in the hands of different social classes. Zera Fink struggles hard to link Montesquieu to the mixed government doctrine, but the reasoning he employs in support of this makes the notion of mixed government so elastic that it can embrace almost any complex political order (1945, 186n.).

80. For a discussion of the antecedents of the idea of separation of powers, see Shackleton (1949, 30f.) and for a more general examination of its history, and its connection with the checks and balances doctrine, Gwyn (1965), and Vile (1967).

Moreover, it is doubtful that such a system could work at all without the establishment of a coordinating institution that would be superior to all of them—in essence the hierarchical model. The countervailance model requires institutional "separation" in order to provide the several entities with sufficient independence to enable them to impose constraints upon each other. In all of the cases examined earlier, this was clearly the nature of their institutional structures. It is also the nature of separation of powers that one finds in Montesquieu's analysis of the English constitution, and in his view of what is necessary in any state, republican or monarchical, whose animating "spirit" is civic liberty.

Montesquieu identifies three distinct state functions: legislative, executive, and judicial. He notes that these tasks should be performed by specialized institutions for efficiency reasons, but he regards their separation as also essential to the control of the coercive authority of the state. He reduces the effective functional entities to two, construing the judiciary as part of the executive. But he insists that the legislative and executive functions must not be institutionally combined if liberty is to be preserved. Even in a republic, where there is no monarch, constraints upon government are necessary. If legislative and executive functions were performed by the same persons, he writes, "there would be an end then of liberty" (1966, 156). The English constitution does even more to protect liberty, he observes, by dividing the legislative branch into two bodies, which "check one another by the mutual privilege of rejecting" the proposals of each (160). Anticipating an argument that was later frequently advanced against such a political system, Montesquieu adds that this arrangement does not necessarily result in stalemate. It requires only that the legislative and executive bodies of the state move "in concert." Obviously, his concept of "separation" is not meant to denote a complex of *completely independent* institutions; he states plainly that the preservation of liberty requires that the executive and legislative organs of the state be dependent on each other. It is not separation in itself that protects liberty, but the arrangement of the separated powers in a system of mutual control.

One need not stretch the text of the *Laws,* nor stitch together selected phrases from it, in order to interpret Montesquieu as a countervailance theorist. He himself makes the matter plain:

Democratic and aristocratic states are not in their own nature free. Political liberty is to be found only in moderate governments; and even in these it is not always found. It is there only when there is no abuse of power. But constant experience shows us that every man invested with power is apt to abuse it, and to carry his authority as far as it will go. Is it not strange, though true, to say that virtue itself has need of limits?

To prevent this abuse, it is necessary from the very nature of things that power should be a check to power. (150)

Earlier, in book 5, noting that most nations are despotisms despite the fact that the love of liberty is natural to all mankind, Montesquieu ascribes this incongruence to the lack of the necessary political machinery:

To form a moderate government, it is necessary to combine the several powers; to regulate, temper, and set them in motion; to give as it were ballast to one, in order to enable it to counterpoise the other. This is a masterpiece of legislation, rarely produced by hazard, and seldom attained by prudence. (62)

As noted earlier, Montesquieu regarded England as essentially a republic, despite having a monarch. Of the three types of government in his classification—monarchy, republic, and despotism—it goes without saying that he saw little merit in despotism, and it is clear that he favored the republic over monarchy. But Montesquieu did not construe England as a republic merely in order to rationalize his admiration of the English constitution with his republican preference. In his view, a monarchy *can* be a "moderate government"—if the monarch is constrained in the exercise of his authority. How can such constraints be exercised, if not by the construction of constitutional machinery, which, as in England, produces "a republic under the form of monarchy"? The necessary constraints, he notes, can be effected through nongovernmental institutions such as churches, by the existence of a powerful nobility, and by long-standing customs that induce the monarch to respect established practice (bk. 2, ch. 4). Montesquieu's appreciation of such factors anticipates the modern theory of pluralistic constitutionalism, which extends the domain of mutual counterpoise beyond the checks and balances that exist among the official organs of the state.

The English system of government was widely admired in the later eighteenth century, not for its abstract qualities as a "beautiful system," but because of the empirical evidence of its ability to serve a variety of desirable objectives: personal freedom, which appealed to people of Whiggish sentiment; stability and order, which appealed to Tories, and the pursuit of material wealth and international hegemony, which appealed to both. When the Americans came to devising a constitution for themselves, there was no better model to emulate. They constructed a political system that differed greatly from the English one in its structural details, but one that was guided by the same basic view of the purposes, and dangers, of political power.

8

American Constitutionalism

Writing in 1901, James Bryce asserted that "Rome and England are the two States whose constitutions have had the greatest interest for the world and have exerted the greatest influence on it" (1901, 1:124). A scholar of great distinction, Lord Bryce's omission of the United States of America is surprising, especially because he had only a dozen years earlier published a celebrated book, *The American Commonwealth*. If the importance of the United States in Western constitutional development was not generally appreciated in 1901, that has certainly changed during the past century. Today, the United States is widely regarded as a prime exemplar of democracy, and its Constitution has captured the attention of political and legal scholars and commentators wherever there is freedom to discuss the foundations of governance.

The literature on the origins and development of American constitutionalism, even in English alone, is so large, and continues to increase so rapidly, that only one who studies nothing else (which is not without peril in itself) can lay claim to a full mastery of it. In this chapter, I shall limit myself to issues that are closely related to the development of the countervailance model of political organization in America, and to the "founding" period— from the beginnings of American government in the colonial era to the establishment of the national Constitution. During the three decades between the Revolution and the Constitution, a flood of political literature was written that, in quality as well as quantity, surpassed any other continuous period in Western history up to that time. Since then, there has been significant development in political organization and practice, in America and elsewhere, but modern political theory largely continues to address the same problems that the American colonists faced when they rebelled against British rule, formed independent governments, and joined together in a federal union.

The Political Theory of the American Revolution

By the time that serious conflict between the British government and its colonial possessions in America began to develop in the mid-eighteenth century, those colonies had existed as political entities for a long time, some of them for more than a century. A prominent theme in recent American historiography is the importance of the colonial experience in generating the sentiment that led to the Revolution—in shaping the forms of governmental organization that the individual colonies adopted when they declared their independence and the national government that was established by the Constitution (see, e.g., McLaughlin, 1932; Adams, 1980; Lutz, 1988). Especially important as both cause and consequence is the relation between the structural organization of colonial government and the political theory that developed during the colonial era. Both of these were derivative from England to a considerable degree, but American constitutionalism cannot be adequately understood without attending to indigenous features that supported the adoption of English forms and principles and, at the same time, demanded significant deviations from them.

The origins of the English colonies in North America were diverse. The first of them, Virginia, was founded in 1606 by a private trading company and received a charter from the Crown in 1624. New Hampshire, Maryland, the Carolinas, and Georgia were similarly established during the following century as proprietary companies with royal charters. New York, New Jersey, Delaware, and Pennsylvania were initially part of the Dutch overseas empire, with many settlers from the Netherlands and Sweden. They fell under English control as a consequence of the Anglo-Dutch War of 1664 and became, in effect, the personal property of the Duke of York (later James II), who farmed them out to proprietary companies. Massachusetts, Connecticut, and Rhode Island were colonized by settlers acting on their own initiatives, without official status or commercial backing—the first by Puritans from England, the other two by migrants from other American colonies.

Some of the colonies were founded with distinct social aims. The settlers who chartered the *Mayflower* for transport to the new world were a highly cohesive, and exclusive, religious group who wished to create a homogeneous Puritan society. Lord Baltimore obtained a charter for Maryland from Charles I with the intention of creating a haven in America for his fellow Catholics who were persecuted in England. The Duke of York's need for ready money overcame his Catholic convictions sufficiently to induce him to grant a proprietary charter to William Penn, who wished to demonstrate the social and philosophical excellence of Quakerism in a less hostile political environment. James Oglethorpe obtained a royal charter for Georgia in 1732 in order to assist English debtors to make a fresh start in the new world—an enterprise that might also prove profitable to himself. As time passed, these differences between the colonies were greatly modified by immigration, which tended to undermine their initial internal homogeneity. Between 1700 and 1770, the population grew from less than 300,000 to more than 2 million. Demographically, the several colonies became more diverse within themselves than they were, as communities, from each other.[1] The most important difference between the colonies was due to the introduction of African slave labor, which commenced as early as 1619 and spread rapidly, but predominantly in the southern colonies. It was a common belief during the seventeenth century that religious homogeneity was the sine qua non of political stability, but in America the most important differentiating factor proved to be the profitability of slave labor in the plantation agriculture of the south.[2]

In 1636, the settlers in Massachusetts adopted a "Pilgrim Code of Laws" that was, in effect, a constitution. By mid-century, the governments of all of the colonies operated under similar foundational organs. More significantly, they were allowed to do so by the mother country and, in fact, to govern themselves in virtually all matters except those that concerned foreign relations.[3] During this period, England's own political energies were absorbed by domestic and European conflicts. The American colonies were, rightly, perceived as attached to the mother country by strong ties of sentiment, language, and economics, and there appeared to be no need to maintain close supervision of their internal affairs. As a result, by the time of the Revolution, most of the colonies had been largely self-governing for generations. More-

---

1. Robert Ferguson emphasizes the role of religion in early American life and political thought, but notes, "Although most colonies follow the European model of an established church, pressure against religious uniformity represents the broadest single trait in colonial religion. Open competition among proliferating denominations and active lay involvement in church government distinguish American religion from its European origins and promote a general resistance to hierarchy" (1997, 46). But this was clearly not so everywhere. In Virginia, where the Anglican Church was officially established, with little lay participation in its governance, non-conformists were subjected to harsh repression and even imprisonment (McCoy, 1991, 228). For a comprehensive review of the relation between organized religion and the law before and since the "free exercise of religion" clause of the Bill of Rights, see McConnell (1990).

2. Some historians have suggested that there were distinct cultures in colonial America: "moralistic" in New England, "individualistic" in the middle colonies and "traditional" in the south (Lutz, 1988, 53–58). Perhaps so, but these differences had no significant impact upon the political thought of the revolutionary era.

3. "Europe exported its method of governing to the overseas territories: absolutism, bureaucratic centralism, military and police rule, religious intolerance. Only England, having evolved a constitutional system, granted its American nationals a certain degree of autonomy through charters" (Lefebvre, 1962, 1:11).

over, the colonists had observed the events in England that led to civil war in the 1640s, and the Revolution of 1688. Although not directly involved in these conflicts, the colonists were aware that issues of great political importance were at stake, which prepared them to believe that similar issues were raised by the change in British colonial policy initiated by passage of the Stamp Act in 1765.

It is a curiosity of history that while England had no written constitution, all of her colonies in America did. But the similarities between the institutional forms of government in the colonies and in England were much greater than the differences. In all of the colonies, from their beginnings or shortly thereafter, the powers of state were lodged in a governor designated by the Crown as the chief executive officer; an appointed advisory council; a legislative assembly (which controlled the public purse) elected by the citizenry on the basis of property qualifications; and a judiciary that was institutionally independent of both the executive and legislative branches (Adams, 1980, 44).[4]

Political development in the colonies during the seventeenth century paralleled that in England. Relations between governors and assemblies were frequently punctuated by disagreements similar to but not of the same magnitude as those that characterized the conflict between king and Parliament in England. As executive officers, colonial governors had great power to control public policy. Moreover, they could veto laws passed by the assemblies and sometimes received instructions from London to do so. Nevertheless, over time, the political power of the assemblies steadily increased. English common law, supplemented by the decisions of the colonial courts, was accepted as having precedential authority, and the colonial judiciaries became increasingly independent. Many of the essential features of constitutional government developed indigenously in colonial America (see Adams, 1980, ch. 11; Morgan, 1989, ch. 6). In the second quarter of the eighteenth century, the governmental structures of England and the colonies began to diverge: the Cabinet system, which became a central feature of British government, was not copied in America. Thus the main similarities—and (except for federalism) the main differences—between the forms of government in present-day Britain and the United States have their roots in the colonial era.

On the plane of political theory, the doctrine of checks and balances can also be traced to colonial times. The concept of "mixed government" appeared frequently in the literature of the period, but its Aristotelian content

4. One should also note that by the time of the Revolution, these offices were largely occupied by colonials. Thomas Hutchison, governor of Massachusetts, who became the chief object of anti-British anger, was a fifth-generation American of Puritan stock who, for eleven years, had been an elected member of the Massachusetts assembly (Bailyn, 1990, ch. 3).

was meager; it was almost invariably interpreted to mean *limited* government, one in which the coercive authority of the state was constrained.[5] The assemblies were widely regarded as not only lawmaking bodies, but also as groups of elected representatives who had the duty of protecting the citizenry from any arbitrary exercise of power by the governor and his officials. The liberty of the citizen was a preoccupation of many political writers, who felt that it must be an essential feature of the communities they were building in the new world. Coherent and systematic expressions of the countervailance doctrine did not appear in America before the several colonies undertook to fashion new constitutions for themselves as independent states, but by this time the view was virtually ubiquitous that good government meant constrained government, and that the only way of achieving it was by structuring the "frame of government" as a pluralistic compound of separated and mutually controlling institutions.[6]

The charter establishing the colony of Virginia specified in detail the rights and privileges of the proprietors, but it also declared that the inhabitants of the colony, like those of every other English "Dominion . . . shall have and enjoy all Liberties, Franchises, and Immunities . . . as if they had been abiding and born, within this our realm of *England*" (Thorpe, 1909, 7, 3788). When this statement was written in 1606, the security that ordinary Englishmen enjoyed in their persons and property was not large, but it grew considerably during the ensuing century of conflict between the king and Parliament and, as constitutionalism developed in England, the American settlers construed themselves as among those embraced by it. The "Glorious Revolution" of 1688 was revered in the colonies as a climactic event in their own histories as much as it was in England. As many historians of the revolutionary period have emphasized, the civic liberties that Americans regarded as sacrosanct were widely construed as "the rights of Englishmen."[7] Nevertheless, these

5. Bernard Bailyn points out that the notion of *limited* government, and even its specification in documents resembling the later Bill of Rights, can be traced back to the early colonial charters (1967, 189f.).

6. John Adams was one of the first to express the central principles on which American constitutionalism was to be based. Writing in November 1775, he explained: "A legislative, an executive, and a judicial power comprehend the whole of what is meant and understood by government. It is by balancing each of these powers against the other two, that the efforts in human nature towards tyranny can alone be checked and restrained, and any freedom preserved in the constitution" (Wright, 1949, 9). Thomas Paine was the only important writer of the Revolution period who rejected the principle of checks and balances. His *Common Sense* (1776) inflamed American opinion against England but did not convince many that America should aim at creating a different constitutional structure.

7. "The colonists' attitude to the whole world of politics and government was fundamentally shaped by the root assumption that they, as Britishers, shared in a unique inher-

liberties were not wholly derivative; they had been part of domestic colonial politics for long enough to be regarded as part of an indigenous tradition. The Revolution was led by Virginia and New England, whose inhabitants were largely of English stock, but the other colonies also appreciated the merits of constrained government. Americans of all origins understood the dangers inherent in political power and were quick to criticize, and resist, their own governments.[8] In the 1760s their concern shifted sharply to the imperial authorities in London.

From his examination of the voluminous pamphlet literature of the pre-revolutionary period, Bernard Bailyn concludes that the American colonists "saw about them, with increasing clarity, not merely mistaken, or even evil, policies violating the principles upon which freedom rested, but what appeared to be evidence of nothing less than a deliberate assault launched surreptitiously by plotters against liberty in both England and America . . . whose ultimate manifestation would be the destruction of the English constitution" (1967, 95). By the 1760s, there was such disaffection in the colonies that any of a number of events could have ignited rebellion, but the Stamp Act of 1765 was one that was virtually guaranteed to do so among people who regarded themselves as possessing "the rights of Englishmen." In itself, the act was both modest and reasonable. British taxpayers had borne the costs of the Seven Years' War, which had relieved the colonists from the French (and Catholic) menace of Quebec, and they continued to bear the costs of colonial defense and administration. But the British government did not *ask* the colonial legislatures to contribute to these costs; it unilaterally imposed a tax by requiring that colonial newspapers and legal documents carry stamps purchased from agents of the Crown. By this time the British had perhaps forgotten what had ensued a century and a half earlier when Charles I had imposed a "ship money" tax for the support of the navy without parliamentary approval. Like their English predecessors, the members of the colonial assemblies knew that their authority over taxation not only protected private property from excessive exaction, but was also the most powerful weapon they possessed for the control of executive power. At the initiative of the

itance of liberty" (Bailyn, 1967, 66). See McDonald (1985, ch. 2) for a discussion of what Americans took to be "The Rights of Englishmen."

8. "The colonists had no doubt about what power was and about its central, dynamic role in any political system . . . 'Power' to them meant the domination of some men over others, the human control of human life: ultimately force, compulsion . . . Most commonly the discussion of power centered on its essential characteristic of aggressiveness: its endlessly propulsive tendency to expand itself beyond legitimate boundaries . . . What turned power into a malignant force, was not its own nature so much as the nature of man—his susceptibility to corruption and his lust for self-aggrandizement" (Bailyn, 1967, 55f.).

Massachusetts Assembly, nine of the colonies sent delegates to an ad hoc congress in New York City, where they declared the Stamp Act to be unconstitutional—thus, in effect, sanctioning the violence that broke out wherever attempts were made to enforce it.

These first overt acts of rebellion horrified many of the colonists. Some condemned them altogether, but others attempted to support them by philosophical argument.[9] It was a British politician, however, William Pitt the Elder, who expressed most concisely the political thought of American resistance to the Stamp Act. Speaking in the House of Commons on January 14, 1766, Pitt declared that except for Parliament's struggle against the Crown in the Stuart era, relations of Britain with America were "a subject of greater importance than ever engaged the attention of this House." He went on:

> It is my opinion, that this kingdom has no right to lay a tax upon the colonies. At the same time, I assert the authority of this kingdom over the colonies, to be sovereign and supreme, in every circumstance of government and legislation whatsoever. They are the subjects of this kingdom, equally entitled with yourselves to all the natural rights of mankind and the peculiar privileges of Englishmen . . . Taxation is no part of the governing or legislating power. The taxes are a voluntary gift and grant of the Commons alone . . . When, therefore, in this house we give and grant, we give and grant what is our own. But in an American tax what do we do? . . . We give and grant . . . [not] our own property . . . [but] the property of your Majesty's commons in America. It is an absurdity in terms. (Blakeley and Collins, 1975, 265f.).

The main elements that punctuated American opposition to the Stamp Act were expressed in this speech: the distinction between "taxation" and regulative "legislation" in defining the authority of Britain over the colonies, and the principle that became the battle cry of the Revolution—no taxation without representation.

Pitt's speech also raised another point that deserves notice: the doctrine of "virtual representation." The disenfranchisement of the great bulk of Englishmen was commonly defended, even by Whigs, on the ground that the members of Parliament represented them "virtually." This doctrine was applied to the American colonists as early as 1733 in refutation of the contention that they could not be taxed by a Parliament in which they had no elected representatives (Buel, 1964, 180f.; Morgan, 1989, 226f., 240f.). In Pitt's

---

9. The diversity of opinion is shown by Bernard Bailyn's study of the literature of the period (1967). See also his essay on Jonathan Mayhew (1990, 125–136), the prominent Boston Congregational minister whose sermons on the Stamp Act reveal "the tension at the heart of American Revolutionary thought."

view, "the idea of a virtual representation of America in this House is the most contemptible idea that ever entered into the head of a man; it does not deserve serious refutation." Nevertheless, this notion continued to be advanced in defense of unilateral parliamentary action. On the eve of the Revolution, Samuel Johnson used the doctrine of virtual representation as the foundation for an attack on American claims in his *Taxation no Tyranny: An Answer to the Resolutions and Address of the American Congress.*

The Stamp Act was repealed, but the British government, still heavily pressed financially, passed the Townshend Acts imposing tariffs on colonial imports. Although masked as an assertion by England of its authority to regulate colonial commerce, these acts were in fact designed to raise revenue for the Crown. The reaction of the colonists was violent, and a British military detachment was sent to Boston to restore order and enforce the acts. On March 5, 1770, troops fired into an unruly crowd, killing five persons. The "Boston Massacre," as this event quickly came to be called, hardened the determination of the anti-imperialist faction and added greatly to its numbers. The repeal of the Townshend Acts quieted matters, but the resentment of the colonists had risen to such a level that they were now prepared to oppose any action by London that impinged upon the colonies. Nothing could have prevented the Revolution short of recognition by the British government that the American colonies were self-governing communities. But in Britain, "the sovereignty of Parliament" had become the dominant political mantra in discourse on America, and the government embarked on what proved to be the largest and costliest overseas military enterprise in history up to that time in order to bring the Americans to heel.[10]

Throughout the ensuing conflict, though it was punctuated by barbarities visited upon civilian inhabitants by the armies of both sides, Americans retained the image of themselves as fighting to defend the liberties of Englishmen. It was in England that these liberties had been undermined, they believed, and Americans were left to preserve them not only for themselves, but also for the future generations of all mankind. In order to understand the political theory of the American Revolution, and to distinguish it from the Revolution that took place a short time later in France, it is essential to recognize that its intellectual leadership (with the notable exception of Tom Paine) had no desire to wipe the slate clean and construct political society de novo; instead it sought to preserve, and develop, the institutions and ideals that had long been the warp and woof of the colonial political fabric. In

---

10. According to Dickinson, "In the final analysis the most serious point at issue between the mother country and her colonies rested on a fundamental disagreement over the nature and location of sovereignty" (1976, 189).

America, the Revolution was a continuation of British constitutionalism; in France, unfortunately, there was no comparable tradition.

The First Continental Congress met in Philadelphia in September 1774, and formed a continuing association for the purpose of restricting the importation of British goods. The second, eight months later, faced a rapidly deteriorating political situation. Numerous colonial assemblies, local councils, and other civic bodies had issued statements declaring themselves to be no longer subjects of the British Crown (see Maier, 1998, chs. 2 and 3), but many Americans were extremely reluctant to foreclose the possibility of an accommodation with Britain. The delegates to the Congress from New York, Pennsylvania, and Maryland were under specific instructions not to agree to anything that would terminate efforts to restore harmonious relations with the mother country. But by mid-June, the Congress had decided that the only alternatives open were complete submission and loss of self-government, or an intensified prosecution of the war and the assumption of independent national status. It set in motion arrangements for coordinated military action and appointed a committee to draft a Declaration of Independence, which was signed by the members of the Congress on July 4.

The Declaration, as such, had little immediate impact on American political opinion, but it subsequently attained canonic status as a foundational document of American republicanism. In modern textbook histories it is typically presented as unique, with Jefferson revered as its creator.[11] This serves the need for sacred icons of nationhood, but distorts its history. There was little in the Declaration that had not been stated in numerous similar documents that had been issued previously by other American civic bodies. It expressed political views that were widespread in revolutionary-era America and had an intellectual lineage extending back to the conflict between Paliament and the Crown in seventeenth-century England. But recognition that it was not novel does not diminish its significance; it enriches appreciation of its historical context.

The idea that the people have a right to rebel against, and replace, a government that does not serve their interests has a long history, but by the mid-eighteenth century it was widely regarded as peculiarly English, and its classic expression was John Locke's *Second Treatise on Civil Government*. Written during Locke's exile in Holland, the treatise was published after the Revolution of 1688. It was embraced in England as providing a philosophical justification of that Revolution.[12] Locke's *Second Treatise* was well known in

11. Jefferson's text was changed little by the committee, but in the Congress it was debated in detail, amended, and considerably abbreviated. Though still bearing the imprint of Jefferson's style, the final document differed considerably from his original draft.

12. Locke's prestige as a political theorist derived largely from his fame as the author of

America and, indeed, was more frequently referred to in the Revolutionary War period than any other document except the Bible (see Hyneman and Lutz, 1983, index).[13]

In considering the political theory expressed in the Declaration of Independence, Locke's *Treatise* is significant both for what it contained and for what it did not. Locke contends that in entering a civil society, the people retain the right to dissolve the association if and when a series of events indicates that their government has ceased to serve their interests—a view reflected in the Declaration's opening passages and by the long bill of indictment it contains against the government of George III. But who is to judge whether, and when, the evidence of governmental malfeasance has become compelling? If every person has the right to determine this matter, then everyone is justified in resisting the established authorities whenever they have a mind to. Under such circumstances, orderly government and the rule of law would be impossible. Locke raises this problem in the final section of the *Second Treatise* but gives no satisfactory answer. He asserts that the right to judge belongs to "the people," by which he seems to mean the majority, but he also suggests that the individual possesses this right. He finally concludes lamely that no one has such a right, noting that "as in all cases where they have no Judge on Earth" the people can only "appeal to Heaven" (see Laslett in Locke, 1960, 425n.).

---

the *Essay Concerning Human Understanding* (1690), the first systematic statement of the epistemic doctrine of empiricism. As Laslett put it, "Everything else which he wrote was important because he, Locke of the *Human Understanding,* had written it" (Locke, 1960, 50). Locke had been charged with treason for conspiring in a plot to replace James II with the Duke of Monmouth and had fled the country. His patron, Lord Shaftesbury, also in exile, played a prominent role in the plan to depose James by means of a Dutch invasion of England. In short, Locke had good credentials as a political philosopher who was prepared, in extremis, to advise rebellion.

13. The classic interpretation of the Declaration as Lockean is Carl Becker's *The Declaration of Independence* (1922). This has been frontally challenged by Gary Wills, who in *Inventing America* (1978) contends that, in composing the document, Jefferson was inspired by the communitarianism of eighteenth-century Scottish moral philosophy rather than by Lockean individualism. Wills's book initially received highly favorable reviews, but has since been shown to be excessively tendentious, and to rest upon severely flawed scholarship (Lynn, 1978; Hamowy, 1979; Jaffa, 1981). We might note in passing that revisionist histories of the American Revolution have been plentiful in recent years. Historians have claimed to have discovered (inter alia) that the Revolution was really a domestic American class struggle rather than a falling-out with Britain, that its driving force was the dissatisfaction of Nonconformists with the dominance of the Anglican Church, and even that its leaders were gripped by a psychotic disorder (see Wood, 1982; Greene, 1994). This literature has some value, however, if only in demonstrating that the search for the "deeper" causes of historical events is sometimes shallow.

As detailed in Chapter 4, this problem was addressed by the Huguenot writers of the sixteenth century when they claimed the right to resist the persecution of Protestants in France. Theodore Beza and Phillipe du Plessis-Mornay clearly perceived that claiming such a right for the individual leads necessarily to anarchy, and argued that it belongs exclusively to the "inferior magistrates" as part of their duty to protect the people from arbitrary and tyrannous government. I am not aware of any references to Beza and Mornay in the American literature of the Revolutionary War period. The Declaration of Independence does not confront this issue at all, but the members of the Second Continental Congress certainly qualify as "inferior magistrates" in the sense employed by Beza and Mornay.[14]

It is evident from the literature of the revolutionary period that the concept of sovereignty retained its status as an indispensable instrument of political analysis. The notion that every polity must have a center of undivided and absolute power was generally accepted as virtually axiomatic.[15] Its alternative, the countervailance model of the state, was central to the political theory of opponents of the monarchy in seventeenth-century England, and was definitively embodied in the settlement that followed the Revolution of 1688. It was also the operative model of colonial government in America. But in the domain of political thought, it did not become prominent in America until the colonies, having declared their independence, set about to construct constitutions for themselves.

The State Constitutions

The Second Continental Congress occupies an important place in American history for sponsoring the Declaration of Independence and for constructing the Articles of Confederation, the formal document of association that remained in force until the ratification of the national Constitution in 1789. But in terms of the development of American constitutionalism, the main importance of the Congress was that it urged the colonies to certify their new status as independent states by adopting constitutions for themselves.[16] Apart

14. There are no references to the Huguenots in the index to the collection of writings by Hyneman and Lutz (1983). Laslett's list of the literature that John Locke was acquainted with at the time he wrote the *Treatises* does not include any of the Huguenots (Locke, 1960, app. B), but he must have encountered references to them in Filmer's writings, which are the main focus of his critique of the doctrine of absolute monarchy in the *First Treatise*.

15. See Bailyn's survey of the doctrine of sovereignty in the literature of this period (1967, 198–229).

16. This was, writes Gordon Wood, "the most important act of the Continental Congress in its history." It was "the real declaration of independence" (1969, 132). For useful discussions of state constitutions, see Lutz (1988, ch. 2) and Morgan (1992, 90f.). "These

from the colonial charters, and documents such as the Roman Twelve Tables, Magna Carta, and the various town charters of Europe—some of which extend back to medieval times—the American state constitutions were the first written constitutions in history.

By the spring of 1777, twelve of the colonies had adopted constitutions. Discussions in the state assemblies and among the general public that accompanied this process engaged issues of fundamental political theory: the best form of government, and the means by which the great power of the state may be controlled. Though subordinate to the more pressing issue of justifying rebellion, the consideration of constitutional principles had generated a large literature by the time that the delegates to the Continental Congress decided that the Articles of Confederation should be replaced by "a more perfect union" of the several states.

In forming governments for themselves as independent political entities, some of the states did little more than adopt the institutions they had as colonies, and none of the others can be said to have perceived any need for radical structural change. Just as the colonial governments were modeled after that of Great Britain, so were the state governments that succeeded them. Monarch, Cabinet, House of Commons, and House of Lords were paralleled in the states by a governor, an executive council, and a bicameral legislative assembly.[17] The principle of judicial independence, formally recognized in England by the Act of Settlement in 1701, was adopted by the American states.

In Britain, devotees of the Aristotelian triad could regard the king and the two houses of Parliament as representing monarchical, aristocratic, and democratic "elements" of a "mixed government," but this notion was not sustainable in America, where there was no royal family and no hereditary aristocracy. If the state governments were to be construed as "mixed," then they were mixtures in some other sense. Apart from this, the greatest difference in formal structure between Britain and the American states was in the terms of office for assembly members and officials. Governors were typically elected for one-year terms. Members of the Commons in Britain were at that time elected for seven years, while in the American states, annual elections for the

---

often-overlooked documents" writes Lutz, "occupy a critical position in the development of American constitutionalism" (1998, 96). According to Rakove, "The states had served, in effect, as the great political laboratory upon whose experiments the framers of 1787 drew to revise the theory of republican government" (1997, 31).

17. Most of the state constitutions initially provided for the election of the governor by the assembly, but in New York, Massachusetts, and New Hampshire they were elected by popular vote. The executive councils were elected by the assemblies. Only Pennsylvania opted for a single-chambered legislature.

lower house were almost universal. In most states, members of the upper house had longer terms, the longest being five years in Maryland. Most of the state constitutions invoked the notion of popular sovereignty, but they clearly did not consider it wise to entrust it for a long period even to elected representatives and officials.

American political writers used the terms "democracy" and "republic" to describe their polity. The states were certainly republics, if that term is meant to denote that their heads of state were not selected by hereditary succession. But if the criterion of "democracy" is that all adult citizens have the right to vote and to stand for election to office, then America was not a democracy, and did not become so, even in law, for two centuries thereafter. Slaves and women were excluded, as were white males who could not meet the prescribed requirements.[18]

The classical mixed-government triad was a standard modus of political thought during the seventeenth century in America as well as in England, but by the time of the Revolution, it was rapidly being superseded by the functional triad and the view that good government required legislative, executive, and judicial functions to be entrusted to different institutions. There is no mention of separation of powers in the colonial charters, but many of the state constitutions expressly invoked it. The Virginia Constitution of 1776 listed actions by the government of George III that had improperly infringed the liberties of the colonists, followed immediately by a declaration that in the new government, "the legislative, executive, and judiciary department shall be separate and distinct, so that neither exercise the power properly belonging to the other" (Thorpe, 1909, 7:3815). The preamble to the Massachusetts Constitution of 1780 emphasized the "natural, essential, and inalienable rights" of the citizenry and declared that it is necessary "to

---

18. The federal Constitution of 1789 did not establish its own franchise criteria, but simply accepted what each of the several states had enacted. The state franchise rules thus became the operative ones for national elections. In the initial state constitutions, all except Vermont had a property qualification for the franchise: typically the ownership of fifty acres of land or, as in England, the ownership of property having an annual rental value of forty shillings or more, which had been established there by statute in 1430. In America land was cheap and more widely distributed. Fewer than 10 percent of adult males were qualified to vote in England, whereas in America the proportion has been estimated as ranging from 25 percent of adult white males in Georgia to 80 percent in the New England states. In the cities and large towns, everyone paying taxes was usually able to vote (Lutz, 1988, 75f.; for more detail see Adams, 1980, appendices). Only one state had religious qualifications for voters, but eight of them restricted membership in the assembly to professed Christians, and half of these to Protestants (Wright, 1949, 20f.). By 1825 all of these restrictions had been repealed, and in the twenty-four states that then composed the union there was universal white male suffrage.

provide for an equitable mode of making laws, as well as for an impartial interpretation and a faithful execution of them; that every man may, at all times, find his security in them." In order to accomplish these objectives, "in the government of this commonwealth, the legislative department shall never exercise the executive and judicial powers, or either of them: the executive shall never exercise the legislative and judicial powers, or either of them: the judicial shall never exercise the legislative and executive powers, or either of them: to the end it may be a government of laws and not of men" (Thorpe, 1909, 3:1889, 3:1893). If we read these statements in context, it seems beyond dispute that institutional separation was construed as serving to protect the liberties of the people from the power of the state. In order to preserve their "inalienable rights," it was not sufficient for Americans to free themselves from Great Britain or declare the "sovereignty of the people"; a pluralist structure of domestic political authority was also regarded as essential.

The phrase "checks and balances" does not appear in these state constitutions, nor does any other term that can be construed as equivalent to it. Evidence that the framers of these constitutions were guided by the countervailance model is indirect—but sufficient, in my view, to foreclose any other conclusion.[19] Consider the following points.

The main literary sources from which the framers would have derived the idea of separation of powers were Locke's *Second Treatise of Government* and Montesquieu's description of the English constitution in his *Spirit of the Laws*. In both of these, the structural principle of institutional separation and the functional notion of countervailance are joined together (Locke, 1960, e.g., 382, 388, 410; on Montesquieu, see Chapter 7). The readers of Locke and Montesquieu were of course free to pick and choose, but they could not have encountered one of these ideas without the other.

Just because the notion of countervailance was not expressed explicitly in the state constitutions does not mean that it was absent from the political thinking of the period. Note the following passage from the instructions given to Boston's representatives to the Massachusetts Bay Assembly of 1776:

'Tis essential to liberty that the legislative, judicial, and executive powers of government, be, as nearly as possible, independent of and separate from, each other; for where they are united in the same persons, or number of persons, then would be wanting that mutual check which is

19. We should note that M. J. C. Vile, in his comprehensive study of the separation of powers doctrine, disagrees. The state constitutions, he writes, "all rejected, to a greater of lesser degree, the concept of checks and balances." It was the federal Constitution that "set the seal upon a new and uniquely American combination of separation of powers and checks and balances" (1967, 133f.).

the principal security against the making of arbitrary laws, and a wanton exercise of power in the execution of them. (Spurlin, 1940, 152n.)

Even James Madison would not write a clearer statement of the purpose of separation of powers.

Gerhard Casper contends that the separation of powers embodied in the state constitutions has been given more significance than it deserves. In his view, these documents reflect the notion that there must be a distinct locus of sovereign authority, and that the framers intended to assign this to the legislatures (1989; 1997, ch. 1). If true, why did all states but one establish bicameral legislatures, with both houses chosen by the same electorate? They cannot have been designed to reflect distinct social class differences, as in England. Bicameralism is featured in most of today's democracies because, as has been said of the Canadian senate, a "sober second thought" is desirable when enacting legislation. What can the framers of the state constitutions have intended but to establish an institutionalized checking mechanism within the legislative branch itself?[20]

The state constitutions provided for the election of governors and their executive councils by the assemblies. The role of the councils is revealing. In the colonial governments, the councils had acted as officers of the executive branch. Now, as Gordon Wood puts it, they were "more controllers than servants of the governor in the business of ruling since most of the constitutions were emphatic in stating that what executive powers the governor possessed must be exercised with the advice and consent of the councils of state" (1969, 139; see also Adams, 1980, 274). It is impossible to understand why the institutional complex devised by the framers included such a body without invoking the principle of checks and balances.

Finally, a general question: What purpose can be served by the separation of powers other than as the means by which a system of power control is effectuated? The only alternative, so far as I can see, is that separation is a requirement of efficiency: different functions should be performed by different agencies in order to obtain the benefits of specialization. This is certainly the principle that motivates modern governments in establishing distinct administrative departments and agencies within the executive branch. But if that

20. Whether the state legislatures should have one house or two was an issue that engendered considerable debate (see Adams, 1980, 262f.). John Adams was the most influential supporter of bicameralism. Benjamin Wright quotes him as saying, in 1776, that "a people cannot be long free, nor ever happy, whose government is in one assembly." For himself, Wright observes that "it is difficult at the present time to understand why the men of this age believed that a bicameral system was essential to liberty, but it is unquestionably true that they believed just that" (Wright, 1933, 178).

were what the framers of the early state constitutions had in mind in separating the legislative, executive, and judicial branches, they failed to say so and, so far as I am aware, it was not a prominent argument for separation in the literature of the period. Lacking any other justification for separation of powers, it would seem inescapable to conclude that the countervailance model of governance was understood by American political thinkers well before they began to consider the shape of a constitution that would convey great power to a national government.

The National Constitution

The Constitution proposed by the Convention of 1787 reflected the long history of colonial government, the several state constitutions, and the deficiencies of the union that had been created to oppose British colonial policy. The terse and tightly organized text of the Constitution gives no hint of the fact that its framers represented states that varied greatly in the size and compositions of their populations and had different, even opposed, economic and political interests. Moreover, as individuals, the delegates held widely different views concerning the appropriate roles of state and national governments and, indeed, on fundamental issues of political philosophy. Slavery was an especially important issue, not only in itself, but as a matter that impinged upon structural considerations, such as the rules of representation in the federal houses of Congress. The coherence of the Constitution masks the fact that it was the result of compromises on virtually every substantive matter. Though the proposed Constitution was presented as unanimously approved by the framers, its articles had been repeatedly debated and revised in the convention, and many of them were finally adopted only by small majorities. James Madison and Alexander Hamilton, the great advocates of the proposed Constitution, defended its general design and specific provisions without reserve in the *Federalist* papers, but at the convention their proposals had often been defeated, and their vision of a union government that could dominate the states was rejected. The most difficult matters were postponed for later consideration, and when at the end of August a committee was struck to deal with them, its deliberations, according to Rakove, were "spirited, inventive, and completely satisfactory to no one" (1997, 164). Modern jurists or political scientists who contend that the Constitution should be construed in terms of "original intent" are free to interpret its text as they wish, but if they consult contemporary documents such as Madison's notes on the Philadelphia Convention, or the debates in the various state ratifying conventions—which Madison himself regarded as the chief evidentiary source on this matter (McCoy, 1991, 76)—they will find little support for any claim of wide, much less unanimous, agreement on specific matters (see Rakove, 1997, esp. ch. 11).[21]

Nevertheless, there is a strong general motif evident in the detailed structure of the federal "frame of government" that was proposed in 1787, a motif that was prominently reprised throughout the Philadelphia meetings, and repeated in the ratification debates in the several states: the state is an inherently dangerous social institution; it must have great power if it is to serve the *salus populi,* but the liberty of the citizenry is threatened if its power is not controlled and limited.

The Articles of Confederation constructed a governing body whose members were delegates of the states, not unlike members of the States General of the Dutch Republic. The national government established by the articles had important responsibilities, especially with respect to defense and foreign affairs, but it had no direct mandate from the people, no independent taxing authority, no executive branch of its own, and its policy decisions required the approval of the states. In that structure, the Congress had no authority to govern the people directly; the state governments stood between it and the populace as instruments of public policy. The articles could be amended only with the unanimous approval of the states, and all attempts to do so failed.[22]

There was a considerable body of opinion that this was as it should be— that the union should continue to be little more than an alliance of sovereign states, with severely delimited powers and responsibilities. Moreover, this view persisted long after the adoption of the Constitution. It reemerged in the fierce controversy over federal tariff legislation in the 1820s, and in the political battles over the Second Bank of the United States and the "nullification" controversy of the 1830s. Hugh Blair Grigsby, an unregenerate Anti-Federalist historian, declared still two decades later that the Articles of Confederation had been "the most perfect model of a confederation which the world has ever seen" (McCoy, 1991, 24). That even seventy years of union had not supressed local loyalties in favor of a national one was demonstrated

21. Some decades ago, many American scholars embraced the view that social class conflict is the key to historical understanding, and construed the framers of the Constitution as intent upon maintaining the political hegemony of the propertied class, *tout court.* The framers were deeply concerned about the threat to private property (including for some, slaves), which they regarded as an inevitable consequence of "unbridled democracy." But the class-conflict theory of the Constitution is incapable of explaining more than a small part of the proposal issued by the Philadelphia Convention, and still less of the Constitution as it has evolved since though amendment and judicial interpretation.

22. On the defects of the Confederation, and the failure of attempts to remedy them, see Rakove (1997, 24–28).

by the Civil War, in which many southerners who abhorred slavery neverthe-less supported succession. Foreign observers such as Walter Bagehot in Eng-land viewed the war as evidence that federalism—a violation of the principle that there must be only one center of sovereignty in a nation—was an unstable form of political organization.

During the debate over ratification the Bodinian theory of sovereignty resurfaced, without explicit reference to its author. Anti-Federalists regarded it as axiomatic that there could be no sharing of sovereignty, and viewed the proposed Constitution as establishing only a paper federalism, in which the states would in fact be reduced to subordinate roles.[23] Moreover, had not the great Montesquieu himself declared that republics must necessarily be small? The large territory and diverse interests embraced by the union would, in their view, prove fatal to the republican concept of government. Madison argued powerfully against both of these criticisms in *The Federalist,* but pri-vately he agreed with the Anti-Federalists on the first point, expressing the fear, in a letter to Jefferson, that the framers may have committed a funda-mental error in seeking to establish *"imperia in imperio"*—powers within power (Rakove, 1997, 197).[24]

In the late eighteenth century, there was little trade among the states; economically, they were more dependent upon overseas markets for supplies and outlets for their productions than upon each other. Accordingly, there were no strong economic reasons for a tight union, and powerful reasons—especially the diversity of the states in the sizes of their populations, and the north-south split over slavery—supported a loose one. But after the end of the Revolutionary War, it quickly became evident that independence was not sufficient to establish the states as secure and stable political entities. There were territorial disputes between them that threatened to result in warfare, and conflicts within them that taxed the ability of their governments to main-tain order.[25] Writing in support of the proposed replacement of the Articles

23. "There could be but one supreme legislative power in every state, the Antifederalists said over and over, and every proposition to the contrary was inconsistent with the best political science of the day" (Wood, 1969, 527; see also Bailyn, 1990, 235, 251f.).

24. By this time it had become a locutional convention to refer to Bodinian doctrine as the principle that *imperium in imperio* is impossible. There are no specific references to Bodin in the index to Hyneman and Lutz (1983).

25. An armed uprising in western Massachusetts in the summer of 1786, which aimed at the abolition of farmers' debts and the redistribution of land, was the most dramatic of these disorders. Led by one Daniel Shays, this rebellion, writes Forrest McDonald, "helped to make the Constitutional Convention a reality. More fundamentally, it shocked a large number of Americans into reconsidering their ideas about republican forms of government and about safeguards to liberty and property" (1985, 178; see also Wood, 1969, 284f.). There were threats of similar disorders in New Hampshire and Connecticut.

of Confederation, James Madison declared that the foundations of civil society were threatened by "the prevailing and increasing distrust of public engagements, and alarm for private rights, which are echoed from one end of the continent to the other" (*Federalist* no. 10, 54). His colleague Alexander Hamilton asserted that America had "reached almost the last stage in national humiliation," which he attributed to "material imperfections in our national system" so grave that "something is necessary to be done to rescue us from impending anarchy" (*Federalist* no. 15, 87; see also no. 22, 140).[26]

The Constitutional Convention met at a time of deep and widespread apprehension that everything that Americans had fought for in throwing off British rule might be negated by their inability to govern themselves. The delegates to the convention met to modify the Articles of Confederation, but they soon decided to start afresh and construct a proposal for a new central government that not only would be able to deal with immediate political problems, but also would serve as an effective instrument of governance for a permanent union. The resulting proposal was an event of outstanding significance in the development of Western political organization and political theory. In the history of constitutionalism, it was not as unique as some American historians have claimed, but it demands recognition on a number of particulars, as follows.

While the Constitution of the United States did not establish the first federal association in history, the resulting union was the first in which the central government was endowed with a large measure of independent authority in domestic affairs, and was provided with the autonomous legislative and fiscal power necessary to service its domain of public policy. The Constitution created what Madison called a "compound republic," one in which state and national governments shared political power, without either level having preeminent authority. In their jointly authored contributions to the *Federalist*, Madison and Hamilton reviewed in detail the histories of past confederacies, from those of ancient Greece to the contemporary Dutch Republic, and concluded that they were negative examples, seriously flawed by their failure to provide the central government with sufficient authority (nos. 17–20; see also no. 45, 299f.).[27]

---

26. John Adams wrote his *Defence of the Constitutions of the United States* in praise of the state constitutions. He favored the Articles of Confederation as, essentially, a treaty of sovereign states. He was abroad during most of the 1780s, but kept in close touch with affairs in America. According to John Howe, his initial faith in the "civic virtue" of Americans was undermined by the news he received, especially of Shays' Rebellion, and when he read a copy of the proposed new Constitution, he decided to support it (1966, 106f., 151f.).

27. "It has been shown," Madison wrote, "that the other confederacies which could be

As initially constituted, the Senate of the federal government was a compromise between centralizing and conservative views. It was construed to represent the states, as had been the case of the unicameral Congress under the Articles of Confederation. Every state, regardless of population, was given two seats in the Senate that, until 1913, were filled by the state assemblies. The geographical distribution of the 465 seats in the House of Representatives is now revised after each decennial census, but the distribution of Senate seats remains unchanged. It is surely notable that with the populations of the states today ranging from less than half a million in Wyoming to almost 30 million in California, demand for variance in the allotment of seats in the Senate is almost absent from contemporary American political discourse. By contrast, any even small attempt to censor the press, to limit religious freedom, to impose taxes without legislative authority, or to corrupt representatives or officials receives immediate attention. This may suggest that Americans are less concerned with the formal requirements of "democracy" than with the control of political power.

The Constitution also provided for direct election of members of the House of Representatives, a process that endowed the legislative branch of the national government with the gloss of "popular sovereignty." Bodinian doctrine had already been severely undermined by the examples of pluralistic constitutionalism that engaged our attention in previous chapters, but it was surely given the coup de grâce by the American "compound republic."

The success of the political system established by the Constitution demolished the proposition that a republican form of government could only be viable in small states. Even before Montesquieu stated this view in the *Spirit of the Laws*, it had been negated by the Dutch Republic, which unlike Athens, Rome, and Venice, was not a city-state polity. The effective quietus to this notion was delivered by the American republic, which in the process undermined the belief, widely prevalent in Europe, that no large national state could do without a monarch. This belief was entertained by some even in America, but George Washington had the good sense to reject suggestions that he should become king, and there was no other possible candidate for that office. Since 1789 we have witnessed many examples of polities, monarchical as well as republican, that have solved the problem of maintaining political unity in large and heterogenous societies by adopting a federal system.

Consider also the long-standing view that the taxonomy of polities contains only four categories: monarchy, aristocracy, democracy, and mixtures of them.

---

consulted as precedents have been vitiated by the same erroneous principles [as the existing American one], and can therefore furnish no other light than that of beacons, which give warning of the course to be shunned, without pointing out that which ought to be pursued" (*Federalist* no. 37, 226).

Prior to America, previous examples of pluralistic republics could easily be accommodated to this schema as belonging to the second category, because in all of them political power was wielded by a very small part of the population. America was not a democracy, but participation in politics was much too large and diverse to qualify it as an aristocracy in terms of the Aristotelian categories. Some American political thinkers of the Constitution era, such as John Adams, clung to the notion of "mixed government" as a heuristic concept, but it was not possible, even with respect to colonial America, to make much headway in political analysis by focusing on the monarchical, aristocratic, and democratic "elements" in American government. The framers of the Constitution clearly did not perceive any need to embody the Aristotelian elements in the institutional structure they proposed for the national government.[28] In the *Federalist,* the most important contemporary commentary on the proposed Constitution, its structure is analyzed in detail without resort to the concept of mixed government. The legislative-executive-judicial frame of discourse is ubiquitous in its pages, whereas the only occasions where the authors used the concept of "mixture" is with respect to the compound of state and national authorities.[29]

By the time of the American Constitution, two strands of political thought had merged into a new modus of analysis: the notion of mixed government had been transformed in England into the idea of "checks and balances," while the functional classification had generated the idea of "separation of powers." The connection of these two concepts in American political thought requires some extended comment, which I will defer briefly in order to note a further point bearing on the significance of the American Constitution in the larger history of Western political thought: its impact on Europe.

In the eighteenth century, the Atlantic Ocean carried only one-way traffic in intellectual cargo. Very few Europeans, even in England, paid any attention to American ideas (Benjamin Franklin's accomplishments in science being the

---

28. Gilbert Chinard asserts, "It is clear that in the opinion of several delegates [to the Constitutional Convention], the executive represented the monarchical power, the senate the aristocratical, and the house the democratic" (1940, 51). The evidence he gives, however, only indicates that some of the delegates stressed the need to protect the wealthy minority from spoliation by the majority, and regarded the proposed Senate as, inter alia, performing this function. In the light of Shays' Rebellion, it seems reasonable to regard this as reflecting a specific concern rather than a general point of constitutional principle.

29. Some European observers regarded the American Constitution as slavishly copying the British system of mixed government. In October 1787, Gasparo Soderini, the Venetian ambassador in London, forwarded an Italian translation of the proposed Constitution to his senate and remarked that it revealed that Americans continued to remain "children of Great Britain" and were copying its system of government, merely changing the names of its institutions (Ambrosini, 1975, 152).

only notable exception). This situation was profoundly altered by the success of the Revolution. European nationalism, nurtured by incessant warfare and religious conflict, thrived upon the hatred and contempt of other nations. Great Britain had become the strongest power in Europe, but nationalist xenophobia on the continent largely confined appreciation of its political system to French eccentrics such as Montesquieu, the philosophes, and Voltaire. The victory of America in the Revolutionary War engendered admiration among Europeans, who rejoiced at any humiliation of Britain. A wide spectrum of Europeans celebrated it, just as their predecessors admired Venice for its striking recovery from the near disaster of the War of the League of Cambrai and its resistance to papal authority, and the Dutch Republic for fighting off the great military power of Spain. The United States was not then a major economic, military, or diplomatic power, but its intellectual influence far exceeded its importance in these material domains. The financial difficulties of the French government were largely due to its support of America in the war with England, but it was American political *ideas* that inspired the revolutionaries who destroyed the ancien régime. What ensued in France was hardly a testament to American constitutionalism, but the French Revolution was only the first of an extended chain of events in which American political ideas and the Constitution that embodied them played a large role in bringing constitutional government to Europe. The rise of the United States to economic and military hegemony during the twentieth century created worldwide interest in the political system that supported it. At present, the literature on the American Constitution, in many languages, is so vast as to constitute almost a genre of its own.[30]

The members of the Philadelphia Convention considered, but rejected, the proposal that the Constitution should include a preamble stating the general political *theory* on which it was based (Rakove, 1997, 316f.). For documentary evidence of this theoretical foundation, one must therefore resort to the record of the convention debates and the commentary that ensued after the proposal was made public. Neither of these sources provides one with a clear picture. In the convention itself there were sharp differences, and the resulting document's coherence masks the compromises that were necessary to achieve its adoption. The debate on ratification of the constitution was fierce. Some commentators objected to specific provisions; others, including George Mason who had been a delegate to the convention, regarded it as fundamentally flawed and advocated its outright rejection; still others, such as Pat-

---

30. "I think it is safe to say that even before the bicentennial celebrations the American Constitution had become the subject of more elaborate and detailed scrutiny and commentary than has ever been given to any document except the Bible" (Bailyn, 1990, 225).

rick Henry, viewed it as seriously incomplete without a specific statement of citizen rights, like those that had been included in the state constitutions. On the other hand, some of its strongest defenders, such as James Madison, Alexander Hamilton, and Benjamin Franklin, had been defeated at the convention on important issues, and their warm advocacy of ratification belied the fact that they were far from satisfied with it. For many Federalists, its merit was only that it proposed a plan for "more [sic] perfect union" that had a chance of being ratified. In later life, Madison frequently observed that the adoption of the Constitution had been "nothing short of a miracle" (McCoy, 1991, 63).

The debate on the proposed Constitution was in itself, apart from its content, important in the development of American constitutionalism in that it generated the formation of distinct political parties. Political factions in contest with each other have a much longer history, but I am referring here to political parties of the modern sort. The significance of such institutions cannot be appreciated without reminding ourselves that, in the later eighteenth century, toleration of opposition to established government was rare. Even where criticism by individuals might be allowed, any attempt on the part of the regime's opponents to organize themselves was regarded as a treasonous conspiracy against the state. Indeed, we do not have to look back in time to inform us of the prevalence of this view. It was a central political doctrine in Marxist one-party states and has not disappeared with their recent downfall. In most of the countries that are members of the United Nations today, organized opposition to their ruling regimes only exists in clandestine form.

At the time of the American Revolution, the only country in which parties were an established part of the political fabric was England. Before the Revolution of 1688, they reflected divergent views on constitutional fundamentals by monarchists and parliamentarians; after it, they became a regular feature of everyday politics. The phrase "Her/His Majesty's Loyal Opposition" refers not only to an alternative body of potential governors, but also to members of Parliament whose criticism of the ruling regime, far from being treasonous, is regarded as a civic duty that they are obligated to perform.

The Revolutionary War divided the American people into two camps, between which no reconciliation was possible. The behavior of the revolutionaries toward their monarchist neighbors did not support any confidence that the English doctrine of "loyal opposition" would take root in America, but the contest over the proposed Constitution demonstrated that it had done so. Federalists and Anti-Federalists engaged in a political donnybrook, punctuated by violence, and in egregious practices that would now be regarded as grounds for invalidating the process. But the Anti-Federalists need not have feared, if any did, that their defeat would cost them their lives, or even their liberty and property, as had the revolutionaries of 1776. In the event, the debate over the Constitution witnessed the formation of organized political parties as established institutions of government, not formally recognized in the Constitution itself, but part of the American political system nonetheless. After the ratification of the Constitution, the Anti-Federalist faction disappeared, and in the 1790s, two opposing political factions emerged: the Federalist party, led by Washington and Hamilton, and the "Democratic-Republican" party, led by Jefferson and Madison. The first two presidents of the union belonged to the first of these, the next four to the second, including James Monroe, who had strongly opposed the ratification of the Constitution in the Virginia Convention. An observer of party politics in early nineteenth century America (and indeed today) might well doubt that political parties contribute to the rational formation of public policy. As an acid that corrodes the brain, partisan conviction is only surpassed by religious certitude. But in a democracy larger than a town government, parties are necessary to an orderly and peaceful transfer of power between political opponents, and that objective, still far from universal in the world, was realized early in the United States.

Let us return now to the concepts of separation of powers and checks and balances. The rich and diverse literature on the proposed Constitution that has been mined by political and legal historians shows that these were the basic analytical tools in service, but their respective meanings—and the relation between them in practice—was unclear, and indeed continues to be debated today. Some modern commentators treat the two phrases as denoting a single idea and often use "separation of powers" in argumentation that resorts to checks and balances. Some regard separation of powers as the primary concept and checks and balances as secondary; others the reverse. Some view the separation of legislative, executive, and judicial powers in the Constitution as reflecting a desire to achieve efficiency through specialization; others as an essential requirement of personal liberty and security of property. Some regard checks and balances as a recipe for deadlock that was only avoided by disregarding it and giving the three branches *unequal* powers (see, e.g., Walsh, 1915, iii; Adams, 1980, esp. ch. 12; Anderson, 1986, 144; Marcus, 1989; Richards, 1989; Casper, 1997; Ferguson, 1997, 139).[31]

31. Walsh (1915), a study of John Adams's political ideas, is a sustained critique of the principle of checks and balances. Casper (1989 and 1997) adopts a similar stance with respect to the principle of separation of powers. In Casper's view, the separation of powers doctrine was contaminated by its association with the notion of checks and balances, and it was not an essential part of basic constitutional theory in any event. The central concept in the political thought of the founding era, he contends, was the notion of mixed government, and the deep problem that Americans faced was how to reconcile the pluralistic

The political thinkers of the Constitution era undoubtedly differed in their conceptions of separation of powers and checks and balances, but little would be gained by examining these variant views. It will suffice for our purposes to attend to the theoretical argumentation of the *Federalist*. This series of eighty-five papers, written by Alexander Hamilton, James Madison, and John Jay in order to persuade the people of New York to support the proposed Constitution, was the most comprehensive analysis of it published at the time, and for a long period thereafter. Moreover, the *Federalist* provides the modern reader with an excellent introduction to the main criticisms of the proposal. Unlike most of the contemporary literature, its authors did not summarily dismiss, misrepresent, or caricature opposing views, but considered them rationally and seriously. The Philadelphia Convention had adopted the rule that if at least nine states ratified the proposed Constitution, it would come into force as binding the ratifying states into a federal union. By the time the New York Convention assembled, ten states had already ratified, but New York was still crucial. Without it, the union would be seriously, perhaps fatally, flawed. the *Federalist* played an important role in securing New York's agreement and, in the process, its authors also created one of the most important documents in the history of constitutionalism.[32]

In expounding the political theory of the Constitution, the *Federalist* maintained a strong and persistent focus on the problem of controlling political power. The federal system was regarded as, in itself, contributing to this end, by subjecting the citizenry to two independent structures of political authority rather than the traditional one. Some critics of the proposed Constitution contended that the powers it gave to the federal government would enable it to dominate the states. Two passages from Hamilton's papers dealing with this issue are worth noting. Considering the authority to deploy military force, he wrote: "Power being almost always the rival of power, the general government will at all times stand ready to check the usurpations of the state governments, and these will have the same disposition towards the general government" (no. 28, 174). The authority of both the national government and the states to establish courts of criminal and civil justice, asserted Hamilton, will prove sufficient of itself to prevent domination by the central authority: it "would insure them [the states] so decided an empire over their

---

notion of mixed government with the indivisibility of political authority implicit in the doctrine of popular sovereignty.

32. Recent scholarship on the literature debating the proposed constitution has somewhat diminished the magisterial stature of the *Federalist* (Bailyn, 1990, 229f.), but it still remains the most important source for understanding the theoretical foundations of American constitutionalism and, more generally. the idea that civic liberty can be protected from the power of the state by an appropriate structure of political institutions.

respective citizens as to render them at all times a complete counterpoise . . . to the power of the Union" (no. 17, 103). History has not vindicated Hamilton's assurances that the federal government would not be able to dominate the states, but his wording in these passages is significant as reflecting a disposition to construe federalism not in terms of exclusive state and federal domains of authority, but as a system of competitive "counterpoise."

The authors of the *Federalist,* however, regarded federalism as only part of such a system. *Federalist* 51, probably written by Madison,[33] asserted, "In the compound republic of America, the power surrendered by the people is first divided between two distinct governments, and then the portion allotted to each subdivided among distinct and separate departments. Hence a double security arises to the rights of the people. The different governments will control each other, at the same time that each will be controlled by itself" (339). In describing how the proposed Constitution would effectuate the self-control of the national government, the *Federalist* repeatedly employs the concepts of separation of powers and checks and balances.[34] The basic argument is that delegates to the Philadelphia Convention had designed a government whose several institutions were both independent and interconnected, in such a fashion that each could exercise constraints upon the others. Historians usually cite no. 47, written by Madison, in this connection, but it is prominent in many of the other papers, including a number written by Hamilton (see nos. 9, 65, 71, 73, 75, 76, and 81).

Federalist 47 has captured the attention of historians of political theory on account of its interpretation of Montesquieu described there as "the oracle who is always consulted and cited on this subject"—on how the liberty of the people may be secured against the power of the state. In Madison's view, Montesquieu admired the English system of government as one in which there was a *partial* separation of powers, which made them in fact *interdependent* in exercising state authority. Exclusive domains of jurisdiction for the legislative, executive, and judicial branches would endanger liberty as much as would the concentration of power in a single agency. It was Montesquieu's theory of partial separation, writes Madison, that had guided the construction of the several state constitutions, and the same principle was also embodied in the proposed federal Constitution.

That Madison's construal of separation of powers here leaves something to be desired is evidenced by the earlier précis of it, as well as by some of the

33. The *Federalist* papers were all published under the pen name "Publius." Historians have not been able to assign specific authorships to all of them, and it remains uncertain whether no. 51 was written by Hamilton or Madison.

34. See especially nos. 52–83, in which the institutions of the proposed Constitution are examined, seriatim, in great detail.

modern commentary on *Federalist* 47, on Montesquieu's interpretation of the English constitution, and on the role of separation of powers in the American Constitution today. Number 47 is not the only paper that attempted to express this notion, with various locutions. Madison wrote of "partial separation" and "partial agency," and noted that the proposed Constitution "connected and blended" the three branches of government. Later, in a speech to the first Congress, he criticized the constitutions of some states for laying down "dogmatic maxims with respect to the construction of the Government; declaring that the Legislative, Executive, and Judicial Branches, shall be kept separate and distinct" (Madison, 1904, 381). Hamilton, too, referred to the "partial admixture" of the branches. Such remarks do little in themselves to clarify the idea. But if one reads all of the papers in the *Federalist* that consider the *purpose* of separation, I think it is evident that the ambiguity is only semantic, and the relation between separation of powers and checks and balances in the authors' thinking becomes clear. By "separation of powers," Madison and Hamilton meant to refer to the establishment of the executive, the judiciary, and the two houses of Congress as separate *institutions*, each with its own constitutional status and none subservient to another.

A recurrent theme during the debates at the Philadelphia Convention had been the necessity of constructing a design that would assure the effective independence of these institutions. The potentiality of one to dominate another was a hazard that punctuated consideration of virtually all of the clauses, especially those dealing with the powers and mode of election of the president. Each institution, the framers believed, would *naturally* strive to enlarge its power and dominate the others if it could. But they did not attempt to solve this problem by defining hermetically sealed domains for them. The legislative, executive, and judicial functions of government are conceptually distinguishable, but the framers did not believe that they could be made operationally disjunct. The principle of separation of powers was construed to mean only that the several institutions should be organized in such a fashion that they would be, and permanently remain, politically independent of each other. Hamilton especially would have preferred a dominant executive, but he accepted the design that had been adopted by the Constitutional Convention. In the *Federalist,* he and Madison treated separation as a device to constrain the power of the state by enabling each institution to negate the acts of the others. It is checks and balances that does the work; separation of powers is needed, but only as the necessary "frame" for that function.

In this connection I should note the views of John Jay. He wrote only five of the *Federalist* papers; four pleading the need for a union in order to defend America from foreign power and influence (nos. 2–5) and another defending the proposed constitution of the federal Senate (no. 64). None of these are germane to the issue at hand, but Jay apparently did not share his colleagues' view of the relation between separation of powers and checks and balances. After the ratification of the Constitution he was appointed chief justice of the Supreme Court. Presiding over the grand jury of the Eastern Circuit in 1790, Jay pointed out that the separation of powers was a fundamental principle of the Constitution and interpreted it as, in itself, guaranteeing the liberty of the people. The checking function, according to Jay, was performed by strictly confining the executive, legislative, and judicial departments to their own exclusive domains.[35] Jay's view was not idiosyncratic. The notion of checks and balances had been fiercely derided by Tom Paine (*Common Sense*, 1776) as no more than an English hypocrisy, and, according to Forrest McDonald, this criticism persuaded many to discard it while continuing to embrace the principle of separation of powers (1985, 84). The view that separation of powers is the central political theory of the American Constitution has been prominent in the literature to the present, especially so in that written by lawyers. In a judicial proceeding, it is much easier to determine when one of the branches of government has trespassed on the domain of another than to discover an impairment of their ability to constrain each other. Though the Constitution itself is silent on the principles of separation of powers and checks and balances, the courts have accepted both as fundamental doctrines of constitutional law. Separation has not been rigorously enforced; far from it. But the courts have often followed John Jay in construing it as the central principle of the Constitution.

Hamilton planned the *Federalist* series and coauthored at least three of its most important essays with Madison. They must have engaged in an intensive exchange of ideas. Later they were to became political enemies, sharply differing in their views of how the new nation should be guided in its development by federal policy, but in 1778 they were united in their interpretation of the proposed Constitution. They clearly did not believe that a free polity depends upon the personal qualities of those who govern. Intelligence, knowledge, and civic virtue are desirable in a nation's governors, but not

---

35. "Wise and virtuous men have thought and reasoned very differently respecting Government, but in this they have at Length very unanimously agreed viz. that its Powers should be divided into three, distinct, and independent Departments—the executive, legislative, and judicial . . . The Constitution of the United States has accordingly instituted these three Departments, and much Pains have been taken so to form and define them, as that they may operate as checks one on the other, and keep each within its proper limits— it being universally agreed to be of the last importance to a free People, that *they who are vested with executive, legislative & judicial Powers, should rest satisfied with their respective Portions of Power, and [not] encroach on the Provinces of each other*" (Jay, 1790, 2, italics mine).

sufficient to maintain liberty. The real threat to personal freedom derives not from the ignorance or venality of governors, but from their insatiable thirst for power. The adoption of a republican form of government secures America from the danger of monarchical despotism—the unhappy state of most of the rest of the world—but it does not, in itself, guarantee that governance in America will not become tyrannous. Liberty cannot be long maintained, even in a republic, without institutional artifacts that constrain the exercise of political power. This conception of the problem is what made the *Federalist* an outstanding document in the history of constitutionalism.[36]

The most basic premise of the authors of the *Federalist* is what they believed to be the politically relevant properties of human nature. Their views on this matter led them to embrace the countervailance model of governance, and it raised another issue that is prominent in the *Federalist* papers: the special problem that inevitably emerges in a polity that takes seriously the proposition that sovereign authority derives from the people. I turn now to examine what the papers have to contribute to these questions.

If John Pocock is correct in his contention that American republicanism was founded on the doctrine of "civic virtue" (1975; 1981), there is very little evidence of it in the *Federalist*. On the contrary, though Hamilton and Madison referred to the American people as virtuous, they made it quite clear that it would be fatal to rely upon this attribute in designing the government of a republican polity. In speaking of the proposed House of Representatives, Madison notes, "The aim of every political constitution is, or ought to be, first to obtain for rulers men who possess most wisdom to discern, and most virtue to pursue, the common good of the society; and in the next place, to take the most effectual precautions for keeping them virtuous whilst they continue to hold their public trust." That representatives are likely to have "motives of a more selfish nature," he goes on to note, should not be disregarded. Frequent elections will do much to maintain their attention to the common good, but more is necessary. "It will not be denied," he asserts, "that power is of an encroaching nature," and he quotes Jefferson's remark that "an *elective despotism* was not the government we fought for." (no. 57, 370f.; no. 48, 321, 324). On the role of the Senate in the making of treaties, Hamilton declares, "The history of human conduct does not warrant that exalted opinion of human virtue which would make it wise in a nation to commit interests of so momentous and delicate a kind . . . to the sole disposal of [the President]" (no. 75, 487).

---

36. On this point the Federalists and Anti-Federalists agreed. They differed only on whether the proposed Constitution was sufficient to the task. The debate between them, writes Gordon Wood, "was an amazing display of confidence in constitutionalism, in the efficacy of institutional devices for solving social and political problems" (1969, 517).

In *Federalist* 51, whose authorship is uncertain, the establishment of checks on power in the proposed Constitution is defended in the following general terms:

> It may be a reflection on human nature, that such devices should be necessary to control the abuses of government. But what is government itself, but the greatest of all reflections of human nature? If men were angels, no government would be necessary. If angels were to govern men, neither external nor internal controls on government would be necessary. In framing a government which is to be administered by men over men, the great difficulty lies in this: you must first enable the government to control the governed; and in the next place oblige it to control itself. (no. 51, 337)[37]

As the passage just quoted indicates, the authors of *The Federalist* did not regard the negative features of human nature as universal. Some men are virtuous, and can be relied on to serve the common interest if not corrupted by unconstrained power. This view is central to their depiction of the role of the legislature. The houses of Congress are described as *deliberative* bodies, not merely delegates of the states or the electorate. Legislation was to result from genuine discussion. To this end, it was desirable for the members of the House and Senate to be intelligent and knowledgeable, capable of rational argument, and willing to be persuaded by it (see nos. 55–58). The "supposition of universal venality in human nature is little less an error in political reasoning, than the supposition of universal rectitude," writes Hamilton (no. 76, 495). The expectation that knowledgeable and virtuous men can be found to debate public policy is not unrealistic; but in framing the structure of government, it is prudent to assume that no person, and no group, is immune to intoxication by the prestige and authority of political office.

Like most American political thinkers of the Constitution era, the authors of the *Federalist* embraced the doctrine of popular sovereignty, which was construed as a normative rather than a positive principle. The concept of sovereignty was not employed for analytical purposes to reveal the true locus of political power, but to provide moral justification for the coercion of the citizenry by the state. Jean Bodin's proposition that sovereignty resides in the institution that makes law was transmuted into the view that legislatures are only derivative repositories of sovereign authority, exercising it pro tempore on behalf of the people. But the doctrine of popular sovereignty cannot re-

---

37. See Wright (1949) for an excellent study of *The Federalist*'s conception of human nature. The Anti-Federalists held the same view of human nature, and rejected the idea that the civic virtue of governors could be relied on to protect the people's liberties (see Bailyn, 1990, 241f.).

alistically be construed to mean that moral justification of law requires unanimous consent. Even in a small direct democracy, this would make collective action impossible. In the political literature of the period, and even today when the principle of popular sovereignty is invoked, it is commonly assumed that laws are justified if approved by the majority. What, then, of minorities? Have they no legitimate claim to protection from the will of the majority? If they have, how can they be effectively protected in a political system based upon popular sovereignty? At the time of composition of the *Federalist,* this was a topic of much discussion; many criticized the proposed Constitution for failing to include a specific statement of basic citizen rights. Madison and Hamilton were not convinced that such a statement should be embodied in the Constitution, but one of the most important contributions of the *Federalist* to political theory was the solution it proffered to the problem of reconciling majority rule with minority rights.[38] On this matter the most important paper in the *Federalist* is no. 10. In it, Madison addresses the problem of "faction," which to his mind poses the greatest threat to the continuance of popular government. Madison defines a faction as a body of citizens "who are united and actuated by some common impulse of passion, or of interest, adverse to the rights of other citizens, or to the permanent or aggregate interests of the community." He makes plain that the majority can constitute such a faction, and his argumentation is directed at the problem of controlling the will of the majority.[39]

The root causes of faction, argues Madison, cannot be eliminated without sacrificing liberty, for people differ in numerous ways. Inequality as to property is the most common source of faction, but there are others as well, such as differences in religion. "The latent causes of faction are . . . sown in the nature of man; and we see them everywhere brought into different degrees

38. Bernard Bailyn traces concern for this issue back to the colonial period, when the dangers of " 'democratical despotism' preyed on the minds not merely of crown officials and other defenders of prerogative, but of all enlightened thinkers" (1967, 283). Shays' Rebellion did a great deal to focus the attention of creditors and large landowners on the danger to their interests of the common people when organized and led by popular demagogues. McDonald notes that a number of delegates to the Constitutional Convention expressed fear of "an excess of democracy" in the state governments (1985, 201f.). But it is a misleadingly limited view of the Constitution they constructed to construe it, as Gordon Wood does, as "intrinsically an aristocratic document designed to check the democratic tendencies of the period" (1969, 513).

39. Writing to Jefferson on October 17, 1788, Madison declared: "Wherever the real power in a Government lies, there is the danger of oppression. In our Governments the real power lies in the majority of the community, and the invasion of private rights is *chiefly* to be apprehended . . . from acts in which the Government is the mere instrument of the major number of the Constitutents" (Madison, 1884, 425).

of activity, according to the different circumstances of civil society." Only in a tyranny can such differences be prevented from influencing public policy—a remedy that is "worse than the disease."

History has shown, explains Madison, that direct democracies inevitably fall victim to majority factions. Herein lies the wisdom of the proposed Constitution: it places the power of governance into the hands of representatives, who may have the wisdom to resist the demands of a transitory majority, and, unlike democracies that necessarily must be small, it creates an extended union that is economically, socially, and culturally diverse. "It is this circumstance," asserts Madison, "that renders factious combinations less to be dreaded." In such a union, more heterogeneous than any of the individual states, it will be difficult to form majorities whose object is to despoil or oppress minorities. The federal government, instead of threatening the liberty of the people as some critics of the proposed constitution contend, will be its chief protector.[40]

At least some of the readers of the *Federalist* would have been unimpressed by Madison's argument. It was still widely believed that the internal stability of any political entity, and its ability to defend itself from foreign powers, depend upon unity, which requires either a homogeneous populace or the suppression of organized factions. Madison argues the exact opposite—that demographic diversity and the presence of many factions in a large republic *serve* the common interest. The proposed union would secure Americans from any new threat of foreign domination, and it would prevent them from destroying their republic themselves by failing to limit the power of majoritarian passions and interests that are easily directed against minorities. Respect for the rights of others is furthered by an enlightened moral sense, but this cannot be relied upon to sustain it. Human nature being what it is, personal interests must be engaged. This is possible in a heterogeneous society, where every citizen, on one dimension or another, belongs to a minority. In effect, Madison viewed a free republic as dependent not only upon its form of government, but also, in a larger sense, upon a pluralistic society. The motto of

---

40. Number 10 is not the only paper in the *Federalist* where this argument appears. See, e.g., nos. 48, 51, 71. Hamilton does not elaborate upon the basic idea, as Madison did, but he appears to have embraced it. John Jay, however, seems to have taken a more traditional view, stressing the benefits of homogeneity: "I have . . . often taken notice, that Providence has been pleased to give this one connected country to one united people—a people descended from the same ancestors, speaking the same language, professing the same religion, attached to the same principles of government, very similar in their customs and manners" (*Federalist* no. 2, 9).

the *Federalist* papers could have been: "In unity there is strength; in diversity there is liberty."[41]

Madison became entangled in acrimonious political controversy as secretary of state in the Jefferson administration, and his own presidency (1809–1817) was not a conspicuously successful one, but by a decade after his retirement from politics, admirers were beginning to call him "the Father of the Constitution," a description oft-repeated by historians since. To my mind, he deserves both a smaller and a larger place in history. He must share the honor of fatherhood with those who fought against prerogative authority in seventeenth-century England and in America during the colonial period, and with those who devised the state constitutions. The honor is also deserved by many other contemporary individuals, and especially by George Washington and Alexander Hamilton. As chairman of the Constitutional Convention, Washington guided intense debates that often threatened to bankrupt the enterprise altogether, and his conduct as the nation's first president demonstrated that the political system devised by the framers was workable. Hamilton played a leading role in the calling of a Constitutional Convention to replace the Articles of Confederation. He planned the *Federalist* papers and wrote most of them, including those that developed the vital doctrine of judicial review. As a member of the New York ratifying convention, he played an important part in securing its decision to join the union. He strongly advocated renewal of friendly relations with Great Britain and supported the negotiation of Jay's Treaty (1794), which was highly unpopular, strongly opposed by Madison, and was ratified only after stormy debate in the Senate. As Washington's secretary of the treasury, Hamilton's prescriptions for federal economic policy reflected a much more acute perception of the nation's potential than Jefferson's romanticized image of a pastoral society.[42]

41. Madison's "most amazing political prophesy, formally published in the tenth *Federalist,* was that the size of the United States and its variety of interests, could be made a guarantee of stability and justice under the new constitution. When Madison made this prophecy the accepted opinion among all sophisticated politicians was exactly the opposite" (Adair, 1956–1957, 348). "The essence of Madison's greatness as a theorist and a politician lay in his insight into how to reconcile the rights of individuals and minorities with the necessity of majority rule. The solution he embraced was the extended compound republic, an idea that turned prevailing theory on its head" (McDowell, 1996, 12). See also, Wright (1949, 24f.); Wood (1969, 504f.); Moore (1977, 837); Shklar (1987).

42. Hamilton's reports on *Manufactures,* on *Public Credit* and on the proposal for a *National Bank* are especially noteworthy. He (or Tench Coxe, his assistant) was well in advance of his time in recognizing that bank deposits function as money, and in perceiving that they are generated by bank lending. He anticipated the economic theory of "external benefits" by more than a century in favoring government promotion of road and canal

It is with respect to the history of political *theory* that Madison deserves even more recognition than he has received. *Federalist* 10 displays a more sophisticated understanding of the countervailance model of political organization than any previous document in its long history. The "constitution" of the United States today is too thinly construed if it is presumed to consist of the frames of government specified for the state and federal governments, the Bill of Rights, and the universal franchise. And it remains so even if one adds the constitutional decisions of the courts. Essential parts of the American political system are political parties, private social-policy research foundations, and the almost innumerable general and special interest groups that attempt to influence the enactment and implementation of public policy—the "factions" of which Madison spoke. He did not, of course, foresee that political participation would come to be mediated more strongly, and more continuously, by such institutions than by the occasional opportunity to vote for representatives, but he clearly grasped the central principle of the countervailance model and perceived it as a means of turning diversity into a central pillar of the republican edifice.[43]

The Bill of Rights and the Judiciary

The Bill of Rights is regarded today as an integral part of the Constitution of the United States (Amar, 1991), but it was not included in the initial proposal. Specific statements of civic rights that were not to be infringed by government were contained in most of the state constitutions, and the inclusion of a similar statement in the proposed national Constitution was strongly urged at the Philadelphia Convention by George Mason of Virginia. But this idea received no support and was rejected.[44] "This," writes Rakove, "was the one serious miscalculation the framers made as they looked ahead to the struggle over ratification" (1997, 288). The Anti-Federalists attacked specific

construction, and in arguing that a policy of import restriction could be effectively used by a young country to accelerate its economic development.

43. Madison employed similar reasoning in considering the issue of religious freedom. At the Virginia ratifying convention, he defended the lack of protection of religion against governmental authority in the proposed Constitution, saying that religious freedom "arises from the multiplicity of sects which pervades America, and which is the best and only security for religious liberty in any society; for where there is such a variety of sects, there cannot be a majority of any one sect to oppress and persecute the rest" (McConnell, 1990, 1479).

44. Virginia was the first of the states to incorporate a declaration of citizen rights in its Constitution of 1776. It was drafted by George Mason. Failure of the Philadelphia Convention to include a similar declaration was one of the reasons why Mason refused to lend his name to the proposal and became a leader of the Anti-Federalist party.

provisions of the proposed Constitution on various grounds, but their main plea that it should be rejected was based on a general assessment that it threatened the independence of the state governments and failed to secure the civic rights of the people against a federal body that could pass laws to govern them directly. In *Federalist* 84, Hamilton noted that many opponents of the Constitution deplored its lack of a statement of rights. Referring to England's Magna Carta, the Petition of Right of 1628, and the Declaration of Right of 1688, Hamilton asserted that although such documents had merit in a monarchy, they were unnecessary in a republic. He argued that the structure of the proposed Constitution would, in itself, serve to protect the citizenry from the undue exercise of governmental power. Others contended that the inclusion of bills of rights in the state constitutions was sufficient (Ferguson, 1997, 142). Such arguments failed to convince, however, and it became apparent that ratification by the states would not be achieved unless it was understood that the Constitution should be amended to include a statement of rights.

Madison was skeptical concerning the necessity, or the desirability, of a federal Bill of Rights. In his view, the state bills had proven to be mere "parchment barriers," ineffective in protecting civic liberty (Madison, 1884, 423f.). Others went further. Benjamin Rush considered it "absurd" and "disgraceful" that a popular republican government would be limited, and called the bills of rights in the state constitutions "idle and superfluous instruments" (Morgan, 1989, 283). But the founders were, above all, pragmatic, and they were sensitive to the existence of a strong body of opinion in favor of amending the federal Constitution to include a statement of rights, and to the danger that ratification by some states was doubtful without it. At the first Congress, Madison proposed that a committee be appointed to draft a Bill of Rights, noting that it would, at least, demonstrate to the opponents of the Constitution that its supporters "were seriously devoted to liberty" (1904, 370–389). In the ensuing debate, he led the campaign for the adoption of the amendments.[45]

The notion that a Bill of Rights, in itself, serves to constrain the state is subject to doubt. If one takes the view that a center of power can be controlled only by other centers of power, it follows that, if no institutions exist that can check the authority of Congress to enact law, a Bill of Rights can

---

45. Most of the states submitted specific proposals for inclusion in a federal Bill of Rights, totaling altogether 186 items. Eliminating duplications, there were still eighty substantive proposals that Madison's committee had to consider. These were reduced to seventeen for debate by the Congress, which adopted twelve of them for submission to the states for ratification (Ringold, 1972, 4, 31f.). For a complete list of the amendments proposed by state ratifying conventions, see Barnett, 1989, app. B.

only exert moral constraint upon legislators, and act as a catalyst of public opinion. The power of public opinion is not negligible in a polity where lawmakers have to submit to reelection, but it cannot secure the liberties of minorities, which clearly was a main objective of the Bill of Rights. The history of American constitutional development is, in large part, the history of the role of the federal courts as guardians of the rights specified in the amendments to the Constitution that are aimed at constraining the power of the federal and state governments.[46]

In his celebrated description of the English constitution, Montesquieu identified the judiciary as one of its three functional branches, but he did not regard it as a significant center of political authority because "it has not the power of either the sword or the purse." This was an underestimate of the political role of the English judiciary. Montesquieu failed to recognize what Sir Edward Coke had achieved by construing the common law as England's constitution and the added significance that common law attained when the independence of the judiciary was affirmed by the Act of Settlement after the Revolution of 1688. But even today, the role of the English courts in protecting the rights of the citizen against Parliament and the administration remains ambiguous—additionally so because of Britain's membership in the European Union, which has courts of its own (see Chapter 9). An outstanding feature of the American political system is the authority of the federal courts to engage in what has become known as "judicial review."

It would seem obvious that a written constitution is meaningless unless some institution that is independent of the legislative and executive branches has the authority to deal with allegations that its provisions have been violated. (Recall Charles I's contention that while England was a "limited monarchy," the king had the authority to determine what those limits were). The notion that the federal courts would have power to interpret the Constitution was expressed en passant, by some delegates to the Philadelphia Convention, but the matter was not confronted explicitly. None of the comprehensive proposals made at the convention included any provision for it, and none was embodied in the proposed Constitution. A system of federal courts was proposed in order to complete the structure of the federal government and secure its independence from the states, but aside from a hint of it that can be read

46. The Bill of Rights established constitutional restraints on the exercise of federal power. Though Madison regarded it as also applying to the states, that was not explicitly stated. The Fourteenth Amendment, passed in the wake of the Civil War, has been construed by the courts (not without considerable dissent) as placing the state governments under the restraints of the Bill of Rights. The first case to engage the Supreme Court's full attention to this issue was *Griswold v. Connecticut* (1965), which concerned a state law prohibiting the use of contraceptive devices (see Lockhart et al., 1986, 286–298, 312–326).

into article 3, the Constitution gave no indication that these courts were to have the authority to adjudicate allegations that the Constitution had been violated.

Madison held that no constitution should (or could) be written in such specific terms that it would not require interpretation, and he recognized that some means of correcting violations was necessary. In accordance with the principle of checks and balances, he argued that "in the first instance" the executive and judiciary would control violations by the legislature, but "in the last resort . . . a remedy must be obtained from the people, who can, by the election of more faithful representatives, annul the acts of the usurpers" (*Federalist* no. 44, 295). In view of his great concern for minority rights, one might think that he would not have been satisfied to leave the matter there, but he did not discuss it further in the *Federalist*. In his speech to Congress recommending a Bill of Rights, Madison noted that it would empower "independent tribunals of justice" to protect the citizenry, but he did not elaborate the point (1904, 385).

The *Federalist*, however, did address the issue forthrightly—in Hamilton's papers on the powers of the federal judiciary (nos. 78–83). Indeed, no clearer statement of the doctrine of judicial review can be found in the literature before this, and Hamilton's exposition of it is at least the equal of Chief Justice John Marshall's in the Supreme Court's decision in *Marbury v. Madison* (1803), which is commonly referred to by constitutional historians as its locus classicus.[47]

I do not know how widely shared was Hamilton's view of the authority of the federal courts, but it is not surprising that they began to act as adjudicators of the Constitution soon after its establishment.[48] No other body had been given this role, and power vacuums are notoriously transitory. The authority of the Supreme Court of the United States to act as the final arbiter of the Constitution went unchallenged until the case of *Marbury v. Madison* came before it. In this case, the government's attorneys contended that the court was not empowered to invalidate a federal statute.

In itself, the *Marbury* case was a small affair, but it resulted from events

47. "The complete independence of the courts of justice is peculiarly essential in a limited constitution . . . [i.e.] one that contains certain specified exceptions to the legislative authority; such, for instance, as that it shall pass no bills of attainder, no *ex-post-facto* laws, and the like. Limitations of this kind can be preserved in practice no other way than through the medium of courts of justice, whose duty it must be to declare all acts contrary to the manifest tenor of the Constitution void. Without this, all reservations of particular rights and privileges would amount to nothing" (Hamilton, in *Federalist* no. 78, 505).

48. The first case in which the Supreme Court undertook to determine the constitutionality of a federal statute occurred in 1796. The issue was whether a tax it had imposed was "direct" or "indirect."

that generated a heated, and partisan, political controversy over the Alien and Sedition Acts, passed by Congress in 1798.[49] In the general elections of 1800, the incumbent president, John Adams, a Federalist, was defeated by Thomas Jefferson, whose Democratic-Republican party also won control of Congress. During the interim between the election and the date on which Jefferson and the new Congress were to take office, legislation was hurriedly passed that, in effect, enabled Adams to pack the judiciary with Federalist supporters. Some of the commissions of appointment were not delivered in time, however, and James Madison, secretary of state in the new administration, withheld them. William Marbury's commission as justice of the peace in the District of Columbia was one of these. Marbury petitioned the Supreme Court for a writ of mandamus ordering Madison to deliver his commission. The Court's judgment (1803), written by Chief Justice Marshall, denied Marbury's petition but asserted unequivocally that the Court had authority to rule on disputed issues of constitutionality.[50] Marshall's expression of the Supreme Court's opinion in the *Marbury* case became a defining document in American constitutional law, and judicial review was established by it as a fundamental component of American constitutionalism.[51]

Over the next half-century, the Supreme Court did not invoke its review powers over federal legislation until the *Dred Scott* case in 1857, and the applicability of the Bill of Rights to state legislation was not established until the Fourteenth Amendment was passed in 1868. Initially, the justices of the Supreme Court also sat on circuit courts, but over the course of time they became more specialized. Today, the exercise of its review power is so prominent in American public policy that the Court is commonly regarded as primarily, if not exclusively, a constitutional court. This role of the judiciary has

49. These acts, ostensibly a reaction to the hostile naval and diplomatic actions of the French revolutionary government, were really aimed at undermining the popularity of Jefferson's party, which had been sympathetic to the new regime in France. The acts defined "sedition" so broadly that, despite the Bill of Rights, it made virtually any criticism of the federal authorities illegal. In terms of the principle of judicial review, the acts are significant as occasioning the first judgment of the Supreme Court invalidating an executive order as lacking statutory foundation (*Little et al. v. Barreme et al.*, 1804).

50. John Marshall was himself deeply involved in the political aspect of the controversy. As acting secretary of state in the Adams administration, he had signed the commissions of the new judges, and had been appointed chief justice of the Supreme Court just before Adams left office. Nevertheless, as the court's decision in the *Marbury* case shows, he understood its profound implications and had a clear perception of the role of the judiciary in a political system that is designed to check the power of the state (see Lockhart et al., 1986, 2f.).

51. Dickinson (1927, ch. 4) provides an excellent exposition of the American doctrine of judicial review and its English antecedents.

never been formally established by constitutional amendment. It remains a convention of American constitutionalism.

Constitutional law, as now taught in law schools, is a rich and complex subject. It consists largely of judgments that the federal courts have rendered in cases where the interpretation of the Constitution is at issue.[52] The terms "separation of powers" and "checks and balances" do not appear in the text of the Constitution, but from the beginning, the courts have construed them as its fundamental principles. Supported by the Bill of Rights and subsequent similar amendments, the courts have often accepted the duty of protecting the citizenry from unjust or excessive exercise of state power—that is, they have construed themselves as part of a checks and balances political system. But there have been numerous occasions when separation of powers, *tout court*, has been the focus of attention, and others where judicial decisions fail to display a clear understanding of the relation between separation of powers and checks and balances. Jurists are not alone in confounding these two principles. Tracing the development of constitutional theory in America to the present is not possible and would not be helpful here. Except for the confrontation over slavery in the 1860s, which signified a profound alteration in the conception of "the people," the fundamental principles of American constitutionalism, and the governmental institutions through which they are mediated, remain much as they were two centuries ago.

A Note on Provenance

Beyond question, the most important external source of American constitutionalism was England. The doctrine of checks and balances that developed in seventeenth-century England, and its institutional realization after the Revolution of 1688, dominated American political thought and informed the practice of American colonial government and the construction of the early state constitutions.[53] But England was not the *fons et origo* of constitutional

52. It is worth noting, however, that in adjudicating constitutional cases the courts have often considered, and themselves employed, statements drawn from the literature of the Constitution era that may be construed as indicating the intent of the framers. In this way, the political theory expounded by the Federalists of the 1780s has been carried forward as permanently authoritative. There is, of course, much room for dispute as to what the framers of the Constitution really intended by this or that provision, and the available documentation is both incomplete and untrustworthy (see Hutson, 1986), but there can be no doubt that they aimed to prevent the concentration of political power, and to allow no agency of the state to exercise uncontrolled authority.

53. From the literature of the Constitution era, it is plain that the chief source of American ideas concerning the fundamental theory of the English constitution was Montesquieu. Some historians have contended that David Hume's essay "Idea of a Perfect Common-

practice and theory. As shown in earlier chapters, the conception of a state whose coercive power is constrained by its own institutional structure extends back to ancient Athens and Rome, and was exemplified in early modern times by the Venetian and Dutch republics. Some brief note is warranted on these as potential sources of American constitutionalism.

Education in the colonial era was modeled after that of England, with its intense emphasis on Greek and Latin literature and history. Pupils in American grammar schools studied little else. Knowledge of the classics was the main condition of entrance to the colleges, and after admission, the student was treated to more of the same. With few notable exceptions, such as Benjamin Franklin, Tom Paine, and Patrick Henry, the political leaders of the time had all been immersed in the classics. The political literature of the Revolution and Constitution periods is full of classical references, and numerous historians have called attention to the classical sources of American constitutionalism (e.g., Chinard, 1940; Bailyn, 1967, 23f.; Panagopoulos, 1985, essay 4).

The most comprehensive study of this to date is Carl J. Richard's *The Founders and the Classics* (1985). There can be no doubt that Americans' focus on civic liberty, and their quickness to see threats to it, was reinforced by their study of classical literature and the histories of Greece and Rome. But it seems to me that Richard goes much too far in contending that "the classics supplied a large portion of the founders' intellectual tools," which they applied to politics, and that "classical ideas provided the basis for their theories of government form, social responsibility, human nature, and virtue" (8, 232). It is clear from the pages of the *Federalist,* as well as from other literature of the period, that the framers of the American Constitution regarded the Greek federations as furnishing historical proof of the instability of loose unions, such as that of the American states under the Articles of Confederation. Most of the references to classical models in the *Federalist* are negative. The framers did not copy the Athenian structure of government and did not establish a system of jury courts similar to the Athenian one, which had served there as the main institution that preserved civic liberty and controlled the exercise of political power. They did not adopt the dual con-

---

wealth" (1752) had a strong influence, especially on James Madison and Alexander Hamilton (see Adair, 1956–1957; Moore, 1977; McDonald, 1985, 234). No direct evidence has been supplied to support this view, however, and it does not seem to me that there is a great deal of similarity between Hume's proposal and the constitutional ideas of the Federalists. A better case could perhaps be made for the influence of volumes 5 and 6 of Hume's *History of England* (1754–1762), where he depicts the contest between Parliament and the Stuart monarchs as hinging upon whether political power in England should be concentrated and absolute, or dispersed and limited.

sulate of republican Rome, its tradition of very brief terms for elected officers, its system of voting, or its most important institution for the protection of personal liberty, the plebeian tribunate. Polybius's checks and balances theory of the Roman system of government was well known in America, but was seldom mentioned in the political literature of the 1780s.[54] If classical ideas and political institutions constitute a thread in the historical tapestry of American constitutionalism, it is a faint one.

The Venetian Republic was still extant when the American colonies rebelled against British rule and established republican forms of government at state and national levels. But the repute of Venice had by then turned from myth to anti-myth. The references to Venice in the literature of the period are almost universally negative.[55] Though the framers were undoubtedly familiar with Venice's earlier history and its system of government, they did not copy any of its institutions. Some historians perceive a Venetian influence on some of the early colonial charters (Fink, 1940, 172; Haitsma Mulier, 1980, 53), but it is evident that it had disappeared by the time of the Revolution. I have encountered no references in the literature to Contarini or Guicciardini, the main writers who celebrated the political system of Venice.

In view of the Dutch component of the American population, the early support of the American Revolution by the Dutch Republic, its own origin in a revolt against foreign domination, its repute as a land of liberty, and its federal political system, one might expect to find evidence that the framers of the Constitution would have looked to the Dutch union for instruction on how to construct an American one. But the framers copied none of its political institutions. The federal form of the Dutch union was similar to that of America under the Articles of Confederation, which the delegates at the Philadelphia Convention determined to supplant by a radically different one.[56] On the plane of political theory, as we have seen (Chapter 6), Dutch thinkers focused their

54. The index to the large collection of political writings of the founding era by Hyneman and Lutz (1983) contains only one reference to Polybius.

55. See, for example, the *Federalist* no. 48, 324. Forrest McDonald notes that Thomas Otway's *Venice Preserved*, a popular American play of the Revolution period, depicted Venice as a "wretched, corrupt oligarchy" (1985, 88). Ambrosini (1975) entitles section 4 of her study of Venetian-American relations during the late eighteenth century "Venezia vista dei Founding Fathers: Una republica decaduta."

56. Ricker (1957) examines in great detail what Americans knew, or thought they knew, about the Dutch Republic and concludes that, apart from providing an example of a federal form to be avoided, it had no influence on the framers. In *Federalist* 37, Madison castigated the Dutch for having failed to reform "the baneful and notorious vices of their constitution" (231f.). Of all the framers, Madison was undoubtedly the most knowledgeable about the federal form of political organization. In 1786 he had undertaken a special study of "ancient and modern confederacies" and made copious notes on them (Rakove, 1997, 42n).

main attention on affirming the principle of provincial sovereignty, which the American framers would have been anxious to depreciate.

In general then, we have to conclude that American constitutionalism was a modification of English constitutionalism in its fundamental principles and, except for federalism, in much of the institutional structure that was designed to translate those principles into practice.

The originality, or otherwise, of the American conception of constitutionalism, and of the proper frame of government, continues to be debated by historians, who differ greatly in their appraisals.[57] To contend that the Constitution was something fundamentally new, or that it was entirely derivative, is to adopt extreme views that are easily negated by empirical evidence, but it is impossible to locate its degree of uniqueness definitively on a scalar between them.

The great influence of the American Revolution and the Constitution on Western political thought and events during the nineteenth century, however, is uncontestable, and that influence has broadened and deepened during the twentieth. American political events are followed closely today throughout the world, with reactions that range from admiration, to perplexity and apprehension, to disparagement and even contempt—and negative appraisals are not confined to nations whose political masters reject out of hand the idea that the coercive power of the state should be constrained. In countries where democratic political systems have been established, or reestablished, since World War II, American constitutionalism has been very influential in promoting the universal franchise, political parties, religious toleration, freedom of the press, an independent judiciary, and other lineaments of democracy, but the structural frame of American governmental institutions has been copied by few. Great Britain is now a secondary world power, but its parliamentary system continues to be a positive exemplar, and not only in countries that are, or once were, parts of the British Empire or Commonwealth. At least since Walter Bagehot argued in *The English Constitution* (1867) that there is a fundamental difference between the English and American political systems, it has been common among political scientists to contend that there are two distinct structural models of democratic government, exemplified by Great Britain and the United States. In this book I have been tracing the history of only one basic model: in my view, *all* democracies are based upon the countervailance principle.

In Chapter 7, we examined the development of the countervailence principle in seventeenth-century England. Political scientists might nevertheless

---

57. See, for example, Dwight (1887, 3); Wood (1969, viiif., 92, 564, ch. 14); McDonald (1985, 262, 281); Kammen (1988, 123); Lutz (1988, 1, 8f.).

contend, as Bagehot did, that the emergence of Cabinet government during the eighteenth century constituted a distinct change of course, one that re-established the Bodinian principle of sovereignty and located it in Parliament. Many English jurists and political scientists today speak of "parliamentary sovereignty" as the central principle of the English constitution. In the domain of politics there can be no definitive tests of a theoretical hypothesis, but the one-model thesis would clearly be severely weakened if British governance were shown, by empirical analysis, to be based on another. In the following chapter I will examine the structure and dynamics of the modern British political system in order to ascertain whether it can be validly interpreted as an exemplification of the countervailance model.

9

Modern Britain

During the century after the Glorious Revolution, Britain became the most prosperous nation in Europe and the leading economic and military power in the world. The industrial revolution that began in later eighteenth-century Britain continued the development of its international hegemony. When A. V. Dicey composed his interpretation of the English constitution in the early 1880s, he could assume, without appearing arrogant, or even presumptuous, that he was describing the constitution of the most successful nation since the fall of Rome. Today, Britain's position in world affairs is very different. Her overseas empire is gone, and the United States has become the dominant nation in world affairs. Even within the European Union, Britain carries less weight than Germany or France. But Britian's "decline" is only in terms of international comparison. Domestically, the past fifty years has been an era of economic and social progress. The common people of Britain enjoy a much higher material standard of living than they did in 1939; educational and economic opportunities are much more broadly distributed; access to health services is universal; provisions for the poor, the unemployed, and other unfortunate members of society are generous. And, withal, Britain remains a society in which personal freedom has a high place on the political agenda, and it has a governmental administration and judicial system that is notably short on corruption and sectarian bias.

Among the many changes that have taken place, the reduction in the influence of religion in British politics deserves special note. Religious conflict constituted a prominent element in the Civil War of the 1640s and the Revolution of 1688. The place of religion in people's lives, and the political influence of religious institutions, remained substantial throughout the eighteenth century. As late as 1917, when Harold Laski wrote his *Studies in the Problem of Sovereignty*, he could plausibly emphasize the special role of churches as independent centers of political power. The source of their influence identified by Laski—their ability to command the loyalty of their members—has now virtually evaporated. Britain is today one of the most secular societies in the world.[1] The countervailing role that Laski viewed churches as playing as centers of moral authority is now largely exercised by secular organizations, such as the League Against Cruel Sports, or the Society for the Protection of Unborn Children, which mobilize the personal and financial support of members and contributors to lobby Westminster and Whitehall for, or against, particular public policies. The relation between religion and politics is one of the sharpest points of contrast between Britain and the United States. In American society, active membership in religious institutions is high, and religious leaders are very prominent in politics. It is moderately ironic that Britain today still has an officially established church, while Americans have now lived for more than two centuries with a Constitution that specifically prohibits any official connection between church and state.

Measured in terms of the proportion of the gross domestic product that is taken up by the government sector, the British state is much larger today than it was even up to World War II. In the 1930s it amounted to some 10 percent; today it is more than 40 percent. In 1945 the prominent Austalian-English economist Colin Clark, a strong opponent of big government, advanced the proposition that there was an absolute upper limit to the proportion of the national income that the state could appropriate by taxation. If it attempted to collect more than 25 percent, the real value of its receipts would simply be eroded by inflation (Arndt, 1979, 123f.). Perhaps because social scientists labor under the difficulty of having no fixed numerical magnitudes to which general propositions can be anchored, Clark's 25 percent was embraced, for a time, as if it were a natural constant like the coefficient of acceleration or the boiling point of water.

A complementary notion, which has a longer lineage, is that there is a fundamental incompatibility between "socialism"—defined as the state taking up a large share of the national income—and the preservation of personal freedom. This proposition was forcefully expressed by F. A. Hayek's *Road to Serfdom* (1944), which was widely discussed in the British journalistic media. *Capitalism and Freedom* (1962), by the prominent American economist Milton Friedman, added considerably to the notion that the price that must inevitably be paid for substantially expanding the role of the state is the loss of personal freedom. In some quarters this contention has been embraced as a foundational ideology, but events have failed to support it. In considering

1. "Religious divisions are no longer of any general significance, largely because of the decline of religious convictions. Less than 5 percent of the population attend church on a normal Sunday, and the attitude of a great majority of the people towards religion is one of indifference" (Birch, 1991, 6).

the threats to personal freedom that appear in constitutional polities, we have to look in a different direction—to the lacunae in their networks of power control.

Britain is commonly described today as a "parliamentary democracy." As we saw in Chapter 7, the conflict of the early Stuart era focused on the power of Parliament vis-à-vis the Crown. The settlement that was reached after the Revolution of 1688 permanently established Parliament's central role in British government. But Parliament was not then a "democratic" institution. The proportion of the population that participated in politics was very small. Its enlargement beyond the aristocracy and substantial land-owning gentry did not commence until the early nineteenth century. In the era between, the supremacy of Parliament was stressed by Whig commentators on the constitution and was accepted—more or less—by Tories who continued to regret the passing of absolute monarchy. But "Parliament" is not an unambiguous term in political discourse. William Blackstone in his *Commentaries on the Laws of England* (1765–1769), and A. V. Dicey in his *Law of the Constitution* (1885), expressed the supremacy doctrine but construed Parliament as including the Crown as well as the House of Lords and the House of Commons. In the late twentieth-century journalistic, and scholarly, literatures, the word is frequently used to refer only to the House of Commons, as distinct from the "government," whose most senior officials are in fact members of that house.

The government of modern Britain is complex. The object of this chapter is not to parse the concept of "parliamentary democracy," but to question the sovereigntist notion that there is an institution, however defined, that is "supreme." Our attention will be concentrated upon the structure and dynamics of British governance that demonstrate the necessity to adopt a different view.

The need for reform of the British constitution is a prominent subject in contemporary political discourse. The distinguished constitutional scholar Sir Ivor Jennings published his *Parliamentary Reform* in 1933 and followed with *Parliament Must Be Reformed* in 1941. Jennings contended that the maintenance of democracy in Britain was conditional upon substantial changes in the constitution. The issue was suppressed by the different concerns of wartime politics, and remained dormant until the 1960s. Since then, there has been a growing body of constitutional criticism and demands for fundamental reform. Some of this groundswell has been concerned with the special problem of Northern Ireland and the demands for "devolution" by Scottish and Welsh nationalists, but the general theme of most of it is that the long British tradition of individual liberty is now at risk, and measures must be taken to constrain the power of the government more effectively.[2]

As one might expect, different critics of the constitution emphasize different issues: decline in the stature and effectiveness of the House of Commons (Lenman, 1992); inadequate accountability of public servants (Drewry, 1994); violation of basic civil rights by the police, with and without the sanction of law (Dearlove and Saunders, 1992, 451f.; Marshall and Loveday, 1994); excessive secrecy in governmental activities (Sedgemore, 1980, 13–24; Frankel, 1990; Mount, 1993, 183f.; Austin, 1994; Turpin, 1994, 146); inadequate control of the security agencies (Dearlove and Saunders, 1992, 242–252). Some writers contend that there has been a general trend toward concentration of political power in Britain and a weakening of the traditional system of checks and balances (McAuslan and McEldowney, 1986; Mount, 1993, 80).[3] In 1976, a former lord chancellor, Lord Hailsham described the British system of government as an "elective dictatorship" in which the old checks and balances had ceased to operate, a theme he reiterated in subsequent addresses and in his book *The Dilemma of Democracy* (Dearlove and Saunders, 1992, 162; Lenman, 1992, 1; Mount, 1993, 3). Hailsham's apprehensions were muted after his reassumption of the office of lord chancellor in Mrs. Thatcher's government, where he steadfastly opposed proposals for constitutional reform, but his striking phrase attained a life of its own and continues to reverberate in the political literature as an ominous proclamation of constitutional crisis.[4]

Proposals for reform of the constitution have varied: abolition of the House of Lords (advocated officially by the Labor party since 1935, but now scaled down to reform); the adoption of a "Freedom of Information Act" similar to that of the United States (Austin, 1994, 434f.); the use of referenda to

2. See Dearlove and Saunders (1992, ch. 5) for a good review of this literature. The contention that there has been a significant general trend toward authoritarian government has been forcefully argued by Hillyard (1988).

3. "The last few years have seen the deliberate and steady dismantling of all those checks on governmental power which did indeed slow it down, forced it, often unwillingly, to take account of interests which it would have preferred to ignore . . . Elected authorities can be abolished or financially undermined; judicial decisions can be reversed by retrospective legislation; ministers can mislead Parliament and the public; the media can be harassed. In such a situation it is a refusal to face reality to continue to write in terms of a constitution which enshrines limited government, when clearly there is no such constitution in existence" (McAuslan and McEldowney, 1986, 515).

4. Lord Hailsham's *On the Constitution* (1992) expresses great satisfaction with the constitution, praising its flexibility and denying the need for any great change. He is particularly critical of suggestions for reform that are inspired by American government, which he regards as a fundamentally different system.

decide especially important issues such as ratification of the Maastricht treaty, or ones that engage passionate popular sentiments, such as abortion or capital punishment (see Norton, 1984, 213f.);[5] the creation of a specific body of administrative law in order to increase the accountability of government officials (Partington, 1985); and numerous others. The most general proposal, which has been widely advocated, is that Britain should adopt a written constitution with an explicit and entrenched bill of rights. In 1964 two private member's bills to enact a specific bill of rights were introduced, ineffectively, in the House of Commons. The House of Lords passed such a bill in 1979, and again in 1980, but both failed to make their way through the Commons (Norton, 1984, 245).[6]

The discussion of the structure of British government that follows cannot avoid entanglement with the current constitutional debate, but it is not my purpose to evaluate the proposals for reform that have been advanced. I am in search of the underlying "model" of the British political system. Some commentators specifically refer to the British polity as exemplifying the checks and balances principle, but many do not, and notions that derive from the hierarchical model as resurrected by Bagehot and Dicey persist. My object is to demonstrate that the countervailance model enables one to achieve a better understanding of the British political system as a whole, and a more accurate perception of the roles played by its various institutions.

The notion that a state has three "branches"—legislative, executive, and judicial—refers to conceptually distinguishable state functions. Like any taxonomic scheme, however, it is an instrumental artifact that may, or may not, serve the purposes of empirical investigation and theoretical analysis. For Britain this traditional triadic schema fails to render much heuristic service, mainly because its legislative and executive functions are deeply entangled. So I will focus here on the institutions themselves.

---

5. When Leader of the Opposition, Margaret Thatcher opposed referenda on the ground that it would violate the constitutional principle of the sovereignty of Parliament (Norton, 1984, 220). The only occasion thus far on which a matter has been submitted to a nationwide referendum was in 1975, concerning Britain's membership in the European Community.

6. According to Andrew Marr, the central constitutional difficulty facing Britain is the ambiguity concerning the locus of sovereignty, which he proposes to remedy "with a one-clause, one-sentence Act of Parliament declaring simply that the British people were sovereign, the ultimate masters of their own political destiny" (1995, 337). This bathetic statement is only worth note because it demonstrates that the Bodinian tradition of political analysis continues in the democratic era, sustained by the metaphysical notion that "the people" may be construed as an entity that is capable of making public policy decisions.

Archaic Remnants: The Monarchy and the House of Lords

The United Kingdom, as that term implies, is formally a monarchy, and its governmental officers are officially described as agents of the "Crown," but the monarchy is now anachronistic in substance. New legislation still formally requires the assent of the monarch, but the power to veto legislation by withholding assent has not been exercised for almost three centuries, and it is safe to say that it is now obsolete. The monarch's ability to exercise behind-the-scenes political influence through personal contact with the prime minister has at times been considerable, and it is not completely negligible even today. In addition, the activities and opinions of members of the royal family are "front page" items for the mass media, and should any of them choose to express views on some matter, it is likely to initiate widespread debate that can indeed influence public policy. Britain is more like a republic than the monarchies of earlier times, but "the royals" must still be included among the multiple centers of political influence in its pluralistic political system.

The House of Lords is equally anachronistic, consisting mainly of hereditary descendants of landed aristocrats who, in feudal times, constituted the primary structure of political organization.[7] The last attempt of the Lords to exercise power over legislation occurred in 1909, in connection with Lloyd George's budget, which at the time was regarded as exceedingly radical. In 1911, finance bills were removed from the jurisdiction of the Lords, and its power over other bills was limited to delaying them for two years—reduced to one year in 1949. Members of the House of Lords may become Cabinet ministers, but it is customary that most of them are selected from the Commons. The prime minister must be a member of the Commons.[8] Though its formal authority is now severely restricted, the House of Lords remains a center of political power.

Writing in 1941, Sir Ivor Jennings observed that even among conservatives, there was "complete agreement" that the existence of the House of Lords cannot be justified. But then he went on to note that even supporters of the Labour party regard some of its functions as useful (1941, 54). One finds similar ambiguities in the debate on constitutional reform that has punc-

---

7. There are now some 1,200 members of the House of Lords, about two-thirds of whom hold hereditary titles. The other third consists of peers appointed only for their own lifetimes, plus twenty-six bishops of the Church of England and twenty-one Law Lords, who constitute the final court of appeal in the British judicial system.

8. The last peer to be prime minister was Lord Salisbury (1885, 1886, and 1895–1902). Lord Home became prime minister in 1963, but only after resigning from the peerage.

tuated British politics since the 1960s.[9] That the House of Lords is an anachronistic institution in a modern democratic state is universally conceded, but hardly anyone has called for its abolition *tout court*. Various proposals for its reconstitution as a nonhereditary body have been advanced, reflecting the widespread belief that the bicameral structure of Parliament should be retained. In searching out the theory of the British constitution, this point is revealing. Why is it considered desirable to preserve the bicameral nature of the British Parliament?

Bicameralism is a feature of many modern governments, and Britain's House of Lords is not unique in its apparent defiance of democratic principles. The Senate of the United States is composed of two members from each of the fifty states, regardless of their populations. Occasional grumbles may be heard from populous states that they are underrepresented in the Senate, but this has not become a political issue of any great moment, and American constitutional scholars rarely give it more than passing notice. The history of American constitutional development demonstrates that the theoretical foundation of bicameralism was the principle of countervailance. Two legislative organs were viewed as better than one, regardless of how they may be constituted, reflecting the idea that the lawmaking complex should have the capacity to check itself, in addition to whatever other checks and balances might exist in the political system as a whole.

That critics of the British constitution do not advocate the simple abolition of the House of Lords reveals an implicit assumption that British government is a checks and balances system. "The main argument against abolition," writes Norton, "is that a second chamber is essential as a constitutional safeguard . . . An effective second chamber was needed to act as a constitutional check" (1984, 128f.). Bicameralism is fundamentally incompatible with the hierarchical model of political organization. Anthony Birch, stressing the fact the powers of the House of Lords "are not negligible," observes that "it cannot properly be ignored simply because it cannot be fitted into the chain of command that the liberal [sic] view assumes to be the central feature of the constitution" (1991, 25). Quite so; but it is not difficult at all to fit the House of Lords into the countervailance model.[10]

9. The role of the House of Lords in the system of government has been a continuing issue of debate since the early seventeenth century. See Weston (1965) for a detailed review of how the Lords was widely perceived as a necessary element in the structure of a "mixed government."

10. The authors of the minority report of the Royal Commission on the British Constitution (1973) seem to have clearly recognized this point in recommending that, while being retained much as it is, the House of Lords should be strengthened so as to enable it to act more effectively as "a countervailing force against the centralizing tendencies of the

The House of Commons and the Cabinet

Though the monarchy and the Lords are not negligible entities in the British political system, it is the Commons that demands primary attention. Commentators who continue to talk of the "sovereignty of Parliament" really mean the sovereignty of the House of Commons, but they are not alone in taking the view that democracy is secure in Britain if the Commons is strong, and endangered if it is not. This political tradition was forged by the hot and cold civil warfare of the seventeenth century and certified by the terms under which William of Orange was recognized as monarch. But the House of Commons of the Stuart era could not act in an organized fashion without leaders, and in order to play the role in which it had been cast by the settlement of 1689, leadership was also necessary. In the 1720s, the Commons found a strong leader in Robert Walpole, who became Britain's first prime minister and created the Cabinet system that still pertains today. Walter Bagehot was right to emphasize the significance of the Cabinet in his mid-nineteenth-century appraisal of the constitution, but he was wrong in describing it as the *link* between the legislative and executive branches of the state. Even by his time, the Cabinet had itself become the government. The prime minister and his Cabinet colleagues are members of the Commons, each representing individual electoral constituencies, but it is they, not the House of Commons at large, who have inherited the political status and prerogative powers of the Crown. Indeed, it is doubtful that the traditional distinction between legislative and executive branches is applicable to modern Britain, because the function of lawmaking is also effectively in the hands of the Cabinet. The approval of the House of Commons is necessary for a bill to become law, but virtually all important legislative proposals are introduced by the government. Private members' bills seldom get as far as being voted on.[11] The role of the House of Commons in modifying government bills is, by all accounts, almost negligible. In sum then, the Cabinet is the central legislative and executive organ in the British political system. Bagehot and Dicey would have come closer to the mark if they had found the locus of sovereignty not in Parliament, but in the Cabinet.

Taking into account the ministerial parliamentary assistants as well as the

---

United Kingdom government." In 1978, a Conservative Party review committee chaired by Lord Home proposed a reformed structure for the House of Lords in order to create a body with sufficient moral authority to, in its words, "provide an effective constitutional check" on the Commons (Norton, 1984, 123f.).

11. The only important exceptions in recent years have been bills respecting abortion and capital punishment. On both of these matters public opinion was strong, but split. It was politically convenient for the government to allow private member's bills to come to a vote without its own explicit sponsorship.

ministers themselves, over 100 of the 651 members of the Commons are members of the government, obligated to support the policies determined by the Cabinet. At the head of this group is the prime minister, whose powers, though purely conventional because the office itself has never been given legal status, are awesome. The prime minister chooses whom to appoint to which ministerial posts, and which areas of policy to keep under his own direct administration. If a prime minister wishes, he can become engaged even in the details of a particular area of policy or administration, as Winston Churchill did with respect to military strategy and operations during World War II. The prime minister presides over the meetings of the Cabinet, sets its agenda, and interprets the import of its discussions without necessarily taking a vote. On the principle of "Cabinet solidarity," all members of the Cabinet must support the prime minister's announcement of Cabinet decisions, even if they believe that he has disregarded or misrepresented the consensus of views expressed in Cabinet meeting. The prime minister can, at will, shift ministers about, elevating some to more prestigious ministries and/or bringing them into the Cabinet, demoting others to lower status ministerial posts, or sending them to the back benches. The prime minister decides when to call a general election, which is a strategic political weapon that may be flourished in order to intimidate MPs who, for one reason or another, may be reluctant to submit themselves at that time to the judgment of their constituents. If he can maintain sufficient support in the Cabinet, the prime minister can even declare war on behalf of the state, without seeking the approval of Parliament.[12]

Would Bodin have demanded more as evidence of sovereign power? Must we, after all, resurrect the hierarchical model in examining modern British government? There are some who would do so. In his introduction to a new edition of Bagehot's *English Constitution* in 1963, R. H. S. Crossman spoke of British government as having been profoundly altered by "an immense accretion of power to the Prime Minister." He continues, "He is now the apex of not only a highly centralized political machine, but also of an equally centralized and vastly more powerful administrative machine. In both of these machines, loyalty has become the supreme virtue, and independence of thought a dangerous adventure. The post-war epoch has seen the final transformation of Cabinet government into Prime Ministerial government" (quoted in Mount, 1993, 148f.). This view has been prominent in the recent literature on the British constitution, with some commentators accepting it as an accurate appraisal, others rejecting it.

If one restricts attention to the above list of the powers of the prime min-

---

12. See Dearlove and Saunders (1992, 41f.) for a more complete review of the powers of the prime minister.

ister, one might well conclude that characterizing British government as "prime ministerial," or as an "elected dictatorship," is not inaccurate. But further investigation negates that thesis. The prime minister holds office by virtue of being leader of the political party having a majority of seats in the House of Commons. He may lose that position in two ways: if his party fails to win a majority in a general election, or by an intra-party démarche. Since World War II, both of these events have accounted for the fall of numerous prime ministers. Britain has had ten prime ministers since 1945, only three of whom were able to hold that office for more than five years. Margaret Thatcher was by far the most durable, serving for more than eleven years—twice as long as any other prime minister since 1945—but the rapidity with which she fell from power was breathtaking, and instructive: once a few leading political figures found the courage to offer themselves as candidates for party leadership, the imperial prime ministry, which she had elevated to an unprecedented height, collapsed like a house of cards. But vulnerability to dismissal is only part of the story. Published memoirs and other revelations by former Cabinet ministers show that the prime minister has not been able to dominate Cabinet meetings. Strong opposition by a few key ministers can be effective in persuading him to abandon a favored policy (Norton, 1984, ch. 1; Hennessey, 1991; Mount, 1993, 136f.). If the British prime minister is a dictator, he is a singularly curious one: unable to determine state policy unilaterally, required to endure unremitting and unrestrained public criticism, and subject to dismissal without a shot being fired. Ferdinand Mount's characterization of Crossman's prime ministerial government thesis as "a grotesquely melodramatic picture" appears to be wholly justified.

This is not to deny that governmental power is highly concentrated in Britain, or that this concentration presents dangers. One of the main advantages of the countervailance model is that it directs attention to developments that significantly diminish the checks to which political power is subject and/or undermine the institutional balance of a pluralist constitution. The notion of a prime ministerial dictatorship can be discarded, but a more serious case can be made that the British political system is deficient in the degree of accountability it imposes on officials. That issue has been the focus of much of the constitutional reform literature that has appeared in recent years, and it is the reason why many reformers have advocated a written constitution that would delimit the powers and responsibilities of the various organs of government and specify the inviolable rights of the citizenry.

Ministers of large departments cannot supervise all of its activities. They seldom remain in charge of a particular department for more than a few years, and their work there is part-time because they have numerous other governmental and political responsibilities that make heavy demands upon them.

While they may be held responsible for determining the general policy stance of their departments, it is unrealistic to demand that they accept accountability for its day-to-day administration. This activity, the cutting edge of government, is necessarily in the hands of the department's permanent full-time officials, and what the ministers know of it is little more than what the officials choose to tell them. The officials' responsibility to the ministerial head of the department is largely pro forma. The role of the bureaucracy in British government will be discussed more fully later. At this point, it is sufficient to note that the traditional doctrine of ministerial responsibility is unsustainable. In recent years, ministers have frequently declined to accept personal accountability to the House of Commons for departmental actions that they did not specifically certify, a development that, while disemboweling the principle of ministerial responsibility, is unquestionably realistic.[13]

Colin Turpin takes the view that the doctrine of ministerial responsibility is an indispensable element in the British system of government, and he calls for its "reinforcement" as a "central aim" of constitutional reform (1994, 151). It is not easy, however, to specify how ministerial responsibility might be restored. As we shall see later, there are some recent developments that tend to increase the accountability of officials—especially the creation of "Select Committees" of the House of Commons, and the adoption of the practice of "judicial review" by the courts. From the standpoint of constitutional theory, however, these developments do not constitute a reinforcement of the links in the traditional hierarchical chain of responsibility, as Turpin advocates, but the creation of new centers and new instruments of checking power.

Accountability depends critically upon the provision of information. In a constitutional democracy, the thickest insulation that can be wrapped about a government and its officers is the ignorance of the public. Many critics of British politics have focused upon the high degree of secrecy with which the government functions, not only in its security agencies, but throughout the whole range of its activities (e.g., Frankel, 1990; Austin, 1994). The insulation of the governmental bureaucracy is provided by conventional notions of prerogative confidentiality and the Official Secrets acts of 1911 and 1920, which were passed at times of exceptional concern for national security. A new Official Secrets Act in 1989 reduced somewhat the powers of the government to limit the disclosure of information, but repeated demands for a "Freedom of Information Act," such as that in force in the United States and some other countries, have been consistently rejected.

---

13. See Norton (1984, ch. 2) and Turpin (1994) for good discussions of the principle of ministerial responsibility.

The traditional method of extracting information from the government is for a member of the Commons to direct a specific request to a minister on the floor of the House at "Question Time." By all accounts, this has ceased to be an effective vehicle. A minister who does not wish to disclose the information need only say that it is not available, or that it can be provided only at "disproportionate cost," which he is at liberty to determine himself.[14] Question Time is the parliamentary activity that receives the most attention from the media, not because of the new information it discloses, but because it presents the most available opportunity for an ambitious Opposition member to display his cleverness as a political tactician in phrasing requests that will embarrass the government, while allowing the minister to demonstrate his own political adroitness in ad-lib verbal swordplay.

Many commentators complain that the House of Commons has degenerated into a mere platform for partisan politics, to the exclusion of serious substantive debate on issues of public policy. The phrase "Loyal Opposition" originated in the eighteenth century as part of the checks and balances concept of the constitution. Englishmen took pride in the fact that while in other countries opposition to the government was treated as treason, in Britain it had been made into an established political institution. The loyalty of the parliamentary Opposition no longer needs defense or theoretical explanation, but it seems that minority members of the Commons have adopted a rather too literal view of their role as official opponents of the government, taking the stance that it is their duty not only to criticize, but obdurately to condemn *whatever* the government proposes, regardless of its merits as public policy. This leads the government to dismiss summarily any criticism the Opposition might make, lowers the deliberative quality of parliamentary debate, and induces the press and the general public to regard the proceedings of the House of Commons with a mixture of amusement and contempt. This development, important in itself, is especially worth noting by the advocate of constitutional pluralism. The theory of checks and balances becomes a mere dogma if it leads one to reject categorically any possibility that a checking process might be detrimental to good government.

Political parties have no formal status in the organization of British government, but they are vital institutions in the working constitution. The member of the Commons invited by the monarch to form a government is the one who, by virtue of his leadership of the leading party, appears likely to receive majority support for his policy program. In the standard textbook

14. On one occasion, Margaret Thatcher was asked how many times during her administration she had refused to accede to a request for information on grounds of disproportionate cost. She calmly replied that such information "can be supplied only at disproportionate cost" (Frankel, 1990, 40).

rendition, the government remains in office only as long as it can command that support; should the government be defeated in the Commons, it is obligated to resign. A general election will immediately ensue, unless it appears that some other member of Parliament might be able to form a government that the House will support. This version of the meaning of "responsible government," which schoolchildren are taught to regard as a fundamental principle of the British constitution, is in fact inconsonant with actual practice. Philip Norton has carefully examined governmental defeats in the House of Commons as far back as the mid-nineteenth century, and has found that they have been quite numerous and have rarely culminated in the resignation of the government. In recent years the House has not even bothered to adjourn following a defeat of the government, but has proceeded with its business as if nothing of special significance had occurred. "The popular views of the Government's required response to defeats in the lobbies," Norton concludes, "rest upon no continuous basis in practice, and hence, in this sense, may be described as myths" (1978; see also Norton, 1984, 67f.). As Dicey noted, there is no legal means by which a prime minister may be forced to resign if defeated in the Commons—it is not part of the *law* of the constitution (Blackburn, 1985, 684). Norton's historical research has shown that it is not part of the *convention* of the constitution either.

How is it possible for a government to be defeated in the House of Commons, where its party holds a majority of the seats? Here we encounter another principle of the constitution that seems to be more mythical than operational. According to the standard textbook presentation, the government can count on the solid support of its "backbench." An MPs chances of political preferment, support in forthcoming elections, and so forth depend upon his standing with the prime minister, who needs only to turn on the party Whip to assure the necessary votes. Not so—at any rate since the early 1970s. The Conservative government of Edward Heath (1970–1974), with a clear majority in the Commons, suffered six defeats due to the defection of its backbenchers. The Labour governments of Harold Wilson and James Callaghan (1974–1979) experienced forty-two defeats, twenty-three of which were due to the revolt of the party's backbench (Norton, 1985, 27; see also Giddings, 1989, 371f.; Norton, 1991). These defeats must have been only the tip of the iceberg. How much criticism of government policy must have taken place in party caucuses and other unreported forums if overt rebellion was so common? How much modification in government policy must occur because the backbench can no longer be counted on to support everything the Cabinet wishes to do?[15] It is perhaps too early to regard this as a per-

15. The most contentious intraparty issue in recent years has been Britain's role in the

manent change in House of Commons behavior, but if it proves to be, the view that the Commons is of negligible importance as an institutional center of political power will have to be revised.[16]

The renewed independence of the backbench was one of the causes of undoubtedly the most important change in the activities of the House of Commons in recent years—the creation, in 1979, of a new system of "Select Committees." Like virtually everything in the British constitution, the historical antecedents of this institution can be traced back many years, but it has recently become much more important. The committees are composed of eleven members each, selected from the backbench members of both parties in the House of Commons by a Committee of Selection that is independent of the party whips. For the large number of MPs appointed to them, Select Committee work now constitutes a substantial part of their parliamentary activities. Each committee corresponds generally to a department of government; collectively, virtually all executive agencies of the state have been brought under committee scrutiny. The committees operate under broad terms of reference that empower them to inquire into the administrative activities as well as the policy decisions of the executive agencies. Each committee selects its own chairman; sets its own agenda; and, subject to established parliamentary rules and law, is free to determine its own methods of inquiry. Most committees meet weekly and, up to the present at least, in an atmosphere that is notably free of party politics. The reports issued by a committee represent the consensus of its members.[17]

The special significance of Select Committees derives from the appearance before them of witnesses, including ministers and senior departmental officials as well as private individuals, whose submissions and responses to questions are on open record. "Civil servants give copious and increasingly frank evidence in public to Select Committees," notes Mount (1993, 110). "Sub-

---

European Union. After their party's victory in the 1992 elections, the Conservative MPs who opposed the government's official policy on the Maastricht treaty organized themselves as a party within the party, with their own whip, separate offices, and their own staff, supported by independent financing. Their persistent opposition led Prime Minister John Major to call for a party leadership election in 1995. His victory quieted, but did not end, intraparty conflict over European policy (Marr, 1995, 124f.).

16. From the standpoint of checks and balances theory, a comment by Giddings is noteworthy: "There is some evidence that a growing number of MP's perceive their role as much in terms of *executive control* as in supporting the party programme of the front bench" (1989, 372, italics mine). The supporters of the theory of "elective dictatorship" however, have chosen to turn a blind eye to the development of backbench independence in the House of Commons (see,. e.g., Brazier, 1991, 8f.).

17. The articles in the symposium edited by Drewry (1989) provide an excellent review and appraisal of the Select Committee system.

jecting ministers and their officials to sustained questioning," writes Norton, "helps to elicit information that would otherwise be unavailable; it also helps to keep departments sensitive to parliamentary reaction" (1991, 73). In essence, the role of the new Select Committees in the British political system is to increase the accountability of ministers and civil servants (Rush, 1990, 139f.). They have no authority to bring charges against an official, or to order that a practice be discontinued or altered, or to award compensatory payments to someone who may have been improperly treated by the government. Those powers are still the exclusive domain of the courts. But the select committees have begun, at least, to provide the information that is an essential precondition of effective accountability.[18]

The Select Committees do not take part directly in the legislative process, and there is little evidence that they have had any significant impact upon the formation of state policy (Giddings, 1989, 368, 373f.). The monopolistic power of the Cabinet in these matters remains intact. The Select Committee system was, however, not established to diminish the legislative role of the Cabinet, but to subject the government, in both its legislative and executive roles, to the checking disciplines of informed criticism and accountability. Reviewing the historical background of the system's establishment, Baines points out that the impetus behind it was the view that "the House [of Commons] had lost the capacity effectively to challenge the government of the day on its policies or to act as a check on the actions of ministers and those acting on behalf of ministers in carrying out those policies" (1989, 14). The system was initially proposed in 1976 by a Commons committee that was established to review the procedures of the House and make recommendations. That committee reported: "We believe that a new balance must be struck . . . [which would enable] the House as a whole to exercise effective control and stewardship over Ministers and the expanding bureaucracy of the modern state for which they are answerable" (quoted in Baines, 1989, 27). That committee apparently had no doubt that the British government is a checks and balances system and should be maintained as such. Norman St. John-Stevas, in introducing the first motion for a standing order to establish the Select Committees in 1979, a proposal that, he observed, "could constitute the most important parliamentary reforms of the century," noted that they were "intended to redress the balance of power to enable the House of Commons to do more effectively the job it has been elected to do" (15).

18. "A great deal more information from the private world of Whitehall is entering the public domain. Senior civil servants are becoming public figures . . . widely read and quoted by those with specialist interests in particular areas: and their performances are open to critical inspection, not just by outside observers but by their own colleagues" (Drewry, 1989, 389).

What *is* the job that the House of Commons is supposed to do? The standard classification of governmental functions construes them as either "legislative," "executive," or "judicial." Acceptance of this schema as complete means that the House of Commons must be a legislative organ, for it is clearly not an executive nor a judicial one. Moreover, theories of "representative government," including the "public choice" theory of the state that has been widely embraced by political scientists, regard the electorate as choosing representatives to act on their behalf in determining public policy. But, as we have seen, public policy in Britain is made by the Cabinet, a very small subset of the House of Commons. Even if we include all the MPs with ministerial duties as engaged in the "legislative" function, some three-quarters of the Commons would be excluded. The role of these MPs in public policy formation is purely negative: they can reject a governmental proposal, but they cannot craft legislation of their own. The traditional triadic classification of governmental functions is inadequate, failing as it does to provide explicit recognition of institutions within the governmental complex whose duty is to impose restraints on political power and maintain the public accountability of those who exercise it. In Britain, this is the main task of the House of Commons.[19]

It may appear strange, if not perverse, to deny that the British House of Commons is a legislative body, but in fact it never has been. In the great conflicts of the seventeenth century, Parliament struggled not to replace the king as sovereign lawmaker, but to do away with the doctrine of sovereignty itself, by establishing a pluralistic system in which the Commons would have the authority to countermand the policies and action of the Crown. The development of Cabinet government clouded the essential issue by reposing the powers that had formerly belonged to the Crown in a subsection of the House of Commons, which pretended to act for the whole, thereby enabling Bagehot and Dicey to claim that "the sovereignty of Parliament" is the fundamental principle of the British constitution. But, in fact, Britain has no sovereign authority. Parliament is, as Norton says, a "multi-functional" body, whose main task is to subject the government of the day to the controlling discipline of public scrutiny.[20]

19. We should note in passing that the Select Committees are not the only parliamentary agencies that have recently been established to strengthen the performance of this function. The Parliamentary Commission for Administration was created in 1965 with considerable powers to act as an ombundsman, investigating citizen complaints against administrative actions forwarded to it by individual MPs (Birch, 1991, 234f.). The National Audit Act of 1983, significantly increased the powers of the Comptroller and Auditor General to investigate the financial activities of the departments and other state agencies, and reaffirmed his status as an officer not of the government, but of the House of Commons (Austin, 1994, 424; McEldowney, 1994, 196).

20. "Parliament is a multi-functional body. It not only serves as a reactive body in the

The Bureaucracy

Prior to the mid-nineteenth century, the officials who operated the day-to-day administration of state policy in Britain were largely recruited through political patronage. In a society where the custom of primogeniture obtained, there was great need of respectable and remunerative employment opportunities for the younger male members of the families of the aristocracy and propertied gentry. The army, the church, and the civil service provided this employment, the last of these being the least demanding of personal talents or educational attainment. The typical civil servant, high and low, obtained his post through political connections that, as long as they remained intact, guaranteed his tenure. The Northcote-Trevelyan Report of 1854 initiated the replacement of that system by a professional civil service whose members would be recruited, and promoted, on the basis of demonstrated capacity to perform the duties required. The notion of the "professional administrator" was born, which the great sociologist Max Weber, in his theory of "bureaucracy," later identified as one of the most significant developments of the modern age. It is ironic that this system, which aimed at creating a body of officials detached from "politics," is now heavily criticized on the ground that the distinction between the professional bureaucracy and the political centers of British government has been blurred. Some commentators have even advanced a "Whitehall theory" of the British constitution—that Britain is really ruled by its bureaucratic establishment.[21]

After 1854, the civil service became an independent entity in the British

---

process of law making, it carries out several other tasks as well. Its principal tasks were established within the first two centuries of its development. In the fourteenth century the king accepted that taxes should not be levied without the assent of Parliament. The giving of such assent was variously withheld until the king responded to petitions requesting a redress of grievances. At the same time, Parliament began to take an interest in how money was spent and began to look at the actions of public servants. It became, in a rather haphazard way, a body for the critical scrutiny of government" (Norton, 1994, 315).

21. The contention that the civil service had usurped the constitutional role of Parliament was argued many years ago by Lord Hewart in a book entitled *The New Despotism* (1929). It was revived in the 1970s as part of the more general discussion of the need for constitutional reform that captured widespread attention. A series of BBC Radio talks by Lord Crowther-Hunt, published in *The Listener* in December 1976 and January 1977, provided a strong stimulant. Lord Crowther-Hunt had been a member of the Fulton Committee on the Civil Service and the Royal Commission on the Constitution, had acted as Prime Minister Harold Wilson's constitutional adviser, and held a high ministerial post as secretary of state for higher education. Drawing upon his extensive personal experience, he painted an alarming picture of the growth of bureaucratic power in Britain in his first two talks. In the third, however, he noted compelling practical reasons why the policymaking and decision-making roles of professional bureaucrats should not be significantly reduced and identified the constitutional problem as the need for more openness and accountability. To achieve this end, he suggested that many central government functions might be transferred to

system of checks and balances, but its powers were meager until the expansion of the scope of government after World War II created the need for a large bureaucracy capable of administering governmental programs of great complexity. Indeed, it appears that many of these programs are not only administered by bureaucrats but are also initiated and designed by them. As I have noted already, the senior officials of a department have typically spent many years in its service, whereas its minister rarely occupies his post for more than a year or two, and usually begins his tenure totally ignorant of the department's policies and operations. Even though the saying "knowledge is power" is a cliché, it is correct, and in the modern governmental department, it is the bureaucrat who has the knowledge.[22]

New public policies may originate with the Cabinet, especially when, as during the postwar Attlee administration and the Thatcher administration of the 1980s, a party comes into power with a perceived mandate to carry out radical change. Under such circumstances, public policy is driven by high philosophical principles that transcend the mundane expertise of the bureaucracy. But in most circumstances, proposals for new legislation represent incremental and sometimes only technical changes in established policies, changes that mainly derive from the experience of administrative officials.

In recent years, it has become common for the government to request the House of Commons to enact "outline" or "enabling" legislation, which only states the purposes and general shape of the policy and authorizes a department to make whatever regulations it considers necessary to accomplish the desired objectives. These regulations have the full force of law, attenuated only by the authority of the courts to undertake "judicial review" (discussed later). For the most part, the ordinary citizen comes into contact with the coercive authority of the state through the powers embodied in such regulations rather than the authorizing statute itself. The celebrated constitutional principle of the "rule of law" has become, over a wide range of practice, rule by administrative regulation. This shift has enlarged enormously the power of the bureaucracy because it can design such regulations to suit its own policy preferences and administrative convenience, and embody them in massive

---

regional and municipal authorities, and that Select Committees of the Commons should be established for each of the main departments in Whitehall to enable MPs to participate in the processes of policy formation and to subject administrative actions to public scrutiny.

22. The contrast between the minister and the senior civil servant in this respect was the persistent theme of a popular British television series ironically called *Yes, Minister*. For a more extended discussion of the factors bearing on the relationship between a minister and his department's officials, see Norton (1984, ch. 2, entitled "The Civil Service: Masters or Servants? Which is Which?").

arcane documents that deny effective accessibility to all but highly specialized experts.

If one rigorously maintains that the sovereignty of Parliament is the central principle of the British constitution, then lawmaking by civil service officials is clearly unconstitutional. The bureaucracy must be deprived of this power, and the ministers of the departments, who are members of Parliament and accountable to it, must take into their own hands the crafting of laws that are sufficiently detailed and explicit in themselves to require no body of subordinate regulations.[23] Moreover, in doing this, the ministers must not receive any policy advice from the professional staffs of their departments; only bare factual information. Such a strategy is clearly unworkable. As Lord Crowther-Hunt acknowledged in his radio addresses that called attention to the great increase that had taken place in the exercise of political power by civil servants, the problem is not to find means of depriving them of this power, but to find ways of responding, constructively, to the dangers it poses.[24]

From the standpoint of the countervailance theory of the constitution, lawmaking power in the hands of bureaucrats is not in itself problematic. The bureaucracy, is composed of many competing centers of power; it is part of the complex of institutions that act, and interact, in the political system. In such a pluralist order, an entity only requires special attention if and when its power grows to a point that places the "balance" of the system at jeopardy,

23. The lawyer might contend that administrative regulations, though written by civil servants, are nevertheless acts of Parliament. A "sovereign" Parliament can determine its own procedures, and if it decides to authorize another body to translate its general intent into specific rules, no derogation of its sovereignty is involved. This reasoning is impeccable, but the issue is not a legal but a political one: who, in actuality, has the power to determine the rules that obligate the citizen, on pain of punishment, to behave in one way rather than another?

24. Concern over the growing use of outline legislation has been prominent in the recent constitutional literature but goes back, at least, to the interwar period. In his *New Despotism* (1929), Lord Chief Justice Hewart attacked the "administrative lawlessness" of the practice. A year earlier, an academic jurist, William Robson, had proposed in his *Justice and Administration* (1928) that a new system of administrative courts be established to control the increased powers of executive agents. The lord chancellor responded by setting up a committee of inquiry into ministers' powers, which, in its 1932 report, rejected Robson's proposal as "inconsistent with the sovereignty of Parliament and the supremacy of the law" (Blackburn, 1985, 689f.). In this, the committee was undoubtedly influenced by A. V. Dicey's criticism of the French system of administrative jurisprudence as inconsistent with, and inferior to, the British constitutional principle of the rule of law. Recently, there have been renewed proposals for the establishment of an administrative law system in Britain. Partington notes that Australia's administrative appeals tribunals have proved adaptable to parliamentary government and recommends their emulation by Britain "to act as a check and balance to the exercise of state power" (1985, 197f.).

or if it has become insulated from accountability within its own domain of action.

Until quite recently, only a few executive agencies were regularly singled out for such special attention in the literature on constitutional reform, most notably the security services and the Bank of England.[25] Attention has now come mainly to bear upon a class of administrative bodies generically entitled "quasi-autonomous non-governmental organizations" or, acronymically, "quangos." In association with its zeal for privatization, the government of Margaret Thatcher took the view that the tasks of many state agencies could be better performed by organizations that were not part of the regular bureaucracy and had a great deal of independence. This argument, frequently made previously with respect to the British Broadcasting Corporation and the Bank of England, was extended in the 1980s to a wide range of governmental activities. The typical quango is a small committee composed of persons who are not civil servants and are appointed by the government to act as the chief administrative officers of an agency with specific functions. In such an agency, the top civil servants who had previously determined administrative policy (with the approval of the responsible minister) have now been demoted to purely executive roles.

There are now a large number of quangos in operation—5,681 of them as of 1997 according to the *Economist* (Nov. 21, 1998, 60). The departments have not been disbanded, but they have been reorganized into many discretely identified functional units, headed by quangos. The Inland Revenue Department, for example, with its 63,000 civil servants, was reorganized into

---

25. The national security services must necessarily work in secrecy. This opens a door to abuses, through which the British services have not refrained from traveling, even on one occasion attempting to bring down a legally elected government (Leigh, 1988). The abuses that have been revealed to the public may only represent a small part of those that have occurred and, at any rate, their exposure fails to justify any complacency concerning their place in the system of political power (see Dearlove and Saunders, 1992, 242–252). The Bank of England also operates beneath a heavy cloak of secrecy, which in this case is more traditional than pragmatically necessary. But even if its decisions were matters of public record, monetary policy is arcane business, understandable only by a small number of experts. An action of a central bank is unlikely to impact the civil liberties of the people, but in the modern economy, it can exert a potent effect, for good or ill, on their material welfare. The Bank of England was nationalized in 1946 and was subjected in the late 1960s to the scrutiny of the Select Committee on the Nationalized Industries. A report by that committee in 1970 demanded much greater accountability from the bank, but this elicited only a yawn from Parliament (see Moran, 1980). Since this was written, the Blair government has increased the independence of the Bank of England in the determination of monetary policy.

thirty such units. More than 60 percent of all civil servants work in agencies administered by quangos (Drewry, 1994, 167).[26]

The development of this system has greatly attenuated the accountability of the bureaucracy. Ministers, already reluctant (for good reasons, as noted earlier) to accept personal responsibility for all of their departments' actions, can now claim that they are institutionally detached from the policies and actions of "autonomous" quangos. According to one study, only a very small number of quangos permit public attendance at their policy meetings and only a third of them are under the supervision of the National Audit Office or the Audit Commission (Marr, 1995, 80), so they are insulated both from public criticism and the scrutiny of professional accountants who report directly to Parliament. Moreover, the "independence" of the quangos is more formal than real. Their members are appointed for short terms by the government, so they are more subject to the will of the government of the day than are permanent civil servants. There is, apparently, evidence that commitment to the ruling party, or at least to its political ideology, has been a condition for receiving, and holding, a quango appointment. In effect, the trend of British civil service development that began with the Northcote-Trevelyan reforms of the 1850s has been reversed.[27]

To date, however, Whitehall is not where the impact of the quango system has been most acutely felt. As of 1994, more than four-fifths of the quangos were appointed to take over local government functions (Marr, 1995, 78). The United Kingdom is not a federal state, but local governments are not merely branches of the national government, as they are in France. Historically, local governments developed autonomously, and until the late nineteenth century, no uniform system of local government existed in Britain. With the great expansion of the scope of government after World War II, many of the new responsibilities came into their hands to implement, with a great deal of financial and administrative independence.[28] Over the long term, however, the general trend has been a transfer of political authority from the local councils to the central government. Since the mid-1970s, the decline

26. Referring specifically to the "Next Steps Initiative" of 1988, which proposed further extension of the quango system, Drewry remarks that this "has effected a transformation in the structure and culture of the Civil Service and has had a massive impact upon the organizational arrangements of Governmental departments" (1994, 157).

27. "The 'quangos' ... have ... been widely criticized for being filled largely with known government supporters who are then used to implement government policies without adequate democratic accountability" (Grant, 1995, 7).

28. "British central government is 'non-executant': that is, central departments do not directly deliver services to citizens. Apart from the obvious exceptions of defence and social security, major services such as housing, education, health and personal social services are provided by, for example, local authorities" (Rhodes, 1991, 84).

of local government has accelerated, with additional functions transferred to the center and others privatized.

Legally, local governments in Britain are subordinate to the central government. During the 1980s a series of acts greatly limited their independence, most notably the Rates Act of 1984, which enabled the central government to control local taxation—"an unprecedented centralization of political power" according to one commentator (Loughlin, 1994, 280). The implementation of the quango system has gone further, replacing locally elected governments whose deliberations are open to public scrutiny and participation with centrally appointed committees that operate in camera.[29] In terms of the hierarchical model, this system is commendable; it promotes uniformity and, perhaps, efficiency. But it erodes the pluralist nature of British government by virtually eliminating local institutions as elements of a checks and balances system. In general, the quango system, especially its replacement of elected local governments, constitutes the largest and most distinct movement away from pluralistic constitutionalism that has occurred in Britain since the Revolution of 1688.[30]

The Judiciary

The British judicial system consists of a hierarchy of courts. Cases may be appealed from the courts of original jurisdiction, such as the county courts in civil cases and the Crown courts in criminal ones, to the Court of Appeal, and from there to the Lords of Appeal in Ordinary, usually referred to as the Law Lords.[31] Twelve members of the House of Lords are Law Lords, including the lord chancellor, who is also the minister in charge of a large government department, and invariably a member of the Cabinet. Panels of Law Lords are established for each case. If he wishes, the lord chancellor may

29. "Since 1979 successive Conservative governments have embarked on a radical programme for reorganizing the role of local government in social life . . . The [central] government has . . . asserted its preeminence and, by stripping local government of much of its powers and much of its capacity for independent action, has accentuated the dependent position of local government" (Loughlin, 1994, 261f.).

30. Since this chapter was written, the Labour party, which had strongly advocated the strengthening of local government when in opposition, has come to power, but the Blair government has not introduced any general measures to achieve this objective. It did, however, allow a referendum on whether London should have an elected mayor. The proposal received a large majority of the votes cast—perhaps a harbinger of local government revival.

31. For a more complete but still simplified description of the court system, see Griffith (1991), 38–41.

be a member of such a panel. All Law Lords are selected for Crown appointment by the prime minister, with the advice of the lord chancellor. Judges of the lower courts are appointed by the lord chancellor. In the United States, the doctrine of "separation of powers" forbids any member of the Supreme Court from also occupying a formal office in the Congress or the executive branch, though some presidents have informally sought the advice of Supreme Court justices. In Britain this separation is not maintained. Indeed, through the lord chancellor, there is a formal linkage between the highest court in the legal system and the effective lawmaking authority (the Cabinet), and with an important executive department. As a member of the House of Lords, the lord chancellor also constitutes an institutional link between the highest court and Parliament. Nevertheless, the judiciary is an independent center of power in the British political system, as is any entity that can exert an autonomous influence on the determination of public policy and/or its quotidian application to concrete cases.

According to traditional constitutional theory, the judiciary has no role in lawmaking. In adjudicating a specific case, the bench is obligated to restrict its attention to the relevant statutes and previous cases. Francis Bacon, who held the office of lord chancellor under James I (until impeached for taking bribes), declared that "judges ought to remember that their office is . . . to interpret law and not to make law" and warned them to be "circumspect that they do not check or oppose any points of sovereignty." A century and a half later, the Law Lords, in *Millar v. Taylor* (1769), enunciated the "exclusionary rule," which forbade the courts from consulting any documents (not excepting the record of Parliamentary debates) that might have been useful in clarifying the intent of an ambiguous statute. This rule was reaffirmed by the British Law Commissions in 1969, and only in 1992 *(Pepper v. Hart)* did the Law Lords relax it to permit reference to parliamentary materials (Lester, 1993, 269–275).

The fact that the Law Lords themselves have the power to determine, without parliamentary sanction, what documents the courts may consult would seem to mean that, in this respect at least, they have the power to make important alterations in the law. But more important is that the courts, in accepting the admissibility of previous judicial judgments, do not confine themselves to the statutes as the orthodox theory would seem to require. The exclusionary rule could be defended for a country like France, where the Roman system of code law pertains, but it is simply incompatible with the long-standing English tradition of case law. Unless one takes the view, which no legal historian would accept for a moment, that the operative substance of a statute is never altered appreciably in the course of being interpreted in a series of specific cases, then the process of adjudication is necessarily a process of lawmaking.[32] While defining a "law" as "a rule that will be enforced by the courts," Dicey himself acknowledged, "A large proportion of English law is in reality made by the judges." Adhesion to precedent "leads inevitably to the gradual formation by the courts of fixed rules for decision, which are in effect laws." He went on to defend his principle of the sovereignty of Parliament as the exclusive lawmaking body by contending that "judicial legislation is . . . subordinate legislation, carried on with the assent and subject to the supervision of Parliament" (1960, 60f.), but this distinction justifiably carries little weight with modern jurists and political scientists.[33]

The role of the courts in lawmaking has been a subject of considerable discussion in recent years. Defense of the orthodox doctrine is motivated by the commonsense notion that, in a good society, the judicial system must be impartial. When the line between lawmaking and law adjudication is breached, this impartiality appears to be threatened. One of the contributors to this literature, J. A. G. Griffith, a prominent academic jurist, raised the intensity of the discussion considerably with his book *The Politics of the Judiciary*, originally published in 1977 and reissued frequently since then. Griffith extended the argument that the courts make law to contend that the fifty or so members of the higher judiciary—chosen exclusively from the corps of barristers, with a distinct concentration of men from high social class families—consistently exhibit class bias and political party preference in their judgments. Griffith's charges raise serious questions about the role of the courts in the British polity—and, indeed about the role of courts in any system in

32. In a sermon preached before King George I in 1717, Bishop Hoadley stated, "Whosoever hath an absolute power to interpret any written or spoken laws, it is he who is truly the lawgiver, to all intents and purposes, and not the person who first spoke or wrote them" (Lockhart et al., 1986, 1).

33. Before 1991, a man could not be convicted of the crime of rape if the victim of his assault was his wife. In that year, the Law Lords decided otherwise and "thereby boldly changed the law so as to impose criminal liability upon the appellant" (Lester, 1993, 280). The crime of "conspiracy to corrupt public morals" did not exist before 1961, when the Law Lords created it (Griffith, 1991, 264). In such cases, the court not only made new laws, but also gave them retroactive effect. A statute that imposes criminal liability upon acts previously committed is likely to be looked upon askance by jurists on the principle *nullum crimen sine lege* (no crime without law) but, as these two illustrations show, this rule is disregarded when the courts themselves create a new crime in the course of adjudicating a particular case. We might note that just as the courts can adopt legislative functions when adjudicating a case, so the executive branch almost unavoidably adopts a judicial function in its part of criminal proceedings. It is up to the agents of the Crown to determine whether or not a charge will be laid, and what that charge should be. And, even after the court has spoken, the home secretary has the authority to overturn a conviction. The boundary between the executive and judicial domains is permeable from both sides.

which the incumbents of the superior courts of justice are recruited exclusively from the cadre of professional lawyers, a highly differentiated minority segment of the population. Important as these issues are, we cannot discuss them here. In terms of the matter we are addressing, it is sufficient to note that the judiciary in Britain is indisputably an independent center of political power, one among the many such centers that constitute its pluralist polity.[34]

With respect to public law, the primary and indispensable task of the courts is to apply to particular cases the general rules embodied in statutes and subsidiary regulations. No political system could function without an agency that supports public policy by dealing with specific offenses against it. In constitutional democracies, however, the notion is widely held that the exercise of coercive power by the state must conform to generally accepted principles of *justice*, which means that in the process of law administration, more is required than that an agent of the state declare a particular person to have behaved contrary to law. An institution—one sufficiently detached from the legislative and executive branches of the state to be impartial—must evaluate the merits of the charge before the state may exercise its power to coerce or punish. In performing such an evaluation, the courts act to *legitimize* the exercise of that power—in the moral, not merely the legal, sense of that term. It goes without saying that the legitimizing function of the courts rests upon its authority to declare an alleged offender innocent of the charge and to effectuate his or her liberation from threat of punishment. As a consequence, the courts necessarily play a complex and somewhat ambiguous role in a constitutional polity: on the one hand they serve as the agents of the state's coercive power, while on the other, they protect the citizenry from it.

As we saw in examining the political system of classical Athens, its jury courts had great independent power, which they employed to impose constraints upon the officers of the state. As the celebrated case of the condemnation of Socrates shows, however, an accused Athenian was at the mercy of contemporary popular sentiment, which may not serve the interests of justice as reflective judgment might construe it. The jury courts of a modern nation such as Britain and the United States also have great independent powers. If it wishes, a jury may completely disregard both the law and the evidence in the case before it. This may protect the citizen from excessive actions on the part of officials, but as many cases attest, it may expose him to the fury of popular bigotry or to condemnation by entrenched beliefs that lack defensible philosophic or empirical foundations.

---

34. Griffith himself rejects this view of the matter. The purpose of his book is to show that Britain is ruled by an oligarchy, of which the judiciary is a part. In effect, he adopts the hierarchy model as applicable to modern British government.

When Americans were constructing the Constitution of their new republic, distrust of majority rule led them to enact a Bill of Rights in order to protect individuals and minority groups from the coercive authority of state and federal governments. The structure of the judicial system established by the Constitution assured that the power to interpret the Bill of Rights was to be exercised by the superior federal courts, where decisions would be rendered not by ad hoc juries, but by permanently tenured judges. This process became known as the power of "judicial review." In English jurisprudence, the courts have broad powers to interpret the laws passed by Parliament, but until 1977, there was no explicit use of the practice of judicial review. In that year, the Supreme Court Rule Committee introduced a procedural change allowing private individuals to apply to the courts for a judicial review of administrative orders, and permitting the courts to nullify an order if it found grounds to do so.[35] The courts promptly began to receive applications and ruled on them, thus commencing to build up a new body of case law that, in effect, established test criteria for the invalidation of administrative decisions. In a 1984 case, Lord Diplock summarized these criteria under three general headings: "illegality," "procedural impropriety," and "irrationality" (Griffith, 1991, 125).

Taken together, these criteria establish very broad powers to countermand administrative orders. Unlike their American counterparts, the British courts do not have the power to declare primary legislation invalid, but in view of the great reliance on administrative regulations throughout almost the whole range of public policy, the confinement of judicial review to such "subordinate legislation" does not greatly restrict the authority of the courts to check governmental authority. Under the heading of "illegality," the courts have adopted the view that an administrative order is invalid if it fails to serve the purpose of the legislation under which it was issued; "procedural impropriety" allows administrative orders to be negated if the officers of the Crown have not adhered to established procedures; and "irrationality" is almost open-ended, meaning in effect that the court can invalidate an administrative order if it feels that a convincing argument in its defense was not presented during the review. Griffith remarks that the criteria are "sufficiently imprecise to enable judges to jump with the cat in any direction they choose" (1991,

35. Note that the practice of judicial review was not established by an act of Parliament. The British judiciary clearly has the power to make new laws, even ones that any alert observer would classify as "constitutional law."

326). It remains to be seen what the judiciary will make of its new practice of judicial review over the long run, but there can be no doubt that the power of the courts in the countervailance system of British politics has been substantially increased.[36]

As a coda to this review of the British judicial system, I must note again the significance of Britain's membership in the European Union and its ratification of various European conventions specifying human rights. These measures have, in effect, moved the highest level of British judicature from the House of Lords to the European courts established to enforce these conventions.[37] Since 1965, British citizens have had the right to appeal directly to the European Court of Human Rights in Strasbourg. Such appeals are slow and expensive, but nevertheless that court has already rendered numerous decisions that affect the formation and administration of British domestic policy.[38] As a member of the European Union, Britain has acquired one feature at least of a written constitution: an explicit statement of citizen rights, which is indeed more heavily entrenched than is the American Bill of Rights. In effect, the European courts have become important centers of power in Britain's political system of checks and balances. "The European Court of Justice," notes Dawn Oliver, "has been quite explicit about the fact that citizens are allowed to bring . . . cases, not just to vindicate their own rights but also to put pressure on governments to obey the [European] law" (1994, 452). This extension of the pluralist domain, rather than the question of where "sovereignty" lies, is the significant constitutional implication of Britain's membership in the European Union.

36. Providing opportunity to petition for judicial review would have been of little significance if such petitions were infrequently made or rarely granted. The change in rules, however, disclosed a large latent demand for the opportunity to complain against administrative practices, and the number of petitions for review has increased steadily from year to year: from 491 in 1980 to 2,129 in 1990, with around 50 percent being granted. Mount calls this "little short of a judicial revolution" (1993, 261). In 1993 the number of petitions was 2,886 (Marr, 1995, 284).

37. "Our membership of the European Community is profoundly altering the constitutional role of British judges . . . by widening the scope of judicial review of substance and merits as well as of forms and procedure" (Lester, 1993, 288).

38. Lester gives a number of examples of important cases in which the European Court of Human Rights has found Britain to have violated the Human Rights Convention (Lester, 1994, 42f.). Mount points out that although the judgments of the European Court of Human Rights (unlike those of the European Court of Justice) are not binding upon British courts, "In practice, the moral authority behind them is now so powerful that the British government usually has no choice but to implement them" (1993, 221).

Unofficial Political Institutions: Pressure Groups

In this section I consider the fact that the traditional tripartite classification of functions does not embrace all of the institutions that have the capacity to exert political power. In the Constitution of the United States, no mention is made of political parties, religious institutions, labor unions, trade associations, the press and other media of information and discussion, special interest groups, "think tanks," and various other institutions that undeniably influence the determination and administration of public policy. Similar institutions are part of the structure of British government, as they are in all countries that may be validly described, in vernacular speech, as "democracies." The countervailance model of political organization easily accommodates the existence of such institutions; so far as the exercise of political power is concerned, there is no categorical distinction between official and unofficial institutions. The proposition that power derives from organization is as fully appreciated in the private sector of the polity as in its halls of government. It is unnecessary to examine all of these various institutions, but one broad category of them, "pressure groups"—organizations that seek to influence particular items of public policy—deserves some attention.

Until quite recently, British political scientists tended to regard pressure group influence as a feature of American government that was not significant in Britain. This distinction has now been discarded.[39] Norton points out that lobbying has its roots in ancient English practice: the role of Parliament in seeking "redress of grievances" by the Crown (1991, 58). He attributes its recent growth to various factors such as the adoption of redistributive policies by the state; the emergence of professional lobbying firms that offer their expertise for sale; the greater independence of backbench MPs, who are thereby more accessible to outside influence; and the creation of the Select Committees, which offer lobbyists a ready vehicle for the promotion of their aims (65f.). At any rate, there are today in Britain a large number and great variety of pressure groups. Some, like the National Farmers' Union or the Chemical Industries Association, are "interest" groups seeking to influence public policy in their favor. Others, such as the League Against Cruel Sports or the Ancient Monuments Society, are "cause" groups, which try to propel

---

39. According to Dearlove and Saunders, academic political science underwent a significant change in the 1960s: "The intellectual centre of gravity within the discipline of politics slowly moved from political parties to interest groups and a new theory—pluralism—emerged that quickly gained wide acceptance as *the* theory to make sense of British politics" (1992, 131). For a good general review of pressure groups and their activities, see Grant (1995) or, more briefly, Birch (1991, ch. 7).

public policy toward specific social objectives. Some of these pressure groups are very large—the Royal Society for the Protection of Birds has more than 800,000 members—while others, such as the United Kingdom Men's Movement, are very small. It seems that there is an organized lobbying institution for every interest and every cause. There is even a lobby that promotes the interests of professional lobbyists: the Public Relations Consultants' Association. These groups obtain the funds for their activities from membership fees, service charges, contributions, bequests, and even, in some cases, from the public purse.

Pressure group activity varies a great deal. Some of it aims at influencing general public opinion—an enterprise that over time can be expected to affect official policy. At the other end of the scale are attempts to persuade a member of Parliament to introduce a specific bill in the House of Commons. Pressure groups may also try to achieve their aims by initiating legal proceedings in the courts, but this strategy is inhibited by rules of "legal standing" that are more restrictive in England than in America (Grant, 1995, 80, 89f.). The bulk of pressure group activity is concentrated upon attempting to influence ministers, senior civil servants, and the mass media (Rush, 1990, 272). Unlike the United States, backbench and Opposition MPs are regarded as inferior objects of investment, a view that undoubtedly reflects the very different roles that individual representatives play in the two systems of government. Pressure groups that choose to focus on MPs, however, have much more latitude than in the United States because rules specifying what an MP may do on behalf of a paying client are not as restrictive as those pertaining to members of Congress (253f.).

In some areas of governmental action, it has become established practice for departmental officials to consult the organized pressure groups representing interests that would be directly affected by a specific policy or administrative decision. This kind of relationship has become more evident since the establishment of the new system of Select Committees, whose public hearings show that some lobbies, called "insider groups" by some commentators, have been able to exert a great deal of influence on public policy. Awareness of this influence has recently generated a new theory of British government in which the determination of public policy is distributed among various "policy networks" or "policy communities," composed of both officials with particular areas of public responsibility and lobby organizations representing the corresponding domain of private interest.[40]

40. In concluding his chapter on "How Pressure Groups Influence Whitehall and the Policy Agenda," Wyn Grant writes, "It is apparent from the evidence . . . that there are extensive contacts between pressure groups and the executive branches of government during the development of policy and its implementation . . . Many decisions are clearly

If democracy is a political system in which the actions of the state are determined by the people's representatives in Parliament, the development of effective pressure group activity would seem to be a deleterious trend of development in modern British government. In terms of the pluralist theory of checks and balances, however, evaluation of it is likely to be more favorable because pressure groups increase the number of independent entities operating in the system of countervailing powers (Grant, 1995, 28f.). More specifically on the positive side, it may be argued that pressure groups offer the citizen enhanced opportunities to participate in the processes of government, in that the variety and intensity of an individual's views on public policy are better served by the interest groups and cause groups he or she joins, contributes to, and promotes than by casting a single vote for a single parliamentary candidate every few years. On the other hand, because most of the actual lobbying is done by professional consultancy firms, it may be argued that pressure groups increase the political influence of those who are well financed, which may simply be those who already have a great deal of it. In the sphere of economic interests, producers in a particular industry are much easier to organize than consumers of their products, thus adding a "mercantilist" dimension to public policy formation. Some individual business firms are large enough to employ expensive lobbying agencies to promote their interests, or to establish well-staffed "public relations" departments of their own. The recent history of British economic and commercial policy indicates that the political influence of large business firms needs to be considered.

But it would be misleading to focus entirely upon such economic interests, as is very often the case when "pressure group politics" is under discussion. The largest (in membership), best financed, and probably the most influential group in Britain is the Royal Society for the Prevention of Cruelty to Animals, which does not seek to advance or protect sectional economic or commercial interests. In recent years, "cause" groups have proliferated in England, focusing their efforts on many areas of general social policy such as pollution abatement, the preservation of old buildings, the safety and nutritional value of food products, medical research, forest preservation, civil rights, Britain's relations with the European Union, and so forth. The influence of such groups upon public policy in Britain is patent.

The net effect of pressure groups taken as a whole, for good or ill, cannot be derived by argumentation, and quantitative empirical assessment is exceedingly difficult. Wherever freedom of association is regarded as a basic

---

taken within relatively closed policy communities in which the complexity of the problems being discussed constitutes a significant entry barrier" (1995, 64; see also 34f.; and Rhodes, 1991, 107). Marsh and Rhodes (1992) contains a good collection of papers on policy networks.

civic liberty, the political system will have to accommodate pressure groups among the many institutions that function in a pluralist political system. Like other entities in such a polity, a pressure group is likely to become a focus of special attention when and if it succeeds in insulating itself from the countervailing power of other entities. Nongovernmental institutions, being private, are not subject to the same degree of public accountability as governmental ones. Many pressure groups work "behind the scenes," and information concerning their activities is difficult to obtain. In the United States, numerous legal constraints have been imposed upon the activities of organizations that engage in direct lobbying of the Congress or governmental departments, and the Freedom of Information Act, by opening governmental files to public scrutiny, indirectly subjects their actions to exposure. Britain has not moved as far in this direction, but pressure groups are receiving increasing scrutiny by journalists and political scientists.

A more general thesis concerning the political significance of pressure groups has been advanced by Mancur Olson in his *Rise and Decline of Nations* (1982), which has been widely discussed by political scientists in both Britain and the United States. Olson here extends the argument of his earlier seminal work, *The Logic of Collective Action* (1965), to contend that the general discovery of the principle that organization confers power has led to such a proliferation of pressure groups that democracies are becoming economically inefficient and politically ungovernable. The empirical evidence he supplies to support this thesis is, however, unconvincing. The political processes of nations such as the United States or Great Britain certainly appear to be turbulent and undirected—"no way to run a railroad" as the saying goes. But if we compare these polities with the far more systematic and methodical power arrangements of absolutist regimes, we find that the latter not only deny the civil rights of their citizens, but are invariably inferior in their economic and other public policies. The success of pluralist nations in providing for the material wants of their citizens continually surprises many observers who assume that the only effective form of social organization is hierarchical. In the economic sphere, the common view of market processes as a chaotic struggle for personal advantage is only maintainable if one does not understand the general equilibrium model of economic organization. In the political domain, without the insights provided by the countervailance model, competitive politics similarly appears to be a disorderly muddle.

Epilogue

The history sketched in the preceding pages reveals that the continuous development of constitutionalism is a comparatively recent phenomenon, traceable no further than to seventeenth-century England. The basic elements of a constitutional order can be found in earlier polities, but until then its history was episodic and confined to a small number of cases. Its spread beyond the English-speaking world dates only from the later nineteenth century, but since then, its reach has been extensive. Although a large part of the world still lies outside its domain, constitutionalism is now widely embraced as the paragon political system, celebrated in countries that have adopted it—and inspiring political reformers in those that have not—as a form of governance that controls the power of the state and protects the liberty of the citizenry. Most commonly, such a political system is referred to as a "democracy," but this term is inadequate, and when construed literally, palpably erroneous.

In common perception, a democratic polity is one in which "the people" determine public policy. As we have seen, this is an inaccurate description even of Periclean Athens, and it is clearly inappropriate for republican Rome, Venice, the Dutch Republic, and eighteenth-century England, all of which were aristocracies in terms of Aristotle's classification—governed by the few. In many countries today, the franchise is held by all adult citizens, and the opportunity to achieve political office is not restricted by religious, racial, or property qualifications. Nevertheless, it is simplistic and naive to construe such polities as ones in which the people govern themselves.

In pure terms, we can speak of the people as governing themselves only in a polity where public policy is determined in an assembly of all the citizenry operating with the decision rule of unanimity. Under that rule, no collective action could be instituted without universal assent—but each citizen would have absolute power to negate any proposal. This procedure would clearly be unjust, as well as impractical. If the rule of unanimity is broached, however, it follows necessarily that public policy will be coercive, violating the perceived values or interests of some members of the community. The adoption of majority rule as the modus of determination does not change this fact and, in itself, it has no ethical foundation. Its merit is only that it guarantees that a proposal for legislation will only be enacted into law if more favor than oppose it. Aristotle pointed out that the majority rule procedure of the Athenian assembly exposed the individual citizen and minority groups to the coercion of a tyrannous state. This observation is commonly disregarded by writers who regard Periclean Athens as the ideal that we should seek to emulate and by those who embrace the doctrine of "popular sovereignty."

If majority rule is adopted, further difficulties emerge in polities where public policy is determined by elected representatives. If 50 percent plus one of the voters is sufficient to elect a representative, and 50 percent plus one of the representatives is sufficient to pass legislation, it is possible for a proposal to be enacted that would have received little more than 25 percent of the votes if it had been submitted to a popular referendum. When there are more than two candidates for legislative office, and/or they pledge their support for more than one specific issue, the approving proportion of the citizenry could be even less.

In most "democracies," the majority vote of a singular legislative assembly is not sufficient to authorize the exercise of state power. In the United States, for example, the president and the Senate must also approve. The electoral system does not assure that the successful candidate for the presidency will have received a majority of the votes cast, and it makes certain that the Senate, having an equal number of members from each state despite their great differences in population, will *not* represent the majority.[1] In addition, there is the unelected Supreme Court, whose members have security of tenure until voluntary retirement; it has the power to declare a statute void if it is found to violate the Constitution.[2] The proscriptions embodied in the Constitution themselves reflect a widely held view that there are domains of privacy that should be immune to state action, as well as activities that should be accorded special protection against the will of the majority because of their long-run contributions to the public good, to the nation's cultural and intellectual progress, or, indeed, to the proper operation of the political system itself. The

1. According to the 1990 census, out of a total population of 249 million, the least populous twenty-five states had only 41 million. Accordingly, senators elected by less than one-fifth of the American voters could pass legislation against the opposition of all the others.

2. Some American jurists have argued that this power of the Supreme Court is undemocratic and violates the central principle of American government, which they construe as rule by the majority. William R. Bishin (1977) undertakes to demolish this contention, but his paper is more significant as a trenchant critique of the notion that democracy is such a principle than as a defense of judicial review.

framers of the Constitution did not establish a majoritarian democracy, and many of the developments of the past two centuries have reduced the power of the majority to determine public policy.

The United States today is clearly not a majoritarian democracy; nor is any other state; nor can they be; nor ought they to be. Nevertheless, "democracy" has become the standard test that other nations must pass to win American approval. As a shorthand referent in political discourse, it is a convenient term, but "democracy" often serves as a mantra, generating an aphasic trance that is impervious to critical reason and empirical evidence. To describe a person, practice, or institution as "undemocratic" is the secular equivalent of excommunication.

Representative government is not simply a technical device that enables the political system of a small community to be applied to a large nation while preserving popular rule. It introduces a profoundly different mode of governance. Elections legitimize the authority of those who hold power, but this is not their main role. Elections are the means by which representatives are chosen, but they are also the means by which they may be *dismissed*. The significant election is not the one that has most recently been held, but the one that is soonest to come. In effect, elections are part of the system of accountability and control. They play a vital role in such a system, for which there is no effective substitute—as, indeed, there is no effective substitute for an uncensored press, freedom of association, an independent judiciary, and other institutions that are widely recognized as essential features of a political system that serves the *salus populi* and controls the power of the state.

The successful candidate for election is authorized to "represent" the people of his constituency. But here we encounter another term that requires examination. Is the representative obligated to be a faithful carrier of his constituents' preferences, or is he elected to perform a significantly different role? According to Edmund Burke's famous conception, a representative stands in place of his constituents to engage in face-to-face debate in the legislative assembly; to devote a great deal of time to detailed study of public policy and legislative proposals; to listen to those who will be affected by them and others who favor or oppose them; and to cast his vote as the balance of merit appears to himself. Unlike a "delegate," he is not morally bound to vote as his constituents might wish him to. This distinction is even more important today than in Burke's time, when the electoral constituencies were very small and much more socially homogeneous. The notion that the legislature of a modern state is not a mere voting machine, but a deliberative institution, depends upon a Burkean conception of representative government.

This construal of the role of elections and the responsibilities of representatives cannot be accommodated to the notion of democracy. Nevertheless, the harmonic resonances of that term include many of the features of political systems that are admirable, and it would be perverse to recommend that it be abandoned in scholarly and vernacular discourse. Numerous commentators have adopted the term "constitutional democracy" as more accurate. The semantic purist might reject this as an oxymoron because "constitutional" denotes that the power of the state is constrained, while "democracy" implies that it is not, nor need be. But if "democracy" is construed less literally, as a generic term for polities in which there is widespread opportunity for free participation by the citizenry in the processes of governance, then "constitutional democracy" would seem to be the best shorthand description of polities like the United States and Great Britain.

The thesis argued in this book is that efficient government and constrained government are not incompatible, and I have endeavored to show that both objectives have been realized, in practice, in numerous states dating back as far as ancient Athens. These cases display great variety in the institutional structures of political organization, but I have sought to show that all of them have been modeled on a pluralist distribution of political power and the principle of countervailance. In stressing this point, I do not contend that the protection of the citizenry from arbitrary or unwarranted state action is *guaranteed* by a system of checks and balances. Such a proposition could be easily negated by historical evidence, and indeed, by reference to the state of personal liberty in present-day constitutional democracies. These polities have avoided the general and unremitting suppression of freedom that is common in regimes based on the hierarchical model, but gross injustices are not unknown, or even rare, in them. In wartime, or when the safety of the established order appears to be threatened by domestic subversion, the checks and balances system has proved incapable of protecting civic liberty, and the abuse of state power has not been confined to such special occasions, even in countries where personal rights are entrenched in a written constitution adjudicated by an independent judiciary. A pluralist distribution of political power is necessary to the preservation of liberty, but not sufficient to assure it.

Constitutional democracies have not succeeded in constructing a perfect system for controlling the state, and like other dimensions of social perfection, such an ideal is unlikely to come within our grasp. But while perfection is impossible, improvement is not, and the next step in the journey that I have pursued in this book would seem to be an investigation of "constitutional failure"—the lacunae that are evident in the systems of power control of constitutional democracies. That is a big subject in itself, on which a large and rapidly growing literature exists, and I have already tried the patience of the reader more than enough for one volume. If time allows, I hope to contribute to the debate on this matter in another.

References

Adair, Douglass. 1956–1957. "'That Politics May Be Reduced to a Science': David Hume, James Madison, and the Tenth Federalist." *Huntingdon Library Quarterly* 20: 343–360.

Adams, Willi Paul. 1980. *The First American Constitutions: Republican Ideology and the Making of the State Constitutions in the Revolutionary Era.* Chapel Hill: University of North Carolina Press.

Adeleye, Gabriel. 1983. "The Purpose of the *Dokimasia.*" *Greek, Roman, and Byzantine Studies* 24: 295–306.

Aiken, William Appleton, and Basil Duke Henning, eds. 1960. *Conflict in Stuart England.* London: Cape.

Allen, J. W. 1949. "Jean Bodin." In Hearnshaw, 42–61.

———1967. *English Political Thought, 1603–1644.* Hamden, Conn.: Archon Books.

Amar, Akhil Reed. 1991. "The Bill of Rights as a Constitution." *Yale Law Journal* 100: 1131–1210.

Ambrosini, Federica. 1975. "Un Incontro Mancata: Venezia e Stati Uniti d'America, 1776–1779." *Archivo Veneto.* 5th ser., 105: 123–171.

Anderson, Ann Stuart. 1986. "A 1787 Perspective on Separation of Powers." In Robert A. Goldwin and Art Kaufman, eds., *Separation of Powers—Does It Still Work?* Washington: American Enterprise Institute. 138–167.

Andrewes, A. 1966. "The Government of Classical Sparta." In *Ancient Society and its Institutions: Studies Presented to Victor Ehrenberg on his 75th Birthday.* Oxford: Blackwell, 1–20.

Aristotle. 1981. *The Politics.* Trans. T. A. Sinclair and Rev. T. J. Saunders. London: Penguin.

"Aristotle." 1984. *The Athenian Constitution.* London: Penguin.

Armstrong, Karen. 1993. *A History of God.* New York: Ballantine Books.

Arndt, H. W. 1979. "Clark, Colin." *International Encyclopedia of the Social Sciences: Biographical Supplement.* New York: Macmillan. 121–124.

Aron, Raymond. 1965. *Main Currents in Sociological Thought.* 2 vols. New York: Basic Books.

Austin, Rodney. 1994. "Freedom of Information: The Constitutional Impact." In Jowell and Oliver, 393–429.

Bagehot, Walter. 1928. *The English Consitution.* London: Oxford University Press. Intro. the First Earl of Balfour.

Bailyn, Bernard. 1967. *The Ideological Origins of the American Revolution*. Cambridge: Harvard University Press.

——— 1990. *Faces of Revolution*. New York: Knopf.

Baines, Priscilla. 1989. "History and Rationale of the 1979 Reforms." In Drewry, 13–36.

Barker, Ernest. 1945. *Essays on Government*. Oxford: Clarendon Press.

Barlow, Frank. 1967. *William I and the Norman Conquest*. New York: Collins.

Barnes, Harry Elmer, ed. 1948. *An Introduction to the History of Sociology*. Chicago: University of Chicago Press.

Barnett, Randy E., ed. 1989. *The Rights Retained by the People: The History and Meaning of the Ninth Amendment*. Vol. 1. Fairfax, Va.: George Mason University Press.

———, ed. 1993. *The Rights Retained by the People: The History and Meaning of the Ninth Amendment*. Vol. 2. Fairfax, Va.: George Mason University Press.

Beard, Mary, and Michael Crawford. 1985. *Rome in the Late Republic: Problems and Interpretation*. London: Duckworth.

Behrens, B. 1941. "The Whig Theory of the Constitution in the Reign of Charles II." *Cambridge Historical Journal*. 7: 42–71.

Beinart, B. 1952. "Sovereignty and the Law." *Tydskrif vir Hedendaagse Romeins-Hollandse Reg*. 101–134.

Bell, Roderick, David V. Edwards, and R. Harrison Wagner, eds. 1969. *Political Power: A Reader in Theory and Research*. New York: Free Press.

Benn, Stanley I. 1967. "Power." In *Encyclopedia of Philosophy*. New York: Macmillan. 6: 424–427.

——— 1969. "The Uses of Sovereignty." In Stankiewicz, 67–85.

Bergsma, Wiebe. 1995. "Church, State, and People." In Davids and Lucassen, 196–228.

Berlin, Isaiah. 1991. *The Crooked Timber of Humanity: Chapters in the History of Ideas*. New York: Knopf.

Berman, Harold J. 1983. *Law and Revolution: The Formation of the Western Legal Tradition*. Cambridge: Harvard University Press.

Beza, Theodore. 1969. *The Right of Magistrates*. In Franklin, 100–135.

Birch, Anthony H. 1991. *The British System of Government*. London: Harper-Collins. 8th ed.

——— 1993. *The Concepts and Theories of Modern Democracy*. London: Routledge.

Bishin, William R. 1977. "Judicial Review in Democratic Theory." *Southern California Law Review*. 50: 1099–1137.

Black, Antony. 1980. "Society and the Individual from the Middle Ages to Rousseau: Philosophy, Jurisprudence, and Constitutional Theory" *History of Political Thought*. 1: 145–166.

Blackburn, R. W. 1985. "Dicey and the Teaching of Public Law." *Public Law*. 679–716.

Blakeley, Brian L., and Jacquelin Collins, eds. 1975. *Documents in English History: Early Times to the Present*. New York: Wiley.

Bodin, Jean. 1992. *On Sovereignty: Four Chapters from the Six Books of the Commonwealth*. Ed. and trans. Julian H. Franklin. New York: Cambridge University Press.

Bogdanor, Vernon. 1994. "Britain and the European Community." In Jowell and Oliver, 3–31.

Boholm, Asa. 1990. *The Doge of Venice: The Symbolism of State Power in the Renaissance.* Gothenberg: University of Gothenburg.

Bondanella, Peter E. 1976. *Francesco Guicciardini.* Boston: Twayne.

Boone, Marc, and Maarten Prak. 1995. "Rules, Patricians and Burghers: The Great and Little Traditions of Urban Revolt in the Low Countries." In Davids and Lucassen, 99–134.

Boughner, Daniel C. 1962. "Lewkenor and 'Volpone.' " *Notes and Queries.* 124–130.

Bouwsma, William J. 1968. *Venice and the Defence of Republican Liberty.* Berkeley: University of California Press.

—— 1973. "Venice and the Political Education of Europe." In Hale, 445–466.

Bradley, A. W. 1994. "The Sovereignty of Parliament in Perpetuity?" In Jowell and Oliver, 79–107.

Braudel, Fernand. 1981–1984. *Civilization and Capitalism, 15th to 18th Century.* New York: Harper and Row. 3 vols.

Brazier, Rodney. 1991. *Constitutional Reform.* Oxford: Clarendon Press.

Briggs, Asa. 1972. *Victorian People: A Reassessment of People and Themes, 1851–1867.* Chicago: University of Chicago Press.

Brinton, Crane. 1952. *Anatomy of Revolution.* New York: Prentice-Hall.

Bromley, J. S., and E. H. Kossmann, eds. *Britain and the Netherlands.* Vol. 1: London, Chatto and Windus, 1960; vol. 2: Groningen, Wolters, 1964; vol. 4: The Hague, Nijhoff, 1971; vol. 5: The Hague, Nijhoff, 1975.

—— 1968. *Britain and the Netherlands in Europe and Asia.* 2 vols. London: Macmillan.

Brunt, P. A. 1966. "The Roman Mob." 111: *Past and Present.* 3–27.

—— 1971. *Social Conflicts in the Roman Republic.* New York: Norton.

—— 1988. *The Fall of the Roman Republic and Related Essays.* Oxford: Clarendon Press.

Bryce, James. 1901. *Studies in History and Jurisprudence.* 2 vols. New York: Oxford University Press.

Buchan, Alastair. 1954. "Walter Bagehot." *History Today.* 764–770.

Buchanan, James M. 1975. *The Limits of Liberty: Between Anarchy and Leviathan.* Chicago: University of Chicago Press.

Buel, Richard, Jr. 1964. "Democracy and the American Revolution: A Frame of Reference." *William and Mary Quarterly,* 3d ser., 21: 166–190.

Burke, Edmund. 1991. *Selected Writings and Speeches.* Ed. Peter J. Stanlis. Washington: Regnery Gateway.

Burgess, Glenn. 1996. *Absolute Monarchy and the Stuart Constitution.* New Haven: Yale University Press.

Burke, Peter. 1994. *Venice and Amsterdam: A Study of Sixteenth Century Élites.* London: Temple Smith.

Burn, A. R. 1979. *The Political History of Greece.* Harmondsworth: Penguin.

Burns, J. H. 1959. "Sovereignty and Constitutional Law in Bodin." *Political Studies* 7: 174–177.

————, ed. 1991. *The Cambridge History of Political Thought, 1450–1700.* Cambridge: Cambridge University Press.

Butler, David. 1994. "Electoral Reform." In Jowell and Oliver, 379–391.

Carlyle, Thomas. 1888. *Sartor Resartus, Lectures on Heroes, Chartism, Past and Present.* London: Chapman and Hall.

Carpenter, William Seal. 1928. "The Separation of Powers in the Eighteenth Century." *American Political Science Review* 22: 32–44.

Carswell, John. 1969. *The Descent of England: A Study of the English Revolution of 1688 and Its European Background.* New York: John Day.

Carter, Stephen L. 1988. "The Independent Counsel Mess." *Harvard Law Review* 102: 105–141.

Casper, Gerhard. 1989. "An Essay in Separation of Powers: Some Early Versions and Practices." *William and Mary Law Review* 30: 211–261.

———— 1997. *Separating Power: Essays on the Founding Period.* Cambridge: Harvard University Press.

Chambers, David. 1970. *The Imperial Age of Venice, 1380–1580.* New York: Harcourt Brace Jovanovitch.

Chambers, David, and Brian Pullan, eds. 1992. *Venice: A Documentary History, 1450–1630.* Oxford: Blackwell.

Charles I. 1643. *His Majesties Answer to the XIX Propositions of Both Houses of Parliament.* London. (Excerpts reprinted in Kenyon 1986.)

Chew, Helena M. 1949. "King James I." In Hearnshaw, 105–129.

Chinard, Gilbert. 1940. "Polybius and the American Constitution." *Journal of the History of Ideas.* 38–58.

Chrimes, S. B. 1949. "The Constitutional Ideas of Dr. John Cowell." *English Historical Review.* 64: 461–487.

Cicero. *De re Republica* and *De Legibus.* 1988. Trans. C. W. Keyes. Cambridge: Harvard University Press.

Clark, Evert Mordecai. 1915. Introduction to Milton 1915.

Clark, J. C. D. 1986. *Revolution and Rebellion: State and Society in England in the Seventeenth and Eighteenth Centuries.* Cambridge: Cambridge University Press.

Clinton-Davis, Lord. 1991. "The Community and Britain: The Changing Relationship between London and Brussels." In Norton 1991, 113–132.

Clokie, Hugh McDowall. 1936. *The Origin and Nature of Constitutional Government.* London: Harrap.

Cohen, Hymen Ezra. 1937. *Recent Theories of Sovereignty.* Chicago: University of Chicago Press.

Contarini, Gasparo. 1599. *De Magistratibus et Republica Venetorum.* Trans. Lewes Lewkenor as *The Commonwealth and Government of Venice.* London: John Windet.

Cook, Harold J. 1992. "The New Philosophy in the Low Countries." In Roy Porter and Mikulas Teich, eds. *The Scientific Revolution in National Context.* Cambridge: Cambridge University Press. 115–149.

Cooper, James. 1960. "Differences between English and Continental Governments in the Seventeenth Century." In Bromley and Kossmann 1960, 62–90.

Cowan, Alexander Francis. 1986. *The Urban Patriciate: Lübeck and Venice, 1580–1700.* Vienna: Böhlau.

Cowell, F. R. 1948. *Cicero and the Roman Republic*. London: Pitman.

Cozzi, Gaetano. 1969. Introductory commentaries in Paolo Sarpi, *Opere*. 1969. Gaetano Cozzi and Louisa Cozzi, eds. La Letteratura Italiani: Storia e Testi. Vol. 35, no. 1. N.p.

—— 1973. "Authority and Law in Renaissance Venice." In Hale, 293–345.

—— 1979. *Paolo Sarpi Tra Venezia e L'Europa*. Torino: Einaudi.

Crawford, Michael. 1993. *The Roman Republic*. Cambridge: Harvard University Press.

Crick, Bernard. 1968. "Sovereignty." In *International Encyclopedia of the Social Sciences*. New York: Macmillan. 15: 77–82.

Crowther-Hunt, Lord. 1976—1977. "Whitehall—Just Passing Through." *Listener*, Dec. 16, 1976, 772–774; "Whitehall—The Balance of Power." *Listener*, Jan. 6, 1977, 10–11; "The Case for Civil Service Power." *Listener*, Jan. 13, 1977, 43–45.

Cunliffe, Marcus. 1959. *The Nation Takes Shape: 1789–1857*. Chicago: University of Chicago Press.

Dahl, Robert A. 1957. "The Concept of Power." *Behavioral Science* 2: 201–215.

—— 1968. "Power." In *International Encyclopedia of the Social Sciences*. New York: Macmillan. 12: 405–415.

Daintith, Terence. 1944. "The Techniques of Government." In Jowell and Oliver, 209–236.

Daley, James. 1978. "The Idea of Absolute Monarchy in Seventeenth-Century England." *Historical Journal* 21: 227–250.

Daniel, Glyn. 1968. *The First Civilizations: The Archaeology of Their Origins*. New York: Crowell.

Davids, Karel. 1995. "Shifts in Technological Leadership in Early Modern Europe." In Davids and Lucassen, 338–366.

Davids, Karel, and Jan Lucassen, eds. 1995. *A Miracle Mirrored: The Dutch Republic in European Perspective*. Cambridge: Cambridge University Press.

Davidson, James. 1992. "Lots of Political Power." *Times Literary Supplement*, Apr. 10. p. 10.

Davies, J. K. 1993. *Democracy and Classical Greece*. Cambridge: Harvard University Press.

Davies, Norman. 1996. *Europe: A History*. Oxford: Oxford University Press.

Davis, James Cushman. 1962. *The Decline of the Venetian Nobility as a Ruling Class*. Baltimore: Johns Hopkins University Press.

Dearlove, John, and Peter Saunders. 1992. *Introduction to British Politics: Analysing a Capitalist Democracy*. Cambridge: Polity Press.

Denzer, Horst, ed. 1973. *Proceedings of the International Conference on Bodin in Munich*. Munich: Verlag C. H. Beck.

De Vries, Jan. 1973. "On the Modernity of the Dutch Republic." *Journal of Economic History* 33: 191–202.

—— 1984. *European Urbanization, 1500–1800*. Cambridge: Harvard University Press.

—— 1985. "The Population and Economy of the Preindustrial Netherlands." *Journal of Interdisciplinary History* 15: 661–682.

Dewey, John. 1894. "Austin's Theory of Sovereignty." *Political Science Quarterly* 9: 31–52.

Dicey, A. V. 1930. *Lectures on the Relation between Law and Public Opinion in England during the Nineteenth Century*. London: Macmillan.

—— 1960. *Introduction to the Study of the Law of the Constitution*. London: Macmillan. 10th ed., intro. by E. C. S. Wade.

Dickinson, H. T. 1976. "The Eighteenth-Century Debate on the Sovereignty of Parliament." *Transactions of the Royal Historical Society*. 5th ser., 26: 189–210.

Dickinson, John. 1927. *Administrative Justice and the Supremacy of Law in the United States*. Cambridge: Harvard University Press.

Diggins, John Patrick. 1984. *The Lost Soul of American Politics: Virtue, Self-Interest, and the Foundations of Liberalism*. New York: Basic Books.

Drewry, Gavin. 1989. "The 1979 Reforms: New Labels on Old Bottles?" In Drewry 1989, 382–393.

—— 1991. "Judicial Independence in Britain: Challenges Real and Threats Imagined." In Norton 1991, 37–57.

—— 1994. "Revolution in Whitehall: The Next Steps and Beyond." In Jowell and Oliver, 155–174.

——, ed. 1989. *The New Select Committees: A Study of the 1979 Reforms*. Oxford: Clarendon Press.

Dufour, Alfred. 1991. "Pufendorf." In Burns 1991, 561–588.

Duke, Alastair. 1985. "The Ambivalent Face of Calvinism in the Netherlands, 1561–1618." In Prestwick, 109–134.

Duke, A. C. and C. A. Tamse. eds. 1985. *Britain and the Netherlands*. Vol. 8. Zutphen, De Walburg Pers.

Dunn, John, ed. 1992. *Democracy: The Unfinished Journey, 508 B.C. to A.D. 1993*. Oxford: Oxford University Press.

Dwight, Theodore W. 1887. "Harrington and His Influence upon American Political Institutions and Political Thought." *Political Science Quarterly* 2: 1–44.

Earle, Edward Meade. Introduction to *The Federalist*.

Ebenstein, William. 1968. "Kelsen, Hans." *International Encyclopedia of the Social Sciences*. New York: Macmillan. 8: 360–366.

Eltis, David. 1995. *The Military Revolution in Sixteenth-Century Europe*. New York: Taurus.

Falkus, Christopher. 1992. *The Life and Times of Charles II*. Introduction by Antonia Fraser. New York: Cross River Press.

Farrar, Cynthia. 1988. *The Origins of Democratic Thinking: The Invention of Politics in Classical Athens*. Cambridge: Cambridge University Press.

Federalist, The. Ed. Edward Meade Earle. N.d. New York: Modern Library.

Ferguson, Robert A. 1997. *The American Enlightenment, 1750–1820*. Cambridge: Harvard University Press.

Ferrary, J.-L. 1984. "L'Archéologie Du *De Re Publica*: Cicéron entre Polybe et Platon." *Journal of Roman Studies* 74: 87–98.

Filmer, Robert. 1949. *Patriarca and Other Political Works of Sir Robert Filmer*. Ed. Peter Laslett. Oxford: Blackwell.

Finer, S. E. 1997. *The History of Government from the Earliest Times*. New York: Oxford University Press.

Fink, Zera. 1940. "Venice and English Political Thought in the Seventeenth Century." *Modern Philology* 38: 155–172.

—— 1945. *The Classical Republicans: An Essay in the Recovery of a Pattern of Thought in Seventeenth-Century England.* Evanston: Northwestern University Press.

Finlay, Robert. 1980. *Politics in Renaissance Venice.* New Brunswick, N.J.: Rutgers University Press.

Finley, M. I. 1962. "Athenian Demagogues." *Past and Present* 21: 3–24.

—— 1983. *Politics in the Ancient World.* Cambridge: Cambridge University Press.

Fletcher, Anthony. 1981. *The Outbreak of the English Civil War.* London: Arnold.

Fletcher, F. T. H. 1939. *Montesquieu and English Politics, 1750–1800.* London: Arnold.

Fontana, Biancamaria. 1992. "Democracy in the French Revolution." In Dunn, 107–124.

Forrest, W. G. and D. L. Stockton. 1987. "The Athenian Archons: A Note." *Historia* 36: 235–241.

Foster, Elizabeth Read. 1960. "The Procedure of the House of Commons against Patents and Monopolies, 1621–1624." In Aiken and Henning, 57–86.

Frankel, Maurice. 1990. "Parliamentary Accountability and Government Control of Information." In Norman Lewis, Cosmo Graham, and Deryck Beyleved, eds. *Happy and Glorious: The Constitution in Transition.* Milton Keynes: Open University Press. 32–43.

Franklin, Julian H. 1968. "Bodin, Jean." In *International Encyclopedia of the Social Sciences.* New York: Macmillan. 2: 110–113.

—— 1969. *Constitutionalism and Resistance in the Sixteenth Century.* New York: Pegasus.

—— 1973. *Jean Bodin and the Rise of Absolutist Theory* Cambridge: Cambridge University Press.

—— 1978. *John Locke and the Theory of Sovereignty.* Cambridge: Cambridge University Press.

—— 1991. "Sovereignty and the Mixed Constitution: Bodin and His Critics." In Burns, 298–328.

Fried, Morton A. 1968. "The State: The Institution." *International Encyclopedia of the Social Sciences.* New York: Macmillan. 15: 143–150.

Friedman, Milton. 1962. *Capitalism and Freedom.* Chicago: University of Chicago Press.

Friedmann, Wolfgang. 1967. "Grotius, Hugo." *The Encyclopedia of Philosophy.* New York: Macmillan. 3: 393–395.

Friedrich, Carl J. 1968. "Constitutions and Constitutionalism." In *International Encyclopedia of the Social Sciences.* New York: Macmillan. 3: 318–326.

Gaeta, Franco. 1961. "Alcune cosiderazioni sul mito di Venezia." *Bibliotèque D'Humanisme et Renaissance* 23: 58–75.

Gelderen, Martin van. 1992. *The Political Thought of the Dutch Revolt, 1555–1590.* Cambridge: Cambridge Universiy Press.

——, ed. 1993. *The Dutch Revolt.* Cambridge: Cambridge University Press.

Gewirth, Alan. 1951. *Marsilius of Padua; The Defender of Peace.* New York: Columbia University Press.

Geyl, Pieter. 1956. "A Historical Myth." *Listener,* Aug. 9, 201–203.

——— 1961. *The Netherlands in the Seventeenth Century.* Part 1: 1609–1648. London: Ernest Benn.

——— 1964. *The Netherlands in the Seventeenth Century.* Part 2: 1648–1705. London: Ernest Benn, 1964.

——— 1966. *The Revolt of the Netherlands, 1555–1609.* London: Ernest Benn.

Gianturco, Elio. 1938. "Bodin's Conception of the Venetian Constitution and His Critical Rift with Fabio Albergati." *Revue de Littérature Comparée* 18: 684–695.

Gibbs, G. C. 1969. "The Revolution in Foreign Policy." In Holmes, 59–79.

Giddings, Philip. 1989. "What Has Been Achieved?" In Drewry, 367–381.

Gilbert, Felix. 1967. "The Date of the Composition of Contarini's and Giannotti's Books on Venice." *Studies in the Renaissance* 14: 172–184.

——— 1968. "The Venetian Constitution in Florentine Political Thought." In Rubinstein, 463–500.

——— 1977. *History: Choice and Commitment.* Cambridge: Harvard University Press.

——— 1987. "Venetian Secrets." *New York Review,* July 16, 37–39.

Gilmore, Myron. 1973. "Myth and Reality in Venetian Political Theory." In Hale, 431–444.

Gimpel, Jean. 1976. *The Medieval Machine: The Industrial Revolution of the Middle Ages.* New York: Holt, Reinhart, and Winston.

Girouard, Mark. 1985. *Cities and People: A Social and Architectural History.* New Haven: Yale University Press.

Glazer, Nathan, and Daniel Patrick Moynihan. 1963. *Beyond the Melting Pot: The Negroes, Puerto Ricans, Jews, Italians, and Irish of New York City.* Cambridge: MIT Press.

Gleason, Elisabeth G. 1993. *Gasparo Contarini: Venice, Rome, and Reform.* Berkeley: University of California Press.

Goldsmith, M. M. 1980. "Hobbes's 'Mortall God': Is There a Fallacy in Hobbes's Theory of Sovereignty?" *History of Political Thought* 1: 33–50.

Goldwin, Robert A., and Art Kaufman, eds. 1986. *Separation of Powers: Does It Still Work?* Washington: American Enterprise Institute for Public Policy Research.

Gooch, G. P. 1898. *The History of English Democratic Ideas in the Seventeenth Century.* Cambridge: Cambridge University Press.

——— 1959. *English Democratic Ideas in the Seventeenth Century.* New York: Harper, 1959.

Gordon, Scott. 1976. "The New Contractarians." *Journal of Political Economy* 84: 573–590.

——— 1980. *Welfare, Justice, and Freedom.* New York: Columbia University Press.

——— 1981. "The Political Economy of F. A. Hayek." *Canadian Journal of Economics* 14: 470–487.

——— 1991. *The History and Philosophy of Social Science.* London: Routledge.

——— 1994. "The Theory of Public Choice and the Problems of Constitutional Choice." Atlantic Canada Economic Association, *Papers* 23: 1–6.

Gough, J. W. 1957. *The Social Contract: A Critical Study of Its Development*. Oxford: Clarendon.

Grant, Wyn. 1995. *Pressure Groups, Politics, and Democracy in Britain*. London: Harvester.

Gray, Hamish R. 1953. "The Sovereignty of Parliament Today." *University of Toronto Law Journal* 10: 54–72.

Greene, Jack P. 1994. "Why Did They Rebel? Looking for Deeper Causes of the American Revolution." *Times Literary Supplement* (London). June 10.

Grell, Ole Peter, Jonathan I. Israel, and Nicholas Tyacke. 1991. *From Persecution to Toleration: The Glorious Revolution and Religion in England*. Oxford: Clarendon.

Grever, John H. 1981. "Committees and Deputations in the Assemblies of the Dutch Republic." *Parliaments, Estates, and Representation* 1: 13–33.

———— 1982. "The Structure of Decision-Making in the States General of the Dutch Republic, 1660–68." *Parliaments, States, and Representation* 2: 125–153.

Griffith, J. A. G. 1991. *The Politics of the Judiciary*. London: Fontana.

Griffiths, Gordon. 1959–1960. "The Revolutionary Character of the Revolt of the Netherlands." *Comparative Studies in Society and History* 2: 452–472.

Grubb, James S. 1986. "When Myths Lose Power: Four Decades of Venetian Historiography." *Journal of American History* 58: 43–94.

Guicciardini, Francesco. 1994. *Dialogue on the Government of Venice*. Ed. and trans. Alison Brown. Cambridge: Cambridge University Press.

Gwyn, W. B. 1965. *The Meaning of the Separation of Powers: An Analysis of the Doctrine from Its Origin to the Adoption of the United States Constitution*. New Orleans: Tulane University Studies in Political Science. Vol. 9.

Haak, Bob. 1984. *The Golden Age: Dutch Painting of the Seventeenth Century*. New York: Abrams.

Hailsham, Lord. 1992. *On the Constitution*. London: Harper Collins.

Haitsma Mulier, E. O. G. 1980. *The Myth of Venice and Dutch Republican Thought in the Seventeenth Century*. Assen: Van Gorcum.

———— 1985. "Grotius, Hooft, and the Writing of History in the Dutch Republic." In Duke and Tamse, 55–72.

———— 1987. "The Language of Seventeenth-Century Republicanism in the United Provinces: Dutch or European?" In Anthony Pagden, ed., *The Languages of Political Theory in Early-Modern Europe*. Cambridge: Cambridge University Press. 179–195.

Hale, J. R., ed. 1973. *Renaissance Venice*. London: Faber and Faber.

Haley, K. H. D. 1972. *The Dutch in the Seventeenth Century*. London: Harcourt Brace Jovanovich.

Hall, Jerome. 1937. "Nulla Poena Sine Lege." *Yale Law Journal* 47: 165–193.

Haller, William. 1955. *Liberty and Reformation in the Puritan Revolution*. New York: Columbia University Press.

Hamowy, Ronald. 1979. "Jefferson and the Scottish Enlightenment: A Critique of Gary Wills's *Inventing America: Jefferson's Declaration of Independence*." *William and Mary Quarterly* 36: 503–523.

Hampsher-Monk, Iain. 1976. "The Political Theory of the Levellers: Putney, Property, and Professor MacPherson." *Political Studies* 24: 397–422.

Hampton, Jean. 1986. *Hobbes and the Social Contract Tradition* Cambridge: Cambridge University Press.

Hansen, Morgens Herman. 1981. "Initiative and Decision: The Separation of Powers in Fourth-Century Athens." *Greek, Roman, and Byzantine Studies* 22: 345–370.

—— 1991. *The Athenian Democracy in the Age of Demosthenes: Structure, Principles, and Ideology.* Oxford: Blackwell.

Hart, Marjolein 't. 1989. "Cities and Statemaking in the Dutch Republic, 1580–1680." *Theory and Society* 18: 663–687.

—— 1993. *The Making of a Bourgeois State: War, Politics, and Finance during the Dutch Revolt.* Manchester, Eng.: Manchester University Press.

Hawthorn, J. R. 1962. "The Senate after Sulla." *Greece and Rome* 9: 53–60.

Hayek, F. A. 1973, 1976, 1979. *Law, Legislation, and Liberty: A New Statement of the Liberal Principles of Justice and Political Economy.* Chicago: University of Chicago Press. 3 vols.

Hearnshaw, F. J. C., ed. 1949. *The Social and Political Ideas of Some Great Thinkers of the Sixteenth and Seventeenth Centuries.* New York: Barnes and Noble.

Heichelheim, Fritz M., Cedric A. Yeo, and Allan Ward. 1984. *A History of the Roman People.* Englewood Cliffs, N.J.: Prentice-Hall.

Hennessy, Peter. 1991. "How Much Room at the Top? Margaret Thatcher, the Cabinet, and Power-Sharing." In Norton 1991, 20–36.

Hexter, J. H. 1978. "Power Struggle, Parliament, and Liberty in Early Stuart England." *Journal of Modern History.* 50: 1–50.

—— 1982. "The Early Stuarts and Parliament: Old Hat and the *Nouvelle Vague.*" *Parliamentary History* 1: 181–215.

—— 1983. "The Birth of Modern Freedom." *Times Literary Supplement* (London). Jan. 21, 51–54.

Hibbert, Christopher. 1993. *Florence: The Biography of a City.* New York: Norton.

Hill, Christopher. 1965/1975. *Intellectual Origins of the English Revolution.* Oxford: Clarendon.

—— 1975. *The World Turned Upside Down: Radical Ideas during the English Revolution.* Harmondsworth: Penguin.

—— 1990. *A Nation of Change and Novelty: Radical Politics, Religion, and Literature in Seventeenth-Century England.* London: Routledge.

Hillyard, Paddy, and Janie Percy-Smith. 1988. *The Coercive State: The Decline of Democracy in Britain.* London: Fontana.

—— 1989. "The Coercive State Revisited." *Parliamentary Affairs* 42: 533–547.

Hinsley, F. H. 1986. *Sovereignty.* Cambridge: Cambridge University Press.

Hinton, R. W. K. 1957. "The Decline of Parliamentary Government under Elizabeth I and the Early Stuarts." *Historical Journal* 13: 116–132.

Hobbes, Thomas. 1968. *Leviathan.* Ed. with an intro. by C. B. Macpherson. Harmondsworth: Penguin.

Hofstadter, Richard. 1954. *The American Political Tradition.* New York: Vintage.

Holmes, Geoffrey, ed. 1969. *Britain after the Glorious Revolution, 1889–1714.* London: Macmillan.

Holt, James C. 1972. *Magna Carta and the Idea of Liberty.* New York: Wiley.

Hornblower, Simon. 1992. "Creation and Development of Democratic Institutions in Ancient Greece." In Dunn, 1–16.

Hotman, François. 1969. *Francogallia*. In Franklin 1969, 53–99.

Howe, John R., Jr. 1966. *The Changing Political Thought of John Adams*. Princeton: Princeton University Press.

Howell, James. 1651. A Survey of the Signorie of Venice, of Her Admired Policy, and Method of Government. London: Lowndes.

Hughes, Ann. 1995. "Local History and the Origins of the Civil War." In Todd, 252–271.

Huizinga, J. H. 1968. *Dutch Civilisation in the Seventeenth Century, and other Essays*. New York: Frederick Ungar.

Hulliung, Mark. 1983. *Citizen Machiavelli*. Princeton, N.J.: Princeton University Press.

Hulme, Harold. 1960. "Charles I and the Constitution." In Aiken and Henning, 87–128.

Hume, David. 1953. *Political Essays*. Ed. Charles W. Handel. New York: Liberal Arts Press.

——— 1983. *The History of England: From the Invasions of Julius Caesar to the Revolution of 1688*. 6 vols. Indianapolis: Liberty Classics.

Hunton, Philip. 1689. *A Treatise of Monarchy . . . also, A Vindication of the Said Treatise*. London: E. Smith. The *Treatise* was first published in 1643; the *Vindication* in 1644.

Hutson, James H. 1986. "The Creation of the Constitution: The Integrity of the Documentary Record." *Texas Law Review* 65: 1–39.

Hutton, Ronald. 1991. *Charles II: King of England, Scotland, and Ireland*. Oxford: Oxford University Press.

Hyneman, Charles S., and Donald S. Lutz, eds. 1983. *American Political Writing during the Founding Era, 1760–1805*. Indianapolis: Liberty Press.

Israel, Jonathan I. 1991. "William III and Toleration." In Grell, Israel, and Tyacke, 129–170.

——— 1994. "The noblesse dorée." *Times Literary Supplement*. Jan. 21.

——— 1995. *The Dutch Republic: Its Rise, Greatness, and Fall, 1477–1806*. Oxford: Clarendon.

———, ed. 1991. *The Anglo-Dutch Moment: Essays on the Glorious Revolution and Its World Impact*. Cambridge: Cambridge University Press.

Israel, Jonathan I., and Geoffrey Parker. 1991. "Of Providence and Protestant Winds: The Spanish Armada of 1588 and the Dutch Armada of 1688." In Israel 1991, 335–363.

Jacob, E. F. 1963. *Essays in the Conciliar Epoch*. South Bend, Ind.: University of Notre Dame Press.

Jacob, Margaret C., and Wijnand W. Mijnhardt, eds. 1992. *The Dutch Republic in the Eighteenth Century: Decline, Enlightenment, and Revolution*. Ithaca, N.Y.: Cornell University Press.

Jaffa, Harry V. 1981. "Inventing the Past: Gary Wills' *Inventing America* and the Pathology of American Scholarship." *St. Johns Review* 33: 3–19.

James I. 1918. *The Trew Law of Free Monarchies, or, The Reciprock and Mutual Dutie Betwixt a Free King, and His Naturall Subjects.* Ed. C. H. McIlwain. First published 1598; republished 1603 and 1616.

James, Margaret. 1930. *Social Problems and Policy during the Puritan Revolution, 1640–1660.* London: Routledge.

Janson, H. W. 1986. *History of Art.* 3d ed. revised and expanded by Anthony F. Janson. New York: Abrams.

Jay, John. 1790. "The Charge of Chief Justice John Jay to the Grand Juries of the Eastern Circuit." The Papers of John Jay. Rare Book and Manuscript Library, Butler Library, Columbia University, New York.

Jennings, W. Ivor. 1933. *The Law and the Constitution.* London: University of London Press.

—— 1935. "In Praise of Dicey, 1885–1935." *Public Administration* 11: 123–134.

—— 1941. *Parliament Must Be Reformed: A Programme for Democratic Government.* London: Kegan Paul.

Johnson, Nevil. 1985. "Dicey and His Influence on Public Law." *Public Law.* 717–723.

Jones, J. R. 1968. "English Attitudes to Europe in the Seventeenth Century." In Bromley and Kossmann, 37–55.

—— 1972. *The Revolution of 1688 in England.* London: Weidenfeld and Nicholson.

Jouvenal, Bertrand de. 1948. *Power: The Natural History of Its Growth.* London: Hutchison.

Jowell, Jeffrey. 1994. "The Rule of Law Today." In Jowell and Oliver, 57–78.

Jowell, Jeffrey, and Dawn Oliver, eds. 1994. *The Changing Constitution.* Oxford: Clarendon.

Judson, Margaret Atwood. 1964. *The Crisis of the Constitution: An Essay in Constitutional and Political Thought in England, 1603–1645.* New York: Octagon.

Kammen, Michael. 1988. *Sovereignty and Liberty: Constitutional Discourse in American Culture.* Madison: University of Wisconsin Press.

Keegan, John. 1994. *A History of Warfare.* Toronto: Vintage.

Kelsen, Hans. 1945. *General Theory of Law and the State.* Cambridge: Harvard University Press.

Kenyon, J. P. 1970. *The Stuarts: A Study in English Kingship.* Glasgow: Fontana.

—— 1990. *Stuart England.* Harmondsworth: Penguin.

——, ed. 1986. *The Stuart Constitution, 1603–1688.* Cambridge: Cambridge University Press.

Kingdon, Robert M. 1991. "Calvinism and Resistance Theory." In Burns 1991, 193–218.

Kossmann, E. H. 1960. "The Development of Dutch Political Theory in the Seventeenth Century." In Bromley and Kossman, 91–110.

—— 1968. "Grotius, Hugo." In *International Encyclopedia of the Social Sciences.* New York: Macmillan. 6: 256–259.

—— 1971. "The Crisis of the Dutch State, 1780–1813: Nationalism, Federalism, Unitarism." In Bromley and Kossmann, 156–175.

—— 1981. "Popular Sovereignty at the Beginning of the Dutch Ancien Regime." *Acta Historiae Nederlandica* 14: 1–28.

——— 1991. "Freedom in Seventeenth-Century Dutch Thought and Practice." In Israel 1991, 281–298.

Kunkel, Wolfgang. 1973. *An Introduction to Roman Legal and Constitutional History.* Oxford: Clarendon.

Lane, Frederic C. 1966. *Venice and History: The Collected Papers of Frederic C. Lane.* Baltimore: Johns Hopkins University Press.

——— 1973. *Venice: A Maritime Republic.* Baltimore: Johns Hopkins University Press.

Larsen, J. A. O. 1968. *Greek Federal States: Their Institutions and Their History.* Oxford: Clarendon.

Laski, Harold J. 1968. *Studies in the Problem of Sovereignty.* New York: Fertig.

——— 1977. *A Grammar of Politics.* London: Allen and Unwin.

Laslett, Peter. 1949. *Patriarcha and Other Political Works of Sir Robert Filmer.* Oxford: Blackwell.

Lasswell, Harold Dwight, and Abraham Kaplan. 1950. *Power and Society: A Framework of Political Inquiry.* New Haven: Yale University Press.

Lawson, F. H. 1959. "Dicey Revisited." *Political Studies* 7: 109–126, 207–221.

Leeb, I. Leonard. 1973. *The Ideological Origins of the Batavian Revolution: History and Politics in the Dutch Republic, 1747–1800.* The Hague: Martinus Nijhoff.

Lefebvre, Georges. 1962. *The French Revolution.* 2 vols. New York: Columbia University Press.

Leigh, D. 1988. *The Wilson Plot.* London: Heineman.

Lenman, Bruce P. 1992. *The Eclipse of Parliament: Appearance and Reality in British Politics since 1914.* London: Edward Arnold.

Lessnoff, Michael, 1986. *Social Contract.* Atlantic Highlands, N.J.: Humanities Press International.

———, ed. 1990. *Social Contract Theory.* New York: New York University Press.

Lester, Anthony. 1993. "English Judges as Law Makers." *Public Law.* 269–290.

Lester, Lord. 1994. "European Human Rights and the British Constitution." In Jowell and Oliver, 33–53.

Lewis, J. U. 1968. "Jean Bodin's 'Logic of Sovereignty.' " *Political Studies* 16: 206–222.

Libby, Lester J., Jr. 1973. "Venetian History and Political Thought after 1509." *Studies in the Renaissance* 20: 7–45.

Lindenbaum, Peter. 1991. "John Milton and the Republican Mode of Literary Production." *Yearbook of English Studies.* 21: 121–136.

Lindley, Keith. 1986. "London and Popular Freedom in the 1640s." In Richardson and Ridden, 111–150.

Lintott, A. W. 1968. *Violence in Republican Rome.* Oxford: Clarendon.

Lloyd, Howell A. 1991. "Constitutionalism." In Burns, 254–297.

Locke, John. 1960. *Two Treatises of Government.* Ed. with an intro. by Peter Laslett. New York: New American Library.

Lockhart, William B., Yale Kamisar, Jesse H. Choper, and Steven H. Shiffrin, eds. 1986. *The American Constitution: Cases—Comments—Questions.* St. Paul, Minn.: West Publishing.

Lockyer, Roger. 1989. *The Early Stuarts: A Political History of England, 1603–1642.* New York: Longman.

Logan, Oliver. 1972. *Culture and Society in Venice, 1470–1790: The Renaissance and Its Heritage.* New York: Scribners.

Lossky, Andrew. 1985. "Political Ideas of William III." In Rowen and Lossky, 33–59.

Loughlin, Martin. 1994. "The Restructuring of Central-Local Government Relations." In Jowell and Oliver, 261–293.

Lovejoy, Arthur O. 1936. *The Great Chain of Being.* Cambridge: Harvard University Press.

Luciani, Vincent. 1947. "Bacon and Guicciardini." *Publications of the Modern Languages Association.* 62: 96–113.

Lutz, Donald. 1988. *The Origins of American Constitutionalism.* Baton Rouge: Lousiana State University Press.

Lynn, Kenneth S. 1978. "Falsifying Jefferson." *Commentary* 66: 66–71.

MacMullen, Ramsay. 1980. "How Many Romans Voted?" *Athanaeum* 63: 454–458.

Macpherson, C. B. 1962. *The Political Theory of Possessive Individualism.* Oxford: Oxford University Press.

Maddison, Angus. 1982. *Phases of Capitalist Development.* Oxford: Oxford University Press.

Madison, James. 1884. *Letters and Other Writings of James Madison.* New York: Worthington. Vol. 1.

——— 1904. *The Writings of James Madison.* Ed. Gaillard Hunt. New York: Putnam Vol. 5.

Maier, Pauline. 1998. *American Scripture: Making the Declaration of Independence.* New York: Vintage.

Mann, F. A. 1978. "Britain's Bill of Rights." *Law Quarterly Review* 94: 512–533.

Mann, Michael. 1986. *The Sources of Social Power.* Vol. 1: *A History of Power from the Beginning to A.D. 1760.* Cambridge: Cambridge University Press.

Manning, Brian. 1976. *The English People and the English Revolution, 1640–1649.* London: Heinemann.

Manuel, Frank E., and Fritzie P. Manuel. 1979. *Utopian Thought in the Western World.* Cambridge: Harvard University Press.

Marcus, Maeva. 1989. "Separation of Powers in the Early National Period." *William and Mary Law Review* 30: 269–277.

Maritain, Jacques. 1951. *Man and the State.* Chicago: University of Chicago Press.

——— 1969. "The Concept of Sovereignty." In Stankiewicz, 41–64.

Marr, Andrew. 1995. *Ruling Britannia: The Failure and Future of British Democracy.* London: Michael Joseph.

Marsh, David, and R. A. W. Rhodes, eds. 1992. *Policy Networks in British Government.* Oxford: Clarendon.

Marshall, Geoffrey. 1954. "What Is Parliament? The Changing Concept of Parliamentary Sovereignty." *Political Studies* 5: 193–209.

Marshall, Geoffrey, and Barry Loveday. 1994. "The Police: Independence and Accountability." In Jowell and Oliver, 295–321.

Martin, John. 1993. *Venice's Hidden Enemies: Italian Heretics in a Renaissance City.* Berkeley: University of California Press.

Mayer, T. F. 1989. Introduction to Thomas Starkey, *A Dialogue between Pole and Lupset*. London: Royal Historical Society.

McAuslan, J. P. W. B. and J. F. McEldowney. 1985. *Law, Legitimacy, and the Constitution: Essays Marking the Centenary of Dicey's Law of the Constitution*. London: Sweet and Maxwell.

—— 1986. "The Constitution under Crisis." *Parliamentary Affairs* 39: 496–516.

McConnell, Michael W. 1990. "The Origins and Understanding of Free Exercise of Religion." *Harvard Law Review* 103: 1410–1517.

McCoy, Drew. 1991. *The Last of the Fathers: James Madison and the Republican Legacy*. Cambridge: Cambridge University Press.

McCullough, Colleen, *The First Man in Rome* (New York: William Morrow, 1991); *The Grass Crown* (New York: William Morrow, 1992); *Fortune's Favorites* (New York: William Morrow, 1993); *Caesar's Women* (New York: William Morrow, 1996).

McDonald, Forrest. 1985. *Novus Ordo Seclorum: The Intellectual Origins of the Constitution*. Lawrence: University Press of Kansas.

McDowell, Gary L. 1996. "Madison's Filter." *Times Literary Supplement*. (London). May 24.

McEldowney, John F. 1985. "Dicey in Historical Perspective: A Review Essay." In McAuslan and McEldowney, 39–61.

1994. "The Control of Public Expenditure." In Jowell and Oliver, 175–207.

McIlwain, Charles Howard. 1918. *The Political Works of James I*. Cambridge: Harvard University Press.

—— 1939. *Constitutionalism and the Changing World*. New York: Macmillan.

—— 1940. *Constitutionalism Ancient and Modern*. Ithaca, N.Y.: Cornell University Press.

—— 1950. "Sovereignty in the World Today." *Measure*. 109–117.

McLaughlin, Andrew C. 1932. *The Foundations of American Constitutionalism*. New York: New York University Press.

McPherson, David. 1988. "Lewkenor's Venice and Its Sources." *Renaissance Quarterly* 41: 459–466.

McPherson, David C. 1990. *Shakespeare, Jonson, and the Myth of Venice*. Newark: University of Delaware Press.

McRae, Kenneth Douglas. 1962. "Introduction" to Jean Bodin, *The Six Bookes of a Commonweale*. Cambridge: Harvard University Press.

Mendle, Michael. 1995. *Henry Parker and the English Civil War: The Political Thought of the Public's "Privado."* Cambridge: Cambridge University Press.

Merriam, C. E. 1972. *History of the Theory of Sovereignty since Rousseau*. New York: Garland.

Mill, John Stuart. 1977. "On Liberty." *Collected Works of John Stuart Mill*. Toronto: University of Toronto Press. 18: 217–310.

Millar, Fergus. 1984. "The Political Character of the Classical Roman Republic, 200–151 B.C." *Journal of Roman Studies* 74: 1–19.

—— 1986. "Politics, Persuasion, and the People before the Social War." *Journal of Roman Studies* 76: 1–11.

—— 1989. "Political Power in Mid-Republican Rome: Curia or Comitium?" *Journal of Roman Studies* 79: 138–150.

Miller, John. 1983. *The Glorious Revolution*. London: Longman.

Milton, John. 1915. *The Ready and Easy Way to Establish a Free Commonwealth*. Ed. Evert Mordecai Clark. New Haven: Yale University Press.

Monahan, Arthur P. 1987. *Consent, Coercion, and Limit: The Medieval Origins of Parliamentary Democracy*. Montreal: McGill–Queen's University Press.

Montesquieu, Baron de. 1966. *The Spirit of the Laws*. Trans. Thomas Nugent, intro. by Franz Neumann. New York: Hafner.

—— 1977. *The Spirit of the Laws*. A compendium of the first English ed. by David Wallace Carrithers. Berkeley: University of California Press.

Moore, James. 1977. "Humes's Political Science and the Classical Republican Tradition." *Canadian Journal of Political Science* 10: 809–839.

Moran, Michael. 1980. "Parliamentary Control of the Bank of England." *Parliamentary Affairs* 33: 67–78.

Morgan, Edmund S. 1989. *Inventing the People: The Rise of Popular Sovereignty in England and America*. New York: Norton.

—— 1992. *The Birth of the Republic*. Chicago: University of Chicago Press.

Morgan, Kenneth O., ed. 1984. *The Oxford Illustrated History of Britain*. Oxford: Oxford University Press.

Mörke, Olaf. 1995. "The Political Culture of Germany and the Dutch Republic: Similar Roots, Different Results." In Davids and Lucassen, 135–172.

Mornay, Phillipe du Plessis. 1969. *Vindiciae Contra Tyrannos*. In Franklin 1969, 141–199.

Morrill, John. 1984. "The Stuarts (1603–1688)." In K. Morgan, 286–351.

—— 1991. "The Sensible Revolution." In Israel 1991, 73–104.

Mosse, George L. 1950. *The Struggle for Sovereignty in England: From the Reign of Queen Elizabeth to the Petition of Right*. East Lansing: Michigan State College Press.

Mostov, Julie. 1992. *Power, Process, and Popular Sovereignty*. Philadelphia: Temple University Press.

Mount, Ferdinand. 1993. *The British Constitution Now: Recovery or Decline?* London: Mandarin.

Muir, Edward. 1981. *Civic Ritual in Renaissance Venice*. Princeton, N.J.: Princeton University Press.

Mundy, John Hine. 1961. "The Conciliar Movement and the Council of Constance." In John Hine Mundy and Kennerly M. Woody, eds. *The Council of Constance: The Unification of the Church*. New York: Columbia University Press. 3–51.

Murray, Oswyn. 1994. "Animals of the Polis." *Times Literary Supplement*. (London). Apr. 5, 3–4.

Nenner, Howard. 1993. "The Later Stuart Age." In Pocock, Schochet, and Schwoerer, 180–208.

Nierop, Henk van. 1995. "Similar Problems, Different Outcomes: The Revolt of the Netherlands and the Wars of Religion in France." In Davids and Lucassen, 26–56.

Nisbet, Robert A. 1966. *The Sociological Tradition*. New York: Basic Books.

North, Douglass C., and Barry R. Weingast. 1989. "Constitutions and Commitment: The Evolution of Institutions Governing Public Choice in Seventeenth-Century England." *Journal of Economic History* 49: 803–832.

North, J. A. 1990. "Democratic Politics in Republican Rome." *Past and Present*. 135: 3–21.

North, Michael. 1995. "Art and Commerce in the Dutch Republic." In Davids and Lucassen, 284–302.

Norton, Philip. 1978. "Government Defeats in the House of Commons: Myth and Reality." *Public Law*. 360–378.

——— 1984. *The Constitution in Flux*. Oxford: Blackwell.

——— 1985. "Behavioural Changes: Backbench Independence in the 1980s." In Norton 1985, 22–47.

——— 1991. "The Changing Face of Parliament: Lobbying and Its Consequences." In Norton 1991, 58–82.

——— 1994. "Parliament I: The House of Commons." In Bill Jones, ed., *Politics U K*. London: Harvester. 314–348.

———, ed. 1985. *Parliament in the 1980s*. Oxford: Blackwell.

———, ed. 1991. *New Directions in British Politics? Essays on the Evolving Constitution*. Aldershot: Elgar.

Nozick, Robert. 1974. *Anarchy, State, and Utopia*. New York: Basic Books.

Oakley, Francis. 1964–1965. "Almain and Major: Conciliar Theory on the Eve of the Reformation." *American Historical Review* 7: 673–690.

Oliver, Dawn. 1994. "What Is Happening in the Relationship between the Individual and the State?" In Jowell and Oliver, 441–461.

Ortega y Gasset, José. 1950. *The Revolt of the Masses*. New York: Mentor Books.

Ostwald, Martin. 1986. *From Popular Sovereignty to the Sovereignty of Law: Law, Society, and Politics in Fifth-Century Athens*. Berkeley: University of California Press.

Ozment, Stephen. 1991. *Protestants: The Birth of a Revolution*. New York: Doubleday.

Panagopoulos, E. P. 1985. *Essays on the History and Meaning of Checks and Balances*. Lanham, Md.: University Press of America.

Parker, David. 1981. "Law, Society and the State in the Thought of Jean Bodin." *History of Political Thought* 2: 253–285.

Parker, Geoffrey. 1976. "Why Did the Dutch Revolt Last Eighty Years?" *Transactions of the Royal Historical Society* 5th ser., 26: 53–72.

Parker, Henry. 1642. *Observations upon Some of his Majesties Late Answers and Expresses*. London: n.p.

Parsons, Talcott. 1963. "On the Concept of Political Power." *Proceedings of the American Philosophical Society* 107: 232–262.

Partington, Martin. 1985. "The Reform of Public Law in Britain: Theoretical Problems and Practical Considerations." In McAuslan and McEldowney, 191–211.

Peck, Linda Levy. 1993. "Kingship, Counsel, and Law in Early Stuart Britain." In Pocock, Schochet, and Schwoerer, 80–115.

Pennington, Kenneth. 1993. *The Prince and the Law, 1200–1600: Sovereignty and Rights in the Western Legal Tradition*. Berkeley: University of California Press.

Perkinson, Richard H. 1940. "'Volpone' and the Reputation of Venetian Justice." *Modern Language Review* 35: 11–18.

Peters, R. S. 1967. "Hobbes, Thomas." In *Encyclopedia of Philosophy*. New York: Macmillan. 4: 30–46.

Pirenne, Henri. 1963. *Early Democracies in the Low Countries; Urban Society and Political Conflict in the Middle Ages and Renaissance*. New York: Harper and Row.

Plato. 1980. *The Laws of Plato*. Trans. T. L. Pangle. New York: Basic Books.

—— 1994. *Republic*. Trans. Robin Waterfield. Oxford: Oxford University Press.

Plumb, J. H. 1969. "The Growth of the Electorate in England from 1600 to 1715." *Past and Present* 14: 90–116.

Pocock, J. G. A. 1965. "Machiavelli, Harrington, and English Political Ideologies in the Eighteenth Century." *William and Mary Quarterly* 22: 549–583.

—— 1975. *The Machiavellian Moment: Florentine Political Thought and the Atlantic Republican Tradition*. Princeton, N.J.: Princeton University Press.

—— 1981. "*The Machiavellian Moment* Revisited: A Study in History and Ideology." *Journal of Modern History* 53: 49–72.

—— 1992. "The Dutch Republican Tradition." In Jacob and Mijnhardt, 188–193.

—— 1993. "Political Thought in the English-Speaking Atlantic, 1760–1790." In Pocock, Schochet, and Schwoerer, 246–317.

Pocock, J. G. A. and Gordon J. Schochet. 1993. "Interregnum and Restoration." In Pocock, Schochet, and Schwoerer, 146–179.

Pocock, J. G. A., Gordon J. Schochet, and Lois G. Schwoerer, eds. 1993. *The Varieties of British Political Thought*. New York: Cambridge University Press.

A Political Catechism; or, Certain Questions Concerning the Government of This Land, Answered in His Majesties Own Words, Taken Out of His Answer to the 19 Propositions. 1963. London: Samuel Gellibrand.

Poss, Richard Lee. 1986. *The Myth of Venice in English Drama of the Seventeenth Century*. University of Georgia Dissertation Abstracts Index: 47, 2170A.

Powell, Anton. 1988. *Athens and Sparta: Constructing Greek Political and Social History from 478 B.C.* Portland, Oreg.: Areopagitica Press.

Prak, Maarten. 1991. "Citizen Radicalism and Democracy in the Dutch Republic: The Patriot Movement of the 1780s." *Theory and Society* 20: 73–102.

Prestwick, Minna, ed. 1985. *International Calvinism, 1541–1715*. Oxford: Clarendon.

Price, J. L. 1994. *Holland and the Dutch Republic in the Seventeenth Century: The Politics of Particularism*. Oxford: Clarendon.

Pullan, Brian. 1971. *Rich and Poor in Renaissance Venice: The Social Institutions of a Catholic State, to 1620*. Cambridge: Harvard University Press.

—— 1974. "The Significance of Venice." *Bulletin of the John Rylands University Library of Manchester* 56: 441–462.

Queller, Donald E. 1986. *The Venetian Patriciate*. Urbana: University of Illinois Press.

Rabb, Felix. 1964. *The English Face of Machiavelli: A Changing Interpretation, 1500–1700*. London: Routledge and Kegan Paul.

Rakove: Jack N. 1997. *Original Meanings: Politics and Ideas in the Making of the Constitution*. New York: Vintage Books.

Rawls, John. 1971. *A Theory of Justice*. Cambridge: Harvard University Press.

Rawson, Elizabeth. 1969. *The Spartan Tradition in European Thought*. Oxford: Clarendon.

—— 1983. *Cicero: A Portrait*. Ithaca, N.Y.: Cornell University Press.

Rees, W. J. 1950. "The Theory of Sovereignty Restated." *Mind* 59: 495–521.

Rhodes, P. J. 1984. "Introduction" to Aristotle, *The Athenian Constitution*. London: Penguin.

Rhodes, R. A. W. 1991. "Now Nobody Understands the System: The Changing Face of Government." In Norton 1991, 83–112.

Richard, Carl J. 1994. *The Founders and the Classics: Greece, Rome, and the American Enlightenment*. Cambridge: Harvard University Press.

Richards, David A. J. 1989. *Foundations of American Constitutionalism*. Oxford: Oxford University Press.

Richardson, R. C. 1977. *The Debate on the English Revolution*. London: Methuen.

Richardson, R. C., and G. M. Ridden, eds. 1986. *Freedom and the English Revolution: Essays in Liberty and Literature*. Manchester, Eng.: Manchester University Press.

Riker, William H. 1957. "Dutch and American Federalism." *Journal of the History of Ideas* 18: 495–521.

Ringold, A. F. 1972. "The History of the Enactment of the Ninth Amendment and Its Recent Development." *Tulsa Law Journal*. 8: 1–55.

Roberts, Clayton. 1966. *The Growth of Responsible Government in Stuart England*. Cambridge: Cambridge University Press.

Roberts, Jennifer Tolbert. 1982. *Accountability in Athenian Government*. Madison: University of Wisconsin Press.

Robey, David, and John Law. 1975. "The Venetian Myth and the 'De Republica Veneta' of Pier Paolo Vergerio." *Rinacimento*. 2d ser., 15: 3–59.

Roche, John P. 1968. "Constitutional Law: Distribution of Powers." In *International Encyclopedia of the Social Sciences*. New York: Macmillan. 3: 300–307.

Romano, Dennis. 1987. *Patricians and Popolani: The Social Foundations of the Venetian Renaissance State*. Baltimore: Johns Hopkins University Press.

Rose, Charles J. 1974. "Marc Antonio Venier, Renier Zeno, and 'The Myth of Venice.'" *The Historian* 36: 479–497.

Rousseau, Jean-Jacques. 1913. *The Social Contract*. London: J. M. Dent.

Rowen, Herbert H., ed. 1972. *The Low Countries in Early Modern Times*. New York: Walker.

—— 1985. "Neither Fish nor Fowl: The Stadholderate in the Dutch Republic." In Rowen and Lossky, 1–31.

—— 1988. *The Princes of Orange: The Stadholders in the Dutch Republic*. Cambridge: Cambridge University Press.

Rowen, Herbert H., and Andrew Lossky, eds. 1985. *Political Ideas and Institutions in the Dutch Republic*. Los Angeles: Clark Memorial Library, 1985.

Rubinstein, Nicolai. 1991. "Italian Political Thought, 1450–1580." In Burns 1991, 30–65.

——, ed. 1968. *Florentine Studies: Politics and Society in Renaissance Florence*. Evanston, Ill.: Northwestern University Press.

Ruggiero, Guido. 1980. *Violence in Early Renaissance Venice*. New Brunswick, N.J.: Rutgers University Press.

Rush, Michael. 1990. "Select Committees." In Rush, 137–151.

——, ed. 1990. *Parliament and Pressure Politics*. Oxford: Clarendon.

Russell, Bertrand. 1938. *Power: A New Social Analysis*. London: Allen and Unwin.

Sabine, George H. 1937. *A History of Political Theory.* New York: Holt.

Sarma, G. N. 1984. *Political Thought of Harold J. Laski.* New Delhi: Sterling.

Sartori, Giovanni. 1962. "Constitutionalism: A Preliminary Discussion." *American Political Science Review* 56: 853–864.

Saxonhouse, Arlene W. 1996. *Athenian Democracy: Modern Mythmakers and Ancient Theorists.* Notre Dame: University of Notre Dame Press.

Scarisbrick, J. J. 1985. *The Reformation and the English People.* Oxford: Blackwell.

Schmitt, Carl. 1985. *Political Theology: Four Chapters on the Concept of Sovereignty.* Cambridge: MIT Press.

Schochet, Gordon J. 1975. *Patriarchalism in Political Thought: The Authoritarian Family and Political Speculation and Attitudes Especially in Seventeenth-Century England.* Oxford: Blackwell.

Schoeck, R. J. 1973. "Bodin's Opposition to the Mixed State and to Thomas More." In Denzer, 399–412.

Schöffer, I. 1975. "The Batavian Myth during the Sixteenth and Seventeenth Centuries." In Bromley and Kossmann, 78–101.

Schwoerer, Lois G. 1981. *The Declaration of Rights, 1689.* Baltimore: John Hopkins University Press.

Scullard, H. H. 1951/1973. *Roman Politics, 220–150 B.C.* Oxford: Clarendon.

——— 1980/1992. *A History of the Roman World: 753 to 146 B.C.* London: Routledge.

——— 1982. *From the Gracchi to Nero: A History of Rome from 133 B.C. to A.D. 68.* London: Methuen.

Sealey, Raphael. 1987. *The Athenian Republic: Democracy or the Rule of Law?* University Park: Pennsylvania State University Press.

Sedgemore, Brian. 1980. *The Secret Constitution: An Analysis of the Political Establishment.* London: Hodder and Staughton.

Service, Elman R. 1975. *Origins of the State and Civilization: The Process of Cultural Evolution.* New York: Norton.

Shackleton, Robert. 1949. "Montesquieu, Bolingbrole, and the Separation of Powers." *French Studies* 3: 25–38.

Sharpe, Kevin. 1992. *The Personal Rule of Charles I.* New Haven: Yale University Press.

Shatzman, Israel. 1972. "The Roman General's Authority over Booty." *Historia.* 177–205.

Shepard, Max Adams. 1930. "Sovereignty at the Crossroads: A Study of Bodin." *Political Science Quarterly* 45: 580–603.

Shklar, Judith N. 1987. "Alexander Hamilton and the Language of Political Science." In Anthony Pagden, ed., *The Languages of Political Theory in Early Modern Europe.* Cambridge: Cambridge University Press. 339–355.

Sidgwick, Henry. 1969. *The Elements of Politics.* 4th ed. New York: Kraus Reprint Co.

Skinner, Quentin. 1965. "History and Ideology in the English Revolution." *The Historical Journal.* 8: 151–178.

——— 1978. *The Foundations of Modern Political Thought.* 2 vols. Cambridge: Cambridge University Press.

Smith, Adam. 1937. *An Inquiry into the Nature and Causes of the Wealth of Nations.* New York: Modern Library. First published in 1776.

Smith, David L. 1994. *Constitutional Royalism and the Search for Settlement, ca. 1640–1649*. Cambridge: Cambridge University Press.

Smith, R. E. 1955. *The Failure of the Roman Republic*. Cambridge: Cambridge University Press.

Smith, Thomas. 1982. *De Republica Anglorum*. Ed. Mary Dewar. Cambridge: Cambridge University Press.

Snelders, H. A. M. 1992. "Professors, Amateurs, and Learned Societies: The Organization of the Natural Sciences." In Jacob and Mijnhardt, 308–323.

Sobel, Dava. 1996. *Longitude: The True Story of a Lone Genius Who Solved the Greatest Scientific Problem of His Time*. New York: Penguin.

Sommerville, J. P. 1991. "Absolutism and Royalism." In Burns 1991, 347–373.

Speck, William. 1995. "Britain and the Dutch Republic." In Davids and Lucassen, 173–195.

Spufford, Margaret. 1995. "Literacy, Trade and Religion in the Commercial Centres of Europe." In Davids and Lucassen, 229–283.

Spurlin, Paul Merrill. 1940. *Montesquieu in America, 1760–1801*. Baton Rouge: Lousiana State University Press.

Stankiewicz, W. J., ed. 1969. *In Defense of Sovereignty*. New York: Oxford University Press.

Stockton, David. 1971. *Cicero: A Political Biography*. Oxford: Oxford University Press.

—— 1990. *The Classical Athenian Democracy*. Oxford: Oxford University Press.

Strauss, Leo. 1963. *The Political Philosophy of Hobbes: Its Basis and Its Genesis*. Chicago: University of Chicago Press.

Swart, K. W. 1975. "The Black Legend during the Eighty Years' War." In Bromley and Kossmann, 36–57.

Taylor, Lily Ross. 1966. *Roman Voting Assemblies: From the Hannibalic War to the Dictatorship of Caesar*. Ann Arbor: University of Michigan Press.

Temple, Sir William. 1972. *Observations upon the United Provinces of the Netherlands*. Oxford: Clarendon.

Tenney, Frank. 1930. "Rome." In *The Cambridge Ancient History*, vol. 8, ch. 12. Cambridge: Cambridge University Press.

Thompson, M. P. 1977. "The Idea of Conquest in Controversies over the 1688 Revolution." *Journal of the History of Ideas* 38: 33–46.

Thomson, James. 1986. *Liberty, the Castle of Indolence, and Other Poems*. Ed. James Sambrook. Oxford: Clarendon.

Thorne, Samuel E. 1957. *Sir Edward Coke, 1552–1952*. London: Quaritch.

Thorpe, Francis Newton. 1909. *The Federal and State Constitutions, Colonial Charters, and Other Organic Laws of the States, Territories, and Colonies*. Washington: Government Printing Office.

Tierney, Brian. 1963. "'The Prince Is Not Bound by the Laws': Accursius and the Origins of the Modern State." *Comparative Studies in Society and History* 5: 378–400.

—— 1966. "Medieval Canon Law and Western Constitutionalism." *The Catholic Historical Review* 52: 1–17.

—— 1975. "'Divided Sovereignty' at Constance: A Problem in Medieval and Early Modern Political Theory." *Annuarium Historiae Conciliorum* 7: 238–256.

——— 1982. *Religion, Law, and the Growth of Constitutional Thought, 1150–1650*. Cambridge: Cambridge University Press.

Todd, Margo, ed. 1995. *Reformation to Revolution: Politics and Religion in Early Modern England*. London: Routledge.

Trevor-Roper, Hugh. 1985. *Renaissance Essays*. Chicago: University of Chicago Press.

——— 1991. "Toleration and Religion after 1688." In Grell, Israel, and Tyacke, 389–408.

Tuchman, Barbara W. 1988. *The First Salute*. New York: Ballantine.

Tuck, Richard. 1991. "Grotius and Selden." In Burns 1991, 499–529.

Turpin, Colin. 1994. "Ministerial Responsibility." In Jowell and Oliver, 109–151.

Ullmann, Walter. 1949. "The Development of the Medieval Idea of Sovereignty." *The English Historical Review* 250: 1–33.

Vile, M. J. C. 1967. *Constitutionalism and the Separation of Powers*. Oxford: Clarendon.

von Fritz, Kurt. 1975. *The Theory of the Mixed Constitution in Antiquity*. New York: Arno Press. Appendix 1 contains excerpts from Polybius's "History" that concern political theory.

Wade, E. C. S. 1960. "Introduction" to Dicey.

Wade, H. W. R. 1955. "The Basis of Legal Sovereignty." *Cambridge Law Journal*. 172–197.

Walbank, F. W. 1957. *A Historical Commentary on Polybius*. Oxford: Oxford University Press.

——— 1966. "The Spartan Ancestral Constitution in Polybius." In *Ancient Society and its Institutions: Studies Presented to Victor Ehrenberg on his 75th Birthday*. Oxford: Blackwell. 303–312.

——— 1972. *Polybius*. Cambridge: Cambridge University Press.

Walsh, Correa Moylan. 1915. *The Political Science of John Adams: A Study in the Theory of Mixed Government and the Bicameral System*. New York: Putnam.

Wansink, H. 1971. "Holland and Six Allies: The Republic of the Seven United Provinces." In Bromley and Kossmann, 133–155.

Ward, Paul W. 1928. *Sovereignty: A Study of a Contemporary Political Notion*. London: Routledge.

Watkins, Frederick M. 1968. "The State: A Concept." In *International Encyclopedia of the Social Sciences*. New York: Macmillan. 15: 150–156.

Weber, Max. 1947. *The Theory of Social and Economic Organization*. Glencoe, Ill.: Free Press.

Webster, Charles, ed. 1974. *The Intellectual Revolution of the Seventeenth Century*. London: Routledge.

Weinstein, Donald. 1968. "The Myth of Florence." In Rubinstein, 15–44.

Weston, Corinne Comstock. 1960. "The Theory of Mixed Monarchy under Charles I and After." *English Historical Review* 75: 426–443.

——— 1965. *English Constitutional Theory and the House of Lords, 1556–1832*. New York: Columbia University Press.

——— 1991. "England: Ancient Constitution and Common Law." In Burns 1991, 374–411.

Weston, Corinne Comstock, and Janelle Renfrow Greenberg, eds. 1981. *Subjects and Sovereigns: The Grand Controversy over Legal Sovereignty in Stuart England*. Cambridge: Cambridge University Press.

White, Stephen D. 1979. *Sir Edward Coke and "The Grievances of the Commonwealth," 1621–1628*. Chapel Hill: University of North Carolina Press.

Whitfield, Christopher. 1964. "Sir Lewes Lewkenor and 'The Merchant of Venice': A Suggested Connection." *Notes and Queries*. 123–133.

Williams, E. N. 1965. *A Documentary History of England*. Vol. 2 (1559–1931). Harmondsworth: Penguin.

Wilks, Ivor. 1969. "A Note on Sovereignty." In Stankiewicz, 197–205.

Wilson, Charles. 1968. *The Dutch Republic, and the Civilisation of the Seventeenth Century*. London: World University Library.

Wilson, Woodrow. 1891. "The Elements of Politics." *The Dial*, Nov. 215–216.

Wittfogel, Karl A. 1957. *Oriental Despotism: A Comparative Study of Total Power*. New Haven: Yale University Press.

Wood, Gordon S. 1969. *The Creation of the American Republic, 1776–1787*. Chapel Hill: University of North Carolina Press.

—— 1982. "Conspiracy and the Paranoid Style: Causality and Deceit in the Eighteenth Century." *William and Mary Quarterly* 39: 401–441.

—— 1992. "Democracy and the American Revolution." In Dunn, 91–105.

Woodhouse, A. S. P., ed. 1992. *Puritanism and Liberty*. London: J. M. Dent.

Wooton, David. 1983. *Paolo Sarpi: Between Renaissance and Enlightenment*. Cambridge: Cambridge University Press.

Worden, Blair. 1982. "Classical Republicanism and the Puritan Revolution." In Hugh Lloyd-Jones, Valerie Pearl, and Blair Worden, eds. *History and Imagination: Essays in Honor of H. R. Trevor-Roper*. New York: Holmes and Meier. 182–200.

—— 1991. "English Republicanism." In Burns 1991, 443–475.

Wormuth, Francis D. 1949. *The Origins of Modern Constitutionalism*. New York: Harper.

Worst, I. J. H. 1992. "Constitution, History, and Natural Law: An Eighteenth-Century Political Debate in the Dutch Republic." In Jacob and Mijnhardt, 147–169.

Wright, A. D. 1974. "Why the *Venetian* Interdict?" *English Historical Review*. 534–550.

Wright, Benjamin F., Jr. 1933. "The Origin of Separation of Powers in America." *Economica* 169: 169–185.

—— 1949. "The *Federalist* on the Nature of Political Man." *Ethics* 59: 1–31.

Wrong, Dennis H. 1979. *Power: Its Forms, Bases, and Uses*. New York: Harper and Row.

Yardeni, Miriam. 1985. "French Calvinist Political Thought." In Menna Prestwick, ed. *International Calvinism, 1541–1715*. Oxford: Clarendon.

Young, G. M. 1937. "The Greatest Victorian." *The Spectator*, June 18. 1137–1138.

Zagorin, Perez. 1980. *Culture and Politics from Puritanism to the Enlightenment*. Berkeley: University of California Press.

Zee, van der, Henri, and Barbara van der Zee. 1988. *1688: Revolution in the Family.* London: Penguin.

Zeitlin, Irving M. 1997. *Rulers and Ruled: An Introduction to Classical Political Theory from Plato to the Federalists.* Toronto: University of Toronto Press.

Zorzi, Alvise. 1983. *Venice: The Golden Age, 697–1797.* New York: Abbeville.

Index

absolutism, 3, 57–58, 166, 192, 223
accountability, in modern Britain, 336–338, 341, 342n
Accursius, 116, 117, 117n
Act of Abjuration, 187, 214, 216
Act of Seclusion, 203–204
Act of Settlement of 1701, 227, 267
Act of Supremacy of 1534, 229
Acts of Survivance, 203
Adams, John, 298n, 302n, 304
aediles, Roman, 102n
Aeschylus, 61
African slave labor in America, 286
Aldine Press, 136
Althusius, Johannes, 30, 216, 218, 220
American Constitution, 32, 299–317; framers of, 7–8; Bagehot on, 41; compromises in, 299; federalism in, 300, 302–303; class conflict theory of, 300n; structure of federal government in, 303–304; influence on Europe, 305; ratification of, 305–307, 308–317; provenance of, 322–326
American Revolution, 31–33; political theory of, 285–294; influence of, 325
Anglo-Dutch affinity, 178n, 180
Anjou, Duke of, 218
Aquinas, Thomas, 13, 29, 152
Archons, 65, 73–74
Arendt, Hannah, 11
Areopagus, 63–64
aristocracy, 11, 21; Venetian, 22, 134, 135, 137, 145, 148, 358; government by, 40–41, 237; Roman, 99, 112, 358; Dutch, 221, 227, 358; English, 227, 236, 358; constitutional, 237
Aristophanes, 61
Aristotle: on power, 8; on democracy, 11, 12, 77; importance of, 61, 63; on forms of government, 63, 81, 358; on mixed

government, 82–83; view of state of, 248; Filmer on, 250, 252. *See also Athenaion Politeia*
Arminianism, 173, 174
Arminius, Jacobus, 174
Armstrong, Catherine, 25n
art market in Holland, 182
Articles of Confederation, 294, 300–302, 303
Assemblies, Roman, 104–107, 112; attendance at, 106–107n
Assembly, Athenian, 67–70
Athenaion Politeia, 63, 72, 73, 76
Athenian democracy, 60–85, 358; duration of, 60–61; influence of, 61–63
Athenian political system, 66–75; romanticization of, 77; lack of hierarchy in, 79
Atlantic world, commercial development in, 133–134
Attlee, Clement, 344
Austin, John, 43–44, 54, 55
Avvogaria di Comun, Venice, 142

Bacon, Francis, 225, 244, 349
Bagehot, Walter, 37–43, 278, 325, 334
balance of powers, 82, 111, 345–346
Baltimore, Lord, 285
Batavian Myth, 212–213
Beeckman, Isaac, 178–179
Bellarmine (Cardinal), 152, 154, 250
Bentham, Jeremy, 14, 27, 44
Beza, Theodore, 121, 123–124, 294
bicameralism, 232, 298, 298n, 333
Bill of Rights: English, 266–267; American, 317–319
Birch, Anthony, 333
Blackstone, William, 37, 254, 329
Bodin, Jean, 20–24, 218; on sovereignty, 8,

ECI   **DATE DUE**

aug

5 NOV
NOV 8

ERSITY OF SUDBURY
ERSITE DE SUDBURY